The Legacy of Aristotelian Enthymeme

Bloomsbury Studies in the Aristotelian Tradition

General Editor:

Marco Sgarbi, Università Ca' Foscari, Italy

Editorial Board:

Klaus Corcilius *(University of California, Berkeley, USA)*; Daniel Garber *(Princeton University, USA)*; Oliver Leaman *(University of Kentucky, USA)*; Anna Marmodoro *(University of Oxford, UK)*; Craig Martin *(Oakland University, USA)*; Carlo Natali *(Università Ca' Foscari, Italy)*; Riccardo Pozzo *(Consiglio Nazionale delle Ricerche, Rome, Italy)*; Renée Raphael *(University of California, Irvine, USA)*; Victor M. Salas *(Sacred Heart Major Seminary, USA)*; Leen Spruit *(Radboud University Nijmegen, The Netherlands)*.

Aristotle's influence throughout the history of philosophical thought has been immense and in recent years the study of Aristotelian philosophy has enjoyed a revival. However, Aristotelianism remains an incredibly polysemous concept, encapsulating many, often conflicting, definitions. *Bloomsbury Studies in the Aristotelian Tradition* responds to this need to define Aristotelianism and give rise to a clear characterization.

Investigating the influence and reception of Aristotle's thought from classical antiquity to contemporary philosophy from a wide range of perspectives, this series aims to reconstruct how philosophers have become acquainted with the tradition. The books in this series go beyond simply ascertaining that there are Aristotelian doctrines within the works of various thinkers in the history of philosophy, but seek to understand how they have received and elaborated Aristotle's thought, developing concepts into ideas that have become independent of him.

Bloomsbury Studies in the Aristotelian Tradition promotes new approaches to Aristotelian philosophy and its history. Giving special attention to the use of interdisciplinary methods and insights, books in this series will appeal to scholars working in the fields of philosophy, history and cultural studies.

Available titles:

A Political Philosophy of Conservatism, by Ferenc Hörcher

Elijah Del Medigo and Paduan Aristotelianism, by Michael Engel

Early Modern Aristotelianism and the Making of Philosophical Disciplines, by Danilo Facca

Phantasia in Aristotle's Ethics, by Jacob Leth Fink

Pontano's Virtues, by Matthias Roick

The Aftermath of Syllogism, edited by Marco Sgarbi, Matteo Cosci

The Reception of Aristotle's Poetics in the Italian Renaissance and Beyond, by Bryan Brazeau

The Scientific Counter-Revolution, by Michael John Gorman

Virtue Ethics and Contemporary Aristotelianism, edited by Andrius Bielskis, Eleni Leontsini, Kelvin Knight

Aristotle's Syllogism and the Creation of Modern Logic, edited by Lukas M. Verburgt and Matteo Cosci

The Legacy of Aristotelian Enthymeme

Proof and Belief in the Middle Ages and the Renaissance

Edited by
Fosca Mariani Zini

BLOOMSBURY ACADEMIC
LONDON • NEW YORK • OXFORD • NEW DELHI • SYDNEY

BLOOMSBURY ACADEMIC
Bloomsbury Publishing Plc
50 Bedford Square, London, WC1B 3DP, UK
1385 Broadway, New York, NY 10018, USA
29 Earlsfort Terrace, Dublin 2, Ireland

BLOOMSBURY, BLOOMSBURY ACADEMIC and the Diana logo are trademarks of
Bloomsbury Publishing Plc

First published in Great Britain 2023
This paperback edition published 2024

Copyright © Fosca Mariani Zini and Contributors, 2023

Fosca Mariani Zini has asserted her right under the Copyright, Designs and Patents Act, 1988, to be identified as Editor of this work.

Cover image: Bookbinder in Middle Ages (© history_docu_photo / Alamy Stock Photo)

All rights reserved. No part of this publication may be reproduced or transmitted in any form or by any means, electronic or mechanical, including photocopying, recording, or any information storage or retrieval system, without prior permission in writing from the publishers.

Bloomsbury Publishing Plc does not have any control over, or responsibility for, any third-party websites referred to or in this book. All internet addresses given in this book were correct at the time of going to press. The author and publisher regret any inconvenience caused if addresses have changed or sites have ceased to exist, but can accept no responsibility for any such changes.

A catalogue record for this book is available from the British Library.

A catalog record for this book is available from the Library of Congress.

Library of Congress Control Number: 2023939092.

ISBN: HB: 978-1-3502-4880-9
PB: 978-1-3502-4884-7
ePDF: 978-1-3502-4881-6
eBook: 978-1-3502-4882-3

Series: Bloomsbury Studies in the Aristotelian Tradition

Typeset by Deanta Global Publishing Services, Chennai, India

To find out more about our authors and books visit www.bloomsbury.com and sign up for our newsletters.

Contents

List of Illustrations	vi
Notes on Contributors	vii

Introduction: The theory of enthymeme: Between defective and ampliative inference *Fosca Mariani Zini*		1
1	The theories of the enthymeme between late antiquity and the early Middle Ages (*c.* 325–880) *Renato de Filippis*	23
2	Enthymemes in al-Fārābī's and Avicenna's systems *Saloua Chatti*	47
3	*Argumentum*, *locus* and enthymeme: Abaelard's transformation of the topics into a theory of enthymematic inference *Christopher J. Martin*	75
4	The logic of enthymemes as (incomplete) syllogisms: Thirteenth-century theories and practices *Julie Brumberg-Chaumont*	99
5	Inference and enthymeme in Ockham *Paola Müller*	147
6	Enthymematic inferences in John Buridan *Barbara Bartocci*	169
7	The enthymeme from signs and the study of nature in the Renaissance *Marco Sgarbi*	187
8	The lion's fault: The enthymematic foundation of signatures *Marie-Luce Demonet*	201

Index	215

Illustrations

Figures

8.1	Giambattista Della Porta, *De humana physiognomonia*, 1586	206
8.2	Michel Foucault, Bibliothèque Foucaldienne	208

Table

I.1 The Link between Status Questionis and Loci in Cicero's *Topics*	7

Contributors

Barbara Bartocci is a postdoctoral researcher at the University of Geneva, working primarily in logic, philosophy of language and epistemology from ancient to early modern periods. She had co-edited three volumes (e.g. the critical edition and English translation of Paul of Venice's *Treatise on Insoluble*, co-edited with Stephen Read, will be published in fall 2023).

Julie Brumberg-Chaumont is senior research professor, PSL/EPHE/CNRS/LEM, Paris, and co-author with D. Poirel of *Adam and Bockenfield and His Circle on Aristotle's De memoria et reminiscentia*, *Auctores Britannici Medii Aevi* (2011) and with Claude Rosenthal of *Logical Skills: Social-Historical Perspectives* (2021). She is editor of volume 'Ad notitiam ignoti' L'Organon dans la translation studiorum à l'époque d'Albert le Grand (2013).

Saloua Chatti is a professor at the University of Tunis. Her books include *Arabic Logic from Al-Farabi to Averroes: A Study of the Early Arabic Categorical, Modal and Hypothetical Syllogistics* (2019); *Al-Farabi Syllogism: An Abridgement of Aristotle's Prior Analytics*, translated by S. Chatti and Wilfrid Hodges (2020); and *Women's Contemporary Readings of Medieval (and Modern) Arabic Philosophy* (2022).

Renato de Filippis is a professor at the University of Salerno. His books include *Loquax Pagina. La retorica nell'Occidente tardo-antico e alto-medievale* (2013); *Le ragioni del diavolo. Otlone di Sankt Emmeram* (2015); and as editor, *Pier Damiani. Nuove prospettive sul suo pensiero* (2021).

Marie-Luce Demonet is a professor emerita at the University of Tours. She is Chevalier de la Légion d'Honneur. Her books include several digital editions of Montaigne and Rabelais and the essays *A plaisir. Sémiotique et scepticisme chez Montaigne* (2002) and *Les voix du signe. Nature et origine du langage à la Renaissance (1480–1580)* (1992).

Fosca Mariani Zini is a professor at the University of Tours. Her books include *L'économie des passions. Essai sur le Décaméron* (2012); *La pensée de Marsile Ficin. Itinéraires néoplatoniciens* (2014); and *La Calomnie. Un philosophème humaniste* (2016). She is co-editor with Joel Biard of *Les lieux de l'argumentation. Le syllogisme topique d'Aristote à Leibniz* (2009) and with Gernot M. Müller of *Philosophie in Rom-Römische Philosophie* (2017).

Christopher Martin is a professor of philosophy at the University of Auckland. He had published several seminal papers on medieval logic, Abaelard and Boethius. See 'The

Theory of Natural Consequence', *Vivarium*, 56, 2018, pp. 340–66; and 'The Invention of Relations: Early Twelfth Century Discussions of Aristotle's Account of Relative', *British Journal for the History of Philosophy* 24, 2016, pp. 447–67.

Paola Müller is a professor at the Università Cattolica del Sacro Cuore, Milan. Her main areas of interest are logic and metaphysics, especially of Bonaventura da Bagnoregio, Ockham and John Duns Scot, as well as the philosophy of Ildegarde von Bingen. She is the author of *La logica di Ockham* (2012).

Marco Sgarbi is a professor at the University of Venice, 'Ca' Foscari' and author of several books, including *The Aristotelian Tradition and the Rise of British Empiricism: Logic and Epistemology in the British Isles* (2013); *The Italian Mind: Vernacular Logic in Renaissance Italy* (2014); *Profumo d'immortalità: Controversie sull'anima nella filosofia volgare del Rinascimento* (2016); and *Francesco Robortello: Architectural Genius of the Humanities* (2019).

Introduction

The theory of enthymeme: Between defective and ampliative inference

Fosca Mariani Zini

I.1 The enthymeme as 'imperfectus syllogismus'

The standard doctrine of the enthymeme as *imperfectus syllogism* was well established by the time of Boethius, in the sixth century AD.[1] The enthymeme would be an incomplete syllogism, in which the conclusion is inferred without all the premises having been set down beforehand. Therefore, it was characterized by a missing premise.[2]

So far so good. But the history of the logical nature of enthymeme is very amazing because *this* kind of incomplete syllogism can be mainly interpreted in two ways: either incompleteness denotes a *defective syllogism*, a 'minus', something less than a syllogism or it implies a different theory of argumentation and even the possibility of producing *ampliative inferences*, a 'plus', something more than a syllogism or something else.

Let me clarify this point.

First, what does *incomplete* mean here? There are two main possibilities: if the enthymeme designates a constitutive defect, is it still an authentic syllogism, that is, deduction that proves its conclusions? And if it is characterized by a missing premise omission, how can it be completed?

Second, what is the meaning of this *completeness*? Is it the 'fullness' of a defective syllogism and its 'conversion' in a complete one? On contrary, does it bring something more or something else? In this case, either the enthymeme is an expanded syllogism (in the sense that the enthymeme theory T1 adds new vocabulary and new theorems to the standard syllogism theory T but preserves the theorems of T) or it opens the way to any other inference theory, providing different modes of proof as well as different validity criteria.

Finally, this otherness can be considered as a 'weak logic' or as a logic that eludes the strong-weak polarity, because it presents a logic that, compared to the standard conception, offers the possibility of producing *ampliative inferences*, whose conclusions present more information than the premises. In fact, for Aristotle the conclusions of the syllogism must not contain more information than the premises.

However, the meaning of 'weak logic' strictly refers to the inductive probability of an argument, even a deductive one, while ampliative inferences do not necessarily imply probability but they entail *belief, that is, a reasoned assent* on the part of the audience. Moreover, the modern notion of probability itself would be completely anachronistic if it were applied to philosophical texts from Aristotle to the Renaissance. 'Probable' means plausibility.

Indeed, logical theories and their epistemic frames have a history, since they can answer differently the following two questions: first, which are the validity criteria of true argumentation supporting true knowledge? Could proofs for any plausible argument be found to guide thought and action in the space of contingency so that the 'opinion of the strongest' does not impose itself?

Consequently, the history of the enthymeme offers an original perspective to trace how the reflection on the incomplete syllogism led Middle Ages and the Renaissance authors to question the validity criteria of deductions in a double direction: either they tried to reduce incomplete syllogisms to complete syllogisms or they considered an alternative deontic or epistemological way of valid argumentation.

In both cases, they found new problems as well as new solutions.

Therefore, the authors of this book have been invited to reflect on the difficulties and the inventive solutions given to this tension, which is proper to the enthymeme, switching from an argument *within* the syllogism to an argument *beyond* the syllogism.

The enquiry about this legacy is the original topic of this volume.

In what follows I would like to proceed in two steps.

After summarizing the significant theories of the enthymeme in ancient Greek and Latin thought, by distinguishing their prevalent questions, I will briefly outline the chapters of this volume, identifying their bearing on a prevalent set of questions as well as the answers they propose to give.

I.2 What is a valid syllogism?

Although interpretations of the syllogism are controversial, it is possible to argue the following:

The syllogism is a deduction that has two premises and a conclusion, which is drawn according to the position of a *middle term (i.e. medium)* that is present in the premises and disappears in the conclusion.

Premises can be singular or general, affirmative or negative. There are also indeterminate premises like 'pleasure is not a good', which, for Aristotle, can be considered as particular propositions. For Aristotle,[3] the principle of bivalence is valid: any proposition is true or false. According to the symbols used in Aristotle's Latin posterity,[4] the universal affirmative proposition is abbreviated by *a*, the universal negative proposition is abbreviated by *e*, the particular and affirmative proposition is abbreviated by *i* and the particular and negative proposition is abbreviated by *o* (i.e. *medium*).

Thanks to this quantification, it is possible to establish the relations between propositions, hence what has been called the 'logical square': the universal affirmative and the particular negative as well as the universal negative and the particular affirmative are contradictory, while the universal negative and the particular negative as well as the universal positive and the particular positive are contrary. This point is very important because two contradictory propositions cannot be false together while two contrary propositions can be false.

Therefore, the validity criteria of syllogisms do not depend on the truth or falsehood of the premises but on the disposition of their affirmative or negative or particular universal natures in figures (*schemata*) determined by the position of the *medium* term. In the first figure, the medium is the subject of the predicate (=extreme major) in the first premise and predicate of the subject (=extreme minor) in the second premise; in the second figure, the *medium* is predicate in both premises; in the third figure, the *medium* is subject in both premises.

Aristotle doesn't give criteria of proposition validity but tries to show that any valid proposition must be reduced to a group of perfect syllogisms so that all other syllogisms are valid only if they can be reduced to perfect syllogisms: so, the *imperfectus syllogismus* 'become *perfectus*'. The notion of perfect means that the deduction needs nothing more than what has been explicitly stated to show the necessity of the conclusion, while the notion of imperfect means that a deduction needs one or more elements to show the necessity of the conclusion. However, these elements must be necessary with regard to the terms that have been posited but not made explicit in the premises.[5]

While all four moods of the first figure are perfect syllogisms, the moods of the second and third are imperfect syllogisms and must be reduced to the moods of the first figure. However, Aristotle determines four moods of the second and six of the third figure because they are indeed imperfect, but are potentially deductions, in the sense that they can be reduced to the moods of the first figure thanks to *the rules of conversion*, which allow us to transform a proposition into another one that converts the predicate into a subject and the subject into a predicate, keeping the quality of the original proposition but not necessarily its quantity.

If all syllogisms are deductions, they are also distinguished by the nature of their premises: the premises of the demonstrative syllogism are true and necessary, whereas the dialectical premises are the *endoxa* (what is admitted at the beginning by an opponent and by a respondent), and the rhetorical premises are what is plausible, the necessary signs (*tekmerion*) and the plausible signs. So, any deduction is not a demonstration, but from the point of view of the conclusion, any syllogism posits that something is or isn't the case about something.[6]

Ultimately, all syllogisms that do not belong to the first figure are imperfect because they are completed by positing additional premises and are reduced to the valid moods of the first figure, since this is the only figure that meets the conditions of universal conclusion. So, the additional premise does not introduce an element extrinsic to the terms that are posited, but an element *implicit* in the premises, because the extension of the premises must be greater than, or equal to, the extension of the conclusion.

It should be noted that Aristotle deals at length here with the deduction of contingent conclusions, which are introduced by 'it may be that',[7] a statement with a twofold meaning: on the one hand, it denotes everything that happens in a general way and by nature (e.g. a grey-haired man). It can be converted into: 'which is not necessarily the case'. On the other hand, it denotes everything that happens by chance (e.g. 'an animal walks'; 'the ground is shaking'): It can be converted by 'not more in this way than in that way'. This distinction is fundamental, because Aristotle states that his research deals with the first meaning of contingent, which he distinguishes between 'it may be the case' and 'what it is the case for'. This makes it possible to determine under what conditions the deduction will be a deduction of the kind 'it may be' and when it will be a deduction of the kind 'it is the case'.[8] Aristotle thus determines the conversion rules *of this kind of contingent premises* in the three valid figures of the syllogism.

In a coherent way, Aristotle thinks that not only demonstrative and dialectical syllogisms but also rhetorical syllogisms are built according to the first three figures.[9] Therefore, the validity of rhetorical arguments like induction, example, abduction[10] and enthymeme, that is, rhetorical deduction itself, can be tested by the rules of conversion.[11]

In fact, the enthymeme is a deduction that starts from plausible premises and signs, which must be distinguished according to their position as *medium* in the three figures. Therefore, if the sign plays the role of the *medium* – as in the first figure and the deduction is universal, hence true – then the deduction is irrefutable. If the sign plays the role of the predicate, hence of an extreme term, as in the second figure, then the deduction can be refuted, even if the conclusion is true. If the sign plays the role of the subject (i.e. an extreme term) then the deduction can always be refuted because there is never any deduction when the terms are arranged in this way. That is why the latter case of enthymeme is fallacious.[12]

All in all, even if rhetoric aims not at knowing something, but at persuading others, it uses syllogisms that, like all syllogisms, establish that something is the case or that it isn't, either universally or in a particular way. Proof (*pistis*) is thus the central element of rhetoric, which plays a role in the treatment of the audience's passions as well as in the modalities of the speaker's behaviour. The enthymeme is built according to the three figures established by Aristotle and is tested by the conversion rules. Certainly, the enthymeme obtained by the first figure is the most accepted, while in the other figures it is refutable or completely refutable. In a coherent way, in the *Rhetoric*, Aristotle underlines that only the enthymemes drawn from necessary signs are irrefutable.[13]

I.3 *tis sullogismus/aletes sullogismus*

However, the validity of the enthymeme as a syllogism remains problematic.[14] Certainly, the enthymeme is a syllogism which links proof with belief and persuades the audience.[15] Rhetoric is therefore, according to Aristotle, a *techné* which has a method. Moreover, it is the *antistrophos* (the corresponding part) of dialectic.[16] Rhetoric must speculatively find the proofs that persuade in a general way just as medicine doesn't teach to heal this or that person but to find the means to heal anyone who might be suffering from this or that disease. Like dialectical deduction, the enthymeme too uses the *topoi*, the *loci*, as *entailment warrant* to guarantee the conclusion from the premises.[17]

In fact, topical schemes (like the relations between more and less; whole and parts; similarity or dissimilarity; cause and effect) allow to justify a conclusion by introducing an *additional premise*. For example, I would like to prove the thesis: 'to be temperate is good, since to be intemperate is bad'.[18] The entailment warrant is given here by the *locus* of opposites. It is thus necessary to introduce (at least in the mind) the following premise: 'the opposites of the opposites are opposites' and to apply it to the temperate/intemperate and good/evil opposites. The premise introduced to justify – thus complete – the inference may not be expressed when the audience is able to grasp it by the *mens* without needing to make it explicit. However, sometimes the conclusion needs the introduction of several premises and a more complex topical deduction. Now, for Aristotle, even though a syllogism is formed by three terms and two premises, it can also introduce 'something more' to complete the deduction. In this case, the number of premises must be even, and the number of terms must be odd.[19]

At this point, the nature of the enthymeme as a syllogism can seem problematic for at least two items:

1. The relation between proof and belief
2. The completeness criteria

First, the enthymeme deals with most of our judgements and decisions, which can always receive a different solution. The proof here is closely linked to its possibility of being recognized as such by the audience and thus to its credibility. Indeed, the premises of the enthymeme are often given by the plausible and the unnecessary signs. It is thus a matter of what happens most often or in a possible way and therefore of what could have happened otherwise.[20] Apart from the necessary signs (which are quite rare), the enthymeme seems to designate the contingent, 'it may be that', which is converted by 'not more this way than that way'. But this is precisely what Aristotle excluded in the *Analytica Priora* from his research on the validity of syllogisms. Therefore, the definition of the enthymeme as *tis sullogismos*[21] has raised the question: is the enthymeme a kind of syllogism or a syllogism of kind?[22] In the second case, it would be an argument which would follow a 'weak' logic; in the first case, it would designate a class of syllogisms, which like any deduction can be a true syllogism or a fallacious syllogism. Indeed, Aristotle uses *tis sullogismus* where he establishes the criteria for recognizing and refuting enthymemes as paralogisms, just as there are dialectical deductions as paralogisms.

Anyway, this question entails the determination of the kind of completeness proper to enthymemes. *Are there several kinds of completeness?*

I.4 From Athens to Rome

From Athens to Rome, the conceptual network of the Aristotelian enthymeme has been enriched by new elements that partly changed its structure. Roughly speaking, the decisive step was the influence of the Stoic conditional logic[23] and the integration of Aristotelian topics[24] in theory of inferences which, like analogies and inferences to the best explanation, are not syllogisms but ampliative inferences. Consequently, the enthymeme is considered above all as a dialectical deduction, which can have a rhetorical use.

In this respect, Cicero's conception of the enthymeme is very important.[25] In his rewriting of Aristotle's *Topics*, Cicero considers the enthymeme as a *consequentia* or, to put it more precisely, as the third Stoic indemonstrable. This argument draws his conclusions from a particular copulative negation (¬(p & q)/p / ¬q). However, the ancient philosophy, especially Galen,[26] had underlined the argumentative weakness of the third indemonstrable, since it presupposes the truth value of the elements is known, but he had acknowledged its strength in court cases.[27] Significantly, Cicero reverses the perspective: legal argumentation is the model for dialectical and topical argumentation. This supposes a precise idea of the validity criteria of the topical enthymeme as *consequentia*, as well as of its *epistemic value*. In fact, Cicero considers *consequentia* as a general mode of the relationship between antecedent, consequent and repugnant in all inference grounded from a topical scheme.[28]

At this point, it should be noted that it is not always true that every time the conditional proposition 'if p, then q' is true, there is a valid inference 'p, therefore q'. For this to happen, 'if . . .then' must be an implication. The conditional is a complex true or false proposition of the object language, while the implication is what makes 'if . . . then' valid, that is, always true, independently of the truth value of the propositions involved. Thus, the validity criteria of conditional arguments were discussed by the Stoics. The sceptical philosopher Sextus Empiricus distinguishes four criteria:[29] the first two, from Philo and Diodorus, have often been compared to the material implication (p→ q = p & −q): namely to the falsity of the joint assertion of the antecedent and the negation of the consequent and to the strict implication 'It is false that it is possible for p to be true and q to be false: Df = ¬◊ (p & ¬ q).' The third, which Cicero himself attributes to Chrysippus, introduces the incompatibility criterion: the conditional is true if the contradiction of the consequent is incompatible with the antecedent. The major problem here is to understand the *meaning of the incompatibility or conflict*, logical or empirical, complete or incomplete. The fourth one, anonymous, implies that the consequent must be potentially contained in the antecedent.

Now, in his pleadings as well as in his philosophical works, Cicero develops the criterion of incompatibility, which implies a complete or incomplete conflict. Moreover, since the parties in conflict can rarely be neither true together nor false together – but most of the time they cannot be true together, whereas they can be false together – Cicero seems to choose incomplete conflicts.[30]

However, for Cicero, it's not a matter of wanting to establish a 'weak' logic but of proposing validity criteria for any contingent subject that 'can be so or otherwise' – which Aristotle excluded from syllogistic deduction but which concern most of our moral, juridical and aesthetic discussions. Thus, the enthymeme as a dialectical consequence is only one possible meaning of the 'if . . . then' link, characterized by the necessity of deduction, since it implies the opposition inherent to the third indemonstrable. The other inferences don't have this necessity and use other topical schemes. However, Cicero doesn't just list them but orders them, in an original way, according to the *status quaestionis*. The *status quaestionis* indicate the three main positions from which two parties start to discuss a controversial topic. Cicero attributes them to indeterminate questions,[31] notably to philosophical controversies. He defines the *status quaestionis* as establishing a priori the domains of the answers: the *conjecture* – determining if a thing is; the *definition* – what that thing is; and the *value-based judgement* on the just and the unjust establishing its qualification. Above all, it determines which *loci* are best suited to the three questions. An argument, proving whether a fact has occurred, would not be credible if it did not employ the places that conform to the possible answer.

The distribution is as follows:

Cicero thus elaborates a theory and a practice of inference that cannot be reduced to a syllogism, which is why the enthymeme is a Stoic indemonstrable. Certainly, topics have historically developed the reflection on relations, which account for the link 'if … then' because a topical scheme grounds their relationship. Now, in Cicero's sceptical philosophy, most inferences are ampliative and defeasible. They are ampliative in the sense that their conclusions bring more information than the premises, by contravening the Aristotelian rules of term distribution in the conversion. This is the case of analogy that deals with a case not foreseen by the juridical law or by any normative or scientific system and the strategy of abduction that elaborates an explanatory thesis of an unusual phenomenon such that if the thesis were legitimate the phenomenon would be explained. The enthymeme itself poses an *incompatibility* that is not a contradiction, because it is the construction of two assertions between which one must choose, *unless one renounces both*. Cicero proposes a very famous incompatibility in his *Pro Milone*. In defending Milon from the charge of having killed Clodius, who was hated by the Roman aristocracy, Cicero addresses the hesitant and troubled judges in the following way: 'You judges! You sit here to avenge the death of a man (Clodius) you would not restore life to, even if you believed yourselves capable of doing so!'[32]

This is neither expanded syllogisms nor weak logic but a logic that tries to introduce validity criteria for ampliative inferences. Moreover, these are *defeasible*. Indeed, the conclusions of a legal argument can be challenged by the addition of new premises that invalidate the applicability of a given inference rule. The law also implies a fundamental rule of *defeasibility*, namely the rule that considers an accused person innocent until proven guilty (*donnec probetur contrarium*). In this respect, a presumptive belief is guaranteed if it can be subjected to evidential procedures, which challenge its believability.

Table I.1 The Link between Status Questionis and Loci in Cicero's *Topics*

Conjecture	Definition	Quality
Places of cause, of effects; of necessary relations (*ex causis, ex effectis, ex coniunctis*)	Places of definition, of identity and difference; the dialectical places par excellence: consequences, antecedents and contradictories; of cause and effect (*ex definitione, de eodem et de altero; ex consequentia, antecedentis, repugnantia; ex causis et effectis*)	Places of comparison between greater, lesser or equal things, according to the number, the kind, the force and the relation to other things (*ex comparatione*)

Source: © Fosca Mariani Zini.

Therefore, in Cicero's *Topica*, the link between proof and belief (*fides*) denotes the search for inferences whose *epistemic value* is not so much the necessary, the impossible, the true or the false but *epistemic* or *deontic* values such as permissible, legitimate, forbidden, plausible, probable. More precisely, Cicero privileges what 'it is allowed to believe', or even what it is *preferable to believe*, in the sense of what can produce belief, and hence a motivated assent.

In sum, Cicero presents, in his *Topica*, but also in his other works, a doctrine of enthymeme as a Stoic indemonstrable in a theory of deontic argumentation that aims at devising procedures of proof producing a motivated assent. What is best to believe is not a psychological attitude but an epistemic one. Consequently, Cicero develops the link between topics and inferences, which cannot be reduced to syllogisms. *The topic inferences are ampliative and defeasible*, and as such their completeness does not depend on the Aristotelian rules of syllogism conversion but on the validity criteria of the conditional, namely the criterion of the complete and incomplete conflict and of the *entailment warrant* given by the topical outlines.

In this respect, the V book of Quintilian's *Institution of Oratory* stresses that the proof of the discourse is given by the *overlap* between the topics and the Stoic indemonstrable.[33] However, Quintilian considers that emotion is a central element in persuasive strategies. Indeed, the audience is most often inexpert and ignorant. So, the status of the Ve book is very strange if it is compared to other books of *Institutio*: on the one hand, it deals with discursive proof in an exhaustive way, but once and for all; on the other hand, it is largely a deep explanation of the topical and conditional arguments that Cicero uses in his pleas (especially in the *Pro Milone*).

However, unlike Cicero, for Quintilian the nature of belief denotes primarily a psychological state so that it can also be obtained through the manipulation of passions. In this context, Quintilian presents the different understandings of the enthymeme of his time, without apparently taking a position. He singles out five main meanings of the enthymeme:[34]

1. Anything that can be conceived by the mind
2. A kind of argument not yet clearly formulated
3. A proposition accompanied by its justification (*sententia cum ratione*)
4. The conclusion of a consequence
5. The conclusion *ex repugnantibus*

Like Cicero, Quintilian affirms that the enthymeme drawn from its opposites seems to be the most powerful. These remarks are therefore largely based on Ciceronian thought. However, there are two problems:

1. What is the relation between the enthymeme and the consequence on the one hand and the enthymeme and the conclusion drawn from opposites on the other hand?
2. Isn't one of its forms syllogistic?

In fact, on the one hand, for Quintilian, there are only two discursive proofs: the consequence and the conclusion drawn from opposites, to which the name of enthymeme seems to be more appropriate. But the enthymeme is not so much the *oratorius syllogismus* as a part of the syllogism, since it does not necessarily guarantee its conclusion: 'it limits itself to be understood'. On the other hand, the consequence is a syllogistic deduction, since it can guarantee the logical steps which lead from the premises to the conclusion. Quintilian calls this syllogistic deduction of the consequence *epichereima*[35]: Cicero does not name it, but Quintilian identifies it with the justified argument: *ratio/ratiocinatio*. Sometimes, it seems to be the proof itself of the enthymeme. Moreover, Quintilian says that the consequence or *epichereima* is 'the famous imperfect syllogism', but he also reports that the enthymeme has been called 'imperfect syllogism' because it misses parts of the syllogism.

Therefore, two questions arise:

1. Is it the same incompleteness in both cases?
2. Has the notion of imperfection taken on another meaning?

On the one hand, the rules of conversion are not treated by Cicero or Quintilian, since completeness depends on the conditional inference rules, guaranteed by the topical schemes. So, completeness and incompleteness refer especially to Galen's validity criterion of conditional inferences. On the other hand, whereas for Cicero deduction *ex repugnantibus* and *consequentia* were part of the same *locus*, Quintilian differentiates them. The enthymeme remains the most powerful *locus* because it infers *ex repugnantibus*, but for Quintilian, the *consequentia* is a syllogistic deduction.

But in what sense? It seems to me that for Quintilian *consequentia* is a kind of syllogism because the syllogism itself is considered as a kind of topical and conditional inference. Therefore, the enthymeme is an alternative way of demonstrating the relationship between antecedent and consequent expressed in a topical inference, since the consequence and the conclusion *ex repugnantibus* are the only kind of logical proof. So, the *consequentia* is an inference because the syllogism has been integrated in the *consequentia*, that is, in a formal structure with a variable number of premises.

Moreover, for Quintilian, three propositions are an optimal solution for the speaker's audience. In fact, in any argument, there are two items: what needs to be proved and what proves it. But a third element can be added that agrees with the other two ('tertium adici potest velut ex consensu duorum antecedentium') normally the major premise. Thus, imperfection is not so much a lack as a constitutive element of the deduction concerning the plausible or the contingent, which can be so or otherwise. If the speaker must know how to legitimize all the steps of his speech, he needn't present them all, because the missing premise can be easily recognized (*confessa*). Indeed, *loci* build the premises that are either evident maxims or maxims of common sense or a kind of logical conflicts between terms (good/bad) or situations (being in Rome and Athens at the same time).

In sum, in the *philosophia togata* the topical consequence integrates the syllogism in a completely different kind of inferences which are ampliative and defeasible. Incompleteness is neither a defect nor an omission but the epistemological condition of the topical guarantee of any plausible belief. The law is then, for Cicero as well as

Quintilian, the paradigm of this deontic logic, although for Quintilian the manipulation of emotions plays a significant role.

I.5 The legacy of the enthymeme in the Middle Ages and in the Renaissance

The legacy of the Aristotelian enthymeme implies specific questions: the relation between proof and belief; the criteria of completeness, hence of validity; and the reflection on the syllogistic nature of the enthymeme. At stake is to identify tensions, in the history of philosophy from late antiquity to the Renaissance, between a view of the enthymeme as a *syllogismus imperfectus*, defective, but that can be completed by the conversion rules, and a *syllogismus imperfectus* that designates an extended syllogism, or even an ampliative inference, whose completeness criteria do not indicate a defect but a gain in intelligibility. Thereby, *the analysis of the enthymeme gives a particular point of view that enables us to shed light on the relations between the validity criteria of plausible or contingent arguments and their epistemic value dans la 'longue durée'*.[36] This enquiry could only be a collective one and extends a previous research project that gave rise to a collective volume on the topical syllogism.[37]

The chapters collected here do not claim retracing the history of the enthymeme in an exhaustive way, but they propose to examine some very significant theses with respect to the principal questions suggested. It is in this perspective that I will present this volume's chapters. The aim is indeed to suggest the most important interpretation lines in their historical context, without presupposing a teleological history of enthymeme theories.

In Chapter 1, 'The theories of enthymeme between late antiquity and the early Middle Ages (*c*. 325–880)', Renato de Filippis analyses the theory of the enthymeme in classical Latin texts. The enthymeme is considered in three ways: as an 'imperfect syllogism', as the demonstration of a contradictory (and therefore as *a contrario* or *ex repugnantibus*) argumentation; or as 'mental consideration' (*mentis conceptio*). This polysemy by Cicero and in the *Rhetorica ad Herennium* is inherited from the so-called *rhetores latini minores*, a group of manuals, *compendia* and repertoires written after Quintilian (from the fourth century until the eighth century AD). The readings of the enthymeme are different between Fortunatianus, Iulius Rufinianus and Iulius Victor, Cassiodorus, Victorinus and Isidor of Seville, but the most important claim is to distinguish – or not – the enthymeme from the *epichireima* in order to define the *imperfectus syllogsmus* as an incomplete or as an expanded syllogism.

Between the sixth and ninth centuries, the leading philosophers and theologians dealt with all three ancient conceptions of the enthymeme. Boethius, in the second book of his *De differentiis topicis*, for example, clearly states that the enthymeme is *imperfectus syllogismus* because it is similar to a logical syllogism, even though it does not use all *quae convenient* elements of the latter (i.e. it lacks a premise). Moreover, the concept of enthymeme is important to distinguish dialectic from rhetoric. Scotus Eriugena, for his part, follows Cicero, because he considers the enthymeme as the Stoic third indemonstrable, which concerns the things that 'simul esse non possunt'. Besides, he uses the *De praedestinatione* to demonstrate that the *ousia* cannot be corporal. If Scotus Eriugena considers the enthymeme as irrefutable evidence, Cassiodorus thinks that Bible stories use the *enthimemata*.

In sum, de Filippis shows that from late antiquity to the early Middle Ages, not only where there several doctrines of the enthymeme but also different theories about the nature of the enthymeme as a syllogism and its completeness criteria. The enthymeme was considered as a syllogism with missing premise as well as irrefutable evidence and sometimes as an argument extending knowledge.

In mediaeval Islamic philosophy, Averroes, in twelfth-century Andalusia, extended the canon of Aristotle's logical works to rhetoric and poetics. For Averroes, the enthymeme is a kind of syllogism and as such must be studied by logic, even though its conclusions may not be true. In fact, the aim of logic is to produce both an act of conception and a motivated assent since proof does not demonstrate without the recognition of its validity as plausible belief by the audience. The study of *enthymemata* must therefore focus on this form of assent, which is not the manipulation of pathos. Averroes's enthymeme doctrine has – rightly – been the relevant object of attention in historiography. Perhaps a little less well known are al-Fārābī's and Avicenna's (eleventh-century philosophers) doctrines of enthymeme in Islam.

So, in Chapter 2, 'Enthymemes in al-Fārābī's and Avicenna's systems', Saloua Chatti proposes a carefully comparative study on the two authors of the Islamic mediaeval philosophy. While al-Fārābī provides a full analysis of the notion of enthymeme (called *ḍamīr*, in Arabic) – mainly in his treatise entitled *al-Khaṭāba* (corresponding to *Rhetorics*), where he makes a difference between enthymemes, analogies and syllogisms – Avicenna deals with enthymemes not only in his *al-Khaṭāba* but also in *al-Qiyās*, where he analyses it in relation with the concept of logical consequence and shows its limits in this respect. Chatti shows how different these views are from each other, although they are both clearly influenced by Aristotle. In his *al-Khaṭāba*, al-Fārābī compares the enthymeme with both analogy (*tamthīl*) and syllogism (*qiyās*). He says that the enthymemes are closer to syllogisms than to analogies because they produce a kind of certainty, like syllogisms, which deduce their conclusions necessarily. Nevertheless, they are not identical to syllogisms, since they are only convincing; that is, they lead to an opinion, not necessarily to true knowledge. In other words, the conclusion of an enthymeme is a conviction, while the conclusion of a syllogism is true knowledge when its premises are themselves true. In several passages of *al-Khaṭāba*, al-Fārābī insists that the real specificity and power of an enthymeme is precisely that one of its premises is hidden: this feature makes the enthymeme convincing. On the contrary, for Avicenna, enthymemes are valid, and consequently convincing, only when their missed premise is added. Otherwise, they are neither consequent nor convincing. Moreover, by analysing these two approaches, Chatti relates them to their general views about logic. As a result, Avicenna believes logic should be a formal science, while al-Fārābī's claims logic is more an art than a science, which can be formal in some fields but less formal in rhetoric.

In short, al-Fārābī stresses the power of persuasion of the enthymeme because it is incomplete, especially when the added premise is clearly false or when the moods they rely on are clearly invalid. So, he sees enthymemes as some acceptable kind of reasoning in the context of rhetoric. Their incompleteness and even their invalidity in some cases do not seem problematic for him: he explicitly says they should remain incomplete; otherwise they would become something else and would not have the same power and utility.

By contrast, Avicenna does not consider them as persuasive because they are incomplete. Indeed, in his *al-Khaṭāba*, he gives several examples of enthymemes, which are generally admitted by common people but are not persuasive. Although, in *al-Khaṭāba*, he stresses the utility of rhetoric and rhetorical arguments, enthymemes among others, in *al-Qiyās*, he explicitly says that enthymemes are far from persuasive without their missing premise. All in all, not only the enthymemes are not persuasive without their missing premise but also they are not even admissible – as logical arguments – if that premise is not added.

In Chapter 3, 'Argumentum, locus and enthymeme: Abaelard's transformation of the topics into a theory of enthymematic inference', Christopher Martin argues that before the recovery of Aristotle's *Prior Analytics* around the mid-twelfth century and for a considerable time afterwards, the major research area in logic consisted in developing accounts of warranted enthymematic inference prompted by Boethius's presentation of the topics. In this regard, Martin points out Abaelard's theory of completeness in developing a unified theory of the conditional inference, that is, of enthymematic inference understood as a topical one. In fact, even if Abaelard takes up the standard definition of enthymeme as *imperfectus syllogismus*, such incompleteness is a more general notion and one which is central in his theory of topical inference. First, Abaelard defines the locus as the *vis inferentiae*, that is, 'the power entailment' or 'entailment warrant', grounding the relationship between antecedent and consequent in a true conditional proposition. Martin examines Abaelard's criteria performing completeness as the structural property of entailment possessed only by the conditionalization of the figures and moods of the categorical and hypothetical syllogism. The guarantee of enthymemes as local conditional depends on the topical relationship as well as on the appropriate maximal proposition. However, the criterion 'the antecedent proposition cannot be true when the consequent is false' is not sufficient to prove the truth of conditionals. So Abaelard supposes a 'strong' kind of necessity and a 'weak' one. In sum, Martin demonstrates how enthymemes as topical and conditional inferences cannot be reduced to traditional imperfect syllogisms but denote local conditional inferences, whose criteria of completeness and validity are not the Aristotelian rules of convertibility.

While the twelfth century was, according to Martin, the 'golden age' of topical argumentation, in Chapter 4, 'The logic of enthymeme as (incomplete) syllogisms: Thirteenth-century theories and practices', Julie Brumberg-Chaumont reminds us that the thirteenth century was the 'golden age' for syllogistic. In addition, the full recovery of the two analytics (*Prior* and *Posterior*), of the *Topics*, by adding to the earlier reception of the *Sophistici Elenchi* and of Boethius works, imposed the epistemic paradigm of the *Posterior Analytics* so that logic is considered as the instrument of knowledge in every science, itself included. As a consequence, scientific argumentation was supposed to be syllogistically conducted, but the problem was that it was not, since not a single demonstrative syllogism appears in the Aristotelian corpus.

Therefore, the Latin masters dealt with two significant logical tasks: on the one hand, they attempted systematically to reduce the enthymeme, as *imperfectus syllogismus*, to a valid syllogism of the three Aristotelian figures; on the other hand, they tried to reconstruct the several incomplete syllogisms founded in Aristotle's texts. In each case, completeness is the key issue but in different ways. Brumberg-Chaumont focuses carefully on Robert Kilwardby's answers. Since, for Kilwardby, the enthymeme is a kind of syllogism, he needs to cope with the problematic examples of enthymemes in the second and third figures which are not reducible to syllogisms according to Aristotle according in *Analytics Prior II, 27*. He proposed a sophisticated answer whose main features are: First, he adds a new example, a first-figure enthymeme whose completion leads to a correct syllogism, but with a false added premise. This example helps understanding how some enthymemes can be analyzed as both non-reducible to a syllogism (i.e. yielding an invalid second-figure argument, *Prior Analytics II, 27*) and fallacious (*Sophistici Elenchi 5*), while being grounded on the syllogism all the same, as is every enthymeme (*Prior Analytics II, 23*) — the analysis leads here to a comparison with the 'Caenus argument'. It also suggests that the Arabic theory of the 'hidden' premisse might have had some Latin equivalent. Second, he presupposes that Aristotle's examples are just 'examples' (as did already Ps-Philoponus) so that he can provide a method where enthymemes from a proof, from a sign and from a likelihood are all potentially reducible to syllogisms in the three figures, with all propositions true. Third, he relies on the obvious existence of non-rhetorical, scientific enthymemes, that is, truncated syllogisms, be they from a necessary sign (as physiognomonic signs, *Prior Analytics II, 27*) or not, where the missing premise is 'self-evident'. This feature is connected by Brumberg-Chaumont to the practice of systematically completing incomplete syllogisms in the Aristotelian corpus, a enterprise which can be interpretated as meaning that an 'enthymematic' practice of syllogistic, scientific argumentation is ascribed to Aristotle himself by medieval commentators. The fact that 'following the syllogistic form according to reason' (which the enthymeme does) is valued to the detriment of 'according to the vocal sound' (which the enthymeme does not) offers yet another example of the typically non-formalistic approach to the problem of the logical form displayed by thirteenth-century logical texts. Brumberg-Chaumont's study ends by shortly presenting Giles de Rome's conception of the enthymeme, the author of the first Latin commentary in Aristotle's *Rhetoric*. The change in point of view is significant. For Giles, the enthymeme is a *defectivus* syllogism, or a syllogism of kind. Giles of Rome has lost interest in the logic (or the syllogistic) of enthymemes, since this is 'incidental' to rhetoric and only a side topic for dialectic. During the next century, John of Jandun's commentary shows that the criteria of the formulated or unformulated premisse is no longer under focus. The existence of non-rhetorical, scientific enthymemes is considered as obvious : the difference with rhetorical/dialectical enthymemes lies only in the specialized (as opposed to common) nature of terms and topics that warrant the argument. To sum up, Brumberg-Chaumont shows how Kliwardby's syllogistic agenda is an inventive way to understand the enthymeme as incomplete syllogism, that is, as kind of syllogism, and how the line of thinking the relationship between then can support new views of the enthymeme.

In Chapter 5, 'Inference and enthymeme in Ockham', Paola Müller (Milano) presents a close study of Ockham's enthymeme. Even if Ockham in the fourteenth century does not elaborate a specific doctrine of enthymemes, he deals with them as well as with consequences and fallacies, by attempting to link in a coherent way the semantic approach with the syntactic one. Indeed, thanks to the development of topics into the doctrine of consequences, the enthymeme is placed in this new context, in which elements of terminist logic are correlated. The syllogism is no longer the dominant standard model of valid argument but only a kind of argument that can be considered as a consequence. Given that Ockham applies the hylomorphic language to the doctrine of propositional inference, he distinguishes between material and formal consequences grounded on an intrinsic mean, related to semantic rules that relate terms to each other, or an extrinsic mean which is a general syntactic. Enthymemes fall under formal valid consequences by an extrinsic mean (in a mediately way) and by an intrinsic one (in an immediately way), while formal consequences hold only by extrinsic means. The double condition extrinsic/intrinsic means denote the function of topical logic, whose validity depends on the semantic relationship between the inference terms. Only the intrinsic mean does transform the argument into a syllogism. Therefore, the enthymeme as consequence entails an added premise.

The added premise may be either necessary or contingent. Müller explains carefully how Ockham refers to the enthymeme in the fallacy of the form of expression, the fallacy in an absolute sense or for a specific aspect and the consequent fallacy. Is this regard, Ockham distinguishes between fallacious defective enthymemes in a material way (thus they have false premises and are fallacious *enthymemata secundum quid et simpliciter*) and fallacious defective *enthymemata* in a formal way (because their defect is structural). Nevertheless, Ockham proposes a set of rules in order to resolve these fallacious *enthymemata* and in doing so he opens the way to another view of the enthymeme, that is, the Buridan's theory.

In Chapter 6, 'Enthymematic inferences in John Buridan', Barbara Bartocci examines how John Buridan describes enthymeme as *imperfectus syllogismus*, from a logical and epistemological point of view. From a logical point of view, an enthymeme is a material consequence, so an incomplete deduction that can be reduced to a valid deduction by adding the missing premise thanks to topical rules. From an epistemological point of view, an enthymeme is an inference, that is, a process performed by an agent producing an epistemic gain, and in this case, it meets specific epistemological criteria. Such a theory of enthymeme is grounded on Buridan's adoption of the Arabic 'long *Organon*', which includes Aristotle's *Poetics* and *Rhetoric*. Therefore, Bartocci analyses, on the one hand, the relation between material consequences, that is, enthymemes and topical inference rules, by underlining how Buridan expands them to produce a complete syllogism (*reductio ad syllogismus*), where 'syllogism' has to be understood broadly as including categorical and hypothetical syllogisms. On the other hand, the epistemic side of enthymemes shows that enthymemes as dialectical argumentations produce opinion as well as *suspicion*, belief. The significant issue is how Buridan deals with the material consequences, that is, *enthymemata*, that do not fit the syllogistic figures. Buridan leaves unsaid how this is supposed to work and to which type of material consequences this expansion applies. Bartocci demonstrates this kind of enthymemes, which do not infer their conclusion necessarily, either formally or materially, can produce some useful belief in the agent. Therefore, this kind of *enthymemata* can better be appraised by a dialectical rather than by a deductive standard. Indeed, for Buridan dialectic is the discipline concerned with establishing the epistemic norms for producing 'weak knowledge', namely justified likely true beliefs, and with providing a reliable, though fallible belief-forming method, which yields mostly true beliefs and could be used in those disciplines that deal with contingent subject matters, hence unable to achieve 'strong knowledge' and absolute certainty. Therefore, as Bartocci argues, this expanded conception of Buridan's dialectic implies ampliative inferences, underpinned by a necessary or probable consequence, which produces an imperfect belief in the agent. In fact, Buridan defines arguments in general as inferences that provide justification for assenting to the conclusion and believing a proposition that was unknown or doubted. Finally, he leaves open the possibility that a mental syllogism might be expressed in enthymematic form. Besides, a speaker might have various reasons for preferring enthymemes over syllogisms.

Before presenting the last chapters of this volume, let me introduce few remarks concerning, on the one hand, the relationship between the Middle Ages and the Renaissance and, on the other hand, the humanist theories of argumentation. First, recent historiography has largely demonstrated that Mediaeval and Renaissance philosophy share many aspects, emphasizing moments of continuity. However, not only did the reception of new philosophical works by Plato and the Neoplatonists, along with Galen's or Quintilian's or Lucretius's entire works, besides Cicero's *Academics*, transform private and public libraries, but above all the order of questions. The point was to rethink the links between language or languages – Latin and vernacular at least but also Greek and Hebrew – and thought. Thanks to the pioneering philological work of *grammatici* such as Angelo Poliziano and Lorenzo Valla, it was established that language is not a 'neutral' instrument of logic but a historical institution that resists any attempt at logical 'purification'. *Language is not only one of the main features of human beings' dignity but also a possible obstacle to the conception as well as to the expression of thought.* Beyond polemical criticisms towards mediaeval logicians, humanists like L. Valla, R. Agricola, A. Nizolio or Ramus underlined that the theory of consequences and obligations does not account for the 'art of arguments' in an historical language.

Consequently, the philosopher can speak without knowing what he says, hence disavowing himself. The reforms of the language arts the humanists tried to propose – often in an unsatisfactory way – therefore aim at elaborating the rules of an argumentation that they often called 'natural'. It is not a matter of spontaneous argumentation but of an argumentation theory and practice that takes into account not only the defence and refutation of theses but also the elaboration of value judgements and beliefs transmitted by this or that culture, in order to coherently link proof procedures for defeasible and ampliative inferences (such as induction and abduction), which require a motivated assent. Belief here is not only a psychological state but above all a cognitive state. That is why the 'natural' argumentation model is often law juridic argumentation, as it was for Cicero and Quintilian. This line of reasoning goes through the recompositing of the functions of rhetoric, dialectic and topic, in a sometimes implicit confrontation with the most significant mediaeval theses on the enthymeme as *imperfectus syllogismus* and on its different validity and completeness criteria.

Now, this topic would deserve a collective volume of its own, since traditional historiography, on the one hand, has not produced such a synthetic and exhaustive essay on the subject since Cesare Vasoli's book *La dialettica e la retorica dell'umanesimo. Invenzione e metodo nei XV e XVI secoli* (1964)[38] and, on the other hand, tends to reduce humanist reforms to an enterprise of 'rhetorization' of dialectics – a thesis I find very problematic, even though it is still very widespread. In saying this I do not mean to argue that the fifteenth and sixteenth centuries are characterized only by these argumentation reforms. Since the history of thought is not teleological, other accounts of the enthymeme are simultaneously present, whether it be the adaptation of the enthymeme to the writing of history or poetry or the development of reflection on consequences, in the wake of the mediaeval tradition.

In this context, the two following chapters approach the doctrine of the enthymeme in the Renaissance from the original point of view of scientific thought: the first, as a conjecture from the necessary signs and, the second, as a signature, that is, 'visual' argument from plausible signs in physiognomy.

In Chapter 7, 'The enthymeme from signs and the study of nature in the Renaissance', Marco Sgarbi deals with the reception and influence of Philoponus's and Simplicius's enthymeme on the philosophy of nature in the Italian fifteenth and sixteenth centuries, notably by Agostino Nifo, Alessandro Achillini, Marcoantonio Zimara, Bernardino Tomitano, Girolamo Balduino and Jacopo Zabarella. Sgarbi shows how the Aristotelian kind of enthymeme, whose premises are the necessary signs (*tekmeria*), is considered by these authors as valid conjecture in order to investigate the causal explanation of the natural phenomena. Indeed, the Greek Aristotelian commentators, Philoponus and Simplicius, extend the conception of enthymeme based on necessary signs or evidence to the syllogism from effect to cause – that is, the inference from what is a posteriori to what is a priori, while this causal relation is missing in Aristotle's rhetorical enthymeme. In fact, the most important aspect is the introduction of a causal relation that was missing in Aristotle in the proof-based inference. This idea enables Philoponus to conceive the induction also as a form of reasoning based on evidence. However, for Simplicius, inference would be based on refutable signs, thus on a more conjectural inference. All in all, for both Philoponus and Simplicius, the enthymeme by evidence becomes an inference that characterizes the foundations of natural investigation while, for Aristotle, the enthymeme from necessary signs cannot explain causality. Then, Sgarbi shows how many Renaissance philosophers inherited this incorrect interpretation of the Aristotelian enthymeme originating from Greek commentators, in order to elaborate the so-called *demonstratio ex signis*. Philoponus's and Simplicius's Renaissance translation develops a deep and original investigation about the distinction between *propter quid* demonstration and *quia* demonstration. What is very remarkable is that Philoponus's inference from necessary signs is called 'conjecturalis syllogism'. At this point, Sgarbi outlines two important ways of interpreting inference by signs as inference by conjecture: the first underlines the nature of the argument of the sign as conjecture, while the second follows the transformation of conjecture into demonstration. So, the Aristotelian enthymeme becomes an instrument for the investigation of nature and the knowledge of particulars coming from experience. In this respect, it is not defective or incomplete but implies an ampliative inference, discovering the cause from the effect. In doing so, it is very powerful in the philosophy of nature.

In Chapter 8, 'The lion's fault: The enthymematic foundation of the signatures', Marie-Luce Demonet deals with the enthymeme, relying on *semeia eikota* (probable signs) in *Rhetorica*, in the physiognomic tradition. She focuses on Della Porta's *De humana physiognomonia* (1586) and *Physiognomonica* (1588), by examing on the example of the large lion's paws that bring out his fortitude (ps. Aristotle, *Analytica Priora*, I-2, 2 because this passage is doubtful). The most important question is where ps. Aristotle's physiognomic opens the way to the signature. It would seem so, since the big paws warrant the construction of a valid enthymeme of the first figure. However, to demonstrate that conjecture from signs is a *scientia*, he skips the first lines of the Aristotelian chapter to quote the lion and his large paws. Nevertheless, Demonet prefers to define the physiognomic enthymeme, especially the example of the lion, as a 'visual enthymeme'.

In fact, on the one hand, the authentic signature theory (owed to Paracelsus) is widely ignored during most of the sixteenth century, particularly in France; on the other hand, even if the illustrated physiognomic as well the emblematic tradition underline the visual and commonplace correspondences between animals, objects and plants – in order to signify human qualities or vices, they admit that several signs can be interpreted in different ways. Della Porta himself considers the syllogism of the lion as an enthymeme, valid in Barbara, but admits the relationship between exterior (body) and interior (soul) is only a problematic similitude. In fact, *Fortis* can be translated either by 'strong' or by 'courageous', enlarged by the addition of another feature of the lion, magnanimity – a quality of the soul, not of the body. Furthermore, what about the round nose? Some other physiognomics suppose that the round nose is not a sign of magnanimity but of the lion's boastful character. Hence, if there is more than one propriety at stake for one *indicium*, the necessity of the connection between body and soul remains uncertain.

To summarize, Demonet shows how the physiognomic visual enthymeme as *imperfectus syllogismus* can be reduced with great difficulty – indeed almost never – to the valid syllogism. In fact, Aristotle and his commentators warn about the risk of *fallacia* by finding similitude, especially in scientific matters. However, the visual enthymeme is acting as an inventing conjecture. This is useful to grasp important and hidden elements in our experience of physical and human natures, though human souls should not forget the pleasant and convincing power of the image as an image.

So, the problematic legacy of enthymeme bears on various topics in logic, epistemology, metaphysics, theology and visual signs. So, this volume explores the history of enthymeme from different points of view and hopefully will bring it a little more of the attention it deserves.

Notes

1 Boethius 2004b; see Marenbon 2003; Pinzani 2003; Magnano 2014.
2 Kraus 1994; Green 1995; Rapp 2002.
3 Aristotle 1969, 1973, 2020. See Rose 1968.
4 *Aristoteles latinus* 1938-. See Ebbesen 1981; Anderson 1986; D'Onofrio 1986; Jacobi 1993; Kraus 2002; Bianchi 2011; Coda & Martini Bonadeo 2014.

5   Mignucci 1975.
6   Brunschwig 1994; Slomkowski 1997.
7   An. pr., I, 13–22.
8   An. pr., I, 22, 40b 9–16.
9   An.pr., II, 23, 68b 10–14.
10 An. pr., II, 23, 68b15-26, 70a3.
11 An. pr., II, 27, 70a4-70b5.
12 Tabarroni 2002.
13 Rhet., I, 2, 1357 a22-b21.
14 See Sorensen 1988; Piazza 2000; Piazza 2012.
15 Rhet., I, 2, 1356a 19-20; 1356b2-4, *passim*.
16 Rhet., I, 1 1354a1-9.
17 See De Pater 1968; Green-Pedersen 1984.
18 Rhet., 1397a.
19 An. pr., I, 25, 42b30-35.
20 Rhet., 1,2, 1357a7-33.
21 Rhet., II, 24, 1400 b37-40.
22 Burnyeat 1994.
23 Striker 1979; Bobzien 2003; Speca 2001.
24 Bird 1962.
25 Cicero 1949, 1994. See Mariani Zini 2009a; Mariani Zini 2010a; Mariani Zini 2019.
26 Galen 1964.
27 Galen, Inst., XIV, 4, p. 271.
28 Cicero, Top., 54–7.
29 Sextus Empiricus, Adversos Math., VIII, 110–12.
30 Galen, Inst., XIV, 5.
31 Cicero, Top., 68–89.
32 Cicero, Pro Milone, 79.
33 Quintilian 2002.
34 Quintilian, Inst. or., V, 10, 1–6 and XIV, 1–10.
35 Klein 1994.
36 See Etchmenendy 1990; Black 1990, 1990a; Demonet 1992; Street 2005; Mariani Zini 2008; Martin 2004; Pinzani 2005; Martin 2009; Biard 2009; Mariani Zini 2008; Mariani Zini 2009; Pasnau 2010; Müller 2012; Biard 2012; De Filippis 2013; Brumberg-Chaumont 2013; Read 2015; Klima 2016; Perreiah 2018; Duthil Novaes 2007; Chatti 2019; Mariani Zini 2021.
37 Biard and Mariani Zini 2009.
38 But see Leinkauf 2017, I, pp. 315–604.

Bibliography

Anderson, H. R. (1986), 'Enthymeme and Dialectic: Cloister and Classroom', in *From Cloister to Classroom: Monastic and Scholastic Approaches to Truth*, E. Rozanne Elder (ed.), Kalamazoo, Cistercian Publications, pp. 239–74.

Aristoteles (1947–1972), *Aristoteles Latinus*, L. Minio-Paluello (ed.), Brill, Leiden; H. P. Cooke et alii (trans.), Cambridge, MA, Harvard University Press, Loeb Classical Library, 23 vols, 1970–1993.

Aristoteles (1969), 'Topica, Translatio Boethii', in *Aristoteles Latinus*, L. Minio-Paluello (ed.), Bruxelles/Paris, Desclée de Brouwer, vol. 5.
Aristoteles (1973), *Analytica priora*, H. Tredennick (trans.), Cambridge, MA, Harvard University Press.
Aristoteles (2020), *Rhetorica*, J. H. Freese (trans.), G. Striker (rev.), Cambridge, MA, Harvard University Press.
Bianchi, L. (ed.) (2011), *Christian Readings of Aristotle from the Middle Ages to the Renaissance*, Turnhout, Brepols.
Biard, J. (1989), *Logique et théorie du signe au XIVe siècle*, Paris, Vrin.
Biard, J. (2009), 'Le lieu de la croyance: le traité sur les Topiques de Jean Buridan', in *Les lieux de l'argumentation. Histoire du syllogisme topique d'Aristote à Leibniz*, J. Biard and F. Mariani Zini (eds), Turnhout, Brepols, pp. 359–83.
Biard, J. (2012), *Science et nature. La théorie buridanienne du savoir*, Paris, Vrin.
Bird, O. (1962), 'The Tradition of the Logical Topics: Aristotle to Ockham', *Journal of the History of Ideas* 23 (3), pp. 307–23.
Black, D. (1990), *Logic and Aristotle's 'Rhetoric' and 'Poetics' in Medieval Arabic Philosophy*, Turnhout, Brepols.
Bobzien, S. (2003), 'Logic', in *The Cambridge Companion to the Stoics*, B. Inwood (ed.), Cambridge, Cambridge University Press, pp. 85–123.
Boethius Severinus (=Boethius) (2004a), *De differentiis topicis*, D. Z. Nikitas (ed.), Athens/Paris/Bruxelles, Akademia Athenon/Vrin/Ousia, 1990: E. Stump (trans.), Ithaca, NY, Cornell University Press. 1978.
Boethius Severinus (=Boethius) (2004b), *In Topica Ciceronis*, E. Stump (ed. et trans.), Ithaca, NY, Cornell University Press.
Brumberg-Chaumont, J. (2013), 'Les divisions de la logique selon Albert le Grand', in *'Ad notitiam ignoti' L'Organon dans la translation studiorum à l'époque d'Albert le Grand*, J. Brumberg-Chaumont (ed.), Turnhout, Brepols, pp. 335–416.
Brunschwig, J. (1994), 'Rhétorique et dialectique. Rhetorique et Topiques', in *Aristotle's Rhetoric. Philosophical Essays*, D. Furley and A. Nehemas (eds), Princeton, NJ, Princeton University Press, pp. 57–96.
Burnyeat, M. F. (1994), 'Enthymeme: Aristotle on the Logic of Persuasion', in *Aristotle's Rhetoric. Philosophical Essays*, D. Furley and A. Nehemas (eds), Princeton, NJ, Princeton University Press, pp. 3–56.
Chatti, S. (2019), *Arabic Logic from al-Fārābī to Averroes*, Basel, Birkhäuser/Springer.
Cicero, Marcus Tullius (1949), *De inventione*, H. M. Hubbell (trans.), Cambridge, MA, Harvard University Press.
Cicero, Marcus Tullius (1994), *Topica*, G. Di Maria (ed.), Palermo, L'Epos.
Coda, E. and Martini Bonadeo C. (eds) (2014), *De l'antiquité tardive au Moyen Age. Etudes de logique aristotélicienne et de philosophie grecque, syriaque, arabe et latine, offertes à Henri Hugonnard-Roche*, Paris, Vrin.
Demonet, M.-L. (1992), *La voix du signe. Nature et origine du langage à la Renaissance*, Paris, Champion.
De Pater, W. A. (1968), 'La fonction du lieu et de l'instrument dans les Topiques', in *Aristotle's on Dialectic. The Topics*, Oxford, Oxford University Press, pp. 164–88.
D'Onofrio, G. (1986), *Fons scientiae. La dialettica nell'Occidente tardo-antico*, Napoli, Liguori.
D'Onofrio, G. (2009), 'Topica e sapere teologico nell'alto Medioevo', in *Les lieux de l'argumentation. Histoire du syllogisme topique d'Aristote à Leibniz*, J. Biard and F. Mariani Zini (eds), Turnhout, Brepols, pp. 141–70.

De Filippis, R. (2013), *La retorica nell'Occidente tardo-antico e alto-medievale*, Roma, Città Nuova.
Duthil Novaes, C. (2007), *Formalizing of Medieval Logical Theories: Supposition, Consequentia and Obligations*, Berlin et al., Springer.
Ebbesen S. (1981), *Commentators and Commentaries on Aristotle's Sophistici Elenchi. A Study of Post-Aristotelian Ancient and Medieval Writings on Fallacies*, Leiden, Brill, 3 vols.
Etchmenendy, J. (1990), *The Concept of Logical Consequence*, Cambridge, MA, Harvard University Press.
Galen (1964), *Institutio logica*, J. S. Kieffer (trans. and ed.), Baltimore, MD, The John Hopkins Press.
Green, L. D. (1995), 'Aristotle's Enthymeme and the Imperfect Syllogism', in *Rhetoric and Pedagogy*, W. B. Horner, M. Leff, R. Gaines, J. Dietz Moss, B. S. Bennett (eds), London, Routledge, pp. 19–41.
Green-Pedersen, N. J. (1984), *The Tradition of the Topics in the Middle Ages*, München-Wien, Philosophia Verlag.
Jacobi, K. (ed.) (1993), *Argumentation Theory. Scholastic Research on the Logical and Semantic Rules of Correct Inference*, Leiden, Brill.
Klein, J. (1994), *s. v. Epicheirem*, In *Historisches Wörterbuch der Rhetorik*, II, coll. 1251–1258, von G. Ueding (ed.), Tübingen, Niemeyer.
Klima, G. (2016), 'Consequence', in C. Dutilh Novaes and S. Read (eds), *The Cambridge Companion to Medieval Logic*, Cambridge, Cambridge University Press, pp. 316–41.
Kraus, M. (1994), *v. Enthymem*, in *Historisches Wörterbuch der Rhetorik*, II, coll. 1197–1222, von G. Ueding (ed.), Tübingen, Niemeyer.
Kraus, M. (2002), 'Theories and Practice of the Enthymeme in the First Centuries', in *Rhetorical Argumentation in Biblical Texts. Essays from the Lund 2000 Conference*, A. Eriksson, T. H. Olbricht, W. Übelacker (eds), Harrisonburg, PA, Trinity Press, pp. 95–111.
Kraus, M. (2012), 'Teorie dell'entimema nell'antichità', in *Pan. Rivista di filologia latina*, N.S., 1, pp. 17–30.
Leinkauf, Th. (2017), *Grundriss. Philosophie des Humanismus und der Renaissance (1350-1600)*, Hamburg, Meiner, 2 vols.
Magnano, F. (2014), *Il De topicis differentiis di Severino Boezio, Palermo, topique d'Aristote à Leibniz*, Officina di Studi Medievali.
Marenbon, J. (2003), *Boethius*, Oxford, Oxford University Press.
Mariani Zini, F. (2008), 'Sprache and Argumentation in Lorenzo Valla', in *Sol et homo. Mensch und Natur in der Renaissance*, Th. Ricklin et alii (eds), München, Fink, pp. 63–79.
Mariani Zini, F. (2009a), 'Les Topiques oubliées de Cicéron', in *Les Lieux de l'argumentation. Histoire du syllogisme topique d'Aristote à Leibniz*, J. Biard et F. Mariani Zini (éds.), Turnhout, Brepols, pp. 65–92.
Mariani Zini, F. (2009b), 'Topique et argumentation dans le premier humanisme italien', in *Le langage mental du Moyen Âge à l'Âge classique*, J. Biard (éd.), Louvain-la-Neuve/Paris, Éditions de l'Institut supérieur de philosophie, Éditions Peeters, pp. 221–40 (Philosophes médiévaux, 50).
Mariani Zini, F. (2010a), 'Cicero on Conditional Right', In *Approach to legal Rationality*, D. M. Gabbay et alii (eds), New York/Berlin/Amsterdam, Springer-Kluwer, pp. 45–70.
Mariani Zini, F. (2010b), 'Crédibilité, croyance, confiance. Le legs de la tradition romaine', *Revue de métaphysique et de morale, numéro thématique « Concepts rhétoriques, raisons topiques »* 2, pp. 179–94.

Mariani Zini, F. (2019), 'Argumentation als Trost. Bemerkungen über Ciceros *Tusc. I*', in *Philosophie in Rom-Römische Philosophie. Kultur-, literatur-und philosophiegeschichtliche Perspektive*, G. M. Müller et F. Mariani Zini (eds), Berlin, Walter de Gruyter, pp. 327-43.

Mariani Zini, F. (2021), 'La réflexion de Politien sur l'enthymème', in *Politien, humaniste aux sources de la Modernité*, E. Seris and P. Viti (eds), Paris, Garnier, pp. 221-37.

Martin, C. J. (2004), 'Logic', in *The Cambridge Companion to Abaelard*, J. Brower and K. Guilfoy (eds) Cambridge, Cambridge University Press, pp. 158-99.

Martin, C. J. (2009), 'The Development of Abaelard's Theory of Topical Inference', in *Les lieux de l'argumentation: Histoire du syllogisme topique d'Aristote à Leibniz*, op. cit., pp. 249-70.

Mignucci, M. (1975), *L'argomentazione dimostrativa in Aristotele*, Padova, Antenore.

Müller, P. (2012), *La logica di Ockham*, Milano, Vita e Pensiero.

Pasnau, R. (2010), 'Medieval Social Epistemology: Scientia for Mere Mortals', *Episteme* 7, pp. 23-41.

Perreiah, A. R. (2018), 'Ideology and Reception in Renaissance Logic', in *The Aftermath of Syllogism. Aristotelian Logical Argument from Avicenna to Hegel*, M. Sgarbi and M. Cosci (eds), London, Bloomsbury, pp. 35-57.

Piazza, F. (2000), *Il corpo della persuasione. L'entimema nella retorica greca*, Palermo, Novecento.

Piazza, F. (2012), 'Non solo sillogismo. Per una lettura retorica dell'entimema aristotelico', *Pan. Rivista di filologia latina, N.S.* 1, pp. 32-4.

Pinzani, R. (2003), *La logica di Boezio*, Parma, Franco Angeli.

Pinzani, R. (2005), *Le conseguenze di Ockham. Appunti e proposte interpretative*, Roma, Aracne.

Quintilian (2002), *Institutio oratoria*, D. A. Russell (ed. and trans.), Cambridge, MA, Harvard University Press.

Rapp, Ch. (2002), 'Die Syllogismus-truncatus-Lehre – ein Nachruf', in *Id., Werke in deutscher Übersetzung, Aristoteles, Rhetorik*, C. Rapp (trans. and comm.), Berlin, Akademie Verlag, vol. 2, 187-9.

Read, S. (2015), 'The Medieval Theory of Consequence', *Synthese* 187 (3), pp. 899-912.

Rose, L. E. (1968), *Aristotle's Syllogistic*, Springfield, Thomas, 1968.

Slomkowski, P. (1997), *Aristotle's Topics*, Leiden, Brill.

Sorensen, R. A. (1988), 'Are Enthymemes Arguments?', *Notre Dame Journal of Formal Logic* 29, pp. 155-9.

Speca, A. (2001), *Hypothetical Syllogism and Stoic Logic*, Leiden, Brill.

Street, T. (2005), 'Logic', in *The Cambridge Companion to Arabic Philosophy*, P. Adamson and R. Taylor (eds), Cambridge, Cambridge University Press, pp. 247-67.

Striker, G. (1979), 'Aristoteles über Syllogismen 'aufgrund einer Hypothese'', *Hermes* 107, pp. 33-50.

Tabarroni, A. (2002), 'Fantastiche argomentazioni: lo studio logico delle fallacie da Aristotele a Whately', in *Quando il pensiero sbaglia. La fallacia tra psicologia e scienza*, G. Mucciarelli and G. Celani (eds), Torino, UTET, pp. 3-38.

Vasoli, C. (1964, reprint 2007), *Dialettica e retorica nel Rinascimento*, Reggio Calabria, La Città del Sole.

Walton, D. and Reed C. A. (2005), 'Argumentation Schemes and Enthymemes', *Synthese* 145, pp. 339-70.

1

The theories of the enthymeme between late antiquity and the early Middle Ages (*c.* 325–880)

Renato de Filippis

1.1 *The enthymeme in the Greek and Latin theories.* In the Latin philosophical tradition of the West between the fourth and ninth centuries, it is difficult to find two authors who agree on the nature and *status* of the enthymeme, one of the elements of the logical-rhetorical theory which lacks a clear and undisputed definition.[1] We could ironically define the enthymeme as 'the great mystery' of this theory, and its enigma continues in the historiography of late antiquity and the early Middle Ages with very few studies devoted to describing its history and its evolution during those times.[2]

It is well known that this ambiguity of sense and classification of the enthymeme goes back to Greek thought, where there are at least two main theories about it. The first, and perhaps oldest, is in the *Rhetorica ad Alexandrum*, in which the enthymeme is the demonstration of a contradiction in the line of reasoning of an adversary. Then there is the Aristotelian theory, which we can find in both the *Rhetoric* and the *Prior Analitics* and which is partially ambiguous from the start because the two texts do not present exactly the same theory. Aristotle considers the enthymeme a 'rhetorical syllogism', that is, a syllogism which does not have all the features of scientific deduction but tries, using evidence, signs and examples, to persuade rather than demonstrate in a strict, apodictic way.[3] In the second book of the *Rhetoric*, he further specifies that there are two typologies of enthymeme: one 'demonstrative' and one 'confutative'.[4] Manfred Kraus observes that in the common Greek language there is also a third sense for the words *enthymema* and *enthymeisthai*, which mean both 'consideration' and 'mental reflection': this is the meaning understood, for example, by Sophocles or Isocrates.[5] In this context, the idea of enthymeme as 'imperfect' or 'elliptic syllogism', which is typical in modern and contemporary theories as well as in common language, is substantially absent. It 'appears' later, as result of a process we cannot determine precisely with the sources at our disposal.[6]

If we turn to the Latin classical rhetorical context, we observe that this ambiguity is still present, perhaps even more so. The *Rhetorica ad Herennium* does not use the term *enthymema*, but it does mention, among the rhetorical figures of speech, a *contrarium* which bears some similarity to what the *Rhetorica ad Alexandrum* considered to be an enthymeme. It is the figure through which we argue something deriving from the opposite concept, behaviour or element. As in its possible Greek source, it has to be concise. Although included among the figures of speech, it seems to have some, albeit weak, argumentative value.

> Reasoning by contraries is the figure which, of two opposite statements, uses one so as neatly and directly to prove the other, as follows: 'Now how should you expect one who has ever been hostile to his own interests to be friendly to another's?' Again: 'Now why should you think that one who is, as you have learned, a faithless friend, can be an honourable enemy? Or how should you expect a person whose arrogance has been insufferable in private life, to be agreeable and not forget himself when in power, and one who in ordinary conversation and among friends has never spoken the truth, to refrain from lies before public assemblies?' Again: 'Do we fear to fight them on the level plain when we have hurled them down from the hills? When they outnumbered us, they were no match for us; now that we outnumber them, do we fear that they will conquer us?' This figure ought to be brief and completed in an unbroken period. Furthermore, it is not only agreeable to the ear on account of its brief and complete rounding-off, but by means of the contrary statement it also forcibly proves what the speaker needs to prove; and from a statement which is not open to question it draws a thought which is in question, in such a way that the inference cannot be refuted, or can be refuted only with much the greatest difficulty.[7]

Cicero's theory is far more complex. In his *De oratore* he notes a *contrarium* among the figures of speech but provides no further explanation.[8] The *De Inventione* lacks a theory of the enthymeme, although it does have a very specific theory of syllogism, which is called *ratiocinatio* and which should not ever have less than three parts[9] (this notion, we incidentally observe, seems to go against the already mentioned theory of 'elliptic syllogism'). We must then recur to the *Topica*, which we know are heavily influenced by Stoic doctrine. In the long list of argumentations in the text, and specifically within the *loci* 'ex iis rebus quae quodam modo affectae sunt ad id de quo quaeritur',[10] we find the *locus ex repugnantibus*, or 'tertium modum conclusionis' ('Not at the same time *p* and *q*; but *p*; therefore, not *q*'). It is, together with two other *loci, ex consequentibus* and *ex antecedentibus*, considered 'proprius dialecticorum'.[11] Here, Cicero is speaking of Stoic hypothetical syllogisms:

> The logicians give the name of 'first form of conclusion' to this way of concluding an argument, in which when you have assumed the first statement, that which is connected with it follows as true; when you deny what is connected, with the result that that statement with which it is connected must also be denied, this is called the second form; when, however, you deny that certain things are associated and assume the truth of one or more, so that the remaining statement must be excluded, this is called the third form. To this belong those forms of conclusion from contraries adopted by teachers of rhetoric, to which they themselves have

given the name ἐνθυμήματα. Not that any expression of thought is not properly called an ἐνθύμημα, but just as among the Greeks Homer by his outstanding merit has made the name of poet peculiarly his own, although it is common to all poets, so although every expression of thought may be called ἐνθύμημα, that one which is based on contraries has, because it seems the most pointed form of argument, appropriated the common name for its sole possession. . . . This kind of argumentation has doubtless a relation to your discussions when you give answers on legal problems, but it more closely concerns the philosophers, who share with orators that method of drawing a conclusion from contradictory statements which the logicians call the third form, and the teachers of rhetoric, the ἐνθύμημα.[12]

It is most interesting to observe the link that Cicero creates here between the *locus ex repugnantibus* or third hypothetical syllogism (from a logical point of view) and the enthymeme (from a rhetorical point of view). They would appear to be the same thing, seen from two different perspectives. He also seems to understand that the word can generally indicate a 'thought' or 'consideration' (this is the first meaning of the Latin word *sententia*) and is thus quite aware of the third sense of the Greek term, the most general one. Nevertheless, he states that as it is the cleverest (*acutissima*), this *sententia ex contrariis* can 'take possession' of this common name. Even if he connects his meaning of the enthymeme to a contrariety and we can therefore assume that there is some connection with the almost contemporary theory of the *Rhetorica ad Herennium*, Cicero sees something quite different with more argumentative value.

With Quintilian we may have reached the highest peak of ambiguity and complexity. He himself is aware of this when in the fifth book of his *Institutio oratoria*, he tries to create order out of the intricate previous tradition.[13] Discussing the *probationes artificiales* which an orator could include in his discourse, Quintilian affirms that for the Greek rhetorical essayists there are three similar typologies of *argumenta*: enthymemes, epicheiremas and apodosis. Regarding the enthymeme, which he hesitantly translates as *commentum* or *commentatio*, he in turn distinguishes three meanings of the word: all the mind's reflections (the more ancient Greek meaning which matches his translation but is immediately excluded from his analysis); 'sententia cum ratione' (another sense which he does not debate but which could refer to the Aristotelian one[14]); and, finally, a 'certa conclusio' of an *argumentum ex consequentibus* or *ex repugnantibus*. This dichotomy might also originate with the Aristotelian division of the demonstrative and refutative enthymeme. However, if we read it with reference to the Stoic hypothetical syllogisms of the first and third type, the theory corresponds with Cicero's only in relation to the last element.[15]

I now turn to Arguments. Under this name we include all that the Greeks call enthymēmata, epicheirēmata, or apodeixeis; in Greek usage there is some difference between these, but the general sense is much the same. Enthymēma (which we may render as *commentum* or *commentatio*, though, as we have no other term available, we shall do better to use the Greek) means (1) anything conceived in the mind (this is not the sense we are speaking of here); (2) a proposition with a reason; (3) a certain mode of completing an Argument, derived either (a) from Consequents or (b) from Conflicts. There is however no agreement about this.[16]

It is in terms of this third sense, the one which he thinks it is most important for an orator, that Quintilian observes the greatest ambiguity ('de hoc parum convenit'). First, many refute his identification with the *argumentum ex consequentibus*, considering it substantially equivalent to the *epichirema*. This notion is likewise ambiguous in Greek and classical Latin theory.[17] Quintilian seems to consider it close to syllogism *tout court* and links it with the Ciceronian theory of the *ratiocinatio*.[18] Second, some authors – and he may be referring to the *Rhetorica ad Herennium*, if, as many scholars accept, its author is the unacknowledged orator Cornificius[19] – limit the field of enthymemes to the *contraria*. Finally, others refer to it as 'rhetorical syllogism' or *inperfectum syllogismum*: here Quintilian is likely thinking of the followers of the Aristotelian theory, but it is even more interesting to observe that in the first century AD. the theory of the enthymeme as 'truncated syllogism' is finally widespread.

> Some call the former of these two an Epicheireme, and you will find a majority to maintain that only that which is based on a conflict is an Enthymeme. Hence Cornificius calls it a 'contrary'. Others called this a 'rhetorical syllogism', others an 'imperfect syllogism', because its parts are not distinct or of the same number as those of the syllogism. Completeness of argument is of course something not necessarily required of the orator.[20]

Thus, through the dissertations of the *auctor ad Herennium*, Cicero and Quintilian, the notion of enthymeme comes to the late antique and early mediaeval Latin world, as we have seen, with neither clarity nor uniformity. Quintilian himself simply seems to expose all possible theories about it, without really choosing one of them. For him, it can be not only a figure of speech, a rhetorical or (from Quintilian on) elliptic syllogism but also the 'oratorical version' of the *argumentum ex repugnantibus*. Its meaning as 'sentence' also stands in the background. All of this implies that while Greek theory considers at least three meanings of the word, there are four in the Latin context, although two of them – the enthymeme as *contrarium* and as *argumentum ex repugnantibus* – are in some way similar as both deal with the ideas of comparison and antithesis, although not at the same argumentative level. It is also important to observe that, at least from the first century BC, the various conceptions are not antithetical or exclusive in writers who are well acquainted with rhetorical theory; while Seneca the Elder and (obviously) Cicero prefer to use enthymemes founded on contradictions and incompatibilities, the younger Seneca favours elliptic syllogisms and Paul – even in Greek – uses both.[21]

2. The theories of enthymeme between Iulius Rufinianus and John Scottus Eriugena. It would be an error to think that in the centuries following Quintilian, rhetorical theory in the Occidental world develops no further and gradually disappears. At the time of Augustine of Hippo, it is still a strong force and in subsequent ages, thanks to the efforts of Boethius, Cassiodorus, Alcuin of York and other, virtually unknown, authors, it maintains an important role in Latin culture.[22] Its elements continue to evolve and mature, progressively adapting themselves to the new Christian world while maintaining the presence of the enthymeme. It is therefore possible to continue to track its history, which is not the history of a simple and unintelligent repetition of Roman notions.

First of all, the legacy of the classical Latin authors was passed on to the so-called *rhetores latini minores*, the variegated group of writers of manuals, *compendia* and repertoires who are active following the Quintilian age (most of them write in the fourth and fifth centuries) until the end of the eighth century AD.[23] Their efforts ensure that ancient rhetorical theory remains alive and studied – sometimes with great simplifications, sometimes even with errors and misunderstandings, but ever more adapted to a new role in the Christian world. However, as expected, there is no homogeneous enthymeme theory.

The first of them to talk anew and explicitly of enthymemes is the mysterious Iulius Rufinianus, who lives in the first part of the fourth century and writes a bare repertoire of thirty-eight rhetorical figures, *De figuris sententiarum et elocutionis*.[24] Considering the enthymeme a figure, he no doubt follows the tradition of the *Rhetorica ad Herennium*: in his words, the enthymeme originates 'cum periodos orationis ex contrariis sententiis astringitur'.[25] He is also the last one to offer such an explicit correlation: no subsequent author uses the word *enthymema* to identify the well-known figure of *contrarium* or *contentio*.

Most probably during the same period, or a little later, Consultus Fortunatianus pens his popular (at the time) *Ars rhetorica*, written in a question-and-answer format and later used as a source by Cassiodorus.[26] While discussing the *argumentationes* in the second of the three books of his work, he quotes the *enthymema*, connecting it without hesitation to the Ciceronian *ratiocinatio*. The differences between the two typologies are only in the nature of their *probatio* (the logical one originates *alte*, the rhetorical one *ex proximo*) and in the number of the parts of those *probationes* themselves.

> How many types of argumentations are there? There are two types of argumentations, through inductive reasoning, which the Greeks call *epagoghen* and through syllogism, which the Greeks call *enthymeme*. What is syllogism? Syllogism is what we use to prove something. What is the difference between philosophers' syllogism and enthymeme? Syllogism is confirmed from afar whilst enthymeme is confirmed from near us. Furthermore, syllogism is complete of all the parts of the demonstrations (partibus probationis) while enthymeme is not.[27]

Fortunatianus lives in a time in which the works of both Cicero and Quintilian are still available, and this particular passage illustrates the influence of the latter.[28] It also harks back to the widespread division between θέσις and ὑπόθεσις, *quaestio infinita* and *quaestio finita*, the first one typical of philosophy, the second one characteristic of rhetoric, which always takes the elements of discussion from specific events.[29] As he himself says immediately following this passage, the *probatio* is the development of categorical syllogistic reasoning ('Quae sunt partes probationis? Propositio, exsecutio eius, conclusio'),[30] which means that the doctrine of the elliptic enthymeme is also included in his theory.

Up to this point, Fortunatianus's doctrine seems to be sufficiently coherent, but what follows illustrates two problems which are typical of the *rhetores latini minores*, that is, frequent confusion due to the use (and sometimes misuse) of different and not always compatible sources and the frequent absence of explanations and contextualization of the doctrines. In the following paragraph, the orator describes the *epichirema*, which is identified with the *exsecutio* of a *probatio*: this implies that it is simply a part of a *ratiocinatio* or of an *enthymema* (and, in this second case it could also be absent as the enthymeme should not necessarily be complete).[31] What in the previous sources was at least at the same level of an enthymeme, if not something more precise and valuable, is here deprived of its role (and we will see that this declassification will continue in Iulius Victor). Finally, Fortunatianus very briefly suggests dividing the enthymeme into five parts and offers some other 'user advice'. We can no longer identify the sources of this section, which is too cursory to be really useful, but it provides a glimpse of the practical work of composition of a late antiquity orator. In any case, it is interesting to note that far from the positions of the *Rhetorica ad Alexandrum* and the *Rhetorica ad Herennium*, Fortunatianus does not think that an enthymeme needs to be brief.

> How many types of enthymeme are there? There are five types of enthymeme, *elenktikon, deiktikon, gnomikon, paradeigmatikon, syllogistikon*. Is it possible to develop a single argumentation using two types of enthymeme? Yes, it is possible. In the inductive reasoning and in the enthymeme what must we observe? We must use them with variety and mix them, although using the enthymeme more frequently. What do we have to observe in relation to the enthymeme themselves? We have to use them with variety, sometimes the ones that accuse, sometimes the ones that demonstrate and for the others it depends on the typology of the genre of the speeches, of the lawsuits, and of the persons, considering both the plaintiffs in question and the judges. How should we do the *exergasia*, i.e. the manner of exposing the enthymemes? Variously, not always brief, which we call *braxy enthymema*, i.e. 'abbreviated' and not always ample, which we call *pleres enthymema*, i.e. 'long'.[32]

The most complete (and intricate) theory of the enthymeme of the entire Latin late antiquity can be found in another *Ars rhetorica*, this one by Julius Victor, likewise written in the fourth century, possibly in Gaul.[33] His work is a compendium of the writings of previous orators,[34] but what renders it particularly interesting for modern scholars is the fact that many of its sources have been lost, and what we read in his book is precious testimony of the evolution of rhetorical theories following Quintilian. For these reasons, his section on the argumentations sounds 'original'.

For Iulius Victor, 'ratiocinatio, id est syllogismus'[35] is divided into two parts, or *membra*: enthymeme and epicheirema.[36] The first one is elliptic syllogism, in which it is possible to omit the first premise or the conclusion itself, if we think that they can be argued by the judge or the public. This is a possible strategy for orators because their job is to persuade more than to demonstrate apodictically and to safeguard the beauty of style more than the strictly logical passages.

> The enthymeme is an imperfect syllogism; in fact, it is not necessary to set the question first, then to argue and to finally draw a conclusion, but: it is possible to skip the first proposition – because it can be simply included in the suppositions of the judge or of the listener – and conduct the reasoning reaching a conclusion; or undoubtedly omit the conclusion and leave the task to conclude what the reason is up to the intelligence of the judges. But why it is always necessary to the dialecticians, but not to the orators, to enumerate all parts? Because the dialecticians have the task to find the truth, but the orators have the task to persuade. And the orators should not persuade, if for the sake of precision itself and because of the repetition of the parts of the reasoning they obscure what they conclude. For the dialecticians, then, it is not relevant to be pleasing and enjoyable in their speeches; the orators have to maximally apply this, to avoid the risk of offending the ears of the listeners; and in fact, it is disagreeable to often use the same words and to refer to the same conclusion.[37]

The enthymeme is then the favourite weapon of the orator, who in most cases is only concerned with *probabilia*.[38] The theory of Iulius Victor (or of his source, if he acritically transcribes it) is completely positive: he proudly claims that the enthymeme is not a 'simplified syllogism' for orators but something of value in itself, adherent to the 'common sense' which guides the majority of people and far from the *subtilitas disputationum* and the logicians' prolixity.[39]

But then something occurs: Iulius Victor probably changes his source and in just a few lines offers a different doctrine. Now, enthymeme and epicheirema are different, but substantially the same ('est autem diaphora utrumque, sed vi et substantia idem'), and he surprisingly reports the doctrine that we already know from Fortunatianus, defining the first as 'correptior probatio' (and so, a part of itself!) and the second the 'exsecutio' of the first (and so, a part of it, which is in turn a part of itself!).

> We have already said what the difference is between syllogism and enthymeme, so it is not out of place to speak about the epicheirema also, given that it is frequently asked what sets epicheirema and enthymeme apart. There is indeed a difference in the terminology, but the sense and the substance are the same. Therefore, what is the difference? The enthymeme is the most correct development of a categorical syllogism while the epicheirema is the exposition of an enthymeme.[40]

Iulius Victor 'clarifies': sometimes an enthymeme can be *nudus*, *viduus* and *circumcisus*, without explanations (and he uncommonly quotes, as example, an enthymeme in form of a *contrarium*). On the other hand, sometimes, it requires explanations when it seems 'parum probabile' and so – even if he does not repeat the word – needs to be reinforced with an epicheirema.[41] Eventually, he reports the five categories already quoted by Fortunatianus, this time with full explanations, saying (although it seems very hard to assert) that they are characteristic of both enthymemes and epicheiremas.

There are five types of enthymemes or epicheirema, the *elencticon*, the *dicticon*, the *gnomicon*, the *paradigmaticon*, the *syllogisticon*. The *elencticon*, which was discussed only by the ancient authors, is the one in which the conclusion derives from opposite elements. . . . Others, afterwards, added the *dicticon* enthymeme: . . . the terms are not opposite, but the latter result from the former, and this is the form of enthymeme, which is called *dicticon*, and comes from the consequent elements. The third one is the *gnomicon*: a *gnomicon*, indeed, is a maxim. . . . But the *gnomicon* enthymeme differs from the maxim in this way: in the latter, just a simple maxim is pronounced, in the first also the explanation of the maxim is at the same time given. . . . The *paradigmaticon* enthymeme, although refers to an example, from it differs in this way: the example considered alone support the argumentation, changed in the form of an argument takes the shape of an example structured as an enthymeme. . . . The *syllogisticon* enthymeme is the one that, as a syllogism, from many elements concludes something.[42]

This list is as interesting as it is puzzling. The *elencticon* seems to correspond to the *contrarium* typology: Iulius Victor's sources seem to be aware of the antiquity of this meaning ('quod solum apud veteres tractabatur'), which was prevalent, as we have seen, before the appearance of the notion of elliptic syllogism. The *dicticon* clearly corresponds to the *argumentum ex consequentibus*, accepted in the Latin world only by Quintilian; the *gnomicon* is not only a *sententia* but a *sententia cum ratione*, again in the Quintilian sense. To explain this typology, Iulius Victor quotes Marcius Porcius Cato: 'Carthaginienses nobis iam hostes sunt; nam qui omnia parat contra me, ut quo tempore velit, bellum possit inferre, hic iam mihi hostis est, tametsi nondum armis agat'.[43] The phrase has some oppositional structure, and only in this sense could we accept it as enthymeme (it would be easier to accept it as epicheirema, precisely because it includes an explanation). Even less justifiable, in this list, is the *paradigmaticon*, which is an *exemplum* in the form of an argumentation;[44] but the real paradox comes with the *sillogisticon*, which should be, if enthymemes and epicheiremas are syllogisms, a sort of 'syllogistic syllogism'.

It would be far too easy to ridicule the efforts of Iulius Victor. While it is true that his enthymeme theory is not coherent, neither is Aristotle's. His *Ars rhetorica*, which at least provides a different, and in large part alternative, framework to examine the matter, also shows how the enthymeme 'survived' the decadence of the Roman Empire to arrive at the dawn of the Middle Ages.

Significantly absent in Martianus Capella,[45] the enthymeme has a noteworthy role in the work of Severinus Boethius.[46] First, he is the translator of most of the logical tractates of Aristotle, in which he finds several mentions of it. As far as we know, he did not read the *Rhetorica*, but he studies both the *Analytics* and the *Topica*. His versions of *De interpretatione*, *Categoriae* and Porphyrius's *Isagoge*, along with his own works on syllogisms, form the so-called *logica vetus* – which encompasses nearly all early Middle Age knowledge in the field of logic. His translation – based on a corrupted test[47] – of *Analityca priora* II, 27 marks the definitive victory of the theory of elliptic syllogism:

> A probability is not the same as a sign. The former is a generally accepted premise; for that which people know to happen or not to happen, or to be or not to be,

usually in a particular way, is a probability: e.g., that the envious are malevolent or that those who are loved are affectionate. A sign, however, means a demonstrative premise which is necessary or generally accepted. That which coexists with something else, or before or after whose happening something else has happened, is a sign of that something's having happened or being. An enthymeme is a syllogism from probabilities or signs.[48]

In his own works, Boethius obviously defends this interpretation and finds a theoretical explanation for it. In the second book of his *De differentiis topicis*, for example, he clearly states that the enthymeme is *imperfectus* because it is similar to logical syllogism, even though it does not use all elements 'quae conveniunt' of the latter (i.e. it lacks a premise). Far from the position of Iulius Victor, he sees rhetoric as somehow subordinate to logic, because the first regards something particular, the latter something universal.

> An enthymeme is an imperfect syllogism, that is, a discourse in which the precipitous conclusion is derived without all the propositions having been laid down beforehand, as when someone says: 'Man is an animal; therefore, he is a substance', he omits the other proposition, 'Every animal is a substance'. So, since an enthymeme argues from universals to particulars which are to be proved, it is, as it were, similar to a syllogism; but because it does not use all the propositions appropriate to a syllogism, it deviates from the definition of a syllogism and so is called an imperfect syllogism.[49]

We find the same definition in the first book of the vast commentary which Boethius dedicates to Cicero's *Topica*.[50] However, in the fifth book, Boethius widely discusses §§ 54–57, which contains the references to the enthymeme quoted earlier; here, he recalls all other meanings, mentioning the *argumentum ex repugnantibus* (which he calls *ex contrariis*[51]) and even the *mentis conceptio*.

> Cicero says that the third typology is the one in which two things that are related to each other are negated, and to those is then further added another negation, for example: as 'man' and 'animal' are related, we can say: 'It is not possible that he is a man and he is not an animal', and from these things we affirm one in order to delete the other, this way: let us affirm that he is a man, saying: 'But he is a man'; what is left, 'He is not an animal', it is deleted, and we conclude 'He is then an animal'. The argumentation is formed as follows: 'It is not possible that he is a man, and he is not an animal; but he is a man; he is then an animal'. From those things, Cicero says that the enthymemes that are derived from the contraries, which the orators usually use often, come from; and they are called 'enthymemes', not because with this name it is not possible to designate every other element which is found by our mind (the enthymeme, indeed, is a 'conception of the mind', and then the word can be used for everything elaborated by the mind), but because those things found by the mind through a quick conclusion based on opposite things, are very sharp. Therefore, thanks to the excellence and the beauty of this finding, the common

name of enthymeme becomes proper of this typology. So, it is called 'enthymeme' by the orators, as if this was its exclusive name.[52]

This time, this apparent discrepancy should not be viewed in a negative light. We must not forget that here Boethius comments on Cicero's text, which leads him to consider these alternative meanings, and we should remember the great respect Boethius always demonstrates for his sources, a respect which leads him in some way to 'adapt' his mental horizon to the one of his authorities.[53] In the continuation of the comment, he also recalls the theory of elliptic syllogism, strongly reducing the possible contrast between *Topica* and *De differentiis topicis*.[54] We can thus consider this last concept as his 'official one'.

Moreover, this idea of enthymeme is one of the four basic elements (regarding *materia*, *usus* and *finis*) on which Boethius establishes the difference between dialectic and rhetoric and, as already stated, 'encloses' the second one in the first. Logic deals with general questions (as we already know, the *thesis*) and is expressed in debate, through the rapid succession of questions and answers; speaks to an adversary; and 'perfectis utitur syllogismis'. Rhetoric, on the other hand, deals only with certain matters (the *hypothesis*); chooses long and continuous discourses; addresses a judge; and is founded ('contenta est') on brief enthymemes.

> The dialectical discipline examines the thesis only; a thesis is a question not involved in circumstances. The rhetorical [discipline], on the other hand, investigates and discusses hypotheses, that is, questions hedged in by a multitude of circumstances. Circumstances are who, what, where, when, how, by what means. Again, dialectic is restricted to question and answer. Rhetoric, on the other hand, goes through the subject proposed in unbroken discourse. Similarly, dialectic uses complete syllogism. Rhetoric is content with the brevity of enthymemes. This too produces a differentia, namely, that the rhetorician has a judge someone other than his opponent, someone who decides between them. But for the dialectician, the one who is the opponent also gives the decision because a reply [which is], as it were, a decision is elicited from the opponent by the cunning of the questioning. So, every difference between these [disciplines] consists in matter, use, or end. In matter, because thesis and hypothesis are the matter put under the two of them. In use, because one disputes by question, the other by unbroken discourse, or because one delights in complete syllogisms, the other in enthymemes. In end, because one attempts to persuade a judge, the other attempts to wrest what it wants from the opponent.[55]

As Boethius is the direct or indirect source for nearly all subsequent early Middle Ages writers who address logical and rhetorical themes, from now on the doctrine of the enthymeme as elliptic syllogism (and of its 'minor value' in the face of perfect logical syllogism) becomes dominant. At any rate, 'contaminations' between the various theories still exist. We can see this immediately in the *Institutiones* of Cassiodorus, who uses both Boethius and Fortunatianus as sources, as well as lost tractates of Marius Victorinus.

According to Cassiodorus, who once again remembers the etymology of the enthymeme as *mentis conceptio*, it has only two parts: the first premise (*propositio*) and the conclusion (*conclusio*). It therefore lacks the second premise (*assumptio*).

> An enthymeme (Latin: mental intention) is what writers in the art usually call an incomplete syllogism. This form of proof is made up of two parts. It employs the means of gaining credence by passing over the rules of the syllogism, as the following: 'If we are to avoid the storm, you must not sail'. It is complete in a major premise and thus is judged more suitable to orators than logicians.[56]

Cassiodorus also mentions a five-member division similar to those of Fortunatianus and Iulius Victor, although his terminology is in Latin.[57] Half a century later, Isidorus, Bishop of Seville, quotes (with some abbreviations) Cassiodorus's text in his impressive encyclopaedia, *Etymologiae*.[58]

This theoretical *excursus* could well end with John Scottus Eriugena, who in his *De praedestinatione* considers the enthymeme as the *locus* of the opposites in an original way. From Cassiodorus, or more probably from Isidorus, whose encyclopaedia he much appreciates, he knows the ancient definition of it as 'animi conceptio' – and thus renders the enthymeme as the strongest of those *conceptiones*, the one that is best articulated from thought into words thanks to the force of opposites:

> We still have to speak of the expressions taken from the topic of the contraries, in which resides such a force of significance, that for the privilege of their excellence they are rightfully called by the Greeks *entimemata*, i.e. 'conceptions of the mind'. Although everything which is spoken is first conceived in the mind, not everything which is conceived in the mind seems to have the same force of significance, when it is transmitted vigorously to the senses. As the strongest of all reasoning is the one which is taken from the contraries, the clearest of all vocal signs is the one which is taken from the very topic of the contraries; of those, some are called 'absolute', some others are called 'connected'.[59]

In the first book of his *Periphyseon*, he specifies his position and refers directly to Cicero's *Topica*, identifying the enthymeme with the *argumentum ex repugnantibus*, which concerns the things that 'simul esse non possunt'. Thanks to his exquisite philosophical skills, he exposes it through a metaphysical example.

> If you want to hear a syllogism in form of an enthymeme (i.e. a common conception of the mind), which, between all the conclusions, achieves first place, because it derives from things that can not be together at the same time, look at this formulation. 'It is not possible that the ΟΥΣΙΑ exists, and that it is not incorporeal; but the ΟΥΣΙΑ exists; therefore, it is incorporeal'. Indeed, it is not possible that the ΟΥΣΙΑ exists and that it is not incorporeal. Again: 'It is not possible that the ΟΥΣΙΑ exists, and that it is corporeal; but the ΟΥΣΙΑ exists; therefore, it is not corporeal'. Again: 'It is not possible that something is not ΟΥΣΙΑ, and that it is incorporeal; but it is ΟΥΣΙΑ; therefore, it is incorporeal'.[60]

We can conclude, then, that the ancient Greek theories on the enthymeme are still alive in the Latin world during late antiquity and the early Middle Ages. They are discussed, analysed and sometimes confused, but none are abandoned to the oblivion of history. On the contrary, in Boethius they are at the core of his theories on the role and *status* of the liberal arts. The fact that Latin culture recognizes *one more theory* in relation to classical Greek culture is a sure sign of interest in and the vitality of this element.[61] The different traditions intersect and sometimes are entwined, and it is very difficult (if not useless), then, to try to create a kind of family tree. Rather, it is more important to observe that the theory of 'elliptic syllogism' and the 'contrary theories', with the 'consideration theory' in the background, all flow towards the late Middle Ages and the direct rediscovery of Aristotelian texts.

3. *The argumentative use of the enthymeme*. In light of this summary, it is further possible to ask how and how much late antiquity and early Middle Age theologians and philosophers use the enthymeme for their argumentative purposes. Such research could be far reaching, but it is not simple to approach, because those authors, of course, use enthymemes in their thought structures without explicitly mentioning them. However, if we limit ourselves to an introductory inquiry based only on the explicit mentions, we can observe that very few authors know the word, and they often give it a negative sense. In the *Commentarium in Amos* of Hieronymus, for example, it is equated to the sophisms of the heretics:

> For example: it is called 'entrance' he who conceived and gave birth to a false dogma, as Arius in Alexandria; his latches and very firm bolts are Eutychius and Eunomius, who strived to reinforce him with syllogisms and enthymemes – or even sophisms, paradoxes and sorites, things that are disgracefully conceived by others.[62]

And in a *Carmen de contemptu mundi*, once attributed to Anselm of Canterbury, the enthymemes have not saved Aristotle from his destiny, which is to perish with all other things in the world:

> And so, nothing stays long with the mortals; so,
> No honour, no glory avoids death.
> The great Aristoteles, clever investigator of logic,
> Exposed many things found with his intelligence.
> But no syllogism, no enthymeme was created
> Which wanted to spare his fate to such man.[63]

In any event, there are also some positive statements. In a letter written in his youth, the monk Peter Damian, future Cardinal-Bishop of Ostia, complains that his readers approach his compositions only to appreciate their rhetorical-logical qualities – the mention of the enthymemes at least shows that Peter knows and uses them, and for this reason he cannot have a negative perception of them.

> I know well that, as soon as a letter of mine comes into the hand of the secular grammarians, they immediately observe if in it the politeness of a polished style is present, they search the vividness of rhetorical elegance, and the curious mind follows the misleading turns of words of syllogisms and enthymemes. So, as a matter of fact, they search the science that inflates, and they do not see the charity that ennoble.[64]

It is important to note that some other theologians, *in primis* Cassiodorus in his *Expositio psalmorum*, recognize enthymemes in Bible prose: if the Holy Scripture utilizes them – and, as we have seen above, even Paul is a good example on this point – they cannot be something to reject. Let us look at just one occurrence of many which are mentioned:

> *Against you and you only I have sinned, and done what is evil in your sight; so you are right in your verdict and justified when you judge (Ps 50, 6)*. Here the syllogism in form of enthymeme which we already wrote about in Psalm 20 appears again. Its first premise is: the Lord is right is His verdict and justified when He judges. Added to the conclusion is the sentence which is written first: 'Against you and you only I have sinned, and done what is evil in your sight'. This is done without fault in exposing syllogisms, and is permitted according to the custom of the ancients.[65]

However, the most significant and informed uses of enthymemes in a structure of thought come from John Scottus Eriugena. We have already seen how he uses them in a key point of his metaphysics, that is, to clarify his doctrine of the *ousia*: it cannot be corporeal, precisely because it radically excludes corporeity. Two enthymemes are also at the basis of a crucial argumentation of the *De divina praedestinatione*, in which John excludes the possibility that God could predestine some men to evil.

> Thus, there is no predestination which binds life, justice, happiness with an inevitable necessity, as there is no predestination which binds to the contrary of these mentioned goods, i.e. death, sin and misery. The reason of this is concluded with the argument of the enthymeme, which always comes from the contraries, and of which the first premise is: 'It is not true that God is the supreme essence and at the same time He is not the cause of only those things which comes from Him. But God is the supreme essence. Then He is the cause of only those things which comes from Him. Sin, death and misery do not come from God. God is not the cause of those things'. Such a syllogism can be also expressed in this way: 'It is not true that God is at the same time the cause of things being and the cause of things not being. But God is the cause of things being. Therefore, He is not the cause of things not being'. Sin and its consequences, such as death, which misery is connected, do not exist. Therefore, neither God nor His predestination, which is what He is, can be the cause of them.[66]

Here, then, we have found at least one 'moment of glory' of the enthymeme in the context of the early Middle Ages. Further research could potentially unveil many other similar cases without specific mention of the word and give us further examples of its presence in the structure of the philosophical-theological thought of those centuries and in the minds of its users.[67]

Notes

1. In using the plural in the title of this chapter, I refer to M. Kraus (2012), accepting his point of view; see p. 17: 'Sì, il plurale nel titolo di questo articolo è corretto. Non si tratterà de*lla* teoria, ma de*lle* teorie dell'entimema nell'Antichità. Infatti ce n'era una pluralità'.
2. For an exhaustive bibliography up to the year 2000, see the list compiled by Carol Foster at https://rhetjournal.net/RhetJournal/Enthymemes.html; here I simply refer to the recapitulatory pages of G. d'Onofrio 1986, pp. 248, 254–5, 293–4. The scarcity of studies on this period is even more remarkable compared to the abundance of studies on the Greek and classical Latin tradition.
3. See Aristoteles 2011, pp. 526–8 ('Enthymemes are contraries not only in word and action, but also in all other ways. You will obtain many of them by proceeding as has been described regarding the investigative species and examining whether the speech contradicts itself somehow or what has been done contradicts what is just, lawful, advantageous, noble, possible, easy, plausible, the character of the speaker, or the pattern of the facts. We must select such enthymemes against the opponents; but we must say what is contrary to them for ourselves, pointing out that our actions and speeches contradict the unjust, unlawful, disadvantageous, the characters of bad people, and, in short, what is thought to be base. We must collect each of these as briefly as possible and state them in the fewest words. We shall create many enthymemes in this way and so use them best'); Aristoteles 1973, II, 27, 70a 12–29; Aristoteles 2020, *Rhetorica*, I, 2, 8–11, 1356b; II, 22–5, 1395b–1403a, pp. 18–20; 286–340. Aristotle knows that 'one of the topics of demonstrative enthymemes is derived from opposites' (Aristoteles 2020, *Rhetorica*, 23, 1397a, p. 295), but this is only one aspect of his complex and stratified theory. For a brief but incisive presentation of the enthymeme in the *Rhetorica ad Alexandrum* see F. Piazza 2012, pp. 35–8. For a concise and useful presentation of the Aristotelian theory, see (among many other essays) M. F. Burnyeat 1994, pp. 3–55.
4. Aristoteles 2020, II, 22, 1396b 22–5, p. 293: 'There are two kinds of enthymemes, the one demonstrative, which proves that a thing is or is not, and the other refutative, the two differing like refutation and syllogism in dialectic.'
5. M. Kraus 2012, pp. 18–19. See also F. Piazza 2012.
6. M. Kraus 2002, pp. 95–111, here pp. 107–9. According to the scholar, this meaning emerges with the rediscovery of Aristotelian works in the first century BC: the text of the *Analytica Priora* was at the time somehow corrupted. In addition, influenced by Stoic logic, syllogism and enthymeme both end up being considered scientific syllogisms with only one difference: the second one was incomplete, with one of the premises being not explicit.
7. Cornificius 1993², pp. 293–5: 'Contrarium est, quod ex rebus diversis duabus alteram breviter et facile confirmat, hoc pacto: "Nam, qui suis rationibus inimicus fuerit semper, eum quomodo alienis rebus amicum fore speres?" Item: "Nam, quem in amicitia perfidiosum cognoveris, eum quare putes inimicitias cum fide gerere posse?

Aut qui privatus intolerabili superbia fuerit, eum commodum et cognoscentem sui fore in potestate qui speres et qui in sermonibus et conventu amicorum verum dixerit numquam, eum sibi in contionibus a mendacio temperaturum?" Item: "Quos ex collibus deiecimus, cum his in campo metuimus dimicare? Qui cum plures erant, paris nobis esse non poterant, hi, postquam pauciores sunt, metuimus, ne sint superiores?" Hoc exornationis genus breviter et continuatis verbis perfectum debet esse, et cum commodum est auditu propter brevem et absolutam conclusionem tum vero vehementer, id quod opus est oratori, conprobat contraria re et ex eo, quod dubium non est, expedit illud, quod est in dubio, ut dilui non possit aut multo difficillime possit.' In his comment, Gualtiero Calboli observes that here the *auctor ad Herennium* follows the characteristic tendency of his times to include many elements among the rhetorical figures which were originally of another nature – as the enthymeme itself. Cfr. Cornificius 1993[2], pp. 328–9.

8   M. T. Cicero 1942, III, 207, p. 164: 'Est etiam gradatio quaedam et conversio et verborum concinna transgressio et contrarium et dissolutum et declinatio et reprehensio.'
9   M. T. Cicero 1949, I, 37, 67, p. 110: 'Quae plurimas habet argumentatio partes, ea constat ex his quinque partibus; secunda est quadripertita; tertia tripertita; dein bipertita; quod in controversia est. De una quoque parte potest alicui videri posse consistere.'
10 M. T. Cicero 1994, pp. 8, 14–15.
11 M. T. Cicero 1994, respectively 13, 53, pp. 22, 10; 13, 54, pp. 23, 12–13.
12 M. T. Cicero 1949, pp. 421–5: 'Appellant autem dialectici eam conclusionem argumenti in qua, cum primum adsumpseris, consequitur id quod adnexum est, primum conclusionis modum; cum id quod adnexum est negaris ut id quoque cui fuerit adnexum negandum sit, secundus is appellatur concludendi modus; cum autem aliqua coniuncta negaris, <aliam negationem rursus adiunxeris> et ex iis primum sumpseris ut quod relinquitur tollendum sit, is tertius appellatur conclusionis modus. Ex hoc illa rhetorum ex contrariis conclusa, quae ipsi ἐνθυμήματα appellant; non quod omnis sententia proprio nomine ἐνθυμήμα non dicatur, sed, ut Homerus propter excellentiam commune poetarum nomen efficit apud Graecos suum, sic cum omnis sententia ἐνθυμήμα dicatur, quia videtur ea quae ex contrariis conficitur acutissima, sola proprie nomen commune possedit. . . . Hoc disserendi genus attingit omnino vestras quoque in respondendo disputationes, sed philosophorum magis, quibus est cum oratoribus illa ex repugnantibus sententiis communis conclusio quae a dialecticis tertius modus, a rhetoribus ἐνθυμήμα dicitur.'
13 About the status and the practice of the rhetoric between first century BC and first century AD see M. Kraus 2002, pp. 95–7. The scholar observes the lack of any mention of the enthymeme between Aristoteles and the *Rhetorica ad Herennium*.
14 Aristoteles 2011, II, 21, 1394a 26-1394b 6, pp. 277–9.
15 M. Kraus 2002, pp. 106–7, propends for a Greek origin of this dichotomy.
16 Quintilian 2002, V, 10, 1–2, pp. 366, 1–10 : 'Nunc de argumentis: hoc enim nomine complectimur omnia quae Graeci enthymemata, epichiremata, apodixis vocant, quamquam apud illos est aliqua horum nominum differentia, etiam si vis eodem fere tendit. Nam enthymema (quod nos commentum sane aut commentationem interpretemur, quia aliter non possumus Graeco melius usuri) unum intellectum habet quo omnia mente concepta significat (sed nunc non de eo loquimur), alterum quo sententiam cum ratione, tertium quo certam quandam argumenti conclusionem vel ex consequentibus vel ex repugnantibus: quamquam de hoc parum convenit.'

17 For a very useful summary see J. Klein 1994, s. v. *Epicheirem*, in *Historisches Wörterbuch der Rhetorik*. According to Klein, this word has three principal meanings: an expanded form of syllogism, with at least one 'reinforcing' argumentation (this sense corresponds to Cicero's); an argumentation normally composed of *intentio, assumptio, complexio*; and a general term for 'rhetorical argumentation' or 'rhetorical conclusion'. Klein declares that the notion is substantially absent in Aristoteles (he claims that the section of the *Topica* where it is mentioned is spurious), and it is first developed by his disciple Theophrastus.

18 Quintilian 2002, V, 10, 4–6, pp. 367, 17–368, 13: 'Epichirema Valgius adgressionem vocat; verius autem iudico non nostram administrationem, sed ipsam rem quam adgredimur, id est argumentum quo aliquid probaturi sumus, etiam si nondum verbis explanatum, iam tamen mente conceptum, epichirema dici. Aliis videtur non destinata vel inchoata sed perfecta probatio hoc nomen accipere ultima specie, ideoque propria eius appellatione et maxime in usu posita significatur certa quaedam sententiae comprensio, quae ex tribus minime partibus constat. Quidam epichirema rationem appellarunt, Cicero melius ratiocinationem, quamquam et ille nomen hoc duxisse magis a syllogismo videtur: nam et statum syllogisticum ratiocinativum appellat et exemplis utitur philosophorum. Et quoniam est quaedam inter syllogismum et epichirema vicinitas, potest videri hoc nomine recte abusus.' 'Valgius' is Valgius Rufus, grammar and poet of the first century BC: see Gundel 1955, s. v. *Valgius*, in *Paulys Realencyclopädie der classischen Altertumswissenschaft*, VIII A.1, Stuttgart 1955, coll. 272–6.

19 G. Calboli has devoted many of his essays to demonstrate this identification. For a summary of his theories, see G. Calboli 1965, 58 [Memorie, vol. 51–52, 1963–1964].

20 Quintilian 2002, V, 10, 2–3, pp. 366, 10–16: 'Sunt enim qui illud prius epichirema dicant, pluresque invenias in ea opinione ut id demum quod pugna constat enthymema accipi velint, et ideo illud Cornificius contrarium appellat. Hunc alii rhetoricum syllogismum, alii inperfectum syllogismum vocaverunt, quia nec distinctis nec totidem partibus concluderetur: quod sane non utique ab oratore desideratur'.

21 M. Kraus 2002, pp. 103–5, 109–11.

22 I tried to describe the history of this 'survival' in R. de Filippis 2013.

23 They take their name from the edition of their works published by the German philologist Karl Halm (1863).

24 I. Rufinianus, *De figuris sententiarum et elocutionis*, in Halm 1863, pp. 38–47. See R. de Filippis 2013, p. 150. His work has the aim of continuing the analogous opus of Aquila Romanus, written in the mid-third century. Those lists would have been useful for mnemonic teaching in school at the time: Halm's collection reports eight of them.

25 I. Rufinianus 1863, 30, pp. 45, 27–33. Two examples follow: one from Lucilius and one from Cicero.

26 C. Fortunatianus 1979. See R. de Filippis 2013, pp. 137–49.

27 C. Fortunatianus 1979, II, 28, pp. 135, 5–136, 5, transl. by the author: 'Quot sunt genera argumentationum? Duo, per inductionem, quam Graeci *epagoghen* vocant, et per ratiocinationem, quam *enthymema* appellant. . . . Quid ratiocinatio? Quod aliquid adprobamus. Hoc Graeci quid vocant? Enthymema. Quo differt a se syllogismus philosophorum et enthymema rhetorum? Sillogysmus alte habet probationem, enthymema ex proximo; item quod syllogismus plenus est omnibus partibus probationis, enthymema non omnibus'.

28 For another interpretation see the *Comment* of Lucia Calboli Montefusco in her edition of the text, pp. 415–16: here, she refers directly to Aristotle.
29 See, for example, M. T. Cicero 1994, 21, 79–80, pp. 32, 12–18: 'Quaestionum duo genera: alterum infinitum, definitum alterum. Definitum est quod *ypothesin* Graeci, nos causam; infinitum quod *thesin* illi appellant, nos propositum possumus nominare. Causa certis personis, locis, temporibus, actionibus, negotiis cernitur aut in omnibus aut in plerisque eorum, propositum autem aut in aliquo eorum aut in pluribus, nec tamen in maxumis.'
30 C. Fortunatianus 1979, II, 28, pp. 136, 6–7.
31 C. Fortunatianus 1979, 29, pp. 136, 8–11: 'Quid est epichirema? Exsecutio sive adprobatio propositionis aut adsumptionis. In epichiremate possumus inducere locos communes et exempla et prosopopoeias? Possumus; est enim epichirema latior exsecutio.'
32 C. Fortunatianus 1979, pp. 136, 12–137, 4, transl. by the author: 'Quot sunt genera enthymematum? Quinque, *elenktikon, deiktikon, gnomikon, paradeigmatikon, syllogistikon*. Potest una argumentatio duobus enthymematum generibus fieri? Potest. In epagoge und enthymemate quid observandum est? Ut varie his utamur et ea commisceamus, ita tamen ut enthymemate frequentius utamur. Quid in ipsis enthymematibus observandum est? Ut his varie utamur, tum elencticis, tum dicticis, et ceteris, pro qualitate generum dicendi et causarum et statuum et personarum, tam agentium quam iudicum. *Exergasia*, id est elocutio enthymematum, qualis esse debet? Varia; nec semper brevis, quam *braxy enthymema* vocamus, id est correptum, nec semper lata, quam *pleres enthymema* dicimus, id est longum.'
33 C. I. Victor 1980. See R. de Filippis 2013, pp. 164–71.
34 See the page title of K. Halm 1863, p. 371: 'C. Iulii Victoris Ars rhetorica Hermagorae, Ciceronis, Quintiliani, Aquili, Marcomanni, Tatiani'.
35 C. I. Victor 1980, p. 50, 27.
36 C. I. Victor 1980, p. 51, 1: 'Syllogismi membra sunt enthymema et epichirema'.
37 C. I. Victor 1980, pp. 53, 5–17, transl. by the author: 'Enthymema est imperfectus syllogismus: non est enim in eo necesse primum proponere, deinde argumentari et postremo concludere, sed vel primam propositionem praeterire licebit, propterea quod ipsa tantum praesumptione iudicis vel auditoris contenta esse poterit, et solam ratiocinationem exsequi et conclusionem superaddere, vel certe conclusionem praetermittere et sensibus iudicis id, quod ratiocinatus est, colligendum relinquere. Quare ergo dialecticis illud necessarium est, ut omnibus partibus colligant, oratoribus non semper? Quoniam illis veri inveniendi ratio, his suadendi proposita est. Persuadere autem non potuerunt, si ipsa diligentia et redditione partium obscuraverint quae colligunt. Deinde ad illos non pertinet, ut suaves et iucundi sint in disserendo, oratori autem maxime, ne aures auditoris offendat, studendum est; offendit porro et iisdem nominibus utendo saepius et eadem collectione referenda.'
38 C. I. Victor 1980, pp. 53, 18–21: 'Debemus etiam illam differentiam scire, quod is, qui disserit, interim longe probationem petit et multis in ratiocinatione positis colligit: orator autem, quo sit lucidior probatio eius, ex proximo petet nec spectabit, quam vera sint ea, quibus colligit, sed quam probabilia.'
39 C. I. Victor 1980, pp. 54, 6–7: 'Est enim illi oratio apud homines, qui non recondita disputationum subtilitate, sed communi sensu universa percipiant'.
40 C. I. Victor 1980, pp. 54, 9–14, transl. by the author: 'Et quoniam diximus, quid differat syllogismus ab enthymemate, non alienum hoc loco videtur et de epichiremate dicere, quoniam quaerere quidam solent, quid inter epichirema et

enthymeme intersit. Est autem diaphora utrumque, sed vi et substantia idem. Quid ergo interest? Quod enthymeme correptior probatio, epichirema autem exsecutio enthymematis est.'

41 C. I. Victor 1980, pp. 54, 14–55, 8.

42 C. I. Victor 1980, pp. 55, 9–56, 11, transl. by the author: 'Enthymematon vel epichirematon formae sunt quinque, elencticon, item dicticon, item gnomicon, item paradigmaticon, item syllogisticon. Elencticon, quod solum apud veteres tractabatur, in quo repugnantia colliguntur . . . Alii postea adiecerunt enthymema dicticon: . . . non enim pugnant haec inter se, sed consecuntur, et est haec forma enthymematon, quod appellatur dicticon, et fit a consequentibus. Tertium gnomicon; nam gnomicon est sententia. . . . Sed enthymema gnomicon hoc a sententia differt, quod ibi tantum simpliciter sententia pronuntiatur, hic autem simul et ratio sententiae redditur . . . Paradigmaticon enthymema quamquam ad exemplum se refert, hoc tamen differt ab exemplo, quod exemplum per se positum probationem adiuvat, conversum autem in speciem argumenti formam accipit paradigmatis enthymematici. . . . Syllogisticon enthymema est, quod ad imaginem syllogismi ex multis aliquid colligit.'

43 M. P. Cato 1967, pp. 78–9.

44 For a classical definition of the *exemplum* see Cornificius 1993², IV, 49, 62, ed. cit., p. 196: 'Exemplum est alicuius facti aut dicti praeteriti cum certi auctoris nomine propositio'.

45 He is clearly aware of the *argumentum ex repugnantibus*, but he does not link it to the enthymeme. See Martianus Capella 1983, IV, 416, pp. 143, 6–16.

46 For a summary of his rhetorical theories see R. de Filippis 2013, pp. 296–315.

47 See note 6.

48 Aristoteles 1938, II, 27, PL 64, 711A, pp. 523–5: 'Eicos autem et signum non idem est, sed eicos quidem est propositio probabilis. Quod enim ut in pluribus sciunt sic factum ; vel non factum, aut esse vel non esse, hoc est eicos, ut odire invidentes, vel diligere amantes. Signum autem vult esse propositio demonstrativa, vel necessaria, vel probabilis; nam quo existente est, vel quo facto prius vel posterius res, signum est vel fuisse vel esse. Enthymema ergo est syllogismus imperfectus ex eicotibus et signis.' Another reference is at the very end of the translation of the *Topica*. See Aristoteles 1969, VIII, 14, p. 178, 20–3 (PL 64, 1007B): 'Oportet autem et rememorationes universaliter facere orationum, et si fuerit disputans particulariter; sic enim et plures possibile erit unam facere. Similiter autem et in rethoribus in enthymematibus.'

49 Severinus Boethius 2004, p. 45: 'Enthymema quippe est imperfectus syllogismus, id est oratio, in qua non omnibus antea propositionibus constitutis infertur festinata conclusio, ut si quis sic dicat: "Homo animal est, substantia igitur est". Praetermisit enim alteram propositionem, qua proponitur "Omne animal esse substantiam". Ergo quoniam enthymema ab universalibus ad particularia probanda contendit, quasi simile syllogismo est; quod vero non omnibus quae conveniunt syllogismo propositionibus utitur, a syllogismi ratione discedit atque ideo imperfectus vocatus est syllogismus.'

50 Severinus Boethius, *Commentaria in Topica Ciceronis*, I, PL 64, 1050BC: 'Argumentum vero nisi sit oratione prolatum, et propositionum contexione dispositum, fidem facere dubitationi non poterit. Ergo illa per propositiones prolatio ac dispositio argumenti, argumentatio nuncupatur, quae dicitur enthymema vel syllogismus, cujus definitionem in Topicis differentiis apertius explanabimus. Omnis vero syllogismus vel enthymema propositionibus constat; omne igitur argumentum syllogismo vel enthymemate profertur. Enthymema vero est imperfectus syllogismus, cujus aliquae

partes, vel propter brevitatem, vel propter notitiam, praetermissae sunt. Itaque haec quoque argumentatio a syllogismi genere non recedit. Quoniam igitur syllogismus omnis propositionibus constat, propositiones vero terminis, terminique inter se differunt, eo quod unus major est, alter minor, fieri non potest ut ex propositionibus conclusio nascatur, nisi per terminos progressae propositiones extremos terminos alicujus tertii medietate conjunxerint'.

51 He chooses this expression in relation to the specific example used by Cicero. See M. T. Cicero 1994, 13, 56, ed. cit., pp. 23, 21–5: 'Hoc metuere, alterum in metu non ponere! / Eam quam nihil accusas damnas, bene quam meritam esse autumas / male merere? Id quod scis prodest nihil, id quod nescis obest?'; Severinus Boethius, *Commentaria in Topica Ciceronis*, V, 1143C: 'Sed haec quidem Ciceronis similitudo non tam ex repugnantibus quam ex contrariis argumentum intelligitur continere'.

52 Severinus Boethius, *Commentaria in Topica Ciceronis*, V, 1142C–43A, transl. by the auhor: 'Tertium vero modum ait esse Cicero cum ea quae conjuncta sunt, denegantur, et his alia negatio rursus adjungitur, ut quia animal homini conjunctum est, ita dicamus: Non et homo et non animal est, atque ex his unum ponitur, ut quod relinquitur auferatur, hoc modo: Ponimus hominem esse, dicentes: Atqui homo est; quod ergo relinquitur, non est animal, aufertur, atque concluditur, animal igitur est. Fit argumentatio hoc modo: Non et homo est, et non animal, atqui homo est, animal igitur est. Ex his nasci dicit enthymemata ex contrariis conclusa, quibus plurimum rhetores uti solent; atque haec enthymemata nuncupantur, non quod eodem nomine omnis inventio nuncupari non possit (enthymema namque est mentis conceptio, quod potest omnibus inventionibus convenire), sed quia haec inventa, quae breviter ex contrariis colliguntur, maxime acuta sunt, propter excellentiam speciemque inventionis commune enthymematis nomen proprium factum est, ut haec a rhetoribus quasi proprio nomine enthymemata vocentur'. Curiously, the theory of the enthymeme as *mentis conceptio* is also mentioned (next to the one of elliptic syllogism) in the pseudo-Boethian *Liber de geometria* (PL 64, 1353CD: 'Nonne et eloquentiae, ex prioribus geometria probat insequentia, et certis incerta, propter quod plures invenies, qui dialectici similiter et rhetorici ingrediantur hanc artem. Dialectico namque syllogismo si res poscit utitur, et qui sunt potentissimi grammatici, qui apodixis Graece dicuntur, idem probant, et certe enthimemate, qui rhetoricus est syllogismus, quod Latine interpretatur mentis conceptio, quem imperfectum solent artigraphi nuncupare, et ipse denique probat cujus sit formae circuitus, quot lineis rectis continetur').

53 I supported this thesis in my recent paper R. de Filippis 2020–1, pp. 289–304, here pp. 303–4.

54 Severinus Boethius, *Commentaria in Topica Ciceronis*, V, 1143C: 'Sed quia non totus (ut supra posuimus) in his argumentationibus ponitur syllogismus, sed propositio, cujus assumptio et conclusio notae sunt, idcirco enthymema dicitur, quasi brevis animi conceptio'.

55 Severinus Boethius 2004, IV, pp. 79–80: 'Dialectica facultas igitur thesin tantum considerat. Thesis vero est sine circumstantiis quaestio. Rhetorica vero de hypothesibus, id est quaestionibus circumstantiarum multitudine inclusis, tractat et disserit. Circumstantiae vero sunt: quis, ubi, quando, cur, quomodo, quibus adminiculis. . . . Rursus dialectica interrogatione ac responsione constricta est. Rhetorica vero rem propositam perpetua oratione decurrit. Item dialectica perfectis utitur syllogismis. Rhetorica enthymematum brevitate contenta est. Illud etiam differentiam facit, quod rhetor habet aliquem praeter adversarium iudicem, qui inter

utrosque disceptet. Dialectico vero ille fert sententiam, qui adversarius sedet. Ab adversario enim responsio veluti quaedam sententia subtilitate interrogationis elicitur. Quae cum ita sint, omnis earum differentia vel in materia vel in usu vel in fine est constituta: in materia, quod thesis atque hypothesis materia utrisque subiecta est; in usibus, quod haec interrogatione, illa perpetua oratione disceptat, vel quod haec integris syllogismis, illa vero enthymematibus gaudet; fine vero, quod haec persuadere iudici, illa quod vult adversario extorquere conatur.'

56   Cassiodorus Senator 2004, pp. 185–6: 'Enthymema igitur est quod Latine interpretatur mentis conceptio, quam imperfectum syllogismum solent artigraphi nuncupare. Nam in duabus partibus haec argumenti forma consistit, quando id quod ad fidem pertinet faciendam utitur, syllogismorum lege praeterita, ut est illud: "Si tempestas vitanda est, non est igitur navigandum". Ex sola enim propositione <et conclusione> constat esse perfectum, unde magis oratoribus quam dialecticis convenire iudicatum est.' This is not, however, the only possibility Cassiodorus contemplates. He also quotes the theory of the above-mentioned Marius Victorinus, who thinks that an enthymeme could be composed only of *assumptio* and *conclusio*, or even of one element. See Cassiodorus Senator 2004, 14, pp. 106, 17–107, 5.

57   The typologies are named *convincibile, ostentabile, sententiale, exemplabile* and *collectivum*. See Cassiodorus Senator 2004, 13, p. 106, 1–16.

58   See Isidorus Hispalensis 1911, II, 9, 7–14.

59   John Scottus Eriugena 2003, IX, 3, pp. 92, 11–19, transl. by the author: 'Restant ea quae contrarietatis loco sumuntur, quibus tanta vis inest significandi, ut quodam privilegio excellentiae suae merito a Graecis entimemata dicantur, hoc est conceptiones mentis. Quamvis enim omne quod voce profertur prius mente concipiatur, non tamen omne quod mente concipitur eandem vim significationis, dum sensibus fervore infunditur, habere videtur. Sicut ergo argumentorum omnium fortissimum est illud quod sumitur a contrario, ita omnium signorum vocalium apertissimum est quod ducitur ab eodem contrarietatis loco, quorum quaedam absolute dicuntur, quaedam coniuncte.' Cfr. G. d'Onofrio 2013, p. 157, note 64; G. d'Onofrio 2009, pp. 141–70, here pp. 157–70; and, for an analysis of the logical elements of the *De divina praedestinatione*, G. d'Onofrio 1986, pp. 275–320. D'Onofrio observes as this theory is also mentioned by Remigius of Auxerre, Eriugena's disciple or co-worker, who, in a comment to the *Opuscula theologica* of Boethius, defines the enthymeme as follows: 'Conceptiones animi Graeci... appellant... ENTYMEMA. Entymema autem dicitur quasi "in anima": TYMH enim Graece dicitur, latine anima' (R. Autissiodorensis 1906, pp. 50, 6–9).

60   John Scottus Eriugena 1996 (CCCM, 161), pp. 69, 2113–20, transl. by the author: 'Si autem enthymematis (hoc est conceptionis communis animi) syllogismum, qui omnium conclusionum principatum obtinet quia ex his, quae simul esse non possunt assumitur, audire desideras, accipe huiusmodi formulam. Non et ΟΥΣΙΑ est et incorporalis non est; est autem ΟΥΣΙΑ; incorporalis igitur. Non enim simul esse potest ut et ΟΥΣΙΑ sit et incorporea non sit. Item non et ΟΥΣΙΑ est et corpus est; est autem ΟΥΣΙΑ; non est igitur corpus. Item non et ΟΥΣΙΑ est et incorporalis est; est autem ΟΥΣΙΑ; incorporalis igitur.' This theory is also confirmed in the *Adnotationes in Martianum*, a collection of glosses devoted to the *De nuptiis Mercurii et Philologiae* of Martianus Capella: speaking of syllogisms, John annotates: 'Primus modus ab antecedentibus vocatur quoniam in eo argumentum praecedit questionem; secundus a consequentibus propterea dicitur, quia in eo questio precedit et argumentum sequitur; tertius a Grecis *enthymema*, hoc est mentis conceptio dicitur; a contrario assumitur,

hoc est per negationem negationis' (John Scottus Eriugena 1939, pp. 103, 28-32). As a matter of fact, he traces the link that Martianus Capella himself didn't recognize between enthymeme and *argumentum ex repugnantibus*.

61 This interpretation differs somewhat from the one that M. Kraus offers in the *Historisches Wörterbuch der Rhetorik*. He also identifies four possible modalities of the enthymeme, but he thinks that they are the following: the 'topical enthymeme'; the probable syllogism; the elliptic syllogism and the maxim. The antithetic form should only be a possible characteristic of the enthymeme. See M. Kraus 1994, coll. 1197-1222, here coll. 1197-1200.

62 Hieronymus Stridonensis 1969, pp. 220, 269-73, transl. by the author: 'Verbi gratia: ostium vocatur, qui falsum dogma concepit et peperit, ut Arius in Alexandria: vectes eius et firmissimae serae eius, Euticius et Eunomius, qui syllogismis et enthymematibus, immo sophismatibus et pseudomenis atque soritis, quae male ab aliis inventa sunt, roborare conantur'.

63 Pseudo-Anselmus Cantuariensis, *Carmen de contemptu mundi*, PL 158, 701A, transl. by the author: 'Ecce diu res nulla manet mortalibus: ecce / Nullus honor prohibet, gloria nulla, mori. / Summus Aristoteles logicae scrutator acutus, / Edidit ingenio multa reperta suo. / Non syllogismo, non enthymemate factum est, / Ut vellent tanto parcere fata viro.'

64 Peter Damian 1983, pp. 303, 3-7, transl. by the author: 'Non ignoro quia cum mea epistola grammaticorum saecularium manibus traditur, mox utrum adsit artificiosi styli lepor attenditur, rhetoricae venustatis color inquiritur, et captiosos syllogismorum atque enthymematum circulos mens curiosa rimatur. Aucupatur nimirum scientiam, quae inflat, charitatem autem, quae aedificat, non miratur'.

65 Cassiodorus Senator 1958, pp. 456, 170-457, 178, transl. by the author: '*Tibi soli peccavi et malum coram te feci: ut iustificeris in sermonibus tuis et vincas cum iudicaris* (Ps 50, 6). Hic iterum enthymematicus syllogismus apparet quem in vigesimo psalmo iam diximus. Cuius propositio est: Dominus iustificatur in sermonibus suis et vincit cum iudicatur. Huic subiungitur in conclusione praemissa sententia: Tibi igitur soli peccavi et malum coram te feci. Hoc in reddendis syllogismis sine culpa fieri, more veterum constat esse permissum.' Positive evaluations of the enthymeme are also to find in such theologians as Sedulius Scottus, Venantius Fortunatus and Thiofrid of Echternach.

66 John Scottus Eriugena 2003, III, 3, pp. 28, 6-18, transl. by the author: 'Non est igitur illa praedestinatio quae cogat inevitabili necessitate sua vitam, iustitiam, beatitudinem, nec illa quae cogeret praedictorum bonorum contraria, videlicet mortem, peccatum, miseriam. Quae ratio enthymematis argumento concluditur, quod semper est a contrario, cuius propositio talis est: Non et Deus summa essentia sit et eorum tantum quae ab eo sunt causa non sit. Est autem Deus summa essentia. Est igitur eorum tantum quae ab eo sunt causa. Peccatum, mors, miseria a Deo non sunt. Eorum igitur causa Deus non est. Idem quoque syllogismus hoc modo connectitur: non et Deus eorum quae sunt causa sit et eorum quae nihil sunt causa sit. Est autem Deus eorum causa quae sunt. Igitur non est causa eorum quae non sunt. Peccatum eiusque effectus, mors profecto cui adhaeret miseria, non sunt. Eorum igitur nec Deus nec eius praedestinatio, quae est quod ipse est, causa esse potest.'

67 Some pioneering research has already unveiled similar cases. Liutpold Wallach has found enthymemes in the famous *Epistola de litteris colendis*, which is attributed in large part to Alcuin of York: see L. Wallach 1951. Even if it exceeds the chronological limits of this chapter, I must mention that H. R. Anderson has studied the use of the enthymemes in the 28th sermon (*Super cantica canticorum*) of Bernhard of Clairvaux. See. H. R. Anderson 1986, pp. 239-74, here pp. 258-68.

Bibliography

Anderson, H. R. (1986), 'Enthymeme and Dialectic: Cloister and Classroom', in *From Cloister to Classroom: Monastic and Scholastic Approaches to Truth*, E. Rozanne Elder (ed.), Kalamazoo, Cistercian Publications, pp. 239–74.

Aristoteles (1938), *Aristoteles Latinus*, L. Minio-Paluello (1962), Brill, Leiden; H. P. Cooke et alii (trans.), Cambridge, MA, Harvard University Press, Loeb Classical Library, 23 vols, 1970–1993.

Aristoteles (1969), 'Topica, Translatio Boethii', in *Aristoteles Latinus*, L. Minio-Paluello (ed.), vol. 5, Bruxelles/Paris, Desclée de Brouwer.

Aristoteles (1973), *Analytica priora*, H. Tredennick (trans.), Cambridge, MA, Harvard University Press.

Aristoteles (2011), *Rhetorica ad Alexandrum*, D. C. Mirhady (ed. and trans.), Cambridge, MA, Harvard University Press.

Aristoteles (2020), *Rhetorica*, J. H. Freese (trans.), G. Striker (rev.), Cambridge, MA, Harvard University Press.

Autissiodorensis Remigius (=Remigius of Auxerre) (1906), *Commentarius in Opuscula Sacra Boethii*, E. K. Rand (ed.), München, Beck.

Boethius Severinus (=Boethius) (2004), *De differentiis topicis*, D. Z. Nikitas (ed.), Athen/Paris/Bruxelles, Akademia Athenon/Vrin/Ousia, 1990: E. Stump (trans.), Ithaca, NY, Cornell University Press.

Boethius Severinus (=Boethius) (2004), *In Topica Ciceronis*, E. Stump (ed. and trans.), Ithaca, NY, Cornell University Press.

Burnyeat, M. F. (1994), 'Enthymeme: Aristotle on the Logic of Persuasion', in *Aristotle's Rhetoric: Philosophical Essays*, D. Furley and A. Nehemas (eds), Princeton, NJ: Princeton University Press, pp. 3–55.

Calboli, G. (1965), 'Cornificiana. 2. L'autore e la tendenza politica della *Rhetorica ad Herennium*', estratto dagli «Atti della Accademia delle scienze dell'Istituto di Bologna. Classe di Scienze morali», 58 (Memorie, 51–52), Bologna, Tipografia Compositori.

Capella, Martianus (1983), *De nuptiis Philologiae et Mercurii*, J. Willis (ed.), Leipzig, Teubner.

Cassiodorus, Senator (1958), *Expositio Psalmorum*, M. Adriaen (ed.), Turnhout: Brepols.

Cassiodorus, Senator (2004), *Institutiones divinarum ac saecularium litterarum*, R. A. B. Mynors (ed.), Oxford, Clarendon Press, 1937; J. W. Halporn (trans.), Liverpool, Liverpool University Press, 2004.

Cato, Marcius Porcius (1967), 'Orationes. De bello Carthaginiensi', in *Oratorum Romanorum Fragmenta liberae Rei Publicae*, E. Malcovati (ed.), Torino, Paravia.

Cicero, Marcus Tullius (1942), *De oratore*, H. Rackham (trans.), Cambridge, MA, Harvard University Press.

Cicero, Marcus Tullius (1949), *De inventione*, H. M. Hubbell (trans.), Cambridge, MA, Harvard University Press.

Cicero, Marcus Tullius (1994), *Topica*, G. Di Maria (ed.), Palermo, L'Epos.

Cornificius (1969), *Rhetorica ad Herennium*, G. Calboli (ed. e trad. it.), Bologna, Pàtron, (1993²); H. Caplan (trans.), Cambridge, MA: Harvard University Press, 1954.

d'Onofrio, G. (1986), *Fons scientiae. La dialettica nell'Occidente tardo-antico*, Napoli, Liguori.

d'Onofrio, G. (2009), 'Topica e sapere teologico nell'alto Medioevo', in *Les lieux de l'argumentation: Histoire du syllogisme topique d'Aristote à Leibniz*, J. Biard and F. Mariani Zini (eds), Turnhout, Brepols.

d'Onofrio, G. (2013), *Vera philosophia. Studi sul pensiero cristiano in età tardo-antica, alto-medievale e umanistica*, Roma, Città Nuova.

Damiani, Peter (1983), *Epistula 21*, K. Reindel (ed.), Muenchen, Monumenta Germaniae Historica.

De Filippis, R. (2013), *Loquax pagina. La retorica nell'Occidente tardo-antico e alto-medievale*, Roma, Città Nuova.

De Filippis, R. (2020–2021), 'Essence and Substance in Boethius: A Matter of Terminology', *Chora. Revue d'études anciennes et médiévales* 18–19, pp. 289–304.

Eriugena, John Scottus (1939), *Annotationes in Marcianum*, C. E. Lutz (ed.), Cambridge, MA, The Medieval Academy of America.

Eriugena, John Scottus (1996), *Periphyseon*, E. Jeauneau (ed.), Turnhout, Brepols.

Eriugena, John Scottus (2003), *De divina praedestinatione*, E. S. Mainoldi (ed. and trans.), Tavernuzze, SISMEL/Edizioni del Galluzzo.

Fortunatianus, Consultus (1979), *Ars rhetorica*, L. Calboli Montefusco (ed. and trans.), Bologna, Pàtron.

Halm, K. (1863): *Rhetores latini minores*, 2 vol., Leipzig, Teubner; repr. Frankfurt am Main, Minerva, 1964.

Hieronymus, Stridonensis (1969), *Commentaria in Amos*, M. Adriaen (ed.), Turnhout, Brepols.

Gundel, H.G., (1955), s. v. *Valgius 7*, in *Paulys Realencyclopädie der classischen Altertumswissenschaft*, VIII A.1, Stuttgart, Metzler, coll. 272–6.

Isidorus, Hispalensis (1911), *Etymologiae*, W. M. Lindsay (ed.), Oxford, Clarendon Press.

Klein, J. (1994), s. *v. Epicheirem*, in *Historisches Wörterbuch der Rhetorik*, II, coll. 1251–8, von G. Ueding (ed.), Tübingen, Niemeyer.

Kraus, M. (1994), *v. Enthymem*, in *Historisches Wörterbuch der Rhetorik*, II, coll. 1197–222, von G. Ueding (ed.), Tübingen, Niemeyer.

Kraus, M. (2002), *Theories and Practice of the Enthymeme in the First Centuries B.C.E. and C.E.*, in *Rhetorical Argumentation in biblical Texts. Essays from the Lund 2000 Conference*, A. Eriksson, T. H. Olbricht, W. Übelacker (eds), Harrisonburg, PA, Trinity Press, pp. 95–111.

Kraus, M. (2012), 'Teorie dell'entimema nell'antichità', *Pan. Rivista di filologia latina*, N.S., 1, pp. 17–30.

Piazza, F. (2012), 'Non solo sillogismo. Per una lettura retorica dell'entimema aristotelico', *Pan. Rivista di filologia latina*, N.S., 1, pp. 32–4.

Pseudo-Anselmus, Cantuariensis (1864), 'Carmen de contemptu mundi', *Patrologia latina* 158, pp. 687–706.

Quintilian (2002), *Institutio oratoria*, D. A. Russell (ed. and trans.), Cambridge, MA, Harvard University Press.

Victor, Iulius. (1980), *Ars rhetorica*, R. Giomini and M. S. Celentano (eds), Leipzig, Teubner.

Wallach, L. (1951), 'Charlemagne's «De litteris colendis» and Alcuin: A Diplomatic History', *Speculum* 26 (2), pp. 288–305.

2

Enthymemes in al-Fārābī's and Avicenna's systems

Saloua Chatti

2.1 Introduction

While al-Fārābī provides a full analysis of the notion of enthymeme (called *ḍamīr*, in Arabic) mainly in his treatise entitled *al-Khaṭāba* (corresponding to *Rhetoric*), where he makes a difference between enthymemes, analogies and syllogisms, Avicenna evokes the enthymemes not only in his *al-Khaṭāba* but also in *al-Qiyās*, where he analyses it in relation with the concept of logical consequence and shows its deficiencies in this respect.

So the problems that we raise in this chapter are the following: How is the notion of enthymeme viewed by both logicians? What are the main characteristics of enthymemes? In what context(s) can they be used? What are their aims and function in rhetoric? How are they different from logical deductions such as categorical or hypothetical syllogisms?

We will try to answer these questions by considering both al-Fārābī's views and Avicenna's ones and comparing between these views in order to determine the status of enthymemes in their respective frames. We will show that these views are different from each other, although they are both clearly influenced by Aristotle.

2.2 Enthymemes in al-Fārābī's frame

It is in his treatise *Kitāb al-Khaṭāba* that al-Fārābī analyses the concept of enthymeme (*ḍamīr*) by distinguishing between enthymemes, analogies or likenings (*tamthīl*) and syllogisms (*qiyās*) and determining their respective characteristics, the way they are used in several contexts and their usefulness in these contexts. For in *al-Qiyās*, he talks about induction and likening (analogy) in the last chapters, but he does not evoke enthymemes explicitly.[1]

In *Kitāb al-Khaṭāba*, he starts by defining the concept *khaṭāba* itself, by saying what follows:

> Rhetoric is a *syllogistic* art (*ṣinā'a qiyāsīyya*), whose aim is to *persuade* in all ten categories[2] (*gharaḍuhā al-iqnā'u fī jamī'i al-ajnāsi al-'ashara*); and the *conviction* that occurs (*mā yaḥṣulu*) in the listener's mind in the context of these things, is the *ultimate aim* (*al-gharaḍu al-aqṣā*) of the actions of rhetoric (*bi-af'āli al-khaṭāba*).[3] (emphasis added)

In this quotation, al-Fārābī stresses several ideas that clarify the differences between rhetoric and the other syllogistic disciplines. He first says that rhetoric is a *syllogistic art*, thus stressing both the closeness between rhetoric and categorical syllogistic, that is, the syllogistic of categorical propositions, and their differences. For as an art, rhetoric is different from categorical syllogistic as such, which studies the formal and valid syllogisms, but it has some common points with the formal discipline studied in *al-Qiyās* (*Prior Analytics*) in that the arguments studied in it are similar in some respects to the formal syllogistic moods. We will see later in this chapter how these points are analysed and justified in the rest of the text.

Second, he says that the aim of rhetoric is to persuade (*al-iqnā'*) in the sense of producing a *conviction*, that is, an opinion or a belief, eventually a strong one, but not necessarily a true discourse. So, the aim of rhetoric is not to reach the truth, unlike the aim of science, which is studied in *al-Burhān* (*Posterior Analytics*), and of logic, whose syllogistic moods are analysed in *al-Qiyās* (*Prior Analytics*), where the conclusion is necessarily a true one, if the premises are true, due to the formal validity of the moods. Rhetoric just searches for convictions acceptable by the audience but not necessarily for a true knowledge. Convictions are subjective rather than objective. They may be true or false. So, they should not be identified with scientific knowledge or with the conclusions of valid syllogistic moods, for their truth is not warranted, unlike these conclusions and knowledge.

In addition, although al-Fārābī makes a clear distinction between science (*'ilm*) and the convictions that we find in rhetoric, he also talks about a kind of parallelism between the persuasion in the context of rhetoric and the teaching in the context of demonstration, for he says: 'and persuasion (*al-iqnā'*) in the art of rhetoric is like teaching in the demonstrative arts' (Al-Fārābī, *Kitāb al-Khatāba*, p. 456.12–13). Likewise, convictions are parallel or analogous to scientific knowledge. But they are not identical, since science is necessarily true, while convictions are not necessarily true. The parallelism established is just a formal one, which stresses the common points between demonstration and rhetoric without identifying both fields. This parallelism can be shown as follows:

Rhetoric	*Demonstration*
uses persuasion	uses demonstrative arguments
reaches conviction	reaches science
the aim is to persuade a listener	the aim is to teach the truth

As we can see, everything in rhetoric is weaker than in the demonstrative disciplines like mathematics, natural sciences and logic. For convictions are weaker than true propositions, persuasion is weaker than teaching and persuasive syllogisms are weaker than demonstrative syllogisms. The weakness in all these cases can be understood in relation with the notion of truth. The demonstrative arts necessarily produce truths while the rhetoric arts only produce convictions which are not necessarily true: in this respect, what they produce and the way they produce it are both weaker than what a demonstrative science produces and the way it produces it.

Third, the aim of rhetoric is reached in the context of a conversation or a dialogue between a speaker and a (or several) listener(s). It is in this context, which has a dialectic nature, that rhetoric must be understood. The aim is to make the listener(s) reach a conviction by means of several kinds of arguments, which are either external or internal. External arguments are those where the speaker wants to persuade people by stressing his own virtue or the 'weakness of his opponents' (Al-Fārābī, *Kitāb al-Khaṭāba*, p. 471.11) instead of focusing on the subject of the debate. According to al-Fārābī, this is 'what Galen has done when he favoured himself by referring to his father's virtue and the [superiority] of his country and weakened his opponents by mentioning the weaknesses of their ancestors and countries' (Al-Fārābī, *Kitāb al-Khaṭāba*, p. 471.13–14). This kind of arguments is not efficient, according to him, because it is not persuasive, since such arguments do not focus on the main subject of the discussion but rely on external features which do not have anything to do with that subject. For this reason, al-Fārābī considers them as rather weak arguments.

More persuasive arguments are examples and enthymemes (*ḍamā'ir*; sing. *ḍamīr*), the latter being the most powerful one. For this reason, they are both more efficient and more reliable than all other kinds of arguments used in rhetoric. Examples are comparable to inductions while enthymemes are closer to syllogisms, that is, to deductive arguments. For he says:

> The ways by which persuasion can be reached are [the following]: one of them is the enthymemes (*al-ḍamā'ir*), the other one is the examples (*al-tamthīlāt*). The status (*manzila*) of enthymemes in rhetoric is the same as the status of demonstrations in the sciences and syllogisms in dialectic. An enthymeme is like a rhetorical *syllogism* (*ka'annahu qiyāsun khaṭabī*), while an example is like a rhetorical *induction* (*ka'annahu istiqrā'un khaṭabī*).[4] (emphasis added)

We can note, here, that al-Fārābī is very close to Aristotle in his classification, although he does not explicitly mention Aristotle's text, since Aristotle says what follows in *Rhetoric*:

> The enthymeme and the example must, then, deal with what is for the most part capable of being otherwise, the example being an *induction*, and the enthymeme a *deduction*.[5] (emphasis added)

Now, enthymemes are used by the speaker to persuade some listeners of some particular thesis or opinion in the context of a discussion or a debate. Al-Fārābī distinguishes between three kinds of listeners who play different roles or functions. These three kinds are the following: 'The [person] whom the speaker intends to persuade (*al-maqṣūdu iqnāʾuhu*), the opponent or discussant (*al-munāḍir*), and the judge (or the arbiter) (*al-ḥākim*)' (Al-Fārābī, *Kitāb al-Khaṭāba*, p. 469.9). The first kind of listeners is the one who asked for a discussion either by starting it (*ibtabadaʾa*) or because he has been asked for it by the speaker, the second kind, that is, the discussant is either a real opponent whose aim is to refute the speaker's opinion or an apparent opponent whose aim is to gain more evidence in favour of that opinion (*al-Khaṭāba*, p. 469.15–16). As to the third kind, the judge, he plays the role of an arbiter or a referee, and for this reason he must have enough ability to correctly recognize (*jawdat al-tamyyīz*) the most persuasive arguments provided by the two other protagonists (*Kitāb al-Khaṭāba*, p. 469.17). These three kinds are thus different from each other, since the first kind might be the less empowered to distinguish the persuasive opinions while the judge seems to be the most empowered to recognize the most persuasive arguments and opinions and to see the different tricks and ways used by the speaker to persuade his audience. In other words, the kinds of listeners oscillate between the less skilful to the most skilful with regard to the degree of persuasion of the different arguments.

Here too, he is close to Aristotle, who says the following in *Rhetoric*:

> The hearer must be either a judge, with a decision to make about things past or future, or an observer. A member of the assembly decides about future events, a juryman about past events [while those who merely decide on the orator's skill are observers]. From this it follows that there are three divisions of oratory – deliberative, forensic, and epideictic.[6]

In the above-mentioned quotation, Aristotle distinguishes between 'deliberative, forensic and epideictic' oratory. He explains what he intends in the rest of the paragraph by saying that the deliberative discourse 'urges us either to do or not to do something' (*Rhetoric*, book I, §3, 1358a3–a35), forensic discourse 'either attacks or defends somebody' (*Rhetoric*, book I, §3, 1358a3–a35) and epideictic discourse 'either praises or censures somebody' (*Rhetoric*, book I, §3, 1358a3–a35).

As to al-Fārābī, he evokes explicitly the opponent, who is distinguished from the simple listener and the judge. It is the opponent who attacks the speaker's discourse and the speaker who defends his thesis. So, we can say that the forensic dimension in particular is present in al-Fārābī's analysis of the rhetorical speeches, especially enthymemes. Note that Aristotle says in the end of book I that 'Enthymemes are most suitable to forensic speeches' (*Rhetoric*, book I, §8, 1368a19–a33).

Now a conviction is a kind of belief. And belief (*al-ẓann*) and certainty (*al-yaqīn*) are both opinions, as al-Fārābī stresses when he says: 'they share the fact that they are opinions (*yashtarikāni fī annahumā raʾyun*)' (Al-Fārābī, *Kitāb al-Khaṭāba*, p. 457.3). So, the concept of opinion is like a genus with regard to belief and certainty, which are its 'two species' (Al-Fārābī, *Kitāb al-Khaṭāba*, p. 457.4).

We can thus say that beliefs, convictions and opinions, even if they may be certain, are not necessarily true, and consequently that truth and certainty are different from each other. Rhetoric is not the way to reach a true knowledge, which should be necessary. But it might happen that the conclusion of a rhetoric argument is necessary. This necessity, however, is not due to the rhetoric argument by which it had been sought; rather it is necessary by itself, regardless of the argument that leaded to it. For convictions can be necessary as well as possible, as al-Fārābī says in the same passage (Al-Fārābī, *Kitāb al-Khaṭāba*, p. 457.5–6). But necessity, which is either absolute or relative to some context or time, characterizes specifically those opinions that are certain. Those that are not certain are not necessary but simply possible. Nevertheless, both kinds of opinions, whether necessary or possible, can be the objects of some persuasion. One can be persuaded by a possible opinion, whose truth is not warranted, even if he can also be persuaded by a necessary truth.

Beliefs can also have degrees. They can be 'more or less strong (*yaqwā wa yaḍ'ufu*)' (Al-Fārābī, *Kitāb al-Khaṭāba*, p. 458.18). In this respect too, they are different from true knowledge, which does not admit degrees. According to al-Fārābī, the strength or weakness of a belief is related to the notion of conflict: the more conflicted a belief is, the weaker it is; the less it is conflicted, the stronger it is (*Kitāb al-Khaṭāba*, p. 458.19–20). In al-Fārābī's frame, the conflict is exemplified either by contradiction (both opinions can never be true together or false together) or by contrariety (both opinions can never be true together, but they can be false together). So, beliefs should not be contradictory or contrary of each other, since when there is a contrariety or a contradiction between two opinions, at least one of them should be considered as false. However, he adds that 'convictions are not weakened by the conflicts that one [might] feel (*wa laysa yunqiṣu al-qanā'ata an yash'ura al-insānu bi-mu'ānadātin*)' (Al-Fārābī, *Kitāb al-Khaṭāba*, p. 458.19). So, convictions are stronger than beliefs and might be accepted even when they contain some conflict. Their strength should thus be more subjective than objective. It could be related, not only to the rational reasons that make these opinions true but also to other features of human's nature, such as passions or emotions, or else to the usefulness (*al-anfa'*) of some opinion. For according to al-Fārābī, if someone thinks that it would be useful for him to refute some opinion, he would 'refute it' for that reason, even if 'he knows that it is strong (*wa 'araḍahu 'alā 'ilmin bi-quwwatihi*)' (Al-Fārābī, *Kitāb al-Khaṭāba*, p. 459.2). These features could be the main reasons that make some opinion convincing, despite the presence of some conflict. In other words, convictions are not necessarily rational, just as they are not necessarily and objectively true.

In addition, the conflict might be hidden or not clearly available to one's mind, either because the opinion is not easily falsifiable by some experience or some observation (Al-Fārābī, *Kitāb al-Khaṭāba*, p. 459.20–1) or because the conflict is 'confused' (*ghāmiḍa*) (Al-Fārābī, *Kitāb al-Khaṭāba*, p. 460.1), that is, not easily seen or realized by one's mind, who would be unable to understand it because he would 'lack the art' (Al-Fārābī, *Kitāb al-Khaṭāba*, p. 460.2) that could help him arrive at this conflicted conclusion. In sum, as he says,

> As long as some opinion is not refuted by some opposed one, it seems to remain certain [in the mind of those] who are persuaded [by it] (*fa-inna al-ḍanna matā lam yaḍhar lahu mu'ānidun, fa-ka'annahu 'inda mu'taqidihi yaqīnun*).[7]

According to him, this feature of being certain as long as it is not refuted by some argument or proof is characteristic of opinions (*ẓunūn*), even if these opinions might seem as convictions to some people. Opinions are thus different from certainty 'because certainty cannot be removed at all by a conflict (*li-anna al-yaqīna lā yumkinu an yazūla bi-'inādin aṣlan*)' (Al-Fārābī, *Kitāb al-Khaṭāba*, p. 462.13–14). In so far as convictions are opinions, they are not always certain, even if they are believed by the listener.

Now how does al-Fārābī define enthymemes, which, according to him, are the most efficient arguments in rhetoric?

According to the definition he provides, enthymemes are said to be syllogisms where one of the premises is hidden. The conclusion of that incomplete syllogism is the conviction to which the enthymeme leads. Enthymemes are thus defined as follows by al-Fārābī:

> An enthymeme is a discourse containing two connected premises and it is used by removing (*yusta'malu bi-ḥadhfi*) one of the connected premises. It is called an enthymeme (*ḍamīr*) because its user hides (*yuḍmiru*) some of its premises and does not state them (*lā yuṣarriḥu bihā*) and it also relies on the fact that the knowledge of these removed premises is present in the listener's conscience (*ḍamīr*).[8]

He adds that an enthymeme is persuasive *only because* one of its premises is hidden, for he says:

> And it must be clear that [the enthymeme] is persuasive . . . *because of* what has been removed from it (*li-ḥadhfi mā ḥudhifa minhu*), and *if it had not been removed from it (wa law lam yuḥdhaf), it would not have been persuasive (la-mā ṣāra muqni'an)*.[9] (emphasis added)

In the first quotation, al-Fārābī defines the enthymemes by saying that they are syllogistic arguments containing two premises where one of the premises is not stated. This feature is characteristic of the enthymeme and makes it different from a classical categorical, hypothetical or modal syllogism, where all the premises are stated. This kind of argument is called *ḍamīr* by al-Fārābī because in Arabic, the word '*ḍamīr*' means both the hiding (of something) and the (human) conscience. These two meanings are contained in this kind of argument because the hiding of one premise is essential in it and because what is hidden is supposed to be known by the conscience of the listener too. So, the definition highlights the adequacy of the name chosen by al-Fārābī for this kind of arguments used in rhetoric.

The second quotation adds one more idea, which is that the enthymeme is persuasive *only when* one of its premises is hidden. For al-Fārābī says explicitly that if this were not the case, that is, if all the premises of the syllogism were stated, not only this syllogism would not be an enthymeme (by definition, so to say) but also *it would not be persuasive*. So, the reason why the enthymeme is persuasive is precisely the hiding of one of the premises.

This idea is repeated two pages later where al-Fārābī says what follows:

> And it [i.e. the enthymeme] becomes (*yaṣīru*) persuasive (*muqni'an*) in so far as the speaker (*al-mutakallimu*) hides (*yuḍmiru*) one of its two premises

and does not state it (*wa lā yuṣarrihu bihā*). Because of that, it has been called enthymeme (*al-ḍamīr*) and the hidden (*al-muḍmaru*), for the hiding (*iḍmār*) of one of the premises is the *reason* (*sababan*) why it is persuasive. Otherwise, the demonstrations and the dialectic syllogisms (*al-qiyāsāt al-jadalīyya*), if they are used in conversations and books, and if one of their premises is removed in each of them, in most cases for the sake of brevity, or because what is removed is very clear to the listener, *these cannot be called enthymemes*.[10] (emphasis added)

This quotation stresses the idea that the enthymeme must hide one of the premises to be persuasive and adds the idea (expressed in a rather confused way in the last half of the quotation) that this hiding *should not* just be an abbreviation (*ikhtiṣār*) and *should not* be due to the clarity of that premise in the listener's mind, for then the argument is not really an enthymeme; it would be a classical syllogism which is stated in a simplified way because of the obviousness of the hidden premise or because the speaker wants to be as brief as possible, without being disrespectful to the general structure of the argument.

So the enthymeme is more than a simplification of a syllogism, and the hiding of the premise is not due to any kind of obviousness or abbreviation. It has other sources and reasons which are related to the art of rhetoric and makes it different from syllogistic, demonstration and dialectic (*jadal*).

However, when al-Fārābī says that the argument is *no more an enthymeme* if the premise is removed only because of its obviousness, he is not really in accordance with Aristotle, who does not defend such an idea. For according to Aristotle, simplicity should be an essential feature of the enthymeme, as appears in the following passage:

Thus, we must not carry its reasoning too far back, or the length of our argument will cause obscurity; nor must we put in all steps that lead to our conclusion, or we shall waste words in saying what is *manifest*. It is this simplicity that makes the uneducated more effective than the educated when addressing popular audiences – makes them as the poets tell us, 'charm the crowd's ears more finely'.[11] (my emphasis)

So, Aristotle does not reject the idea that the obviousness of some premises might be the main reason for hiding them in the enthymemes. And he does not say that when the premise is removed because of its obviousness, the argument is no more an enthymeme. Rather, he says that this hiding of obvious premises simplifies the whole argument and makes it more acceptable to the 'popular' audience. We can note, though, that here too, Aristotle's text is not mentioned.

But al-Fārābī's opinion about enthymemes raises some questions from a logical viewpoint. For why should an incomplete argument, that is, an argument from which one of the premises has been removed, be persuasive at all, since the very reason that makes a classical syllogism (categorical, modal or hypothetical) lead to a true conclusion is precisely the fact that all its premises are stated and that their particular combination corresponds to a specific valid mood? In categorical, modal and hypothetical syllogistics, this structure and the clear statement of the premises is precisely the reason why the conclusion is true, hence convincing, when both premises are true, for it is this structure that *leads necessarily* to a true conclusion when the premises are true. In these syllogistic moods, if one removes one of the premises, one does not warrant the truth of the conclusion, which depends on *both* premises and their specific combination. And of course, when a conclusion is true, it is *a fortiori* persuasive, precisely because of its truth.

So, one should explain why an enthymeme cannot be persuasive if one of its premises is not hidden. In other words, one should explain the difference between a classical syllogism, where *nothing is hidden*, and an enthymeme, where *something must be hidden* – not only for methodological or pedagogical reasons – in order for it to produce a conviction. We will see later that the explanation of that specific feature of the enthymeme is related to the art of rhetoric and the ability of the speaker to persuade any audience, whether the argument he is using is valid or not. For the persuasive character of the enthymeme has to do with the fact that the hiding of one of the premises makes it possible to hide either the invalidity of the syllogism on which the enthymeme is based or the falsity of the hidden premise. In both cases, if the premise is not hidden the listener can easily see that the conclusion is false and consequently, he would not admit that conclusion. For that reason, the whole reasoning would not be persuasive, because the falsity of the conclusion would appear clearly. But the hiding of that one premise makes it easier to also hide the falsity of the conclusion, which makes the whole reasoning persuasive.

This is what al-Fārābī explains in the rest of his analysis. For he says that the enthymemes can be either: (1) real syllogisms (where the conclusion really follows from its premises) or (2) apparent (= not real) syllogisms (where the conclusion does not really follow from the premises) (Al-Fārābī, *Kitāb al-Khaṭāba*, p. 476.21). In the first case, the syllogism is conclusive and it becomes an enthymeme when one of its premises is removed. In the second case, the syllogism seems to be conclusive but it is not quite so.

Let us examine this idea more closely. Enthymemes may be persuasive with regard to the form or the matter of the syllogisms they are relying on. These syllogisms can be either categorical (or predicative) or hypothetical. In both cases, the arguments can be either really conclusive or not really conclusive. If some syllogism is really conclusive, the conclusion follows necessarily from its premises. The syllogism becomes an enthymeme when one of the premises is removed. In the moods of the first figure, for instance, this removed premise should be the major one, which is universal, for as claimed by al-Fārābī,

> If we want to get enthymemes from the moods of the first figure, we must remove the major premise and hide it and state only the minor premise. And if we decide to state it sometimes, we have to state it as an indefinite.[12]

So, there are two ways of transforming a first-figure syllogism into an enthymeme: (1) by hiding its major premise and (2) otherwise by stating the (universal) first premise as an indefinite. In both cases, the trickery is related to the form of the syllogism. In the first case, the speaker states only the minor premise and deduces the conclusion from it, which is a way to hide the form of the syllogism. This is a way to introduce some kind of conflict in such arguments, since the necessary following of the conclusion from the premises is in fact due to the form or the structure of the syllogism. So, by hiding the first premise, the speaker also hides the general structure of the syllogism and consequently the necessary character of the entailment of the conclusion. In the second case, which has also to do with the form of the syllogism, the speaker may introduce some conflict in the argument by stating the major premise as an indefinite rather than as a universal proposition. This is also a way to hide the general form of the syllogism, since the indefinite propositions are ambiguous: they may be interpreted as universals or as particulars, and in al-Fārābī's frame as well as in Aristotle's one, they are rather interpreted as particulars, although he says that common people tend to interpret them as universal propositions in ordinary discourses. For this reason, there is a conflict related to the entailment of the conclusion because the real structure of the syllogism does not appear clearly to the listener. As al-Fārābī says, 'and if it were stated, it is *not stated* in the way that would make the premise *necessarily entail* the conclusion' (al-Fārābī, Kitāb al-Khaṭāba, p. 478.22–3, emphasis added). Since the indefinite is weaker than the universal, the following of the conclusion from an indefinite proposition is not obviously necessary. For this reason, the argument is not demonstrative. It remains nevertheless persuasive if the listener interprets the indefinite as a universal, as common people tend to do, according to al-Fārābī. In this case, the argument would be an enthymeme because it would be persuasive for the common listener without being really valid.

Second, the trickery can also be related to the matter of the premise. This happens when the premise is *false*. In that case, its hiding becomes indispensable to produce a conviction, as al-Fārābī says in the following quotation:

> Secondly, it may happen that the premise is false, [and even] evidently false (*bayyinatu al-kadhib*), so that the listener would realize its falsity, in which case the discourse would no more be convincing. So, if the speaker keeps it silent (*sakata 'anhā*), then by his silence, he gives the false impression that the reason why he is keeping it silent is because it is obviously true (*ḍāhiratu-al-ṣidqi*). And if it is true, he [i.e. the listener] would not think that it is true only when [considered as] a particular.[13]

So, the hiding of the premise is precisely what produces the conviction, because the listener does not clearly realize that the hidden premise is false or that it is true only when taken as a particular. Rather, he (i.e. the listener) thinks that its hiding is due to its obviousness, and it is precisely this thought that produces in his mind the conviction that the conclusion is itself true. This means that in some cases, the enthymeme is really misleading given that the speaker deliberately deceives the listener by making him think that a given premise is true while he knows perfectly well that it is not true. This way of persuading the listener is therefore based on a deceit (a trickery), since the enthymeme produces a false conclusion which the listener thinks to be true. This makes enthymemes somehow close to sophistic arguments in these specific cases. But not all enthymemes are misleading in that way, which puts rhetoric somewhere between syllogistic and sophistic.

The speaker can also use invalid syllogisms to persuade the listener(s). For instance, he can use a second-figure syllogism with two affirmative premises. This kind of syllogisms is never valid in syllogistic, but the speaker can persuade the listener that the conclusion is true, whether by hiding one of the premises or by selecting the appropriate plausible premises and conclusion. The same can happen with the third-figure moods, where the speaker misleads the listener by deducing a universal conclusion from two universal premises, which is not a valid deduction in this figure since the conclusions of both *Darapti* and *Felapton are and must be* particulars. In that case, the premises as al-Fārābī stresses 'should be considered as indefinite' (Al-Fārābī, *Kitāb al-Khaṭāba*, p. 480.9) in order to hide the invalidity of such syllogisms.

Enthymemes can also be hypothetical arguments where one of the premises is hidden. Recall that al-Fārābī admits all Stoic hypothetical moods, such as *Modus Ponens, Modus Tollens* and so on, plus some variants. Enthymemes based on hypothetical moods state the conditional premise and hide the second detached premise. For instance, instead of stating the whole *Modus Ponens*: 'If p then q, but p; therefore q', one hides 'but p' in stating the enthymeme and deduces 'therefore q' only from the first premise 'If p then q'.

Since these moods can deduce either an affirmative proposition or a negative one, depending on the second (detached) premise, by hiding this second premise, the speaker may give the illusion that the conclusion (whether affirmative or negative) is true, even when it is not. To understand that let us give these valid moods and see what could happen when one hides the second premise.

The main valid moods containing a conditional first premise are the following:

(1) If p then q, but p; therefore q
(2) If p then q, but not q; therefore not p
(3) If not p then not q, but not p; therefore not q
(4) If not p then not q, but q; therefore p

By hiding the second premise in these moods, one can deduce 'p' instead of 'q', or 'not q' instead of 'not p', for instance, if 'the speaker considers this conclusion as more useful for him' (Al-Fārābī, *Kitāb al-Khaṭāba*, p. 480.19–20). The hiding of the second premise makes it easier to persuade the listener about the desired conclusion, because the structure of the mood is no more clearly visible.

For instance, 'If the conclusion is the opposite of the consequent, the detached premise is the opposite of the antecedent. This combination apparently seems conclusive, but it is not really so' (Al-Fārābī, *Kitāb al-Khaṭāba*, pp. 480.23–481.1). In other words, the speaker may use the following invalid argument to deduce the conclusion:

'If p then q, [*but Not p*]; therefore Not q'.

He thus deduces 'Not q' from the stated first premise 'If p then q' but hides the second premise (i.e. 'but not p'), because if this premise were stated the argument would clearly appear as invalid to the listener. So, hiding the premise is a way of confusing the listener who would not be able to realize the invalidity of the whole argument. Therefore, this makes it easier for the speaker to persuade him about the truth of the conclusion.

In other cases, the mood used is really valid, as when 'the conclusion is the opposite of the antecedent, [while] the detached premise is the opposite of the consequent [see (2) above]' (*al-Khaṭāba*, p. 481.7–8), but the speaker still considers it 'persuasive [only by] removing the detached premise, or else by stating the detached premise but then the conditional premise should be hidden in order to keep in it some conflict or some object of request' (Al-Fārābī, *Kitāb al-Khaṭāba*, p. 481.8).

So, it is by hiding the premise that the speaker can persuade his audience. This is so because the art of rhetoric is not only based on the intrinsic validity of the arguments used by the speaker. For if the arguments were valid by themselves, rhetoric would not be needed at all. The art of syllogistic would be quite sufficient and much better than all rhetoric arguments. The use of rhetoric arguments, such as enthymemes, is thus needed when the speaker is talking to a wide audience, since rhetoric arguments are used in all kinds of fields without presupposing a deep mastering or knowledge of these fields by the audience. A speaker can thus talk about everything to everybody. But in talking about everything, the speaker must be persuasive. For this reason, he must possess some ability in persuading people about what he wants them to believe. This ability appears in the power that the speaker has to persuade people about the truth of some conclusion in controversial matters, not in scientific ones, where the aim is to reach the truth in a correct way. Unlike the dialectic and demonstrative arts, rhetoric does not always aim at reaching the truth. Its aim is to persuade people about some idea or theory because the speaker has some advantage or utility in producing this conviction. This requires using enthymemes, when the argument leading to this conclusion is not valid by itself. The art of rhetoric is then the art of making the conclusion appear plausible and true even when it is not correctly deduced.

In this respect, it seems hard to clearly distinguish between rhetorical arguments and sophistic ones, since in both cases the speaker misleads the listener(s) by making him think that the conclusion is true while it is false. But rhetoric is not identical to sophistic, because its aims are not the same as those of sophistic. The aim of a rhetorical argument is not primarily to mislead people. Rather it is to help them understand and admit some useful propositions even if they are not correctly deduced. But he also says that 'rhetoric shares with dialectic and sophistic the fact that all of them are used to track (*ta'aqqub*) the false opinions so that they appear clearly (*fa-tankashifu*) to be false' (Al-Fārābī, *Kitāb al-Khaṭāba*, p. 468.7–8). So, these three disciplines share the fact that they can show what opinions should be considered as false. But al-Fārābī does not say in this short passage what attitude towards the false opinions should be taken by the users of these three methods. In particular, is the rhetorician's attitude towards the false opinions identical to the sophist's one, for instance? If we consider that the sophist intends to persuade people about some opinions which he himself considers as false, should we say the same thing about the rhetorician and the dialectician? Al-Fārābī does not give a precise answer to this question in that part of the text, but as we saw earlier in this chapter, he does admit the fact that in some cases, the rhetorician 'misleads' in some way his audience by hiding the premise that could show clearly that the conclusion is not properly deduced or simply not true.

However, we can also say that according to him, rhetoric is fundamentally different from logic and the rhetorical arguments should not be reducible to the logical ones. For he says what follows:

> And if all the premises are stated, and if the necessary is universal, and all the conditions of the syllogism are completely present, then it reaches the higher degree of certainty instead of simply persuasion (*irtaf'a min rutbati al-iqnā'i ilā rutbati al-yaqīni*). [. . .] Nevertheless, its persuasiveness disappears (vanishes: *yazūlu*) in some other respect (*min wajhin ākharin*), which is that it can be thought of its user that he won not by means of rhetorical ways (*lā bi-ṭarīq al-khaṭāba*), but by means of a logical art (*bal bi-ṣinā'a mantiqīyya*), which makes the discourse follow [from other ones] (*ta'aqqaba bihā al-qawlu*), or by means of some other art, not by his ability (*qudratihi*) to excellently use the ways that are common to him and all his interlocutors and opponents.

> And if someone thinks that his victory over his opponents is due to his mastery of another art, different from the one that is common to him and his opponents, then his specific discourse will not be persuasive, in that (*min qibali anna*) it would be thought that what makes it persuasive is not the power of the question (*quwwatu al-amr*) nor the propositions used in his discourse, but rather a power from which he benefited thanks to another art (*quwwatan istafādahā 'an ṣinā'atin ukhrā*). [This would be comparable to the situation] where one of the fighters makes use of a weapon, unlike the other ones [. . .]; for this recourse shows his weakness in that art and brings him out of the class of fighters. Likewise, with those who dispute by using common ways.[14]

This long passage shows that al-Fārābī sharply distinguishes between the rhetorician and the logician and consequently between rhetoric on the one hand and logic on the other one, for he does not approve the use of logical arguments and moods in the context of rhetoric. Although this would make the speaker reach certainty instead of simply persuasion, this also means that the speaker made use of more powerful arguments in order to arrive at this result. By doing so, he would be in some way unfair with the audience since he would not use the same methods as his opponents and interlocutors. This, he says, would be like a fighter who would use a weapon when fighting with people who do not have such arms. So, for him, rhetoric is different from logic; rhetorical arguments are different from logical ones, and they are also weaker than them. But in a rhetorical context, a rhetorician should restrain himself to rhetorical arguments when speaking with his interlocutors and opponents, who are not supposed to be logicians. In addition, if someone wins a rhetorical debate by using logical arguments, not available to his opponents, this success would not be due to his own abilities as a rhetorician but rather to the logical argument itself. This success does not thus show that he is a good rhetorician. It rather demonstrates the power of the logical arguments themselves, which deduce necessarily the conclusion from the premises. It would then be due to logic as a discipline, not to any kind of rhetorical ability that the speaker would possess.

In addition, while mentioning in a brief way the refutation of enthymemes, which Aristotle analyses in *Rhetoric*, book II, §25, he simply says what follows:

> Some people requested invalidating (*ibṭāla*) the use of examples and replacing them by enthymemes. As to enthymemes, they cannot be invalidated at all. For if they are invalidated, they would be invalidated by enthymemes; they would then be invalidated by themselves, and this is not possible.[15]

So, unlike Aristotle who explicitly mentions the *Prior Analytics* in his analysis of the refutations of enthymemes (see Aristotle, *Rhetoric*, book II, §25, 1403a4–a6), he does not really analyse the ways by which one can refute enthymemes, even when they are clearly invalid and misleading. This seems to show that here too, he clearly separates rhetoric from logic, for it is by using logical arguments that one can show the invalidity of an enthymeme.

Maybe this difference with Aristotle could be understood in the light of the fact that as noted by Frédérique Woerther,

> Al-Fārābī worked with the old and error-filled Arabic translation of Aristotle's Rhetoric, which is still available today (ed. Malcolm C. Lyons). Al-Fārābī attempted to explain Aristotle's thought by clarifying the difficulties of the Arabic translation, which sometimes led him to distort Aristotle's original doctrines.[16]

We will see later in this chapter that unlike al-Fārābī, Avicenna does talk explicitly about what Aristotle calls the 'spurious' (Aristotle, *Rhetoric*, book II, §24) enthymemes and about the refutation of enthymemes in general. His opinion about enthymemes appears to be closer to Aristotle's opinion than it is to al-Fārābī's one, as we will see later.

2.3 Enthymemes in Avicenna's frame

Avicenna evokes enthymemes in several treatises, among which we can evoke *'Uyūn al-ḥikma*, *al-Khaṭāba* (*Rhetoric*), and, unlike al-Fārābī, in his *al-Qiyās* (1964) (the counterpart of *Prior Analytics*).

In *'Uyūn al-ḥikma*, he only says what follows:

> Enthymemes: a syllogism where only the minor is stated, as when they say: 'Mr so-and-so goes around at night (*fulān yaṭūfu lailan*), therefore he is disordered (*mukhtaliṭun*)', the major being removed either to dispense with it (*li-al-istighnā bihi*) or to make a sophism (*li-al-mughālaṭa*).[17]

This unique sentence stresses the fact that the enthymeme is either a way to abbreviate some syllogisms or else one of the ways used by the speaker to mislead the listeners. He thus notes the closeness between rhetoric and sophistic from the start.

In *al-Khaṭāba*, however, Avicenna defines rhetoric by distinguishing between that discipline and dialectic as well as sophistic. In that treatise, he provides a long analysis of rhetoric and its different tools and distinguishes between rhetoric and the two other disciplines with regard to their aims, their subjects and their methods. According to him, rhetoric and dialectic are close to each other, while sophistic is different from them both. For rhetoric and dialectic are close with regard both to their subjects and their aims (Avicenna, *al-Khaṭāba*, p. 791.22–3). Both dialectic and rhetoric aim at winning the debate (or the discussion) (*al-mufāwada*), the first 'by [using] implications (*bi-l-ilzām*)' and the second 'by [using] rather disjunctions (*fa-bi-l-infiṣāl*)' (Avicenna, *al-Khaṭāba*, p. 791). Their aim is thus to win the debate by showing the truth of the speaker's thesis (Avicenna, *al-Khaṭāba*, p. 791.24) and, in the case of dialectic, by also showing the falsity of his opponent's thesis (Avicenna, *al-Khaṭāba*, p. 791.25). But the arguments used by the dialectician are more based on implications, while those used by the rhetorician are more based on disjunctions. In both cases, the aim is not only to win the discussion but also to show that the conclusion reached is true, therefore beneficial. In this respect, both rhetoric and dialectic are different from sophistic, which 'just aims at winning [the debate] (*taqṣidu al-ghalaba*) but does not aim at any benefit (*lā taqṣidu ifādatan al-battata*)' (Avicenna, *al-Khaṭāba*, p. 790.10–11). So, despite the slight differences between dialectical arguments and rhetorical arguments, which rely on different logical operators (implication on the one hand and disjunction on the other hand), both kinds of arguments are different from sophistic ones, which do not have the same purpose, that is, which do not aim at producing a conviction or a true conclusion but only at winning the debate by whatever means.

According to Avicenna, unlike rhetoric which aims at persuading people, sophistic aims 'not at persuading but [rather] at misleading (*al-taghlīṭ*)' (Avicenna, *al-Khaṭāba*, p. 798.18). Therefore, sophistic is not something that 'people use to get some benefit (*yasta'miluhā al-nāssu li-al-manāfiʿ*)' (Avicenna, *al-Khaṭāba*, p. 798.19). So, there is a real difference between rhetoric and sophistic with regard to their respective aims: the first one aims at some benefit for people, even if it relies on some doubtful propositions sometimes, while the second one does not aim at any benefit but rather at misleading people. Sophistic is then radically different from rhetoric at least with regard to its aims. For according to Avicenna, sophistic is characterized by the fact that 'its aim (or its will: *mashīʾa*) is [really] bad (*mashīʾa radīʾa*)' (Avicenna, *al-Khaṭāba*, p. 799.20). It is not different from the other disciplines only because of its methods. While the rhetorician's will is not to mislead people but rather to persuade them about what 'is thought to be praised (*bimā yuḍannu maḥmūdan*)' (Avicenna, *al-Khaṭāba*, p. 799.12). Its aim is then good, unlike the aim of sophistic. But the means by which the rhetorician seeks to persuade people are not always clear as we will see later. Avicenna himself recognizes two lines later that it may happen that the opinions that the rhetorician wants to get people believe can be 'erroneous or misleading (*bal 'an ghalaṭin aw qaṣdin wa mashīʾatin li-al-sharri wa al-talbīs*)' (Avicenna, *al-Khaṭāba*, p. 799.14), which relativizes the difference between rhetoric on the one hand and sophistic on the other one, although the will to mislead people in rhetoric is not the main aim, as it is in sophistic.

Dialectic and rhetoric are also close in that 'they do not have a specific subject (*lā li-wāḥidin minhumā mawḍūʿun yakhtaṣṣu bihi naḍaruhu*)' (Avicenna, *al-Khaṭāba*,

p. 791.26), which means that both dialectical and rhetorical arguments can put on any subject. This is so because the rhetorician can discuss with any kind of people (*al-'amma*), that is, with ordinary people whose knowledge is very common. Rhetoric is not specialized in any particular subject and does not presuppose any specific knowledge either in the speaker's mind or in the listeners' minds. A rhetorician has then some ability to produce convictions in any listeners' minds, although he is not himself a specialist of the field that he is talking about.

Like Aristotle,[18] Avicenna defends the idea that rhetoric does not presuppose any particular knowledge of the subject in the listeners' minds too, for as put by Avicenna rhetoric is 'the [discipline] that aims at persuading ordinary people (*al-jumhūr*) in what they should believe (*fī mā yaḥuqqu 'alayhim an yuṣaddiqū*)' (Avicenna, *al-Khaṭāba*, p. 790.4–5). He adds that rhetoric is beneficial (*nāfi'a*) in persuading ordinary people just as demonstration (*al-burhān*) is beneficial to scientists or knowledgeable people (Avicenna, *al-Khaṭāba*, p. 790.7–8). These specialists (*al-khāṣṣi*) cannot be persuaded only by rhetorical arguments; they need real demonstrations based on real valid arguments, because they just cannot be persuaded by controversial theses or doubtful ones. As Avicenna says, these scientists 'do not hold true what could contain some conflict (*lā taṣdīqa lahu bimā fīhi yu'addu imkānu 'ināḍin*)' (Avicenna, *al-Khaṭāba*, p. 790.17). While ordinary people (*al-'āmmi*), who do not possess the same amount of knowledge and are not always clearly aware of the valid syllogisms used in syllogistic, can be persuaded by doubtful premises or conclusions and by enthymemes, which do not exhibit the real logical structure of the mood used. For instance, he says, like al-Fārābī, that ordinary people can be persuaded by invalid arguments such as those syllogisms which 'deduce' a conclusion 'from two affirmative premises in the second figure' (Avicenna, *al-Khaṭāba*, p. 805.14), because 'they are persuaded by what *appears* [to be correct], even if it is not verified (*yaqna'ūna bimā yalūḥu wa in lam yuḥaqqaq*)' (Avicenna, *al-Khaṭāba*, p. 805.17, my emphasis). This is so because ordinary people do not always know the different logical moods and ways of deducing conclusions in a correct way and have a general tendency to admit what seems to them plausible even if it is not really true. They have thus a tendency to accept the conclusions of enthymemes when they seem to them admissible or compatible with general beliefs.

In this respect, Avicenna distinguishes between different kinds of enthymemes depending on the nature of the propositions involved in these arguments. The first kind makes use of 'possible opinions like consultations (*umūr mumkina ka-al-mashūriāt*)' (Avicenna, *al-Khaṭāba*, p. 805.20), the second kind uses 'the praised opinions among the necessary ones (*al-maḥmūdāt min al-ḍarūriāt*)' (Avicenna, *al-Khaṭāba*, p. 805.28) and the third kind relies on probable ('*akthariāt*') (Avicenna, *al-Khaṭāba*, p. 805.25) propositions or opinions. We can note here some closeness with Aristotle, who says in *Rhetoric* that 'the propositions of rhetoric are evidences, probabilities and signs' (Aristotle, *Rhetoric*, book I, §3, 1359a6–a10), although Avicenna does not mention this text of Aristotle.

As an example of the first kind of such arguments, Avicenna gives the following:

'The person who just says "Mr. so-and-so [1] is calumniating Mr. so-and-so [2] (*fulānun yas'ā bi-fulānin*) because he [the former] was consulting the Emir at the time when the arrest [of the latter] has been suggested (*ī'āzihi*) [to the Emir]", will *perhaps* be persuasive (*robbamā aqna'a*)' (Avicenna, *al-Khaṭāba*, p. 805.22, emphasis added). This enthymeme might appear as persuasive, according to Avicenna, because it relies on the following plausible (but not necessarily valid) argument:

- Mr. so-and-so [1] was consulting the prince when the arrest of Mr. so-and-so [2] has been suggested
- Therefore Mr. so-and-so [1] was calumniating Mr. so-and-so [2].

The hidden premise would be something like the following:

- All those who consult the prince when the arrest of Mr. so-and-so [2] has been suggested are calumniating Mr. so-and-so [2].

When one adds this premise, one gets a *Barbara* syllogism, where the minor term is 'Mr. so-and-so [1]', the middle term is 'consulting the prince when it has been . . .' and the major term is 'calumniating Mr. so-and-so [2]'.

However, the hidden premise is not necessarily true, since not all people talking with the Emir at that time when Mr. so-and-so [2] has been arrested were calumniating Mr. so-and-so [2]. Talking with the Emir does not necessarily mean calumniating other people, even if these people happen to have been arrested at that specific time. So as a universal, this hidden premise is false. As an indefinite, it seems plausible, since it may happen to find people calumniating other people, especially when there is such a coincidence in the times of the arrest and that of the discussion with the Emir. So, if the universal premise is added, its falsity would appear clearly to the listeners, and consequently the conclusion would also be clearly seen as false; hence it would not be persuasive. But even when the premise is hidden, the conviction is not warranted, which Avicenna expresses by saying '*perhaps* he will be persuasive (*robbamā aqna'a*)' (Avicenna, *al-Khaṭāba*, p. 805.22).

So, the validity of the argument is not obvious, since when the second premise is added, its falsity appears clearly, and the conclusion will also be false. If the premise is hidden, the conclusion remains doubtful; therefore, the whole argument is not entirely persuasive. So, either as an enthymeme or as a completed syllogism, this argument is not very persuasive: at best it is doubtful, and at worst it is invalid. Avicenna even says that 'maybe the addition of further explanations can cause more doubt (*wa robbamā kāna al-izdiyādu fi al-sharḥi sababan li-ithārati al-shakki*)' (Avicenna, *al-Khaṭāba*, p. 805.23).

As to the enthymemes of the second kind, that is, those involving necessary and praised propositions, Avicenna illustrates them by the following example:

> 'Zayd is learned and virtuous; therefore he [will be] happy in the afterlife (*al-ākhira*)', where the premise 'All learned and virtuous people will be happy in the afterlife' has been removed or replaced by the indefinite 'Learned and virtuous people will be happy in the afterlife' (Avicenna, *al-Khaṭāba*, p. 805.28–9).

Here too, the complete syllogism is a *Barbara* one, from the first figure, where the first premise is a singular while the second premise is a universal. It could be expressed as follows:

- Zayd is learned and virtuous
- All learned and virtuous people will be happy in the afterlife
- Therefore, Zayd will be happy in the afterlife

But as an enthymeme, the argument does not involve the second premise and deduces the conclusion only from the first premise. This second premise expresses what ordinary people would consider as necessarily true whether it is a universal proposition or an indefinite one. It is thus supposed to be an obvious truth which does not need to be stated.

However, some of these arguments could be seen as invalid whether as enthymemes or even as complete syllogisms. Those arguments rely on signs (*'alāma*) (*al-Khaṭāba*, p. 806.5). As an example, we find the following:

One may deduce 'The jurist is virtuous (or pure) (*al-faqīhu 'afīfun*)' because 'Zayd the jurist is virtuous' (Avicenna, *al-Khaṭāba*, p. 806.7). The complete syllogism would be a third-figure syllogism and would have the following structure:

- Zayd is a jurist
- Zayd is virtuous
- Therefore, all jurists are virtuous

However, in this syllogism, Zayd is considered as the typical example of a jurist as if he were representing all kinds of jurists, while he is not necessarily so. For even if Zayd himself is virtuous, this does not mean that all jurists are like him because he does not necessarily represent all the jurists. As Avicenna says, 'Zayd is not implied by jurists so that all jurists are Zayd' (Avicenna, *al-Khaṭāba*, p. 806.9). By saying that, he is doubting the validity of such a syllogism and *a fortiori* of the enthymeme that is based on it. He is thus admitting that these enthymemes should not be valid, hence they are not persuasive.

So, whether one hides the second premise or does not hide it, the argument could not be persuasive, because this premise is a doubtful proposition which expresses a general idea based on an illegitimate generalization.

Likewise, the following example contains the same kind of confused generalization:

'This [woman] has a blown abdomen; therefore, she is pregnant' (Avicenna, *al-Khaṭāba*, p. 806.10), given that 'the blown abdomen is a sign of pregnancy' (Avicenna, *al-Khaṭāba*, p. 806.11), since all pregnant women have a blown abdomen. So, the complete syllogism would be a second figure one, which one can express as follows:

- This [woman] has a blown abdomen
- Pregnant [women] have a blown abdomen
- Therefore, this woman is pregnant

Where 'pregnant' is the major term, 'woman' is the minor term and 'has a blown abdomen' is the middle term. However, this syllogism is not valid since not all women who have a blown abdomen are pregnant. A woman could have a blown abdomen without being pregnant if she has a disease in her abdomen. So, although the proposition 'All pregnant women have a blown abdomen' could in general be considered as true, this other proposition 'Every woman whose abdomen is blown is pregnant' is not true, because many people with blown abdomens are not at all pregnant. This shows that the enthymeme, here too, relies on an invalid syllogism, which would have the structure of a second-figure AAA mood, since singular propositions are generally considered as universals. But there is no valid AAA mood in the second figure. Consequently, the enthymeme as well as the syllogistic mood that it relies on should not be persuasive, although it could seem plausible at first sight.

This analysis of the enthymemes based on signs shows that Avicenna is in total accordance with Aristotle, who evokes signs too in some of his examples, for instance, the following enthymeme: 'Dionysius is a thief, since he is a vicious man' (*Rhetoric*, book II, §24, 1401b3–b9), and is very sceptical about the validity of such enthymemes, since he adds in the same paragraph 'there is, of course, no deduction here; not every vicious man is a thief, though every thief is a vicious man' (Aristotle, *Rhetoric*, book II, §24, 1401b3–b9).

As to the third kind of enthymemes, it contains probable propositions (*akthariāt*), that is, propositions which are true in most cases.

For instance, the following medical example:

'Zayd is feverish; therefore, he has a quick pulsation (*Zayd maḥmūm fa-huwa idhan sarī'u al-nabḍi*)' (Avicenna, *al-Khaṭāba*, p. 806.15).

This is supposed to be taken from a first-figure syllogism which would be expressed as follows:

- Zayd is feverish
- Feverish people have a quick pulsation
- Therefore, Zayd has a quick pulsation.

However, not all feverish people have a quick pulsation, even if most of them can have it. So, the whole deduction is not valid, even when the enthymeme is completed by its missing premise, although it is common for some people as Avicenna notes in the same paragraph (*al-Khaṭāba*, p. 806.15).

With the same propositions, one can also construct another syllogism from the second figure, which would be expressed as follows:

- Zayd has a quick pulsation
  [- Feverish people have a quick pulsation]
- Therefore, Zayd is feverish. (Avicenna, *al-Khaṭāba*, p. 806.16)

But here, even the completed syllogism is not valid, since a second-figure AAA syllogism is not valid. So, the enthymeme cannot be persuasive, and the conclusion should not be admitted even if the second premise is true, which it is not anyway, since it could be true only in most cases, not in all cases.

Likewise, the following example illustrates an enthymeme constructed starting from a third-figure syllogism, which many people could consider as persuasive but which is not really so, in Avicenna's opinion:

'Courageous people are not parsimonious, because ʿAlī Ibn Abī Ṭālib was not parsimonious' (Avicenna, *al-Khaṭāba*, p. 806.16–17).

This enthymeme, when completed, would be expressed as follows:

- ʿAlī Ibn Abī Ṭālib was courageous
- ʿAlī Ibn Abī Ṭālib was not parsimonious
- Therefore, Courageous people are not parsimonious.

In this argument, which contains a generalization, ʿAlī Ibn Abī Ṭālib is considered as representative of all courageous people. But he is not necessarily so, for courageous people do not necessarily possess all the qualities that he himself possessed. Consequently, although this kind of enthymemes is used quite frequently, it does not rely on a valid syllogistic mood (here an EAE third-figure mood, which is not a valid mood in categorical syllogistic) and cannot be convincing, despite its commonness.

Some enthymemes based on propositions which could seem possibly true when stated as affirmatives and when stated as negatives are not persuasive at all, unless the speaker insists on the fact that the missing premise should be true in most cases (*aktharīyya*), not only in some of them. For if the affirmative proposition is as equally true as the corresponding negative one, the enthymeme could not lead to a real conviction in the listener's mind.

The example that illustrates such a situation is the following:

'(1) Mr. so-and-so, who stands in front of the recently killed Zayd with his sabre, is Zayd's killer

(2) Mr. so-and-so, who stands in front of the recently killed Zayd with his sabre, is *not* Zayd's killer' (Avicenna, *al-Khaṭāba*, p. 806.25–6, emphasis added).

In this example, the conviction occurs only if the missing premise is considered as true in most cases, which is the case with sentence (1) but more hardly with sentence (2). So, if the speaker wants to persuade his audience about the conclusion of the second enthymeme (that this man is not the killer of Zayd), he has to add more additional explanations in order to make the missing premise of that particular enthymeme true in most cases (Avicenna, *al-Khaṭāba*, p. 807.1–7).

All these examples show that Avicenna does not consider all kinds of enthymemes persuasive even if they are common. Furthermore, unlike al-Fārābī, he does not hesitate to say that some of them, in particular those that rely on invalid syllogistic moods, can be not persuasive at all. His attitude towards this kind of arguments is not as positive as that of al-Fārābī, for he tends to consider them as persuasive only under some conditions and for some people who would be unfamiliar with the valid syllogistic moods and the logical rules in general. Therefore, he cannot endorse al-Fārābī's opinion according to which enthymemes are persuasive *because* one of their premises is hidden. According to Avicenna, the hiding of the premise does not always make the enthymeme persuasive, when this enthymeme is based on an invalid syllogistic mood.

Note that Hodges and Druart in their article 'Al-Fārābī's Philosophy of Logic and Language' stress the same kind of confusion in al-Fārābī's interpretation of the Aristotelian treatise *Sophistical Refutations*, for they say: 'Aristotle's treatise is usually understood to be teaching the art of detecting and refuting bad arguments, not that of creating them!' (Hodges and Druart, SEP 2020, section 3).

In addition, unlike al-Fārābī, Avicenna does talk about what Aristotle calls the 'spurious enthymemes' and like Aristotle, he analyses the refutations of enthymemes. We find this analysis in his *al-Khaṭāba* (pp. 862–5), where he says that some enthymemes are 'not genuine' (*laysat ḥaqīqīyya*) or 'spurious' (*muḥarrafa*). The spurious (*muḥarrafa*) character might be due to basically two things: (1) the use of ambiguous words (*lafẓ mushtarak*), that is, words that could have several meanings; and (2) the use of an invalid structure (or form: *shakl*) so that the discourse is not really implied by its premises (*al-Khaṭāba*, p. 862.24–5). By doing so, he says, 'the speaker is tolerant (*yatajalladu*) and moves from the discourse to the conclusion as if he had produced it, hence he spreads it' (Avicenna, *al-Khaṭāba*, p. 862.26).

To illustrate these fallacious enthymemes, he takes some examples, which seem very close to those taken by Aristotle in the *Rhetoric*. The first one is the following: 'Don't you see the dog in the sky, which surpasses by its light the rest of the planets?' (Avicenna, *al-Khaṭāba*, p. 863.2–3), which is supposed to 'praise dogs' (*yamdaḥu* [*al-kalb*]), based on an ambiguous (or a common) word (*bi-ishtirāk al-ism*). This example seems close to the one taken by Aristotle who cites a poem and claims after that the following: 'One may argue that, because there is much disgrace in there *not* being a dog about, there is honour of *being* a dog' (Aristotle, *Rhetoric*, book II, §24, 1401a13–a23). The second one, which is based rather on a fallacious structure, is the following: 'Mr. so-and-so (*fulānun*) who knows the letters and the satire (*al-hijā*), knows then poetry (*fa-ya'rifu idhan al-shi'r*)' (Avicenna, *al-Khaṭāba*, p. 863.4). This also is close to the following example taken by Aristotle when he says: 'There is also the argument that one who knows the letters knows the whole word, since the whole word is the same thing as the letters which compose it' (Aristotle, *Rhetoric*, book II, §24, 1401a24–b2). In both cases, the argument is fallacious because it deduces the whole from the elements or from the parts. In Avicenna's example, the satire is only one kind of poetry, not the whole of it, so knowing the satire does not necessarily mean knowing all kinds of poetry. Likewise, knowing the letters (which are the elements of a discourse) does not necessarily mean knowing how to compose them (Aristotle's example) or how to do poetry (Avicenna's example). So, in all these cases, the argument is fallacious and does not lead to the claimed conclusion. It must then be refuted.

Another kind of fallacious enthymemes can be illustrated by the following example:

> Someone who denies having done something which he is accused to have done, if he does not have enough proofs to show that he is not guilty, can start disfiguring (*taqbīḥ*) the person who accuses him, and glorifying his [own] action.[19]

This argument, according to Avicenna, does not prove that this person is not guilty; it is on the contrary a kind of 'suspicious argument' (*iḥtijāj maẓnūn*) (*al-Khaṭāba*, p. 863.8), which does not prove the desired conclusion but rather diverts the judge from the real subject of the discussion. In this case, the judge does not have the real evidence that would make him understand what happened and decide if that person is guilty or not.

Another kind of spurious enthymeme can be illustrated by the argument which 'provides [only] the consequent (*ya'tī bi-al-lāḥiqi*)' (*al-Khaṭāba*, p. 863.11), that is, without providing what leads to that consequent. This too is considered by Avicenna as 'suspicious' (*maẓnūn*), since it can rely, for instance, on an invalid mood 'using two affirmatives in the second figure (*min al-mūjibatayni fī al-shakl al-thānī*)' (*al-Khaṭāba*, p. 863.11). Since the consequence is presented without a valid justification, it is 'suspicious', because it could result from an invalid syllogism. Here he explicitly mentions Aristotle by saying what follows:

> From this we know that when the first teacher (*al-mu'allim al-awwal*) mentioned in his discourse the oblique and corrupt (*al-mā'il al munḥarif*), as if it was a real reasoning, did not mean by this, that the oblique with regard of the positing of its terms, and the corrupt [of] the real productive figure, is a real reasoning. For he does not consider it as a real reasoning, but rather as a suspicious reasoning.[20]

He thus clearly defends Aristotle's position (see Aristotle, *Rhetoric*, book II, §24, 1401b20–b29) towards the fallacious character of the enthymemes based on invalid syllogisms against some false interpretations of it. But he does not explicitly say who interprets Aristotle's text in this false way. We could perhaps think of al-Fārābī as a possible target of this criticism, since al-Fārābī admits explicitly some enthymemes based on invalid syllogistic moods. But this remains just a hypothesis because Avicenna does not explicitly mention al-Fārābī in this part of his text. Anyway, what we can assume is that Avicenna, like Aristotle and unlike al-Fārābī, rejects the enthymemes which are not based on valid syllogistic moods and considers them as suspicious and fallacious.

Another kind of fallacious arguments have to do with 'representing as causes things that are not causes, on the ground that they happened along with or before the event in question' as Aristotle says in *Rhetoric* (book II, §24, 1401b30–b34). These arguments in Aristotle's theory as well as in Avicenna's one must be rejected because they are fallacious. In Avicenna's text, this is expressed as 'taking as a cause what is not a cause (*akhdhu mā laysa bi-'illatin 'illatan*)' (Avicenna, *al-Khaṭāba*, p. 863.24) and illustrated by the following example: 'As when one says "Had the sinister (*al-mash'ūm*) Mr. so-and-so [1] not come, Mr. so-and-so [2] would not have died."'[21] So, like Aristotle, Avicenna urges to not confuse the concomitance of two events (or even the fact that one of them precedes the other one) with the fact that the first one is the *cause* of the second one. This error is often made by ordinary people. But despite its frequency, it is not acceptable even in rhetoric, according to both Aristotle and Avicenna.

However, some other enthymemes seem to be unacceptable even to an audience of ordinary people. For instance, when someone says: 'If it is true that when Zayd, who is guilty, is sick, he ought not to be punished, then he should not be punished at all' (*al-Khaṭāba*, p. 864.1). This example illustrates an enthymeme which appears to be fallacious even 'to the ordinary people' who 'see the corruption that it contains (*mā fīhā min al-taḥrīf*)' (*al-Khaṭāba*, p. 864.2–3). For it is obvious for everyone that even if a guilty person could not deserve punishment because she is sick, there is no reason why she should not be punished once she recovers. So, this kind of enthymemes appears to be fallacious even to the ordinary and uneducated people.

Now what about the refutation of enthymemes?

Here too, Avicenna appears to be close to Aristotle, who cites various kinds of refutations in his *Rhetoric*. The first kind is 'a counter-deduction' or 'an objection' (Aristotle, *Rhetoric*, book II, §25, 1402a32–a38). In Avicenna's view, these objections may be brought by providing 'a proof against the opponent's argument, which produces the contradictory of the opponent's conclusion' (Avicenna, *al-Khaṭāba*, p. 864.4). Another kind of objections may rather 'target the premises (*yaqṣudu al-muqaddamāt*)' (Avicenna, *al-Khaṭāba*, p. 864.6) most presumably in order to show their falsity. According to Avicenna, the premise can be 'contradicted by showing that it is not always true, in which case, one provides a particular [proposition] that falsifies the judgement [and shows] that it is not necessary (*laysa bi-iḍtirārin*). And if it is assumed to be necessary, it is not assumed to be necessary at every single time' (*al-Khaṭāba*, p. 864.21–2). For this reason, even when the judgement is necessary, it may be so only in some circumstances or at some time, not always. So, the judgement can be invalidated either 'by a [specific] time or by a particular which contradict it' (Avicenna, *al-Khaṭāba*, p. 864.21–2).

The refutation in general can be made by showing that 'the discourse is not productive' or that the 'premise is not true', even if according to Avicenna, the latter way appears difficult, since 'the premises are usually admitted (*musallama*)' (Avicenna, *al-Khaṭāba*, p. 864.28), given that they are usually commonplaces. Here, however, Avicenna is less precise than Aristotle who talks about 'spurious' refutations too, especially those that target probable premises. These spurious refutations show 'not that your opponent's premiss is not probable, but only [. . .] that it is not inevitably true' (Aristotle, *Rhetoric*, book II, §25, 1402b22–1403a3). This is not a real refutation since it does not deny the falsity of the (probable) premise. It just denies the fact that it is not necessarily true, which is compatible with the fact that the premise was considered as only probable from the start.

However, Avicenna is much closer to Aristotle in his analysis of enthymemes that al-Fārābī is, which is quite surprising, since Avicenna's logical systems, such as categorical logic, as well as modal and hypothetical logics, depart in many ways from Aristotle's ones by their original character.[22] So, it seems at first sight astonishing that in his correspondent of *Rhetoric*, Avicenna follows very faithfully Aristotle, although he did criticize him in several ways and developed much more sophisticated logical systems in his *al-Qiyās* (the correspondent of *Prior Analytics*). We might venture a hypothesis to explain this closeness by saying that both Avicenna and Aristotle are primarily logicians and do not, for this reason, reject the idea that rhetorical arguments can and should be evaluated by means of the more powerful logical arguments and moods. If this hypothesis is correct, this would explain why their attitude about the relation between logic and rhetoric is globally the same, unlike al-Fārābī's attitude, which sharply distinguishes between rhetoric and logic.

This attitude is confirmed and further stressed in *al-Qiyās*, where Avicenna says explicitly that an enthymeme is neither persuasive nor valid if one does not add the missing premise and if the thus completed syllogistic mood is not itself valid.

In *al-Qiyās*, he gives several examples like the following:

- [1] 'Mr. so-and-so is going around at night; therefore he is a thief' (Avicenna, *al-Qiyās*, p. 60.1)
- [2] 'Memorizing the Sunna [of the prophet] is the contrary of neglecting it; but memorizing the Sunna is not a bad thing; hence neglecting it is bad; therefore memorizing the Sunna is a good thing.'

These two sentences are examples of enthymemes, and in both cases, Avicenna says that they cannot be conclusive if the missing premise in both of them is not added.

In [1], this missing premise is the following:

'Everyone who is going around at night is a thief' (Avicenna, *al-Qiyās*, p. 60.3).

In [2], the missing premise is the following:

'Everything which is not bad and is contrary to bad [things] is good' (Avicenna, *al-Qiyās*, p. 60.6).

So [1] is valid only if its missing premise is added, and the same can be said about [2]. The word 'therefore', in both cases, does not indicate that there is a real implication, or that the conclusion really follows from what precedes it unless the second premise is added. There is no real implication if the conclusion is 'deduced' only from the unique stated premise, for he says, talking about [2], that 'This does not follow from that discourse, and from what has been stated in it by itself, but [it follows rather] from a removed premise, which is "Everything which is not bad and is contrary to bad things, is good"' (Avicenna, *al-Qiyās*, p. 60.5–6).

So, an enthymeme by itself is neither valid nor persuasive, since it does not contain a real implication which would warrant the truth of the conclusion starting from the premise stated.

In section I part 7, he says that 'the rhetorical [syllogisms] do not imply necessarily what they imply (*wa al-khaṭābiyāt laysa luzūmu mā yalzamu 'anhā iḍṭirāran*)' (*al-Qiyās*, p. 66.7). This means that the following of the conclusion in this kind of arguments is not necessary, that is, the link between the premise and the conclusion does not warrant that the conclusion necessarily follows from that premise. In other words, enthymemes are not formally valid as categorical, modal and hypothetical syllogistic moods are. Are they materially valid? Not quite so since the conclusion in some enthymemes is not always true but only plausible. As to the missing premise, it can be true only for the most part, but not for the whole of the subject, as happens in the examples of *al-Khaṭāba* analysed earlier.

In this section, Avicenna says that according to some people, the following deductions are valid, since 'the unique premise really implies (*tūjibu*) the conclusion: "Mr. so-and-so is moving, therefore he is living" and "Given that Abdullah is writing, he is then moving his hand"' (Avicenna, *al-Qiyās*, p. 66.15–67.2). These are typical enthymemes, since one can express them as follows:

- Mr. so-and-so is moving
- Therefore he is living

And

- Abdullah is writing
- Therefore he is moving his hand

But in these enthymemes, the conclusion follows only because some presupposed premises have been removed, which, for the first example, is 'Every moving being is living' and for the second example is 'Every writer moves his hand' (Avicenna, *al-Qiyās*, p. 70.11–13), which gives rise to two *Barbara* syllogisms, expressed in this way:

- Mr. so-and-so is moving
  [- Every moving being is living]
- Therefore Mr. so-and-so is living

And

- Abdullah is writing
  [- Every writer moves his hand]
- Therefore Abdullah is moving his hand

So, in these enthymemes as well as in the usual categorical syllogisms, the conclusion follows necessarily only because the whole set of premises implies it by *Barbara*, the difference between both kinds of syllogisms being that this whole set is explicitly expressed, while in the enthymemes, one of the premises is left unstated but is nevertheless strongly presupposed. Once stated, it implies together with the other premise the conclusion.

Now can we say that enthymemes are some kind of material consequences, as is the case in Buridan's and Ockham's theories?

According to Buridan, the following sentence 'A man runs, so an animal runs' (Buridan, cited in Read 2012, section 3) expresses an enthymeme, which as such is a material consequence, if one does not add the missing premise, namely the premise 'Every man is an animal', in this example. This is what C. Dutilh Novaes says when analysing Buridan's theory about enthymemes and consequences in the following quotation:

> For Buridan, however, enthymematic consequences are not formal consequences because they do not satisfy the substitutional criterion, e.g. this particular example is not valid for all substitutional instances of 'man' and 'animal'. They do become formal consequences with the addition of the missing premise, but before that occurs, they are merely material consequences.[23]

This is so because the replacement of the terms 'man', 'animal' and 'runs' by other ones may lead to false conclusions, as shown by Stephen Read who gives the following example: 'A horse walks; so wood walks' (Hubien 1976, I.4, cited in Read 2012, section 3), which leads to a false proposition ('wood walks') starting from a true one ('a horse walks'). For if we consider the following enthymeme 'A horse walks; so, an animal walks', both the premise and the conclusion are true. But if in this example, one substitutes 'wood' to 'animal', one gets 'A horse walks; so wood walks', which leads to a falsity, starting from a true proposition. So, the substitution of terms in the enthymemes is not legitimate because the substitution can lead to a falsity. Enthymemes, therefore, are not formally valid in Buridan's frame, because they do not obey the substitution criterion, which says that any substitution of terms in a valid argument must preserve the validity of the argument, that is, must lead from a truth to a truth in all substitutional instances of terms. Enthymemes become formally valid only when complemented with their missing premise. Otherwise, they remain materially valid, because the deduction made in this kind of arguments relies on the meanings of their terms, not on the general structure of the enthymeme.

In Avicenna's frame, the substitution criterion is not stated, but Avicenna says explicitly that if one does not add the missing premise, one cannot deduce the conclusion of an enthymeme. This missing premise can be either stated or meant by the speaker, but in all cases, it legitimates the deduction because without it, the conclusion does not follow, even when there is a semantic link between the premise and the conclusion. For instance, when analysing the example 'Mr. so-and-so is going around at night; therefore he is a thief', he says explicitly, 'This discourse is not a syllogism by itself and it does not *entail by itself* [that this man] is a thief, rather *we have to add something else to it*, namely that 'everyone who goes around at night is a thief'" (Avicenna, *al-Qiyās*, p. 60.1–3, emphasis added).

So according to him, enthymemes are acceptable as inferences only when complemented by their missing premises. Otherwise, they can lead to a falsity starting from a truth. In other words, they are not really what we could call 'material consequences', that is, inferences which lead to a given conclusion only by relying on the meanings of the terms of the premise and the conclusion. If they are not complemented, they are not consequences at all, even in rhetoric, because there is no necessity in the link between the premise and the conclusion.

So, unlike al-Fārābī who says that an enthymeme is persuasive only because the missing premise is hidden, and that enthymemes would not be enthymemes if that missing premise was added, Avicenna does not consider that enthymemes are persuasive for that reason or that they should necessarily remain incomplete. On the contrary, in *al-Qiyās*, he stresses the fact that enthymemes are conclusive, hence persuasive, only when the missing premise is added. In *al-Khaṭāba*, his opinion is less clear since he admits several kinds of enthymemes and recognizes the fact that some of them are constructed starting from invalid syllogisms. But he does not *say* that they are persuasive only *because* the missing premise is hidden. According to him, as some of the examples that he gives show, when enthymemes rely on invalid syllogisms, they are not persuasive, even when their missing premise is hidden, for he says explicitly that 'they are perhaps (*robbamā*) persuasive', which means that they are not always or necessarily so. It seems then that his opinion is not the same as that of al-Fārābī, who admits the idea that an invalid argument can be persuasive in some contexts, for instance, in the context of rhetoric. According to Avicenna, no argument is persuasive if it is not conclusive or valid. Rhetorical arguments may be confused, incomplete and misleading, but for this reason, they are not acceptable as logical arguments, and even their persuasiveness is sometimes doubtful since their conclusions are not properly justified.

This shows that the two authors do not have the same attitude towards this kind of arguments. Al-Fārābī considers that inconclusive arguments are acceptable in rhetoric, and that they are persuasive to the listeners when one of the premises is hidden, for in that case, their inconclusiveness does not appear clearly, while Avicenna seems to consider them as not persuasive even in that case, for their persuasiveness is seriously doubted, when they rely on invalid syllogisms, as some examples given in his *al-Khaṭāba* show. Unlike al-Fārābī, he does not say that enthymemes are persuasive because one of their premises is hidden; on the contrary, in *al-Khaṭāba*, he says that even in that case, their persuasiveness is rather doubtful, and in *al-Qiyās*, he stresses the fact that enthymemes are valid, hence persuasive, only when their hidden premise is explicitly expressed.

This shows that Avicenna's approach is both closer to Aristotle's one and more formal than that of al-Fārābī,[24] for unlike al-Fārābī, who admits some kinds of invalid arguments in rhetoric and says that their power of persuasiveness is real precisely because of their very incompleteness and because they lead to plausible conclusions, Avicenna is more sceptical towards enthymemes in general and does not seem to overestimate their persuasiveness, especially when they rely on invalid syllogisms. He thus gives much more importance to the form of the logical arguments, which is the only thing that warrants the truth of their conclusions. According to him, when an argument is incomplete, it cannot be valid unless one adds the premise that shows its real form. And when it is invalid, it can hardly be persuasive. Avicenna's attitude towards these arguments appears to be more negative than al-Fārābī's one, although he does acknowledge their utility in rhetoric and their commonness. But he also stresses their weakness as logical arguments even in rhetoric and shows by doing so that he does not consider them as logically admissible arguments.

2.4 Conclusion

The analysis in this chapter shows that al-Fārābī's and Avicenna's analyses of enthymemes and their attitudes towards them are rather different. Al-Fārābī seems to consider enthymemes as being the kind of arguments that can be used in rhetoric. In that context, they are helpful and beneficial to many people. He compares them to demonstrative arguments by establishing a parallel between demonstration and enthymemes. He also stresses their utility in rhetoric and says that they are persuasive *because* they are incomplete, for if one complements them, they would no more be persuasive, especially when the added premise is clearly false or when the mood on which they rely is clearly invalid. This means that he sees the enthymemes as some *acceptable* kind of reasoning in the context of rhetoric. Their incompleteness and even their invalidity in some cases do not seem problematic for him, for he says explicitly that they *should remain* incomplete, otherwise they would become something else and would not have the same power and utility.

By contrast, Avicenna does not seem to have the same positive attitude towards enthymemes. For, unlike al-Fārābī, he does not consider them as persuasive *because* they are incomplete. On the contrary, in his *al-Khaṭāba*, he gives several examples of enthymemes, which, he says, are generally admitted by common people but are not, according to him, persuasive. Despite the fact that in *al-Khaṭāba*, he stresses the utility of rhetoric and rhetorical arguments among which enthymemes appear to be the best ones by saying that rhetoric and dialectic are helpful in many respects unlike sophistic, he does not seem to give the same importance to enthymemes as al-Fārābī. For in *al-Khaṭāba* he stresses the weakness of several enthymematic arguments which are generally accepted by most people and frequently used in rhetorical contexts. And in *al-Qiyās*, he explicitly says that enthymemes are far from persuasive without their missing premise. For without that missing premise, they cannot be considered as valid, and they do not legitimately lead to a true conclusion. This means that, according to him, not only enthymemes are not persuasive without their missing premise, but they are not even admissible – as logical arguments – if that premise is not added.

In addition, Avicenna's analysis of enthymemes is much closer to that of Aristotle whose text is followed very faithfully. Even if this closeness appears at first sight surprising, since Avicenna is precisely the one Arabic logician who has introduced the most significant changes to Aristotle's syllogistic, it shows that with regard to rhetoric and rhetorical arguments, especially enthymemes, both Aristotle and Avicenna behave primarily as logicians by evaluating the rhetorical arguments on the grounds of their logical systems and rules.

Notes

1 See for instance, *al-Qiyās*, in R. al-Ajam 1986, pp. 11–64, especially pp. 36–45, and the translation of that treatise entitled 'al-Fārābī, Syllogism': S. Chatti and W. Hodges 2020, especially pp. 138–46.
2 See, for instance, p. 477.20–3, where al-Fārābī uses the word '*ajnās*' as a synonym of '*maqūlāt*', that is, as signifying the Aristotelian categories, such as substance (*jawhar*), quantity (*kamm*), quality (*kayf*) and so on.
3 Al-Fārābī 1988, p. 456.1–3.
4 Al-Fārābī 1988, p. 470.14–16.
5 Aristotle 1991, book I, §2,1357a14–1357a22.
6 Aristotle 1991, book I, §3, 1358a3–1358a35.
7 Al-Fārābī 1988, p. 460.23–4.
8 Al-Fārābī 1988, p. 468.10–13.
9 Al-Fārābī 1988, p. 468.14–15.
10 Al-Fārābī 1988, p. 470.18–19.
11 Aristotle 1991, book II, §22, 1395b20–1396a3.
12 Al-Fārābī 1988, p. 478.18–19.
13 Al-Fārābī 1988, p. 479.1–3.
14 Al-Fārābī 1988, p. 479.13–25.
15 Al-Fārābī 1988, p. 475.18–20.
16 Woerther 2018, p. 41.
17 Avicenna, *'Uyūn al-ḥikma*, p. 7.
18 See Aristotle 1991, where it is said that 'It is clear, then, that rhetoric is not bound up with a single definite class of subjects, but is like dialectic'; (I, §1, 1355a22–-1355b7).
19 Avicenna, *al-Khaṭāba*, p. 863.7.

20 Avicenna, *al-Khaṭāba*, p. 863.12–14.
21 Here the text seems to contain an error since what is written is '*lamā mā fulānun*'. But as it is written, this sentence does not make sense because '*mā*' alone is not a verb. So, the most plausible interpretation seems to be '*lamā māta fulānun*', given the context of the example and what Avicenna wants to show by it.
22 See, for instance, S. Chatti 2019, where the logical systems of al-Fārābī, Avicenna and Averroes are analysed and compared to each other.
23 C. D. Novaes 2008, p. 476.
24 With regard to al-Fārābī's conception of logic see, for instance, W. Hodges and T.-A. Druart 2018, where it is said that 'Al-Fārābī's intellectual background was not so much Aristotle himself. Rather it was the Aristotelian part of the syllabus of the Neoplatonic school of philosophy that flourished in Alexandria (in Egypt) in the fifth and sixth centuries. The formal character of his logic is also relativized for they say: 'All in all, al-Fārābī treats the formal rules of logic as heuristics rather than as laws of a scientific theory. A case can be made for viewing al-Fārābī as one of the creators of what is now known as "informal logic", as in the texts of Hitchcock 2017 and Walton 1989' (W. Hodges and T.-A. Druart 2018, section 7).

Bibliography

Al-Fārābī, A. N. (1986), 'al-Qiyās', in *al-Mantiq 'inda al-Farabi*, R. al-Ajam (ed.), vol. 2, Beirut, Dar al-Machreq.
Al-Fārābī, A. N. (1988), 'Kitāb al-Khatāba', in *al-Mantiqiyāt li-al-Fārābī*, M. T. Danesh Pazuh (ed.), vol. 1, Qum, Ansariyan Publications, pp. 456–92.
Aristotle (1991), 'Rhetoric', in *The Complete Works of Aristotle*, J. Barnes (ed.), vol. 2, Oxford, Oxford University Press, pp. 1–143 (1354a1–1420b5).
Avicenna (1964), *al-Shifā, al-Mantiq 4: al-Qiyās*, S. Zayed (ed.), I. Madkour (rev. and intro.), Cairo, al-Ma and intr.), exa.
Avicenna, Uyūn al-Hikma, available online in www.al-mostafa.com, pp. 1–34.
Avicenna, *al-Khaṭāba*, available online in www.al-mostafa.com, pp. 789–884.
Chatti, S. (2019a), 'Logical Consequence in Avicenna's Theory', *Logica Universalis* 13, pp. 101–33.
Chatti, S. (2019b), *Arabic Logic from al-Fārābī to Averroes*, Basel, Birkhäuser/Springer.
Chatti, S. and Hodges, W. (2020), 'Al-Fārābī Syllogism: An Abridgement of Aristotle's Prior Analytics', in commented translation of al-Farabi's treatise 'al-Qiyas' *Ancient Commentators on Aristotle*, gen. ed. Richard Sorabji, London, Bloomsbury Academic Editions.
Dutilh Novaes, C. (2008), 'Logic in the 14th Century after Ockham', in D. M. Gabbay and J. Woods, (eds), *Handbook of the History of Logic: Medieval and Renaissance Logic*, vol. 2, pp. 433–504, Amsterdam, North Holland/Elsevier.
Hodges, W. and Druart, T.-A. (2020), 'Al-Farabi's Philosophy of Logic and Language', in *The Stanford Encyclopedia of Logic*, E. N. Zalta (ed.), https://plato.stanford.edu/archives/fall2020/entries/al-farabi-logic
Read, S. (2012), 'The Medieval Theory of Consequence', *Synthese* 187, pp. 899–912.
Woerther, F. (2018), 'Al-Fārābī commentateur d'Aristote dans les Didascalia in Rethoricam Aristotelis ex glosa Alpharabii', in *Commenting Aristotle's Rhetoric from Antiquity to the Present*, F. Woerther (ed.), pp. 41–63, Leiden/Boston, Brill.

3

Argumentum, locus and enthymeme

Abaelard's transformation of the topics into a theory of enthymematic inference

Christopher J. Martin

3.1 Introduction

At the beginning of his commentary on Boethius's *De differentiis topicis* (*Diff. Top.*) Peter Abaelard gives an example to illustrate the construction of the argument to prove that Socrates is an animal:[1]

> when I wish to show that Socrates is an animal, I consider human being, which is a species of animal and the nature of a species with respect to its genus, which is expressed by the *maximal proposition* which says: 'Of whatever the species is predicated, the genus is also predicated'. Having considered the species and the mode of proving which the maximal proposition expresses, in virtue of these two, I immediately set down the *argumentum*, showing, that is, that Socrates is an animal by means of the fact that he is a human being. And so 'Socrates is a human being' is the *argumentum* for 'Socrates is an animal'. The *argumentum* is drawn from species which human being contains in accordance with the mode of proof which the maximal proposition demonstrates. Whence both the species and the maximal proposition is called a *locus*, that is *the basis for the argumentum* (*sedes argumenti*).

Although the word 'enthymeme' does not appear in this passage and, indeed, does not occur frequently in Abaelard's works as whole, what we can call *enthymematic inference* is, as we will see, central to his thinking about logic.

Following Boethius in *Diff. Top.*, and what Miles Burnyeat calls the traditional doctrine,[2] Abaelard characterizes an enthymeme as an 'incomplete syllogism',[3] that is, as an argument obtained by omitting one of the premises of a syllogism.[4] While the ultimate Aristotelian source for the theory of the enthymeme, Aristotle's *Rhetoric*, was not available in Latin until the beginning of the thirteenth century, the *Prior Analytics* in Boethius's translation was recovered in the first half of the twelfth century. Abaelard's surviving works, however, reveal only the barest knowledge of the beginnings of Book

I.[5] In particular, he shows no awareness of Aristotle's own definition of an enthymeme in *An. Pr.* 2.27 which in Boethius's translation differs crucially from the definition which he gives in *Diff. Top.* in lacking any reference to incompleteness and characterizing an enthymeme rather as an argument from probabilities or signs.[6]

Aristotle's *Topics*, too, in Boethius's translation, became available in the first half of the twelfth century but again Abaelard shows no direct knowledge of it. While it contains only a single reference to enthymemes, and this only parenthetically to their use in rhetoric,[7] τόπος is translated as *locus* and the work, as Cicero and Boethius advertise, is Aristotle's contribution to the theory of dialectical argumentation.[8] The theory, that is, to which Boethius takes himself to be contributing in his commentary on Cicero's *Topica*, *In Ciceronis Topica* (*In Cic. Top.*)[9] and in his own *De differentiis topicis*. Cicero, as we will see, notes that enthymemes, characterized as a very particular form of argument, are used by philosophers as well as rhetoricians, and Boethius in *Diff. Top.* provides an account of the topics in which some of the examples are enthymematic inferences like that constructed by Abaelard in his illustration.[10]

Latin readers in the twelfth century and for the rest of the Middle Ages read Aristotle's *Topics* in terms of the theory presented in *Diff. Top.* This was no easy task since the technical apparatus and language of Boethian topical theory is not found in Aristotle's work.[11] It is true that forms of '*argumentari*' and '*argumentum*' appear numerous times with *argumentum* as a translation of ἐπιχείρεμα six times and importantly once in the claim that an *argumentum* is a dialectical syllogism.[12] Boethius tells us, however, that Aristotle's *Topics* is concerned with maximal propositions and while that expression does occur once in the work it is not used in a way which obviously connects with the theory of *Diff. Top.*[13] Nor do we find in Aristotle's *Topics* anything corresponding to the claim that a *locus* is the *sedes argumenti*, the basis for an *argumentum*, an expression first found in Cicero which Tobias Reinhardt argues may translate the Greek ἀφορμὴ ἐπιχειρήματος used later by Alexander of Aphrodisias to characterize a τόπος.[14] Finally, '*locus differentia*'e is perhaps Boethius's own invention, used to characterize Cicero's classification of topical arguments as being drawn from a particular *locus* – 'from species' in Abaelard's example.[15]

Burnyeat has proposed a history of the traditional doctrine of the enthymeme tracing its development in late antiquity up to the time of Boethius. In this chapter I will pursue the later history of the theory of enthymematic argumentation in Boethius himself and its reception and development in the early twelfth century by Abaelard. The traditional account of enthymemes is present there as the description of a form of argument (*argumentatio*), the verbal and written expression of an *argumentum* and the conclusion which it supports. Something corresponding to what Burnyeat argues is the original theory of the enthymeme, what he takes to be Aristotle's own account, is developed, I will argue, by Abaelard as the theory of incomplete entailment and the 'probable' *argumenta* employed by dialecticians to answer the kinds of questions of interest to them. The topics are central to this story because, according to Boethius, a rich supply of *argumenta* is provided by the *loci differentiae* through their associated maximal propositions.

The twelfth century was the golden age of topical argumentation. The phrase '*unde locus*?' seems to date from its first decade as the challenge to be addressed to the proponent of a non-syllogistic argument to defend it with an account of why the *argumentum* supports the conclusion. Explanations of *argumenta* as drawn from one *locus* or another are everywhere in twelfth-century commentaries on canonical texts, and a training in the use of the topics was fundamental to the education of a twelfth-century student of dialectics.[16] Let me begin, then, by saying something about the development of the traditional doctrine of the enthymeme and the account of *argumenta* and *loci*, which twelfth-century masters found in the ancient material available to them.

3.2 Enthymeme and *argumentum* in antiquity

As I noted earlier, in the *Topics* Aristotle mentions enthymemes only once and there only to refer them to rhetoric. At the one place in the *Prior Analytics* where rhetoric is mentioned, 2.23, he proposes to show that rhetorical demonstration is effected in the figures of the syllogism catalogued in that work and he finally does this in 2.27. It is there that enthymemes are characterized as arguing from probabilities, and signs and examples are given of rhetorical argumentation involving the latter in each of the three figures with one of the premises unstated.

According to Aristotle in the *Topics* the forms of argumentation employed by the dialectician are the same as those employed by the demonstrator – syllogisms and inductions. Both thus employ syllogisms,[17] defined as having the property that the conclusion follows *necessarily* from the premises without the need for anything other than the explicitly stated premises to be true.[18] They differ in that the dialectician argues from generally accepted premises rather than only from those which are necessarily true.[19] The Aristotelian dialectician thus, it seems, does not employ enthymemes, and the topical apparatus set out in the *Topics* is to be used only in the construction of syllogisms. The work of the twelfth-century dialectician is, as we will see, quite different.

In his *Rhetoric*, Aristotle characterizes an enthymeme as a *rhetorical syllogism*. Burnyeat argues that in saying this he does not intend to assert that an enthymeme is a kind of syllogism but rather that it is a syllogism of a kind.[20] It is a brief argument to be used in public speaking before an assembly or in a court and is not required to be valid in the way that a demonstrative or dialectical syllogism is valid, that is, such that it is impossible for the conclusion to be false when the premises are all true. It is *a fortiori* certainly not necessary that it have one of the canonical forms catalogued in the *Prior Analytics*. Rather, Burnyeat argues, the truth of the premise, or premises,[21] of an enthymeme is connected to the conclusion with what he calls *probabilitas consequentiae*. When it is said that the conclusion of an enthymeme is likely to be true an inferential connective is thus being used and not the modality with which Aristotle characterizes the individual premises of dialectical syllogisms.[22] If the claim made with the premises of an enthymeme is true, then some support is available for the conclusion but it is not impossible for the premises to be true and the conclusion false. Burnyeat, indeed, argues that Aristotle's account of them in *An. Pr.* 2.27 allows for a very 'relaxed' relationship between an enthymeme and the claims they are invoked to prove – so that for particular enthymemes it may even be that in most cases in which the premises are true the conclusion is false. All that is required of an enthymeme is that it is concise, that is, consists of only a small number of premises, and that it is 'respectable' in the circumstances to propose these premises in support of the desired conclusion. As evidence Burnyeat cites Aristotle's example of an enthymeme from a non-necessary sign: 'if a woman is of sallow complexion, then she is pregnant.'[23]

Burnyeat's proposed history of the enthymeme locates as a crucial moment the earliest report that we have of the claim that it is an incomplete syllogism in Quintilian's *Institutio Oratoria*, a work in which we also find an extensive discussion of the nature of *argumenta*. The *Insitutio* was certainly well known in the twelfth century[24] but was not, so it seems, much used as a text in the teaching of rhetoric.[25] As far as I know there are no references to it in the discussions of topical inference in dialectics.

Burnyeat argues that this conception of an enthymeme as an incomplete syllogism is connected with the introduction into the discussion of rhetorical topics by Cicero, or his sources, of material from Stoic logic and his identification of an enthymeme as a concise formulation of the incompatibility of two claims with the use of the Stoic third indemonstrable:

> Next the *locus* which belongs properly to the dialecticians: 'from consequents, antecedents, and repugnants'. . . . When you deny a conjunction and from the conjoined propositions assert one or more of them so that what is left is refuted, this is called the third mode of concluding. From this arise the arguments of the rhetoricians concluding from contraries, which they themselves call ἐνθυμήματα. Not that every thought (*sententia*) cannot be called an *ἐνθύμημα*, but rather just as Homer on account of his excellence made the common name 'poet' his own among the Greeks, so, although every thought is called an *ἐνθύμημα*, because that which is formed from contraries seems the most acute, it alone takes the common name as its proper name.

An enthymeme, then, properly speaking is an instance of an argument 'from repugnants' – from a premise, that is, of the form 'not both *A* and *B*' directly to the conclusion leaving any further assumptions unstated. Burnyeat proposes that the traditional doctrine of the enthymeme as an incomplete syllogism could easily have resulted from someone misunderstanding a Stoic idea that there can be an incompletely expressed but formally valid syllogism and mistakenly formulating this in Aristotelian terms.[26]

Cicero, as I said, provided later writers with the characterization of a *locus* as the basis of an *argumentum*. We learn from him also that an *argumentum* is a reason for bringing conviction where something is in doubt (*ratio rei dubiae faciens fidem*)[27] but this is all that he tells us about it. Quintilian has a great deal more to say, offering a sustained discussion of proof and its various forms of which one part is the use of *argumenta* drawn from *loci*.[28]

Where Cicero seems to be quite indiscriminate in his use of '*argumentum*' and 'argument' ('*argumentatio*'),[29] Quintilian distinguishes between them. Like Cicero he characterizes an *argumentum* as something brought forward to produce conviction and having as its basis a *locus*.[30] An *argumentum* is in the first place something conceived in the mind – what Burnyeat calls a 'consideration'[31] – independently of its presentation in spoken or written words in an argument.[32] Both *argumentum* and argument, however, may be called an enthymeme.[33]

As Burnyeat, notes, Quintilian provides a list of five different meanings which the term 'enthymeme' may have and of these he takes the third and the fifth to be crucial for his history. We are told by Quintilian that 'enthymeme' may refer to (3) an inference from an *argumentum* drawn either (a) from consequents or (b) from repugnants and that many people hold that only (3b) is an enthymeme. Either both forms of argument or only (3b) is then apparently identified by some as (5) an incomplete syllogism and this Burnyeat proposes, is the source of the 'traditional doctrine'.[34] We should also note that the second meaning given in the list is that (2) an enthymeme is a *sententia* with an associated reason (*sententia cum ratione*). '*Sententia*' here probably refers, as it does elsewhere in the *Institutio*,[35] to a maxim of some sort but as we will see in a moment when the same term is used by Boethius to explain the nature of an *argumentum* it seems to have the more general sense.[36]

Earlier, at the beginning of the discussion of proof of which this list of meanings is a part, Quintilian claims that all proof is either from consequents or repugnants in saying which he apparently intends to limit the form that rhetorical arguments may take.[37] Later he notes that properly speaking only an argument from contraries, that is, what he had earlier called an argument from repugnants, is an enthymeme.

In his *Topics* Cicero introduces the consideration of 'theses', that is, general questions, which had previously been the concern of dialecticians, or philosophers, as a legitimate and crucial part of the activity of the rhetorician, thus inventing for the Latins what Reinhardt has called 'thetical rhetoric'.[38] Before Cicero's work rhetoricians had dealt only with 'hypotheses', questions concerning particular individuals and events, but following him they could base their argument on general and abstract principles. The examples he gives in his *Topics* are all supposed to illustrate such general questions and the use of what Cicero presents as Aristotelian *loci* as sources for *argumenta* to answer them. They vary, however, in their generality. Many are drawn from the law but in the final third of the work Cicero gives examples of questions which could well have been discussed by philosophers, such as 'Is there such a thing as honour?' or 'Do only humans suffer from sickness, or do beasts suffer too?' In particular, the example that he gives in his explanation of the use of the *locus* from antecedents, consequents and repugnants is concerned with the general question, though a legal one, of whether if a wife has been bequeathed all the silver she has been bequeathed all of the coined money. Cicero formulates the argument to answer this question in three ways corresponding to each part of what he introduces of a single *locus*, saying that it does not matter in which of these ways one answers the question.

While neither Cicero nor Quintilian, unlike Aristotle, identifies theses as the subject of dialectical argumentation Boethius explicitly does so in *Diff. Top.*[39] He thus hands back to dialecticians, or philosophers, what Cicero had co-opted for the use of rhetoricians and with it he gifts them Cicero's account of the *loci*. He presents this, using his own examples, in the third book of *Diff. Top.* after giving in the second an account of the *loci* which he takes from Themistius's commentary on Aristotle's *Topics* and so already the property of the dialecticians.[40] Crucially this means that they obtain from Cicero the *locus* from antecedents, consequents and repugnants, which does not appear in Themistius's account, the two lists of *loci* being otherwise very similar.[41]

In *In Cic. Top.* Boethius, by his own account, considers the way in which rhetorical *argumenta* are obtained from *loci*. As part of this exercise, he attempts to explain Cicero's characterization of the *locus* proper to the dialecticians as a single *locus* in an exposition which Burnyeat thinks 'is wrong from beginning to end'[42]. Boethius, however, was, if not the only, certainly by far the most important source, for twelfth century thinking about *argumentum, locus* and *enthymeme,* and through the account of them given in *Diff. Top.* and *In Cic. Top.* these become central to the logical theories developed then.

Boethius's *Diff. Top.* provided twelfth-century dialecticians with the canonical explanation of Cicero's description of an *argumentum*, insisting that it be distinguished from an argument (*argumentatio*):

> An *argumentum* is a reason bringing about conviction where something is in doubt. An *argumentum* is not the same as an argument, for the power of the sense and the reason (*vis sententiae ratioque*) which is enclosed in the expression when something which is in doubt is proved is called the *argumentum*. The spoken expression of an *argumentum* is called an argument. So, an *argumentum* is the power (*virtus*), or thought (*mens*), and sense (*sententia*) of an argument.

Here again we have *sententia* and a number of other words quite difficult to translate but all indicating that the *argumentum* is the mental correlate of the premises of an argument. Cassiodorus writing a generation later and perhaps drawing on Boethius offers an etymology – an *argumentum* the expression of a clever mind (*argutae mentis*).[43]

As with his definition of an *argumentum*, Boethius's account of the forms of argument in which *argumenta* are presented defined the terms 'syllogism', 'enthymeme', 'induction' and 'example' for writers in the first half of the twelfth century. His definition of an enthymeme, in particular, as Burnyeat notes,[44] transmitted to the Latin Middle Ages the notion that such arguments are incomplete and to be obtained from syllogisms by the omission of a premise:[45]

> An enthymeme is an incomplete (*imperfectus*) syllogism, that is an expression in which the conclusion is inferred hastily without all the premises having been set down beforehand. For example, if someone says as follows, 'a human being is an animal, therefore it is a substance'. For he failed to state the second premise with which it is proposed that every animal is a substance.

While Boethius does associate enthymemes with rhetoric, he nowhere characterizes such argument forms as rhetorical syllogisms. Quite the contrary, he notes in *Diff. Top.* that dialectics employs complete syllogisms while rhetoric is content with the concision of enthymemes where from his commentary on Cicero's remark on the association of enthymemes with rhetoricians we learn that an enthymeme is a concise conception of the mind (*brevis conceptio animi*).[46] The identification we need for Burnyeat's 'fatal step'[47] is, however, found in Cassiodorus, presumably drawing also on Quintilian, who tells us that an enthymeme is a conception of the mind (*conceptio mentis*) and at once an incomplete and a rhetorical syllogism.[48]

Burnyeat, as I said, argues that Aristotle's characterization of an enthymeme as a syllogism is not to be understood in terms of the technical sense of 'syllogism' deployed in the *Prior Analytics*. Boethius opens *Diff. Top.* by locating his task as that of explaining what *loci* are, how they differ and, crucially, which are suited to which syllogisms (*qui etiam quibus apti sint syllogismis*). His exposition of the forms of argument, which follows in Book 2, indicates that for him 'syllogism' is certainly intended as a technical term. After giving the definition he refers the reader to his own *De Syllogismis Categoriciis*, where the modes and figures are set out, and illustrates with an example of a syllogism in *Barbara*. He notes next that syllogisms may also be formed with hypothetical propositions and illustrates with the usual Stoic example of affirming the antecedent of 'if it's day, then it's light'. Such propositions have been introduced in Book I with a reference there to *De Hypotheticis Syllogismis*[49] in which Boethius provides Latin logic with a theory of the hypothetical syllogism and the catalogues its various forms.

In Book I of *Diff. Top.* Boethius distinguishes the interests of the dialectician from those of the rhetorician as a concern with theses, such as whether pleasure is good or whether one should take a wife, from the rhetorician's concern with hypotheses, involving the specification of particular circumstances. By implication, then, precluding the possibility of a thetical rhetoric.

The questions answered by the dialectician according to Boethius may be further divided into predicative questions, such as those mentioned earlier, and conditional questions, such as whether if the heavens are round, they rotate. It is here that Boethius goes beyond the material which is to be found in earlier writers though perhaps drawing on the work of Themistius.[50] Predicative propositions are classified in terms of the predicables, and predicative questions ask whether the subject falls under the predicate in one of these relationships. Conditional questions, on the other hand, are classified in terms of the quality, affirmative or negative, of the antecedent and consequent propositions. Boethius notes that particular combinations of qualities correspond to different relations between the predicables but can also be used to express other relationships such as that of cause to effect or of part to whole. Despite providing an account of formulation of conditional questions, however, Boethius does not tell us how they might be answered by rather instructs the dialectician only in the use of the topical apparatus to answer predicative questions. The dialectician's tool for doing this according to Boethius is, as Aristotle had insisted, the syllogism, not, note, the enthymeme, the very same inferential structure that is employed by the demonstrator, differing from demonstration, however, in proceeding from probable premises rather than only from those which are necessary.

At the end of Book II of *Diff. Top.* Boethius notes that various of the *loci* are particularly suited for the construction of categorical syllogisms while the rest, the majority, better play that role with respect to hypothetical syllogisms. His remarks here, however, do not properly describe most the examples that he gives. Although some are, or could be, reconstructed as instances of a canonical form of the categorical syllogism, others with two or more premises could not be reformulated in this way, yet others are arguments with only a single premise, and a number are formulated as conditional propositions. These latter are not the answers to conditional questions, however, but rather have the desired predicative proposition as their consequents. In one case, indeed, we are given a complete hypothetical syllogism by affirming the antecedent and so an illustration of its use in the theory of the topics.[51] Despite his initial characterization of the application of topics to syllogisms, the wide range of Boethius examples thus shows that the topical machinery may be used to obtain conditionals and enthymemes as well as syllogisms. This is confirmed by his discussion of the *locus* from antecedents, consequents and repugnants in *In Cic. Top.* where he argues that each of the other topical relationships can appear in an argument in the form of a conditional or a repugnance drawn as an *argumentum* from one of these three, as well as other relationships which can appear only in this form.[52] In drawing up his table of correspondence between the Themistian and Ciceronian *loci* Boethius is thus required to note that Cicero's *locus* from antecedents and consequents is spread out among many of the other *loci*.[53]

The thought behind Boethius's account of the use of the topics is simple enough and well illustrated by Abaelard's example earlier. Presented with a predicative question the dialectician examines its terms and notices some features of the subject and or predicate, for example, that they are both natural kind terms, that one is a species name and the other that of an accident, or one of them the name of an integral whole. Referring to his remembered list of *loci differentiae* he considers the various properties that such things have formulated generally in maximal propositions. These two together, the *locus differentia* and the maximal proposition, are the basis for his *argumentum*. Appealing to a suitable maximal proposition he then constructs an *argumentum* to show in an argument that the answer to the question is either affirmative or negative.

Boethius officially requires that the argument must be a syllogism and in *In Cic. Top.* characterizes the problem of obtaining an *argumentum* as that of discovering a middle term (*mediatatis inventio*).[54] In *Diff. Top.* he gives as his example of the use of a maximal proposition not included in the resulting argument the only case which interests us here, the categorical syllogism: 'Someone who is envious is distressed by the goods that come to others, a wise man is not distressed by the goods that come to others; therefore, a wise man is not envious of others'[55]. With a little tidying up this would be an instance of darii and answer negatively the question of whether a wise man is envious of others. The *argumentum* in this case consists of the two premises which according to Boethius are found in the *locus from definition* which includes among its maximal propositions the principle that things of which the definitions are different are themselves different.

While, as I said, the thought at work here seems straightforward enough, that is, consider the definitions of the subject and predicate and if they differ you can prove that they refer to different things, the claim that Boethius makes about the maximal proposition is much less so. He tells us that it provides the power for the argument (*subminstrat vires argumentationi*) and a little later says that such maximal propositions 'contain other propositions and through them the conclusion follows and is confirmed' (*fit consequens et rata conclusio*). Thus, if not requiring, at least leaving open the possibility that the truth of the maximal proposition is what grounds the inference of the conclusion from the premises. This latter possibility is apparently realized in the examples he gives of conditional propositions and enthymemes, or what mediaeval philosophers will call consequences (*consequentiae*).

A reading of Boethius's theory of the topics which takes it to be concerned with enthymemes and the corresponding conditionals is supported by his commentary on Cicero's remarks on enthymemes, the commentary which Burnyeat takes to be wrong from beginning to end. The ellipsis in my quotation above from Cicero conceals his observation that the *locus* from antecedents, consequents and repugnants, the *locus* belonging properly to dialecticians, is single *locus* presented in three different ways. Boethius reasonably takes this the mean that each form rests upon the same basic relationship which he argues is properly expressed with a conditional proposition and that the *locus* should be called the *locus conditionalis*.[56] In support of this claim he argues that repugnance is best expressed in the form of a proposition derived from a true conditional by negating the consequent and then adding a second negation which is located at the beginning of the sentence but applies only to the consequent, thus returning the original conditional. Cicero's negated conjunction 'not both *A* and *B*' is thus rewritten as 'not if *A*, then not *B*' which for Boethius is equivalent to the conditional 'if *A*, then *B*'.

I have discussed Boethius's treatment of the *locus* from *repugnants* elsewhere, arguing that his replacement of the copulative conjunction with a conditional is a motivated by his denial that the copulative conjunction can be used to form a unitary proposition and his insistence that negation must act on the predicate of a proposition, refusing entirely to let it function in Stoic fashion as a propositional operator.[57] The consequence of this rewriting of Cicero, as Boethius shows, is to reduce the argument form presented as an instance of the Stoic third indemonstrable to a merely verbal variation of the first indemonstrable. More important here is that what had been a distinct argument form, privileged with the name 'enthymeme' is revealed to be no more than an alternative way of formulating the relationship between antecedent and consequent expressed in true conditional propositions.[58]

Even if Boethius is entirely wrong in his interpretation of Cicero's meaning, his commentary thus opens up the possibility of taking enthymemes with conditionals as part of a general account of enthymematic inference.

3.3 Abaelard on imperfect entailment, *Argumenta* and maximal propositions

The traditional doctrine of the enthymeme was, as Burnyeat notes, well established by the time Boethius wrote *De differentiis topicis*. A syllogism for Boethius is an argument of one of the canonical categorical or hypothetical forms and an enthymeme an argument which is incomplete because it is obtained by the omission of a premise from such a syllogism. The general definition of a syllogism given by Aristotle and which Boethius transmitted to the twelfth century allows, however, for a much broader notion of incompleteness, that of an argument which satisfies the condition that the conclusion follows necessarily from the premises but it does so only with the aid of something which is not explicitly stated in the expression of the *argumentum*. Abaelard at one point calls arguments which are instances of the canonical syllogistic forms *complexional* arguments and contrasts them with *local* arguments for which some additional support is required to connect the *argumentum* to the conclusion.[59] His greatest achievement as a logician was to deploy the theory of the topics which he inherited from Boethius to provide a general theory of inference for local arguments and the corresponding conditional propositions. With his work dialecticians acquired a tool to be used in much the same way as rhetoricians according to Aristotle, in Burnyeat's account, employed enthymemes. Abaelard's local arguments are best understood, it seems to me, as a generalization of the notion of an enthymeme as an incomplete argument grounded by him in the theory of the dialectical topics taken from Boethius.

Unfortunately while what has survived of Abaelard's commentary on *De differentiis topicis* is substantial both in content and quantity, what we have of it breaks off just before Boethius's account of the enthymeme. Abaelard also discusses the use of the topics in the construction of arguments, and in particular enthymemes, in his earlier *Dialectica* but only comparatively briefly. As I have shown elsewhere there are very considerable, indeed remarkable, differences between the two presentation and we cannot be sure that what he says in the *Dialectica* represents his final views on the subject.[60] Here, however, I will rely almost entirely on the *Dialectica* since it is where Abaelard sets out at great length his general theory of inference. This is to be found in the section devoted to the topics, placed before the discussion of the hypothetical syllogism because, according to Abaelard, some of the topics at least provide us with reasons for accepting the truth of conditional propositions.

The distinction between complete and incomplete arguments appears for the first time earlier in the *Dialectica* in Abaelard's account of the categorical syllogism. It is here that we have evidence that he had some direct access to the *Prior Analytics* since his definitions of a syllogism and of perfect and imperfect syllogisms are taken from it rather than from Boethius's own formulations.[61] In particular, Abaelard quotes Aristotle's explanation of the requirement that the conclusion of a syllogism holds because of (*per*) the premises as stipulating that nothing provided by an extrinsic term is required in order for it come about necessarily (*nullius extrinsecus egere termini ut fiat necessarium*). Abaelard then offers his own gloss on the same requirement:[62]

> When he says that the conclusion comes about because of (*per*) what has been proposed he means that the entailment of a syllogism (*inferentia syllogismi*) is complete (*perfecta*) in that the form (*complexio*) of the conclusion is in some way already revealed in the form of the antecedent propositions.

Boethius in *De Syllogismo Categorico* explains that this requirement serves to preclude arguments which include more, less or something other than the required premises. Abaelard follows Boethius but with his own example:[63]

> Less is set down in this way 'Every human being is an animal, but every animal is animate; therefore every human is a body'. For lacking for the completion of

the entailment (*perfectio inferentiae*) is the proposition which shows that every animate being is a body.

Later in the *Dialectica* Abaelard characterizes such an argument as an enthymeme, though an irregular one, derived by subtraction from an 'irregular syllogism'[64]. Though neither Boethius or Abaelard say so, a traditional enthymeme suffers from precisely the same fault of providing less than needed and so for Abaelard must fail to be a complete entailment.

While Abaelard presents the notion of completeness of entailment as present in Aristotle's definition of the syllogism he knows that Aristotle himself appeals to the idea of completion in quite a different way to distinguish the first figure of the categorical syllogism from the other two figures in terms of their evidence. All categorical syllogisms according to Abaelard are complete entailments in that it is their form which guarantees, without the need of any external support, that the conclusion follows necessarily from the premises. The second and third figures are incomplete in the sense that it is not evident that this is so. Something needs to be done, that is, reduction to the first figure, to prove that they are compete entailments.[65] Abaelard's introduction of completeness of entailment is clearly related to the traditional characterization of enthymeme as incomplete but for him such incompleteness is a more general notion and one which is central to his theory of topical inference.

Abaelard begins his discussion of the topics in the *Dialectica* by noting that the definitions of a *locus* provided by Boethius are too narrow for his purposes. From Cicero, as we saw, a *locus* is the basis for an *argumentum* and Abaelard takes Themistius's definition to be that it is that from which an *argumentum* is drawn (*id unde trahitur argumentum*). These definitions are too narrow for him simply because they refer to an *argumentum*, and an *argumentum* must be conceded if it is to prove the claim which it is cited to support. The new, general, definition which he proposes is that a *locus* is the *vis inferentiae* literally 'the power of entailment' which I will translate as 'entailment warrant', it grounds the logical relationship between two propositions without requiring that they be conceded in an argument:[66]

> Defining *locus* generally we say that it is an entailment warrant. As when this consequence is proposed: 'if something is a human being, then it is an animal', human being, the relationship of which to animal provides the entailment warrant, is called the *locus*. And since human being is related to animal as species to genus this *locus* is to be assigned *from species*.

The same topical apparatus which we saw at the beginning of the chapter used in the proof of an enthymeme is here used to prove the corresponding conditional. Entailment for Abaelard is thus the relationship which exists between the antecedent and consequent of a true conditional proposition. It exists, he says, where we have the necessity of consecution, the relationship which holds when the truth of one claim follows from that of another. The same relationship may, of course, exist between the premises and consequence of an argument but in the case of the argument, according to Abaelard, the premises must also be conceded.

Aristotle's definition perhaps requires for the conclusion of a syllogism to follow from the premises only that it is not possible for the premises to be true and the conclusion false together. The necessity, that is, established in the *reductio ad impossibile* reductions of second- and third-figure syllogisms to the first. Further constraints on syllogistic inference are revealed later in the *Prior Analytics*.[67] Abaelard, on the other hand, stipulates that for there to be the necessity of consecution the sense (*sensus/sententia*), that is, the meaning, of the antecedent must require, or contain, that of the consequent. He maintains that syllogistic consequences hold with just this necessity in virtue of the form (*complexio*) of the antecedent and consequent and in general characterizes such consequences as *complete* because, as he says, the form (*complexio*) of the antecedent contains that of the consequent.[68]

The formal structure of both categorical and hypothetical syllogisms thus guarantees that their conditionalizations are complete entailments. As I said earlier, Abaelard calls such arguments *complexional* arguments and notes that the corresponding conditionals hold for all uniform substitutions for their terms – so anticipating the Bolzano-Tarski criterion for logical validity employed in contemporary logic.[69] This property alone, however, is not, according to him, enough for completeness. The conditional 'if every animal is animate, then every animal is animate' is, he acknowledges, true and remains true for all uniform substitution of terms for 'animal' and 'animate' but it is not complete, he maintains, because it is not the conditionalization of a categorical or hypothetical syllogism.[70] Completeness is thus a purely structural property of entailments possessed only by the conditionalizations of the figures and moods of the categorical and hypothetical syllogisms.

In the traditional doctrine an enthymeme is obtained from a syllogism by the omission of one of the premises. While all conditionalizations of categorial or hypothetical syllogisms are complete entailments, according to Abaelard, holding with the necessity of consecution, the omission of one of the antecedent propositions, corresponding to the production of a traditional enthymeme, does not, however, necessarily produce a true conditional proposition when the omitted proposition is itself necessarily true. The conditionals 'if every human being is an animal and every animal is animate, then every human being is animate' and 'if every human being is an animal, and no animal is a stone, then no human being is a stone' are true syllogistic consequences; because of their forms they are both complete entailments. The removal of one of the components of the antecedent in one case leaves us with a true conditional:[71]

> There are other entailments which are incomplete, when, that is, only one proposition is antecedent as if with one proposition removed from the same antecedents an entailment should be formed in this way: (1) 'if every human is an animal, then every human is animate', or (2) 'if every human is an animal, then no human is a stone'. Which entailments, although they are incomplete with regard to the construction of the antecedent, nevertheless very often possess necessity in virtue of the nature of the world. As in the case of the one we gave first from animal to animate. Since that it is the nature of animal, in which animate inheres as a substantial form, does not permit animal to exist without animation.

Abaelard's language is rather misleading here but it is completely clear from the discussion that follows that although conditional (1) is true, conditional (2) is false for him because it fails to satisfy the requirement of meaning inclusion. This even though there is no possible situation in which the antecedent is true and the consequent is false. While being animate is part of the meaning of 'animal', not being a stone is no part of its meaning.[72]

For Abaelard there is no guarantee that we may always obtain an enthymematic consequence in the traditional way by the suppression of a necessary premise of a syllogistic consequence. We do have this guarantee in a logic for which an argument is valid if and only if no possible situation are the premises all true but the conclusion false and so if and only if the corresponding conditional is true, that is, a logic for which the deduction theorem holds. In Abaelard's logic, however, the guarantee of the validity, in our terms, of a traditional enthymeme provided by an unstated necessarily true premise is not enough to ground the truth of its conditionalization. Rather he requires a guarantee that the meaning of the antecedent contains that of the consequent and this is to be found in a *locus* from which a proof of the conditional may be drawn. The *locus differentia* and the maximal proposition thus provide, according to Abaelard, the *argumentum* to prove the truth of the conditional proposition.[73] What would have been the *argumentum* in the corresponding enthymeme, the fact that every human is an animal, has become, as it does in some of Boethius's examples, the antecedent of a consequence.

The guarantee that a *locus* provides of the truth of a conditional, according to Abaelard, is to be found in the very general facts about the metaphysical structure of the world or as we would say any possible world, expressed in maximal propositions. In the case of the conditional just mentioned the maximal proposition would be 'of whatever the species is predicated the genus is predicated'.

While it is to the *loci* that Abaelard looks for the guarantee of the meaning relation required for the truth of conditionals his arguments in the *Dialectica* show that relatively few of them can provide it. More will guarantee that the antecedent proposition cannot be true when the consequent is false but this alone for Abaelard is not enough to guarantee of the conditional. Although he acknowledges this connection as a kind of necessity, it is the weaker of the two kinds which he recognizes in his general account of inference in the *Dialectica*. The stronger kind of necessity, that of meaning containment and *a fortiori* inseparability, is needed for the truth of a conditional. The weaker necessity, which he characterizes as 'categorical', exists where the truth of one proposition is inseparable from that of another but the former does not include in its meaning the latter.[74] This weaker necessity, however, is all that is needed to ensure that in an inference from a true premise will necessarily yield a true conclusion. Abaelard refers to the weaker necessity as maximal probability,[75] arguing in his commentary on *Diff. Top.*, much as Burnyeat does for Aristotle, that the characterization by Boethius of premises of a syllogism as necessary or probable must refer to their relationship to the conclusion, that is, qualify the inferential connection, rather than to modal properties that the propositions have of themselves.[76]

Abaelard holds that imperfect, local, entailments are just as necessary as perfect, complexional, entailments; both satisfy the meaning containment requirement for entailment. The difference between them is that to prove that a particular complexional entailment is true all that is required is that one invoke the general rule for such entailments and show that it is a substitution instance. To prove a *local* entailment, on the other hand, one must locate both the relevant topical relationship (*habitudo*) for one or both of the terms in question, or for the proposition as a whole,[77] and the appropriate maximal proposition. The maximal proposition is a rule applicable where the relationship exists and so includes in its formulation the *locus differentia* for that relationship. The *locus differentia* 'species', for example, for the relationship of species to genus, appears in the maximal proposition 'of whatever a species is predicated its genus is predicated'. No such relationship between the terms is required for the application of the rules of syllogistic entailment which hold no matter what the terms are and so contrary to Boethius no *locus* is required for a syllogism.[78]

The topics thus provide, according to Abaelard, a machinery for proving *local* conditionals and justifying the inferences made in *local* arguments. This is much larger range of arguments than traditional enthymemes which share with them the property that something external to the argument is needed to support the inference and so like them are incomplete. The vast bulk of Abaelard's discussion of the topics in the *Dialectica* is concerned to establish just which *loci* can guarantee necessity in the strictest sense, at the end of it; however, he turns to the nature of argument in general and a consideration of enthymemes.

In his brief discussion of the nature of *argumenta* Abaelard moves from considering the use of the *loci* to demonstrate the truth of conditionals to their role in supporting arguments. The machinery involved is the same, but it is put to a different, much less constrained use. In proving that a conditional is true the maximal proposition and the *locus differentia* together constitute the *argumentum* to answer the conditional question.[79] In the case of categorical questions, on the other hand, the *argumentum* is a categorical proposition, or in complexional arguments a pair of propositions, whose truth is conceded by the respondent in a dialectical exchange.[80] For a local argument the *argumentum* is provided by the topical apparatus is located outside the argument to be invoked in answering why, *unde locus*?, the conclusion is supposed to follow from the premise.

Abaelard allows the dialectician the same latitude as Boethius in arguing against an opponent: any *argumentum* may be proposed which his opponent believes to be true and from which he believes that the conclusion follows and so in this sense is probable. The dialectician can thus appeal to *loci* supporting the necessary connection required for the truth of the corresponding conditional, those guaranteeing maximal probability, and in this case if the premise is true then so must be the conclusion, but also to those which have only the probability of general acceptance, acceptance by the appropriate expert or simply those which are accepted by one's opponent.[81] Abaelard's dialectician may thus be quite as relaxed as Burnyeat's Aristotelian rhetorician in the arguments he presents to his opponent.[82] In defending his position, on the other hand, and responding to proposals the dialectician must take care to accept only what he knows to be true and necessary in at least the weaker sense, since only this can guarantee the truth of the conclusion.[83]

Abaelard's discussion of the enthymeme as characterized in the traditional doctrine in the *Dialectica* is very brief but notable because he considers the formation of enthymemes from both categorical and hypothetical syllogisms. Referring to both enthymemes obtained from syllogisms and examples obtained from inductions, he confirms that what we produce by removing a premise are local arguments:[84]

> The entailment in the case of each of these apart from the syllogism is incomplete and needs a *locus* to be assigned to provide evidence for it.

In particular Abaelard notes that from the hypothetical syllogism 'if something is a human being, then it is an animal, but it's an animal; therefore it is a human being', we may form the categorical enthymeme 'it's a human being: therefore it's an animal' in which the truth of the *argumentum*, 'it's a human being', necessitates the truth of the conclusion with the strong necessity of containment. As we have seen, if challenged to justify this inference with the challenge '*unde locus?*' the appropriate response would be 'from species'. The other way of forming an enthymeme from a hypothetical syllogism is to remove the categorical premise, leaving what Abaelard calls a hypothetical enthymeme. In this case, however, the *argumentum*, though it is necessarily true, proves no support for the conclusion because as Abaelard explains earlier in the *Dialectica*, an affirmative categorical proposition cannot follow from a conditional because its truth requires that its subject term not be empty, whereas a conditional is, if true, true quite independently of the existence of the things which it is about.

3.4 Conclusion

As I mentioned Abaelard's commentary on *De differentiis topicis* breaks off just before the point at which Boethius introduces enthymemes. We cannot guess what he might have said there but I believe that I have shown that in his *Diaelectica* he provides a sophisticated account of enthymematic inference understood very generally as the theory of *local* argumentation. Later logicians were thus able to draw on a theory of argumentation as rich as that which Burnyeat argues was lost with the replacement of Aristotle's original account of enthymemes with the traditional doctrine.

Notes

1 P. Abaelard 1969, p. 294: 'cum uolo ostendere Socratem esse animal considero hominem qui est species animalis, et naturam speciei ad genus; quam scilicet naturam maxima propositio exprimit quae ait: De quocumque praedicatur species, et genus; et inspecta specie et modo probandi quem maxima propositio exprimit, statim, secundum haec duo, *argumentum* dispono, conuincens scilicet Socratem esse animal per hoc quod est homo; et ita Socrates est homo est *argumentum* ad Socrates est animal, quod *argumentum* ex homine specie quam continet tractum est, secundum

eum comprobandi modum quem maxima propositio demonstrat. Unde tam ipsa species quam maxima propositio *locus*, id est sedes argumenti, dicitur.'

2   M. F. Burnyeat 1994, pp. 3–55. The same material but without the final sections pursuing the history into the Latin tradition is found in M. F. Burnyeat 1996, pp. 88–113. Burnyeat proposes a reading of Aristotle's theory of the enthymeme which should be contrasted with the 'standard' account found, for example, in W. Grimaldi 1972.

3   D. Z. Nikitas 1990, II.2 p. 17: 'Enthymema quippe est imperfectus syllogismus, id est oratio in qua non omnibus antea propositionibus constitutis infertur festinata conclusio, ut si quis ita dicat: homo animal est, substantia igitur est. Praetermisit enim alteram propositionem qua proponitur, omne animal est substantia.'

4   P. Abaelard 1969, p. 295, 'Enthymema est imperfectus syllogismus, cuius aliquae partes, uel propter breuitatem uel propter notitiam, praetermissae sunt'.

5   See C. J. Martin 2010, pp. 159–92.

6   *Aristotles Latinus* 1962, III, pp. 1–4. *Analytica Priora*, 70a9-11: *Recensio Carnutensis* (p. 189): 'Enthymema ergo est syllogismus ex ikotibus et signis'; / *Recensio Florentina* (p. 137): Enthymema ergo est syllogismus ex verisimilibus vel signis.

7   *Aristoteles Latinus* 1969, V, pp. 1–3, *Topica*, 164a5–6, p. 178. Here Aristotle remarks that in rhetoric as in dialectics one should keep a record of the enthymemes that have been employed.

8   I will use both 'topic' and '*locus*' and their cognates here without intending any difference in meaning.

9   Boethius 1833.

10   In Book IV of *Diff. Top.* Boethius gives an account of rhetorical argumentation and observes that (IV.1, p. 72) 'dialectica perfectis utitur syllogismis. Rhetorica enthymematum breuitate contenta est.' This, of course, does not preclude the use of enthymemes by the dialectician.

11   For the mediaeval reading of Aristotle's *Topics* in terms of Boethius's account of topical argumentation see N. J. Green-Pedersen 1984, II.A, p. 5: 'Aristotle Interpreted Through Boethius'. Green-Pedersen notes that mediaeval commentators took Boethius to provide the theory of the topics and Aristotle to provide an account of their application.

12   Aristotle, *Topica*, 162a15–18, p. 302: 'Est autem philosophima quidem syllogismus demonstratiuus, *argumentum* autem syllogismus dialecticus, sophisma vero syllogismus litigatorius, aporima autem syllogismus dialecticus contradictionis.'

13   'Maxima propositio' at *Topica*, 155b15, p. 288, is used by Boethius for the 'ἀξίωμα' which is elsewhere in the work either simply transliterated or translated as 'propositio'. See S. Ebbesen 1981, vol. 1, pp. 120–1.

14   Referring to Theophrastus's account of the topics to justify the use of the expression. A. of Aphrodisias 1883, vol. 2.2, p. 126.11–21: 'ἔστι δὲ ὁ τόπος ἀρχὴ καὶ ἀφορμὴ ἐπιχειρήματος· ἐπιχείρημα δὲ καλοῦσι τὸν διαλεκτικὸν συλλογισμόν.' Cicero uses the phrase 'sedes argumenti' to characterize the source of the *loci* in *De Inventione*, *Topica* and *De Oratore* and in the *Topica* attributes it to Aristotle. M. T. Cicero 2003, §7–8: 'Ut igitur earum rerum quae absconditae sunt demonstrato et notato loco facilis inventio est, sic, cum pervestigare *argumentum* aliquod volumus, locos nosse debemus; sic enim appellatae ab Aristotele sunt eae quasi sedes, e quibus argumenta promuntur. Itaque licet definire locum esse argumenti sedem, *argumentum* autem rationem quae rei dubiae faciat fidem.' 'Sedes' does not occur in Boethius translation of Aristotle's *Topics*, nor for that matter does ἀφορμὴ occur in the Greek. See S. Ebbesen 1981,

vol. 1, IV.3, p. 5 'Axiomatic Topics' and Reinhardt's commentary on *Topica* 8 for discussions of the possible sources of Cicero's ideas on the topics. In *De Inventione* we also have once (I.49) 'fons confirmationis'.
15 See S. Ebbesen 1981, pp. 120–1.
16 As John of Salisbury notes recalling his years as a student in Paris in the 1130s. J. of Salisbury 1991 (*CCCML* XCVIII), p. 71: 'Apud hos toto exercitatus biennio, sic *locis* assignandis assueui et regulis, et aliis rudimentorum elementis quibus pueriles animi imbuuntur, et in quibus praefati doctores potentis simi erant et expeditissimi, ut haec omnia mihi uiderer nosse tanquam ungues digitosque meos.'
17 That these are hypothetical rather than categorical syllogisms has recently been argued by Slomkowski. We will see later that Boethius takes the topics as used in dialectics to be a source of both categorical and hypothetical syllogisms as well as of conditional propositions and enthymematic arguments. See P. Slomkowski 1997.
18 The definition of the syllogism for early twelfth-century logicians was provided by Boethius in *Diff. Top.* and *De Syllogismo Categorico*. Thus *Diff. Top.*, II.2, p. 3: 'Syllogismus est oratio, in qua positis quibusdam et concessis aliud quiddam per ea ipsa quae concessa sunt evenire necesse est quam sunt ipsa quae concessa sunt.' See Boethius 2008, pp. 69–72, for a slightly different word order. Boethius's definition differs from that given by Aristotle in the *Prior Analytics* and *Topics* by requiring that the premises be conceded (*concessis*) as well being as set down *(positis)*. See later for Abaelard's use of Aristotle's own formulation in the *Prior Analytics*.
19 Aristotle, *Topica*, A, 100a25–30.
20 That is to say that Aristotle does not intend to claim that a rhetorical syllogism can be defined by qualifying the definition of a syllogism with an appropriate differentia but rather that on the basis of some kind of similarity a rhetorical syllogism can be characterized as a syllogism.
21 M. F. Burnyeat 1994, p. 18, notes that the definition of a rhetorical syllogism, that is, an enthymeme, in the *Rhetoric* 1356b16, as proceeding from 'certain things being the case', seems to require more than one premise.
22 Where Aristotle requires that the conclusion of a syllogism follow necessarily, that is, with *necessitas consequentiae*, from its premises, that the premises of a demonstrative syllogism are necessary, and that those of a dialectical syllogism are probable. Aristotle, *Topica*, 100a30-31, p. 5: 'Dialecticus autem syllogismus qui ex probabilibus est syllogizatus.'
23 Thus M. F. Burnyeat 1994, p. 33: 'This is a remarkable enlargement of the scope of enthymeme. It is one thing to endorse the kind of *probabilitas consequentiae* . . . , quite another to accept that deductively invalid sign arguments can be respectable too. It is neither universally nor for the most part true that women of sallow complexion are pregnant.' Grimaldi, on the other hand, apparently believes that most sallow women are pregnant! *Studies*, 112: '*Semeion anonymon,* on the other hand, and any *sign*-enthymeme constructed on it can only give a probable conclusion with respect to its signate, that is, a very strong likelihood grounded in the experience of reality.' In the one other work of Aristotle that became available in the first half of the twelfth century, and was read by Abaelard, the *Sophistical Refutations*, there are five references to rhetoric. The only one to say anything about rhetorical argumentation tells us a little about arguments from signs which do not necessitate the claims they are invoked to support. The example given seems to support Burnyeat's claim that Aristotelian rhetoricians may employ very relaxed arguments indeed. *Aristoteles Latinus* 1972, VI, pp. 1–3, *De Sophisticis Elenchis*, 167b9–12, p. 13: 'Et in rethoricis quae secundum

signum sunt demonstrationes ex adiunctis sunt. Volentes enim ostendere quoniam adulter, quod adiunctum est accipiunt, quoniam compositus aut quoniam in nocte videtur errabundus. Pluribus autem haec quidem insunt, praedicatum vero non inest.'
24 For example, by John of Salisbury, see P. S. Boskoff 1952, 27.1, pp. 71–8.
25 See J. O. Ward 2018.
26 M. F. Burnyeat 1994, p. 46. Though without giving any direct evidence for a Stoic account of incomplete syllogisms which might have suggested the application of the phrase to describe enthymemes. The argument is apparently: Cicero identifies enthymemes as arguments from repugnants with the use of the Stoic third indemonstrable and Quintilian introduces an enthymeme as an incomplete syllogism in a list of meanings of 'enthymeme' which includes, as well Aristotle's description of it as a rhetorical syllogism, Cicero's 'argument from repugnants'. The idea that an enthymeme is an incomplete syllogism is not Aristotelian; therefore it must be Stoic.
27 Cicero used the term *argumentum* in a quite different sense in the *De Inventione*, and it is used in the same sense in the *Rhetorica ad Herennium*, as a fictional but possible event. These two works were the standard texts for rhetorical teaching in the twelfth century.
28 Quintilian 2001, (*LCL* 125). The whole of Book 5 is devoted to setting out the theory of proof.
29 In his translation of Cicero's *Topica* Reinhardt renders the first as 'argument' and the second as 'argumentation' but does not indicate any difference in meaning.
30 Quintilian 2001, 5.10, p. 20: 'Locos appello non, ut vulgo nunc intelleguntur, in luxuriem et adulterium et similia, sed sedes argumentorum, in quibus latent, ex quibus sunt petenda.'
31 M. F. Burnyeat 1994, e.g. p. 12: '<Aristotle> means neither more nor less than this: an enthymeme, a consideration, is a sort of argument.'
32 Quintilian 2001, 5.10, p. 4: 'Epichirema Valgius adgressionem vocat; verius autem iudico non nostram administrationem, sed ipsam rem quam adgredimur, id est *argumentum* quo aliquid probaturi sumus, etiam si nondum verbis explanatum, iam tamen mente conceptum, epichirema dici.'
33 Quintilian 2001, 5.14, pp. 1–2: 'Igitur enthymema et *argumentum* ipsum, id est rem quae probationi alterius adhibetur, appellant et argumenti elocutionem, eam vero, ut dixi, duplicem: ex consequentibus, quod habet propositionem coniunctamque ei protinus probationem . . . Ex pugnantibus vero, quod etiam solum enthymema quidam vocant, fortior multo probatio est.'
34 Quintilian 2001, 5.10, pp. 1–3: 'Nam enthymema . . . unum intellectum habet, (1) quo omnia mente concepta significat (sed nunc non de eo loquimur); alterum, quo (2) sententiam cum ratione; tertium, quo (3) certam quandam argumenti conclusionem vel (a) ex consequentibus vel (b) ex repugnantibus, quanquam de hoc parum convenit. Sunt enim, qui illud prius epichirema dicant, pluresque invenias in ea opinione, ut id demum, quod pugna constat, enthymema accipi velint, et ideo illud Cornificius contrarium appellat. Hunc alii (4) rhetoricum syllogismum, alii (5) imperfectum syllogismum vocaverunt, quia nec distinctis nec totidem partibus concluderetur; quod sane non utique ab oratore desideratur.' The text is frustratingly ambiguous, the identification may be of (5) with both 3(a) and 3(b) or only with 3(b). Russell translates it to give the latter sense. The claim might even be simply others call an enthymeme (4) a rhetorical syllogism and others an imperfect syllogism.
35 See M. F. Burnyeat 1994, p. 39 n. 101. Russell translates 'sententia' as proposition. If it means maxim the ultimate source is presumably *Rhetoric* 2, 2.1394a31, where

Aristotle says that a maxim (γνώμη) stated with a supporting reason (αἰτία καὶ τοῦ διὰ τί) is an enthymeme.

36 Sense (1) of 'enthymeme' is any conception of the mind, which Quintilian says is not his subject, and (2) might thus simply be a narrowing of this sense.
37 See M. F. Burnyeat 1994, p. 43 n. 113.
38 See M. T. Cicero 2003, Introduction.
39 Boethius, *Diff. Top.*, I.5, p. 13ff.
40 Boethius identifies particular Ciceronian topics with particular Themistian topics and this is for the most part a straightforward exercise. Unsurprisingly given Cicero's identification of it with the Stoic indemonstrables, Themistius's list of topics does not include that from antecedents, consequents and repugnants, the last Boethius identifies with Themistius's *locus* from opposites and the first two he says (*Diff. Top.* III.8 p.15) are 'mixed up with many' of the Themistian *loci*.
41 See M. T. Cicero 2003, pp. 29–35, for whom the coincidence in the lists is evidence for a common Peripatetic source for the *loci* apart from that from antecedents, repugnants and consequents.
42 M. F. Burnyeat 1994, p. 42, n. 110.
43 Cassiodorus 1937, II, p. 11.
44 M. F. Burnyeat 1994, p. 50.
45 Boethius, *Diff. Top.* II.2, p. 17 : 'Enthymema quippe est imperfectus syllogismus, id est oratio, in qua non omnibus antea propositionibus constitutis infertur festinata conclusio, ut si quis sic dicat: "homo animal est, substantia igitur est". Praetermisit enim alteram propositionem, qua proponitur "omne animal esse substantiam".'
46 Boethius 1833, p. 365.
47 M. F. Burnyeat 1994, p. 46ff.
48 Cassiodorus 1937, II, p. 12. He tells us it is the 'artigraphi' who call an enthymeme an incomplete syllogism. The word means grammarians according to the *TLL* but there is no indication of who these might be or of why they had an interest in the enthymeme.
49 Boethius 1969.
50 As he has been shown to do in his discussion of the definition of a *locus*. See E. Stump 1974, pp. 77–93.
51 Boethius, *Diff. Top.*, II.7, p. 11.
52 Boethius, *In Cic. Top.*, p. 349.
53 Boethius, *Diff. Top.*, III.7, p. 23.
54 Boethius, *In Cic. Top.*, p. 279.
55 Boethius, *Diff. Top.*, II.3, p. 9.
56 Boethius, *In Cic. Top.*, p. 348: 'Si igitur connexa propositio in conditione est constituta, repugnans quoque in conditione consistit. Quod si et consequentiam propositionum et repugnantiam conditio facit, non est dubium, quin lous hic iure conditionali vocetur.'
57 See C. J. Martin 1991, pp. 277–304.
58 Starting with an enthymeme expressed in the form favoured by the rhetoricians he converts it into a conditional and the third indemonstrable into the first. *In Cic. Top.*, pp. 364–5: Fiunt vero haec enthymemata hoc modo, ex contrariis videlicet texta: *hunc metuere, alterum in metu non ponere* ... Sed hoc breviter Tullius enuntiavit, nos vero *argumentum* in syllogismum redigamus, a repugnantibus scilicet, ex quo enthymemata nasci solent, hoc modo. Sit connexum: *Si quis metuit cives paucos interfici, is metuit interire rem publicam.* Interponitur negatio sic: Si *quis metuit cives paucos interfici, is non metuit interire rem publicam.* Iungitur alia negatio:

Non, si quis metuit paucos cives interfici, non metuit interire rem publicam. Quae duae negationes uni affirmationi pares sunt, quae dicit: *Si quis metuit hoc, metuit et illud.* Cuius quidem assumptio est: *at metuit hoc.* Conclusio sequitur: *metuit igitur illud:* quae tantumdem valet, si negando interrogetur, ita: *Hoc metuis, illud non metuis ?* Sed quia non totus (ut supra posuimus) in his argumentationibus ponitur syllogismus, sed propositio, cuius assumptio et conclusio notae sunt, idcirco enthymema dicitur, quasi brevis animi conceptio. Et in ceteris exemplis idem modus est.

59 P. Abaelard 1933, p. 508 : 'Sed argumentationes quaedam sunt locales, quaedam uero complexionales. <Complexionales> quidem sunt <quae> ex ipsa complexione, id est ex ipsorum terminorum dispositione, firmitudinem contrahunt. Locales uero sunt quibus conuenienter potest assignari *locus*, id est euidentia conferri ex aliquo euentu rerum uel proprietate sermonis.'
60 C. J. Martin 2009, pp. 249–70.
61 L. Minio-Paluello 1954, pp. 211–31.
62 P. Abaelard, *Dialectica*, p. 233: 'Quod uero ait ipsam conclusionem prouenire per proposita, tale est ut ita perfecta sit inferentia syllogismi ut complexione[m] antecedentium propositionum quodammodo iam innuatur complexio conclusionis.'
63 P. Abaelard, *Dialectica*, p. 233: 'Minus autem ponitur hoc modo: omnis homo animal est sed omne animal animatum est igitur omnis homo corpus est Defuit enim ad perfectionem inferentiae ea propositio quae omne animatum corpus esse ostenderet.'
64 P. Abaelard, *Dialectica*, p. 466: 'Sed et sicut syllogismus irregularis est quod plures habet assumptiones, sic enthymema quod ex eo nascitur una propositionum adempta.'
65 P. Abaelard, *Dialectica*, p. 257: 'haec imperfectio non ad inferentiam, sed ad euidentiam refertur. Similiter enim et in istis qui imperfecti dicuntur, inferentia est necessaria sicut in illis, et complexio sequentis propositionis in contexione antecedentium propositionum continetur.'
66 P. Abaelard, *Dialectica*, p. 253: 'Locum ergo generaliter definientes vim inferentiae dicimus. Veluti cum talis proponitur consequentia: "si est homo, est animal", "homo", cuius habitudo ad "animal" vim inferentiae tenet, *locus* dicitur, cumque "homo" ad "animal" utpote species ad genus suum sese habeat, *locus* ipse a specie assignandus est.'
67 For a discussion of whether these various extra constraints commit Aristotle to some kind of relevance logic see P. Steinkrüger 2015, vol. 192, pp. 1413–44.
68 P. Abaelard, *Dialectica*, p. 253.
69 See J. Etchmenendy 1990.
70 P. Abaelard, *Dialectica*, p. 255.
71 P. Abaelard, *Dialectica*, p. 255: 'Sunt autem aliae inferentiae, quae imperfectae sunt, cum videlicet una tantum propositio antecedit, <ut> si de eisdem antecedentibus substracta una fiat ad ultimam inferentiam hoc modo: "si omnis homo est animal, omnis homo est animatus" vel: "si omnis homo est animai, nullus homo est lapis". Quae quidem inferentiae, quamvis imperfectae sint quantum ad antecedentis constructionem, tamen necessitatem ex rerum natura saepissime tenent veluti ista quam prius posuimus de "animali" ad "animatum", cum videlicet natura animalis, cui animatum ut substantialis forma inest, ipsum animai praeter animationem existere nusquam patiatur.'
72 See C. J. Martin 2004, pp. 158–99.
73 P. Abaelard, *Dialectica*, p. 265.
74 See C. J. Martin 2004.

75 E.g. P. Abaelard, *Dialectica*, p. 285: 'Maximam autem probabilitatem in consecutione necessitas ista tenet, cum uidelicet antecedens absque consequenti non potest existere. Quae quidem necessitas, si recte consecutionis necessitatem pensemus, inuenietur uel potius ad enuntiationem categoricam quam hypotheticam pertinere, cum id scilicet intelligitur: hoc non posse esse absque illo.'

76 P. Abaelard 1969, p. 307: '"Necessarium uero", sicut *argumentum*, quantum ad conclusionem dicitur quam arguit, id est probat; ita et probabile et necessarium non in se dicitur, sed quantum ad conclusionem, quia probabile est *argumentum* non quia facile in se recipitur, sed quod statim ut audita est argumentatio ad conferendam fidem conclusioni, idoneum iudicatur.' See P. Abaelard, *Dialectica*, p. 460.

77 See P. Abaelard, *Dialectica*, pp. 269–70, where he notes that two *loci* may need to be assigned where both the antecedent and consequent are conditional propositions and that *loci* are required to ground the various conversions of propositions.

78 See P. Abaelard, *Dialectica*, pp. 257ff.

79 P. Abaelard, *Dialectica*, p. 265: 'Ad *argumentum* itaque ueritatis consecutionis *locus differentia* adducitur, sicut et maxima propositio quae post assignationem differentiae subiungitur, non ad causam inferentiae.'

80 P. Abaelard, *Dialectica*, p. 462.

81 See P. Abaelard 1969, pp. 306–7: 'probabile est quod statim uidetur', id est quod statim, ut auditum est, approbatur tamquam ualens et recipitur tamquam idoneum ad conferendam fidem quaestioni', where this, as with Boethius, *Diff Top*, 1.7.4., can be everyone, the majority, the wise, an expert or finally 'illud est recte probabile quod uidetur ei cum quo disputatur, uel ipsi etiam qui iudicat inter eos'.

82 Allowing the dialectician to deploy an argument as relaxed as that of the rhetorician described by Aristotle, cited n. 23. P. Abaelard, *Dialectica*, pp. 277–8: 'Etsi enim cognoscam non necessarium esse ad amorem puellae quod saepe deprehensa est in nocte cum iuuene loquens secreto, tamen facile per hoc colloquium amorem suspicor et concedo, ex eo scilicet quod huiusmodi colloquia numquam uideamus contingere nisi inter amantes. Ex eo itaque quod ad inferentiam tunc admitto, fidem saepe capio, et quod ad inferentiam non uidetur sufficere, maxime tamen ad fidem uidetur ualere, et quae in inferentiae ueritate probabilitas non consistit, in commendatione fidei recipitur.'

83 P. Abaelard, *Dialectica*, p. 462: 'Sed, ut firmae sit propositionis ostensio omnemque sophismatis nodum effugiat, non alia ille cui propositio proponitur, argumenta debet admittere nisi quae uera ac necessaria cognouerit.'

84 P. Abaelard, *Dialectica*, p. 464: 'Horum autem omnium praeter syllogismi inferentia imperfecta est *loci*que assignatione ad euidentiam egens.'

Bibliography

Abaelard, Petrus (1933), *Logica Nostrorum Petioni Sociorum*, B. Geyer (ed.), Peter Abaelards Philosophische Schriften, Münster, Aschendorff.

Abaelard, Petrus (1956, 1970), *Dialectica*, L. M. de Rijk (ed.), Assen, Van Gorcum.

Abaelard, Petrus (1969), *Super Topica Glossae in Scritti De Logici*, M. Dal Pra (ed.), Firenze, La Nuova Italia.

Alexander of Aphrodisias (1883), *In Topica, Commentaria in Aristotelem Graeca (CAG)*, M. Wallies (ed.), Berlin, Reimer.

Aristotles Latinus (1962), *Analytica Priora, Recensio Carnutensis*, L. Minio-Paluello (ed.), Brussels/Paris, Desclée de Brouwer.
Aristoteles Latinus (1969), *Topica*, L. Minio-Paluello (ed.), Brussels-Paris, Desclée de Brouwer.
Aristoteles Latinus (1972), *De Sophisticis Elenchis*, B. G. Dod (ed.), Leiden, Brill.
Boethius, Severinus (1833), 'In Ciceronis Topica', in *Ciceronis Opera*, J. C. Orelli and G. Baiterus (eds), Zurich, Fuesslini.
Boethius, Severinus *De topicis differentis*, D. Z. Nikitas (ed.), Athens/Paris/Brussels, Academy of Athens/Vrin/Ousia.
Boethius, Severinus (1969), *De Hypotheticis Syllogismis*, L. Obertello (ed.), Brescia, Paidea.
Boethius, Severinus (2008), *De Syllogismo Categorico (DSC)*, C. T. Thörnqvist (ed.), Gothenburg, Acta Universitatis Gothoburgensis.
Boskoff, P. S. (1952), 'Quintilian in the Late Middle Ages', *Speculum* 27 (1), pp. 71-8.
Burnyeat, M. F. (1994), 'Enthymeme: Aristotle on The Logic of Persuasion', in *Aristotle's "Rhetoric": Philosophical Essays*, D. J. Furley and A. Nehamas (eds), Princeton, NJ, Princeton University Press.
Burnyeat, M. F. (1996), 'Enthymeme: Aristotle on the Rationality of Rhetoric', in *Essays on Aristotle's Rhetoric*, A. Rorty (ed.), Berkeley, CA, University of California Press, pp. 88-113.
Cassiodorus, Senator (1937), *Institutiones*, R. Mynors (ed.), Oxford, Oxford University Press.
Cicero, Marcus Tullius (1942), *De Oratore*, H. Rackham (ed.), Cambridge, MA, Harvard University Press.
Cicero, Marcus Tullius (1949), *De Inventione*, H. M. Hubbell (ed.), Cambridge, MA, Harvard University Press.
Cicero, Marcus Tullius (2003), *Topica*, T. Reinhardt (ed.), Cambridge, Cambridge University Press.
Ebbesen, S. (1981), *Commentators and Commentaries on Aristotle's Sophistici Elenchi*, Leiden, Brill.
Etchmenendy, J. (1990), *The Concept of Logical Consequence*, Cambridge, MA, Harvard University Press.
Green-Pedersen, N. J. (1984), *The Tradition of the Topics in the Middle Ages*, München-Wien, Philosophia Verlag.
Grimaldi, W. (1972), 'Studies In The Philosophy of Aristotle's Rhetoric', in *Hermes, Zeitschrift Für Klassische Philologie*, Heft 25. Wiesbaden, Franz Steiner Verlag.
John of Salisbury, J. (1991), *Metalogicon*, J. B. Hall (ed.), Turnhout, Brepols.
Martin, C. J. (1991), 'The Logic of Negation in Boethius', *Phronesis* 36, pp. 277-304.
Martin, C. J. (2004), 'Logic', in *The Cambridge Companion to Abaelard*, J. Brower and K. Guilfoy (eds), Cambridge, Cambridge University Press, pp. 158-99.
Martin, C. J. (2009), 'The Development of Abaelard's Theory of Topical Inference', in *Les lieux de l'argumentation: Histoire du syllogisme topique d'Aristote à Leibniz*, J. Biard and F. Mariani Zini (eds), Turnhout, Brepols, pp. 249-70.
Martin, C. J. (2010), 'They Had Added Not a Single Tiny Proposition' The Reception of the Prior Analytics in the First Half of the Twelfth Century', *Vivarium* 48, pp. 159-92.
Minio-Paluello, L. (1954), 'Note sull'Aristotele Latino Medievale', *Rivista di Filosofia Neo-Scolastica* 46, pp. 211-31.
Quintilian (2001), *Institutio Oratoria*, D. A. Russell (ed. and trans.), Cambridge, MA, Harvard University Press, Loeb Classical Library.
Slomkowski, P. (1997), *Aristotles Topics*, Leiden, Brill.

Steinkrüger, P. (2015), 'Aristotle's Assertoric Syllogistic and Modern Relevance Logic', *Synthese* 192, pp. 1413–44.
Stump, E. (1974), 'Boethius's Works on the Topics', *Vivarium* 12, pp. 77–93.
Ward, J. O. (2018), *Classical Rhetoric in the Middle Ages*, Leiden, Brill.

4

The logic of enthymemes as (incomplete) syllogisms

Thirteenth-century theories and practices

Julie Brumberg-Chaumont

4.1 Introduction

A study of enthymemes as (incomplete) syllogisms focuses on logical analysis, which is only one aspect of rhetorical arguments. It also takes into account the nature of rhetorical premises only in so far as it has an impact on the logical structure of the argument. As a consequence, the enquiry here proposed does not touch rhetoric at large, including theories of passions and characters, 'non-technical' means of persuasion or connections with law, ethics and politics, not to speak of forms of 'applied' rhetoric in the Middle Ages (*ars dictaminis, ars predicandi, ars poetica, ars orandi*).[1]

In the aftermath of the full recovery of the two *Analytics*, and before the marginalization of syllogisms as just one type of formal consequence during the fourteenth century, thirteenth-century logic was a 'golden age' for syllogistic as well as for the general value bestowed on syllogistic form.[2] This context was bound to bring a wealth of reflections about the syllogistic nature of enthymemes.

The history of enthymemes during the thirteenth century divides in two periods. In a first one, Aristotle's *Rhetoric* was only very partially known, as deplored by Roger Bacon,[3] through Hermannus Alemannus's translation, composed before 1256. An important step was then the full university reception of the *Prior Analytics* (and, to a lesser extent for the topic at hand, of the *Posterior Analytics* and of the *Topics*), from the 1240s, which complemented the earlier reception of the *Sophistici Elenchi* and of works from the Boethian/Ciceronian tradition. In a second period, after 1269, the translation prepared by William of Moerbeke began to circulate,[4] with a first commentary redacted by Giles of Rome in 1272/1273.

As is well known, the traditional theory of enthymeme, inherited from Alexander of Aphrodisias and from late ancient commentators,[5] was adopted by Arabic logicians and transmitted to the Latin word mainly by Boethius[6] (it was also present in Quintilian[7]). It defined the enthymeme as an incomplete syllogism, but a would-be syllogism, because it reducible to a syllogism by supplying the missing premise. This interpretation does not fit Aristotle's actual doctrine, as shown by Miles Burnyeat.[8] The twelfth-century theory that describes topical inferences as enthymematic, imperfect inferences, to be warranted, or perfected, by topics, as opposed to syllogisms, originally designed by Abelard, did not play a major role. Many thirteenth-century logicians indeed thought that topics were warrant also for syllogisms, and even, for some topics, for scientific syllogisms, following Boethius's approach.[9] Apart from their being incomplete syllogisms, standard qualifications of enthymemes were generally recorded, especially their connection to civil science, their bearing on particulars circumstances (i.e. on *hypothesis*) as opposed to dialectical reasoning (focused on *thesis*), their using mere plausible premises, the cognitive state they produce, an inferior type of opinion (often labelled *fides* or *suspicio*) – with opinion corresponding to dialectic – and their goal, persuasion. The reflection on the logic of enthymeme was enriched by elements stemming from the *Sophistici Elenchi* and, later on, in a much significant manner, from the *Prior Analytics*, as well as from logical theories inherited from Arabic authors. Alhough the newly recovered *Rhetoric* offered some divergent ideas, especially the notion that only *some* enthymemes have a missing premise, these new elements were not necessarily recognized as such.

If we look at actual logical practices, in addition to logical theories, we realize that the same period witnessed a systematic syllogistic reconstruction for incompletely expressed syllogisms in commentaries on Aristotle. This practice was sometimes justified by the fact that the proposition has not been formulated by the Philosopher (Aristotle) because it was 'self-evident (*patet/manifesta de se*)'. This aspect of syllogistic practices has not yet been taken into account when reflecting on the non-rhetorical uses of enthymemes, as theorized by Latin mediaeval masters. The latter were faced, as they saw it, with a repeated abbreviation practice of syllogisms from the part of Aristotle. This practice may be called 'enthymematic', even if masters of the time did not call it so, for reasons that we will try to make clear in this contribution. They completed everywhere abbreviated syllogisms by adding the missing premise, in order for their students to better follow the demonstration. This 'syllogistic-exegetical' practice was just one aspect of the general 'syllogization' of Aristotle's text, where implicitly syllogistic arguments were made explicit and often described in a metalogical way. This practice, also observed in biblical commentaries, was even recognized by Thomas Aquinas as a trademark of 'philosophers'.[10]

One difficulty raised by the traditional definition of the enthymeme as an incomplete syllogism is that one does not immediately see how a negative property could account for the argumentative virtue of the enthymeme, especially if its incompleteness is quite immaterial, since it can be easily fixed by adding the unformulated premise. The virtues of brevity do not seem enough to do the job. Another issue, even more puzzling, is the idea that most enthymemes (at least in rhetoric) are not from a necessary sign so that they cannot be syllogized (*Rhetoric* I, 2), or can only be reduced to second- and third-figure invalid arguments that are not syllogisms (*Prior Analytics* II, 27). Some of them are even described as a fallacy of the accident (*Rhetoric* II, 24; *Sophistici Elenchi* 5). As a consequence, the question raised by Miles Burnyeat is the following:

> We would like to know under what conditions it is appropriate for a speaker to advance, and for the audience to accept, a sign argument that is deductively invalid. The only answer we get from the *Rhetoric* is: when it is convincing.[11]

The solution adopted by Arabic logicians meant that the enthymeme only belongs to rhetoric, that is, necessarily has a hidden (not just unformulated) premise in order to be 'persuasive', and that it is essentially an incorrect argument (unsound or invalid). As we shall see, this approach was not adopted by thirteenth-century Latin masters. In the same manner as for the 'long *Organon*',[12] the different approaches are probably not due only to the fact that Arabic texts and doctrines were poorly transmitted, but also to a series of in-depth cultural and intellectual differences. We can especially mention the value still bestowed on rhetoric in the Latin context, even if the traditional discipline was challenged in the new university system of education. In addition, we find in the Latin tradition the idea that the examples of invalid arguments offered by Aristotle in *Prior Analytics* II, 27 were just 'examples' (as already formulated by Ps-Philoponus). This analysis combines with the full recognition of a use of enthymemes outside rhetoric, in dialectical and scientific argumentation, be they necessary-sign enthymemes (illustrated at the end of the *Prior Analytics* with physiognomy) or abbreviated syllogisms composed with *per se* propositions, as formulated by Boethius with paradigmatic examples in the *De differentiis topicis*, or as found formulated by Aristotle himself.

The questions this chapter aims at addressing are the following: how this incompleteness is to be understood in each of the two cases we have come to distinguish, that is, in enthymemes and in understated, abbreviated Aristotelian syllogisms? What is the relationship between the latter and scientific enthymemes, enthymemes from a necessary sign? What does the idea of enthymematic syllogistic incompleteness reveal about mediaeval views on syllogistic form? Did access to the full text of Aristotle's *Rhetoric* make a difference, or not?

After a survey of some major topics in the theory of the enthymeme in the Aristotelian tradition, as well as a brief description of mediaeval 'enthymematic' exegetical practices, the chapter focuses on the discussions conducted by Robert Kilwardby, a master who was extremely influential on thirteenth-century syllogistic theories (and beyond).[13] His views on the logic of enthymeme are mainly read in the *De ortu scientiarum*[14] and in his commentary on the *Prior Analytics*, with a look taken at the commentary on the *Sophistici Elenchi* ascribed to him, without certainty. The last part of the chapter consists in a preliminary study of Giles of Rome's commentary on the *Rhetoric*, where the interest for the syllogistic dimension of enthymemes fades away. John of Jandun's commentary on the *Rhetoric* is very briefly evoked in the conclusion.

4.2 Enthymemes as (imperfect) syllogisms: Theories and practices

4.2.1 The logic of enthymeme: an overview of the sources

In the context of the Latin mediaeval history of enthymeme, we observe a first period, when a variety of sources was employed to think about enthymemes, with a major authority represented by Boethius's *De differentiis topicis* IV. The discussion mainly runs there on the relationship between rhetoric and dialectic; enthymemes are defined as incomplete syllogisms. The *Sophistici Elenchi*, already widely read since the second half of the twelfth century, also contained the idea that some enthymemes from a sign would be paralogisms stemming from a fallacy of the accident (chapter 5, 167b8–11), a type of enthymeme also described as an argument 'from adjuncts (*ex adiunctis*)'. The 'Topic from adjunct' is the name of the Ciceronian topic listed by Boethius in *De differentiis topicis* 1198A, a topic connected with the topic of consequent and antecedent (1200B) and identified with the Themistean topic of the 'associated accidents' (*locus a communiter accidentibus*) by Boethius in the *De differentiis topicis* (1190 B). The example offered by the *Sophistici Elenchi* is a typically enthymematic one, that is, when one wants to show that a man is an adulterer because he is fancily dressed or wanders around at night.[15] As reminded by Marmo and Bellucci,[16] this example was split into two by Philoponus, followed by Michael of Ephesus (from 'being fancily dressed' to 'being an adulterer' and from 'wandering around at night' to 'being a theft'). The example of the theft, instead of the Aristotle's adulterer, is recorded for the first time in the *Dialectica monacensis*, a terminist logical treatise from the 1220s. The same example was also taken by Aristotle to illustrate sophistic enthymemes from the fallacy of the consequent in *Rhetoric* II, 24, 1401b20–25.[17] It resembles the one taken by Aristotle in *Prior Analytics* II, 27, for an enthymeme reducible to second-figure invalid arguments (from 'being pale' to 'having given birth'). Marmo and Bellucci have shown that the example of the adulterer/theft was introduced by some thirteenth-century logicians when reflecting on the difference between the fallacy of the accident and the topics 'from adjuncts' or 'from associated accidents', which are not supposed to be fallacious topics.[18]

Even if used before, Aristotle's very important chapter on enthymemes in the *Prior Analytics* (II, 27) was systematically commented only from the 1240s, with Robert Kilwardby's very influential commentary. Aristotle's text contained crucial ideas, such as the classification of enthymemes (from a sign, from a proof (*tekmerion*), from a likelihood) and the reduction of the sole enthymeme from a proof to a first-figure syllogism, the others being reduced to invalid third- and second-figure non-syllogistic arguments. The very beginning of the *Posterior Analytics*, systematically commented upon also from the 1240s, contained a designation of the enthymeme as a 'syllogism' (*Posterior Analytics* 71a11).

Some authors, such as Albert the Great, knew of Alfarabi's commentary on the *Rhetoric* in a fragmentary form, the *Didascalia in Rhetoricam Aristotelis ex Glosa Alpharabi*,[19] translated by Hermannus Allemannus – a text quoted also by Giles of Rome.

A new idea was introduced by Arabic logic, namely the 'long *Organon*', where rhetoric would represent the penultimate part of logic (poetics being the last one) and based upon a type of syllogism. Various sources transmitted this doctrine to the Latin world, some of them as early as the end of the twelfth century, especially al-Fārābī's *De scientiis*, translated by Gerard of Cremone. This was adapted by Dominicus Gundissalinus and recycled in his *De divisione philosophie*, which greatly contributed to popularize Alfarabi's and Avicenna's ideas. It was also transmitted later on, by Algazhali's *Logica*, also translated by Dominicus Gundissalinus.[20] Although only very partially received, this new theory was obviously bound to strengthen the emphasis put on the logical dimension of rhetorical argumentation.[21] It met some previous elements developed in the Latin tradition. These included the strong emphasis put on the relationships between rhetoric and dialectic as developed by Boethius in the *De differentiis topicis* IV, as well as a new type of logical unity bestowed on the arts of the *Trivium*. This took different forms. The *Trivium* as a whole indeed came to be called 'logic' by Hugh of Saint Victor in the *Didascalicon*[22] and it was discussed within the general framework of Roman-Latin versions of a long *Organon*, where the different parts of argumentation were not 'material variations' of the syllogism, as they are in the Arabic version of the long *Organon*.[23] The effects of this complex history can be observed in Dominicus Gundissalinus's *De divisione philosophie* (where rhetoric and poetic appears twice, as parts of the *Trivium* and as parts of logic, within a long *Organon*). They are still felt, during the thirteenth century, in Robert Kilwardby's works and, notoriously, in Albert the Great's logic, where the five last parts of the *Organon* are not variations of the very same syllogistic form, but five different types of argumentation. A non-syllogistically based division of the long *Organon* was also read in Thomas Aquinas.[24] As far as *Rhetoric* was concerned, the Latin reception shows that, in a context where the exact philosophical content of Arabic doctrines was poorly transmitted and met different cultural standards, the enthymemes was conceived not just as a material variation of the very same syllogistic form. When the idea of a 'rhetorical syllogism' was indeed considered (for instance under the influence of *Prior Analytics* II, 23), it was not taken seriously enough as to adopting a syllogistic division of logic that would really include rhetoric.

Aristotle's *Rhetoric* shared many conclusions with other previously read logical treatises, especially the *Prior Analytics* II, 27 (classification of enthymemes from a sign/likelihood/proof; reduction of enthymemes from non-necessary signs to non-syllogistic arguments)[25] and the *Sophistici Elenchi* 5 (about the rhetorical fallacy of the consequent).

It nevertheless contained ideas which slightly departed from those conveyed in previously circulated traditions. One could read in the *Rhetoric* the suggestion that any discipline, sciences included, may use means of persuasion of which rhetoric gives a general theory alone (1355b27 *sqq*.). We also find the constant and repeated designation of the enthymeme as the rhetorical *syllogism* (1356b5 *sqq*., for instance)[26]; and a rhetorical 'demonstration' (1355a35, 1356a 7) *per excellentiam* (1355a5–10; 1356b20–5) with respect to the example (the other rhetorical argument). The beginning of the treatise says that the study of the enthymeme as a 'sort of syllogism' (*syllogismus quidam*) is the task of 'dialectic' or of 'one of its parts' (often identified to rhetoric in the tradition). This is because only dialectic can know what a syllogism is, and what distinguishes rhetorical syllogisms from 'logical syllogisms (*syllogismi logici*)', and also because what resembles the truth (*simile vero*), or the 'acceptable' (*probabilis*), must be investigated by the same one who investigates truth (1355a10–15).[27]

One important, utterly divergent element, however, was Aristotle's idea that *some* rhetorical syllogisms only have a missing premise, that is, when the premise is well known and can be filled up easily (1357a15–22). This is because, generally speaking, the audience of rhetorical discourse is made of common people who are not capable of taking a general point of view and of following a multi-step reasoning (1357a1–5; 1395b22–32). This claim clearly departs from the traditional view, where *all* enthymemes are defined as incomplete syllogisms. The same goes for the peculiarities of the definition of the syllogism (1356b15–20), with the absence of the necessity clause (if compared to the definitions in the *Topics* and in the *Prior Analytics*), and the notion that the conclusion can result from the premises universally (*universaliter*) but also 'for the most part' (*ut de pluribus*), which suggests an attenuation of the necessity of the consequence, as pointed out by Burnyeat.[28] Yet these discrepancies were not necessarily recognized as such when the full text of the *Rhetoric* was recovered, as we shall see with Giles of Rome's commentary.

Important also was the notion that necessary premises could enter rhetorical syllogisms, although they seldom do (1357a27–35), and that some enthymemes, composed from necessary signs, are irrefutable and provide a proof (*tekmerion /progidium*).[29] This idea was previously found in *Prior Analytics* II, 27,[30] with the qualification, however, that this type of enthymemes 'wants to (*vult*) be a demonstration (*demonstrativa propositio*).'[31] Indeed, in *Posterior Analytics* I, 6 75a28–37, syllogisms from signs (*per signa syllogismi*) are said to be not demonstrations, or, at least, not demonstrations in the strict sense of a demonstration *propter quid*.[32] Admittedly, as shown by Marmo and Bellucci,[33] we observe a rather superficial treatment of sign demonstrations in the Latin tradition of the *Posterior Analytics* (as opposed to the Greek and Arabic ones), while enthymemes are not mentioned in this context by Aristotle. Yet the notion that enthymemes can provide a scientific demonstration, although in a weaker sense, could be reinforced by a connection established between necessary-sign demonstrations and demonstration *quia* (from the effect), as well as by the often use by commentators on the *Posterior Analytics* of a typically enthymematic example for necessary-sign demonstrations, namely the 'lactating woman' example, as found in *Rhetoric* 1357b16 and in *Prior analytics* 70a15.[34]

4.2.2 Enthymemes as imperfect syllogisms

As seen, the traditional theory of enthymemes was that the enthymeme is an incomplete syllogism but a would-be syllogism because it is reducible to a syllogism by supplying the missing premise. According to Burnyeat, the theory implies that the two operations which consist respectively in being completed for an enthymeme and being perfected for a syllogism in the second and the third figures are more or less assimilated. The perfection/completion process would apply to both cases, as operations internal to already-syllogistic arguments,[35] as opposed to the reduction of inductions, examples, abductions and objections in *Prior Analytics* II, 23–6, which are not syllogisms despite their being reducible to syllogisms. As we shall see later, a criticism of a homogeneous sense of 'perfection' in both cases is offered by Robert Kilwardby in a line of argument (about conversions being identified to enthymemes) that he eventually rejects: this could indicate that he may have accepted this homogeneous sense, which indeed matches his general views about enthymemes.

The chapter dedicated to the enthymeme in the *Prior Analytics* (II, 27) could be read as conveying the notion that the enthymeme from a sign or a likelihood has a missing premise, since it has a sign instead of the proposition with a middle term: the connection between the extremes operated by the middle term in the added proposition of the syllogism would be signified in a 'sub-propositional way' by the sign as a middle term of the enthymeme, or in a 'propositional way' by the single premise of the enthymeme, depending of the interpretation of Aristotle's text one follows.

The idea that the premise is not formulated because it is obvious is applied only to the enthymeme in the third figure by Aristotle (70a19), but it is most of the time generalized by commentators to first-figure enthymemes. This goes in the direction of the definition of enthymemes as incomplete syllogisms, notwithstanding the fact that the reading 'incomplete' (*ateles*), the one present in the version of Aristotle's text read by Philoponus, was not present in Boethius's Latin text transmitted to the Middle Ages. The definition of enthymemes as 'incomplete (*ateles*) syllogisms from a likelihood or a sign' (70a10) in *Prior Analytics* II, 27 was the reading printed in the Aldine edition in 1495, in accordance to a eleventh-century manuscript (C) close to the text read by Philoponus and some Greek commentators, with some consequences on Renaissance thought. But this was not the authentic version, nor the one translated into Latin by Boethius.[36]

Burnyeat has convincingly shown that the traditional doctrine is not that of Aristotle: the enthymeme, rather than being defined as an incomplete syllogism, that is, as a 'kind of syllogism', just distinguished by the fact that one premise is missing and that the premise is from a likelihood or a sign, is a 'syllogisms of a kind', with an attenuation of the necessity of the consequence, as indicated by the different version of the definition of the syllogism read in *Rhetoric* 1356b15–20.[37]

Some aspects of Burnyeat's reflection about Aristotle's authentic theory of the enthymeme were not available at all to thirteenth-century commentators. This was the case for the systematic comparison with the full text of the *Rhetoric* (not read before the 1270s). The now widely-accepted hypothesis about the chronology of Aristotle's logical works was also unknown. This framework is used in standard scholarship in order to give credit to the idea that there is a non-specialized sense of 'syllogism' (= 'deduction') used in treatises composed before the *Prior Analytics*, a non-technical sense that survived aside the technical one, after the 'discovery' of the 'syllogism' in 'a strict sense', that is, the sense of the syllogistic formulas (*schemata*).[38] On the contrary, for Latin mediaeval masters, *syllogismus* meant everywhere the same and this was just 'syllogism'. There was no 'syllogism of a kind', not to speak of an argument with non-necessarily obtained conclusion which would be a syllogism all the same.

Nonetheless, one aspect of Burnyeat's interpretation was not entirely absent, namely the idea that canonical figures and moods described by the *Prior Analytics* are not included in the very definition of the syllogism, but represent only the formula against which any valid argument can be measured.[39] Most Latin commentators did make figures and moods enter the definition of the syllogism, although they did not agree on the exact part of the definition corresponding to the description of the form of the syllogism and they sometimes offered an exegesis where, in fact, there was none.[40] But many of them did not consider that moods and figures were the only elements contained in the syllogistic form, nor did they think that the presence of a correct syllogistic combination was enough to obtain a syllogistic form, or that the absence of this combination was enough to deny that a given argument had a syllogistic form:

this was precisely the point which allowed incomplete syllogisms to be syllogisms all the same. The adoption of moods and figures in the description of syllogistic form was often done in such a way that a distinction was still possible between 'in-mood', that is, syllogistically arranged (*modificati*) syllogisms, and non-in-mood syllogisms (*immodificati*).[41] In addition, the existence of 'in-mood' arguments which were not syllogisms (as fallacious Barbaras) was generally recognized.[42] The same goes for 'syllogizable' arguments, that is, syllogisms that are only potentially so, with a distinction between being a syllogism 'according to reality', 'according to reason' and 'according to the vocal sound', as we shall see when studying Robert Kilwardby's discussion of the problem. The whole approach means that a non-formalistic understanding syllogistic form is observed, despite an in-depth reflection on the distinction between the form and the matter of syllogisms.

4.2.3 Enthymemes based upon 'invalid syllogisms(?)'

If enthymemes are incomplete syllogisms, the pending question is about enthymemes being fully syllogistic or being 'invalid syllogisms', if we may say. As shown by Burnyeat, Greek commentators such as Alexander and Ammonius, when faced with some elements of the definition of the syllogism potentially at odds with the nature of the enthymeme (like a plurality of premises, and the conclusion being necessarily obtained without the need for an extra term), tried to find a way to save enthymemes as syllogisms, provided the missing premise is added.[43] A similar strategy is followed by Latin commentators, as we shall see when studying Robert Kilwardby.

Far more tricky is the idea that enthymemes from non-necessary signs, or from a likelihood, are not 'syllogizable', as stated in the *Rhetoric*, I, 2, 1357b5–6, where figures are not alluded to,[44] or are reducible to invalid combinations in the second and in the third figure, as asserted in *Prior Analytics* II, 27. How can this view go along with the *Prior Analytics*'s theory about the reduction of all enthymemes into syllogisms as their logical grounding, clearly announced by Aristotle in chapter 23? The text in chapter 27 seems to lead to paradoxically admit as syllogisms 'completed enthymemes' following a non-useful combination in the third and second figures. The two arguments given as an example ('Pittacus is a learned man, Pittacus is wise, learned men are wise',[45] 'women having given birth are pale, this woman is pale, this woman has given birth') are explicitly said to be respectively 'not a syllogism according to the thing at hand 70a32-33 (*ad rem syllogismus*)' and 'not a syllogism with terms having such relationship, 70a35-36 (*numquam fit syllogismus sic se habentibus terminis*)'.[46] The same type of argument as the one taken for the second figure (from 'wandering around by night' or/and 'being fancily dressed' to 'being an adulterer') is even described as a fallacy of the consequent in the *Rhetoric* II, 24 and in the *Sophistici Elenchi* 5, as previously seen.

While the notion of a fallacy of the consequent may well explain how the argument can be persuasive and apparently conclusive, even if it is really inconclusive – especially for the untrained, general public – it does not explain how the ability of this type of enthymemes to produce a 'belief' (*fides*) would be grounded generally in its being reducible to a syllogism, as contended by Aristotle in the introduction of the last section of the *Prior Analytics* (II, 23, 68b8–15), if this very 'syllogism' is invalid.

As reminded by Burnyeat, Ps-Philoponus (Philoponus for Burnyeat) tries to attenuate the signification of Aristotle's examples in *Prior Analytics* II, 27,[47] saying that those are precisely just examples, in order to save enthymemes as incomplete syllogisms but would-be syllogistic, valid arguments.[48] The doctrine adopted by Arabic logicians, despite its being inspired by Greek commentators, differently avoided the problem since it accepted and even defined, for many cases, enthymemes as 'invalid syllogisms' in the second and in the third figure.[49] A superficial reading of Latin commentators on the *Prior Analytics* from the thirteenth century such as Robert Kilwardby could give the impression that they do not really address the problem. As we shall see later (Section 4.3.2.2), this impression comes from the fact that Robert Kilwardby just straightforwardly admits that there are indeed various valid enthymemes based upon syllogisms in the three figures, beyond the two Aristotelian examples of invalid arguments, which are just 'examples' (*exempla*). It also comes from the fact that he would never consider to admit that these examples of enthymemes could be grounded on 'invalid syllogisms'. Contrary to Giles of Rome, who is more careless on this account, he is keen on never calling these second- and third-figure invalid arguments 'syllogisms'.

4.2.4 The theory of the hidden premise

Important in this context is the idea conveyed by the Arabic tradition that the missing premise is hidden, not only for sake of elegance or because ordinary people are reluctant (or even suspicious) about multi-step reasoning, but also because the falsity of the hidden premise[50] or the invalidity of the whole argument might be exposed if the missing premise was to be articulated explicitly.[51] The general application of this principle presupposes that every enthymeme in rhetoric is an unsound argument, at best, and, at worse, an incorrect syllogism. If the enthymeme being a truncated syllogism could be considered by some interpreters as incidental to its logical definition as a reasoning – since one can always just add the understated premise – the *hiding* of one premise can only be essential to its definition as an argument, that is, as dedicated to the production of a special kind of cognitive state, persuasion. If one adds the missing premise, it makes explicit the syllogistic form and matter according to which the conclusion is supposed to be obtained in the enthymematic reasoning, but it necessarily destroys its argumentative force, since it makes clear how the truth of conclusion is only apparently obtained, either because the added premise is false or because the reasoning is not valid.

The technicalities of the Arabic theory of rhetorical syllogisms, in the same manner of those of long *Organon*, were only very partially transmitted to the Latin Middle Ages. They were missing from general presentations such as the *Logica Algazali* (where the enthymeme is not even listed among types of argumentations). Not surprisingly, they were not articulated as such in Alfarabi's *Disdascalia*, since the latter consists only of a general introduction and a gloss on the first sentence of

Aristotle's tract, corresponding to the beginning of Alfarabi's long commentary. The only element of this theory Latin masters could read in this text was the notion that enthymemes are always deficient: either because the propositions are necessary and true, but the combination is inconclusive, or because the combination is correct, but the propositions are 'contingent' (by which Alfarabi may have meant that none of them is a true universal proposition, but as-of-now true propositions), or because both the propositions are contingent and the combination is incorrect.[52]

Some additional hints may have permeated through the late Greek commentators' channel. The idea of a strong motivation for the concealment of one proposition is clearly conveyed by the 'Florentine gloss', a marginal gloss transmitted together with one Latin translation of the *Prior Analytics*, a gloss much influenced by Philoponus's commentary and known to the Latin world. About *Prior Analytics* 70a19 (one premise is not expressed because it is obvious in an enthymeme in the third figure), the glossator says:

> The wise men omit the major proposition because [the proposition] is obvious; the rhetorician, because [the proposition] is false; and this is to be taken in the first and in the third figures (*maiorem propositionem omittunt sapientes quidem eo quod palam sit; rhetor eo quod falsa; et est accipiendum hoc in prima et in tertia figura*).[53]

The gloss cannot really apply to Aristotle's example of an enthymeme reducible to a third-figure argument, since the missing premise is not in this case the major, but the minor (70a19–20): the omitted premise is 'Pittacus is wise', since it is well known (Pittacus being one of the seven sages of Greece). The gloss is thus meant as a different, larger explanation, dealing with cases not mentioned by Aristotle, that is, enthymemes corresponding to the first and the third figure where the major is missing. It can be either so because it is obvious (and true) or because it is false.

The idea of a 'hidden (*occultus*)' premise is mentioned by Albert the Great but without much comment.[54] But the exact example of an enthymeme in the first figure where the major, being false, is not articulated on purpose is offered by Robert Kilwardby who, in the same manner as in the Florentine gloss, envisaged other kinds of enthymemes than the three ones listed by Aristotle.

4.2.5 Non-rhetorical incomplete syllogisms and non-rhetorical enthymemes: The role of abbreviated syllogisms and Boethius's paradigmatic examples of enthymemes

In addition to explaining the rhetorical motivation for omitting a premise in enthymemes, or, at least in some of them, the Florentine gloss suggests that syllogisms with omitted premises can be used by learned people (*sapientes*), namely when the proposition is obvious (and, supposedly, true): this would be a non-rhetorical use of one-premise arguments. The text read in the gloss does not allow us to say if the commentator would have called those incomplete syllogisms enthymemes or not.

Clearly conveyed by Alfarabi in the *Kitab Al-Hataba* was also the notion that not every syllogism with a missing premise is an enthymeme. According to Alfarabi, a premise can be omitted in proofs or in dialectical syllogisms used in exchanges or in letters, either for sake of brevity or because it is very obvious. The author clearly denies that those incomplete syllogisms are enthymemes.[55] The reason for this is that they can indifferently be completed, whereas the addition of the missing premise is always destructive of the persuasion aimed at in the enthymemes of rhetoric. This means that a distinction is drawn between, on the one hand, non-enthymematic incomplete syllogisms and, on the other hand, enthymematic incomplete syllogisms, namely those found in rhetoric.

Latin mediaeval commentators do admit that some enthymemes, at least those from necessary signs, called *progidia* in Latin, are used by scientists. A distinction was drawn in the Latin tradition, between, on the one hand, non-rhetorical, dialectically and scientifically useful enthymematic arguments, where incompletely expressed scientific syllogisms could be fitted in, and, on the other hand, rhetorical enthymematic arguments. This idea could be reinforced when some mediaeval commentators came to apply what Aristotle says about the example of the third figure, that is, that the premise being omitted because it is obvious (Pittacus being obviously wise), to the *progidium*, with reconstructed syllogisms in the first figures.

The idea of scientific enthymemes was probably extended to cases of enthymemes that were not from a sign, be it necessary. This was precisely the case in the paradigmatic example given by Boethius. In addition to the definition of the enthymeme as an imperfect syllogism, Boethius's presentations in the *De Ciceronis topica* and in the *De differentiis topicis* indeed contain two important elements. The first one is the designation of 'brevity' and 'direct acquaintance' with the thing at hand (*brevitas, notitia*) as two motivations for not formulating the premise.[56] The second one, of crucial importance here, is the choice of an example of enthymeme ('homo animal est, substantia igitur est') turned into a syllogism by an added premise ('omne animal est substantia'), where every proposition is universal *per se* and has nothing to do with arguments from a sign, be it necessary, such as the lactating women:

> 'Man is an animal, therefore it is a substance (*homo animal est, substantia igitur est*)',
> with the missing premise:
> 'Every animal is a substance (*omne animal est substantia*)'.[57]

This example is all the more significant that the completed syllogism is the same (except for the universal quantification of the minor and the conclusion) as the one taken for a paradigmatic example of a syllogism just above, at the beginning of the treatise, book II (1183B):

> Every man is an animal, every animal is a substance, every man is a substance (*Omnis homo animal est, omne animal substantia est, omnis homo substantia est*).

The enthymeme appears in this context as an abbreviated syllogism where every proposition can be universal *per se*, entirely disconnected from the issue of signs (like the lactating women for the women having given birth). The same type of example appears, for instance, in a text by 'Master Simon' (Simon of Faversham?, c. 1280) when giving an example of an enthymeme in his commentary on Peter of Spain's *Tractatus* V, 3 (on topics). The missing premise is made of a genus predicated of a species, as in the source of the treatise commented upon (itself based upon the *De differentiis topicis*). After having recalled that the enthymeme is an incomplete and diminished (*deminitus*) syllogism, he says:

> In every enthymeme, a proposition is kept (*retinetur*) in mind: either the minor, like in 'man is an animal, therefore Socrates is an animal', or the major, as in 'every man is an animal, therefore every man is a substance'. Here what is kept is 'every animal is a substance'.[58]

The enthymeme appears as an abbreviated syllogism where every proposition can be universal *per se* and have nothing to do with signs. The method for completing the enthymeme, by fitting the missing premise as a major or as minor in order to have a first-figure argument, is exactly the one described by Robert Kilwardby in his commentary on the *Prior Analytics* (see Section 4.3.3), and it is here explicitly applied to *per se*, essential propositions.[59] This view is obviously very different from the Farabian position.

This approach suggests that scientific reasoning could include arguments that are enthymemes just in the sense they are truncated syllogisms (whether from a sign or not), and that their being syllogistically expanded would make no difference, at worse, or would even be beneficial, for the sake of transparency, at best. This type of enthymemes probably included not fully expressed Aristotelian syllogisms, as reconstructed by mediaeval commentators, in the Aistotelian corpus, some of them from genus and species as in the example given by Boethius, because the missing premise is 'obvious'.

These enthymemes would not be from only 'acceptable (*probablis*)' premises but from true and necessary premises, although, being obvious, they must also be in a way 'acceptable'. The next question is then: to whom are they obvious or by whom are they acceptable? The answer may well be that they are obvious to the communicational community envisaged when reading Aristotle's scientific texts. This was the community of learned, university men, all trained following a similar Aristotelian curriculum, whether at the Faculty of Arts (for secular masters and for religious masters entered in the Orders after university studies) or in Mendicant *studia* (in schools of logic and in schools of philosophy), for Mendicant students, who were not allowed to follow classes at the Faculties of Arts.[60] The missing propositions would be obvious because they are part of what we would today called 'normal science', that is, the Aristotelian paradigm in the Middle Ages, a paradigm that was still unchallenged during the thirteenth century.

This sense of being 'acceptable', that is, as part of normal science, was indeed clearly included in Aristotle's *Topics*, when the text talks about the items widely accepted in sciences and arts, as repeated several times in the treatise, speaking of the opinion (*doxa*) 'according to sciences and arts' (*Topics* I, 10, 103b15).[61] In the same treatise, we also find the notion that an argument can be manifest (*dèlos*) in the sense that 'some strongly admitted [premises] are missing' (*Topics* VIII, 11, 162b1–2). This passage will be explained by Robert Kilwardby saying that the missing premise is not really missing 'according to reason', even though it is missing 'according to the vocal sound', as we shall see later (Section 4.3.2.1).

This approach to the problem of enthymeme may have been reinforced by the current logical practices in the exegesis of Aristotle's text, where not a single demonstrative syllogism was formulated. Non-syllogistic Aristotelian arguments were read as abbreviated syllogisms, and the first task of a university commentator from the 1230s was to constantly complete the would-be syllogistic argument with the missing part(s) of the syllogism, generally one premise. Contrary to the Arabic tradition, these non-rhetorical abbreviated syllogisms could well have been considered as enthymemes, even though the identification, if strongly suggested, is not spelled out as such.

4.2.6 'Enthymematic' practices of syllogisms in mediaeval exegesis: Syllogizing Aristotle

As is well known, there is not a single syllogism formulated according to the correct figures and moods defined in the *Prior Analytics* in Aristotle's works. This created important debates among Aristotelian scholars, on systematic and chronological grounds.[62]

During the Middle Ages, especially in the thirteenth century, this absence should have been considered as highly problematic, since the syllogism was deemed as the argument *per excellentiam*, while logic was considered as the instrument of knowledge in every discipline, including itself. In the same period, every university discipline came to be reconstructed as a science according to the standards of the *Posterior Analytics*. This concerned not only parts of philosophy such as physics, metaphysics or psychology but also ancient disciplines that were not previously described as sciences, like grammar, as illustrated by the theories of the Modists, but also theology, as notoriously contended by Thomas Aquinas. As for logic, it was newly described as a science, in addition to an art, a rational science which was its own underlying logic.

The absence of syllogisms was, however, considered as utterly unproblematic: syllogisms just have to be spelled out where they had been understated by Aristotle. The commentators may have been encouraged in this way by the fact that some reasoning announced as a 'syllogism' by Aristotle did not look at all like a syllogism, at least according to the criteria of the *Prior Analytics*.[63] Even though the idea was not formulated in this way in our texts, we can say that the Philosopher was ascribed an 'enthymematic practice' of syllogisms and proofs: most of the time, the commentators say that Aristotle abbreviated the syllogism because the understated premise was 'self-evident' (*patet/manifesta de se*). Teachers in the Faculty of Arts, whether bachelors or masters, when offering the literal commentary of which consisted the afternoon university classes known as *lectio cursiva*, spent a great energy in reconstructing every syllogism, and sometimes a chain of syllogisms and pro-syllogisms. As shown by John Murdoch, the practice is likely to have been introduced by the discovery of Averroes's commentaries,[64] where such reconstructions abound. It was developed at an immoderate level by Latin masters.[65]

The syllogization of Aristotle's texts was not only operated, but it was also metalogically designated,[66] with terms such as 'premise', 'conclusion', 'major' and so on, as was already the case in Averroes.[67] The phenomenon is utterly systematic, observed almost at every page, in the commentaries composed during the 1240s by Adam of Bockenfield, the first important Master of Arts at the University of Oxford, much influenced by Averroes. Unformulated premises are also often filled in.[68] It can also be observed in works by Robert Kilwardby. His logical commentaries offer, in the recursive manner he has precisely theorized,[69] a syllogistically reconstructed theory of the syllogism and of its parts. The practice is massively read, for instance, in his commentary on the *Categories* and, to a lesser extent, in his commentaries on the *Posterior* and the *Prior Analytics*.[70]

The practice of syllogistic reconstitutions with an unformulated premise can even be observed when Robert Kilwardby recursively defines the enthymeme. We can read in Aristotle's *Prior Analytics*, according to Robert Kilwardby, an abbreviated demonstration about the likelihood from which some enthymemes are composed, and the commentator is keen on reconstructing syllogistically the whole argument. This example shows that the missing part of the syllogism is not always one premise: there can be two missing premises, with only the middle term expressed. In the very definition of the likelihood (*ikos*), as distinguished from the sign, Aristotle shows enthymematically that the likelihood in an enthymeme is an acceptable (*probabilis*) proposition. The philosopher just gives the middle term, without formulating any complete premise at all. Commenting on Aristotle's saying:

> The likelihood is an acceptable proposition [= the conclusion]. What we know to be the case or not be the case, or to or not to be for the most part (*ut in pluribus*), this is the likelihood, *Prior Analytics* 70a3–5.

Robert Kilwardby reconstructs the syllogism as follows:

> What we know to be the case or not be the case, or to or not to be for the most part is acceptable,
>
> but the likelihood is a proposition by which we know something to be the case or not be the case, or to or not to be for the most part,
>
> then the likelihood is an acceptable proposition.

And he comments:

> He [Aristotle] only gives the middle term of this reasoning (*medium huius rationis tantum ponit*) and then gives an example.[71]

As we shall see later (Section 4.3.3), Robert Kilwardby follows here the exact method he will describe in the following pages of his commentary, where he gives a general method for the reduction of enthymemes into syllogisms, second and third figures included (as opposed to the invalid examples given by Aristotle for the third and the second figures). This is done by reconstructing the correct, true missing premise, placing it at the right place, for the necessary inference of a conclusion already known as true (since stemming from Aristotle's authority) to be obtained.

4.3 Robert Kilwardby on enthymemes

Robert Kilwardby's views on enthymemes can mainly be read in the *De ortu scientiarum*, where a general approach is displayed, and in his commentary on the *Prior Analytics* where, following Aristotle, a more technical analysis is offered. The commentary on the *Sophistici Elenchi* ascribed to Robert Kilwardby, without certainty, is just alluded to in this section.

4.3.1 The *De ortu scientiarum*
4.3.1.1 *Rhetoric, logic and enthymemes*
Rhetoric is dealt with inside the general discussion about the sciences of language (*scientiae sermocinales*), especially in chapter 49. Rhetoric is there defined as an 'inquisitive' science of language; it is a part of civil science, bearing on a question which is a hypothesis (i.e. with particular circumstances), and it depends on the universal topics taught by dialectic.[72] Previously, in chapter 46, logic, whether demonstrative or dialectical logic, has been contrasted with rhetoric as another inquisitive, rational science; all of them have been distinguished from grammar, which is not inquisitive.[73]

The section on the definition of logic (from chapter 53), distinct from grammar and rhetoric, says that 'logic' in one sense of the term (which is equivocal) signifies 'science of language': it then includes rhetoric. This is a reference to Hugh of Saint Victor's sense of logic as identical to the *Trivium*[74] we have already seen. In a strict sense, logic does not include rhetoric according to Robert Kilwardby.[75] The section also asserts that the form to be followed in reasoning (*forma ratiocinandi*) is taught in the *Prior Analytics*, and that it applies to demonstrative, dialectical and rhetorical arts, wherever the production of 'belief' (*fides*) (here in a larger sense than *fides* as a cognitive state inferior to opinion, which is sometimes also labelled *suspicio*) is at stake, following Aristotle's *Prior Analytics* 'on induction' (i.e. *Prior Analytics* II, 23, 68b9–13).[76] But the form is adapted to logical reasoning (including demonstrative and dialectical reasoning) by the 'philosopher' who discusses 'thesis' and adapted to the rhetorician, who deals with 'hypothesis'.[77]

In the case of dialectical and scientific reasoning, it is clearly asserted that the form is the same and that matter only varies, although a 'matter' in a more 'simple' sense (i.e. the matter of the syllogism *simpliciter*, terms and propositions regardless of their semantic content) is common to both. It is also the case for sophistic syllogisms, at least for those in which the matter only is defective, the form being syllogistic.[78] But rhetorical syllogisms are not mentioned in this context. Further on, in chapter 60, as we shall see later, Robert Kilwardby suggests that also in the case of syllogisms when used by rhetoricians, the form is the same.

The whole series of the chapters on logic is not meant as a division of the *Organon*, since sophistic appears way after rhetoric, according to the order of the arts in the *Trivium*. In chapter 53 (§509), the author says that the books of dialectic and demonstrative logic, namely the *Prior Analytics*, the *Posterior Analytics* and the *Topics*, offer a complete teaching of logic,[79] a judgement later qualified, when the necessity of sophistic is recognized,[80] but rhetoric, not being part of logic in a strict sense, is not mentioned.

Rhetoric is approached more specifically in three chapters inside the *De ortu scientiarum* (chapters 59–61). In chapter 59, the sources mentioned in the discussion are Boethius, Dominicus Gundissalinus, Cicero, Isidorus and Hugh of Saint Victor. It defines rhetoric as 'a reasoning science of language',[81] as previously done. It connects rhetoric with political questions, as opposed to philosophical questions, dealt with by logic.[82] Its instrument is rhetorical reasoning (*ratiocinatio rhetorica*), as distinct from demonstration, the instrument for the scientist (*demonstrator*). The end of the chapters insists on the role of persuasion.[83]

Chapter 60 faces some possible objections. It distinguishes between rhetoric as a science, theoretical rhetoric, whose 'subject' (the object, in modern parlance) is 'dialectical reasoning' (*ratiocinatio dialectica*), of which the rhetorician is in charge, and rhetoric as an art, as an adjuvant (*adminiculatur*), a practical rhetoric conducted by the orator whose 'subject' is the political question (*quaestio civilis*).[84] Drawing on a parallelism between rhetoric and dialectic, it explains that, in the same manner as dialectical syllogism as a whole (*totus syllogismus dialecticus*) is conducted by discovery (*inventio*) and judgement (*iudicium*), rhetorical discourse (*oratio*) is conducted through its five parts (*inventio, dispositio, elocutio, memoria, pronuntiatio*). Again, in the same manner as dialectic deals with every kind of problem following the very same method, through discovery and judgement, rhetoric deals with its three causes or three species – deliberative, judicial and epideictic (*demonstrativus* in Latin) – according to its five parts.[85] The quoted authorities are Boethius and Ps-Cicero ('Tullius', for the *Rherorica ad Herenium*). Even if not mentioned, Robert Kilwardby probably took the distinction between theoretical and practical rhetoric from Dominicus Gundissalinus's division of logic into theoretical and practical logic,[86] to which a distinction between the 'logician' (*logicus*) and the 'disputant' (*disputator*) corresponds: in the same manner as for rhetoricians and orators, according to Robert Kilwardby, logicians and disputants sometimes do coincide, sometimes they do not.

Chapter 61 focuses on the relationships between logic and rhetoric, which are both reasoning sciences. Only there does Robert Kilwardby engage into a robust discussion on the logic of enthymemes. The four questions raised by the author are crucial for the topic here at hand. They are: (1) Why does not rhetoric teach the logical form in an unqualified sense (*simpliciter*) as does logic? (2) The same for demonstration (this will be entirely neglected here). (3) Why is rhetoric not distinguished according to four problems as dialectic is, since both start from acceptable premises? What are the relationships between rhetoric and dialectic? (this will also be neglected here). (4) Why is judgement part of logic and not of rhetoric and, conversely, why are *dispositio, elocutio, memoria* and *pronunciatio* parts of rhetoric and not of logic?

The answer to question 1 is very important. The different points articulated can appear as somewhat incoherent, at least if we suppose that an enthymeme is a special syllogism but a syllogism all the same; as a consequence, they tend to suggest that enthymemes are not really or not fully syllogisms. Robert Kilwardby gives three reasons why rhetoric is not interested in the form of the syllogism: (1) because the form of the syllogism is common to necessary and acceptable premises (i.e. the one from which rhetoric also starts); (2) because the orator is happy with the brevity (*brevitas*) of the enthymemes (whereas the dialectician uses 'perfect' syllogisms), following Boethius (*De differentiis topicis* IV, 1206C); and (3) because the rhetorician teaches to argue from conjectural propositions (*ex conjecturis*) so that it is not his best interest to formulate universal propositions (which are necessary in order to form a syllogism), since they are bound to be false and even 'maybe non-acceptable' (*forte improbabilis*). Here the example is:

Because he wanders around by night, then he is a theft (*quia circuit de nocte, ideo sit fur*).[87]

The rhetorician should not formulate the universal premise 'everyone who wanders around by night is a theft', lest he would expose the weakness of the argument, since the proposition is false (it is false because it is not because you wander around at night that you are a theft, but the other way around). As already mentioned, we have a similar example, but with an adulterer (who is also identified by 'being fancily dressed', in addition to wandering around by night), in *Rhet.* II, 24, 1041b24, for a sophistic enthymeme, and in *Sophistici Elenchi* 167b 8–10, for the fallacy of the consequent, with the 'Philoponian' subdivision of the example in 'being a theft' (identified by 'wandering around by night') and 'being an adulterer' (identified by 'being fancily dressed'). We shall return to this example in the next paragraph.

The last remark of the text goes back to the first reason: when the rhetorician uses syllogisms, the form, which applied 'to every matter and to every science', is taught by the *Prior Analytics* and has nothing special to do with rhetoric.[88] The answer to question 1 is unclear about the logical nature of enthymemes. Are they variations for the very same syllogistic form described in the *Prior Analytics*? Are they imperfect syllogisms, with a missing premise the rhetorician should not express for sake of persuasion, but syllogisms all the same? Are they *sui generis* arguments? Are they syllogisms that are so imperfect that they can hardly be called so?

The same ambiguity lies in the answer to question 2, where the enthymeme is described again as distinct from 'perfect syllogisms' used in dialectic.[89]

The answer to question 4 explains that judgement is not a part of rhetoric. It is so not because the opponent and the respondent (namely the plaintiff (*actor*) and the defendant (*reus*), since juridical uses of rhetoric are mainly considered here) would not judge the arguments put forward by the adversary, but because the act of judgement is performed by a third party, namely the judge, and according to another discipline than rhetoric, namely civil law and canon law. On the contrary, judgement belongs to logical disputations, whether demonstrative or dialectical, because the judgement to which both the respondent and the opponent stick to is the judgement of the opponent, for scientific disputations, or the judgement of the respondent for dialectical disputations.[90] The issue is also dealt with in Robert Kilwardby's commentary on the *Prior Analytics*, where the answer here offered, based on the judgement being performed by the judge, is deemed insufficient, as we shall see later in the chapter.

The logic of enthymeme described in the *De ortu scientiarum* is quite rich but not entirely clear about the syllogistic nature of enthymemes. It echoes the traditional theory that enthymemes are incomplete syllogisms, but would-be syllogism by supplying the missing. Yet we don't know if they are or not just variations of the same syllogistic form. The work is sensitive to a sense of 'logic' where rhetoric could be included, as a 'rational inquisitive science', and it goes as far as giving to theoretical rhetoric 'dialectical reasoning' as its object. However, rhetoric is clearly separated from a coupled formed by dialectic and demonstrative logics, while the premises from which rhetorical argument starts are distinguished from those of dialectic by their being not only 'acceptable' but also often 'false' and even sometimes 'not-acceptable (*improbabilis*)'. This feature suggests that 'brevity', mentioned just earlier, is not enough to account for the functioning of enthymeme as truncated syllogisms. It suggests that the Arabic idea of an on-purpose, hidden premise has permeated, maybe through the Florentine gloss, while the notion of a scientific use of non-rhetorical enthymemes, clearly emphasized in the commentary on the *Prior Analytics*, is absent from de *De ortu scientiarum*.

4.3.1.2 Enthymeme as reducible to first-figure syllogisms with a false premise, second-figure invalid/fallacious arguments (Prior Analytics/Sophistici Elenchi) and second-figure non-fallacious invalid scientific arguments (the 'Caeneus argument')

The example taken in the answer to question 1 is very significant. Robert Kilwardby uses a perfectly all-right syllogism in the first figure, similar to a Darii syllogism (one universal proposition, two particular propositions, all three affirmative):

> Everyone who wanders around by night is a theft,
> He wanders around by night
> He is a theft.[91]

This example is given in order to syllogistically 'complete' the enthymeme, but the major is just false. On the face of it, this example of syllogism is identical to none of the three cases envisaged by Aristotle in *Prior Analytics* II, 27: an enthymeme from a necessary sign, corresponding to a syllogism in the first figure with one necessary true premise; an enthymeme from a probable sign, which can be reduced to an invalid argument in the third figure with two singular premises and an indefinite conclusion; an enthymeme from an acceptable sign which is reduced to an inconclusive argument in the second figure. The possibility of an example of the type taken in the *De ortu scientiarum* is envisaged in the *Prior Analytics*, however, since, for the enthymeme reducible to the first figure, Aristotle says that the conclusion is irrefutably obtained *provided that the major proposition is true* (70a30), a condition also articulated in the *Rhetoric* when necessary-sign enthymemes are described (1357b15–20). Indeed, we have seen that the Florentine gloss envisaged a rhetorical enthymeme in the first figure whose unformulated major premise would be false (see Section 4.2.3).

As seen, the *De ortu scientiarum* example of a theft stems from the transformation of the example of the *Sophistici Elenchi* 5 by splitting the properties, 'wandering around by night' and 'being fancily dressed', and by matching them respectively with 'being a theft' and 'being an adulterer'. The relationships between the properties involved additionally resembles those implied in the example of the invalid argument in the second figure, in the *Prior Analytics* II, 27. The enthymeme is: 'this woman is pale, so she has given birth', and it corresponds to a syllogism with 'woman' as a minor term, 'having given birth' as a major term and 'being pale' as middle term in predicate position in both affirmative premises, arranged in a second-figure combination, a combination which always constitutes an inconclusive argument:

> Whoever has given birth is pale
> She is pale
> Therefore she has given birth.[92]

In the example, both premises are true (or supposedly so): 'a woman who has given birth is pale' and 'this woman is pale'; the conclusion ('this woman has given birth') can be true or false, but if true, this would not result from the truth of the premises. What Aristotle does not say, but is generally articulated by commentators, is that this syllogism is not only inconclusive but also fallacious. This is explained by Robert Kilwardby in own commentary on the *Prior Analytics*, as we shall see later. More precisely, it was considered as a fallacy of the consequent, as explicitly said by Albert the Great[93] and very probably thought by Robert Kilwardby.

The connection among the examples in the *De ortu scientiarum*, the *Sophistici Elenchi* and the *Prior Analytics* for enthymeme in the second figure, can also be made on the basis of the commentary on the *Sophistici Elenchi* ascribed, without certainty, to Robert Kilwardby. In this text, the example of a fallacy of the consequent which corresponds to a rhetorical enthymeme (whose terms are 'being fancily dress' and 'being an adulterer', and with 'wandering around by night' and 'being a theft'), when reformulated into a 'pseudo-syllogistic' paralogism with two premises and a conclusion, does not contain as an added major a fallacious proposition, as underlined by Marmo and Bellucci. It rather contains a true[94] proposition, namely 'a theft is wandering around at night', but within a non-useful combination in the second figure, exactly as in the case of *Prior Analytics* II, 27 (but with 'being pale' and 'having given birth'):

> If someone is an adulterer, he is fancily dressed, but this one is fancily dressed, therefore he is an adulterer [. . .] If someone is a theft, he wanders around by night, but this one wanders around by night, therefore he is a theft (*si aliquis est adulterer, ipse est comptus, sed iste est comptus, ergo iste est adulterer* [. . .] *Si aliquis est fur, est errabundus de nocte, sed iste est errabundus de nocte, ergo est fur*).[95]

We can therefore only suppose that it is fallacious because it appears as convertible into a first-figure syllogism by conversion of the major, where the major would be false: we would then obtain the exact example taken in the *De ortu scientiarum* with 'everyone wandering around at night is a theft'.

A further element in this direction is contained in the answer to a third doubt, about the topic associated to the subject (*ex adiunctis*), in the same passage of the commentary on the *Sophistici Elenchi*. The dialectical topic '*ex adiunctis*', the one described by Cicero and Themistius, obtains when a 'proper sign' is used, as is the *progidium* in the first figure (the terms being 'having milk', 'woman' and 'having given birth'),[96] with convertibility. On the contrary, a fallacy of the consequent is obtained with 'common signs'. The extension of these common signs is greater than that which they signify (like with 'being pale' in relation to 'having given birth') and this leads to invalid arguments in the second figure, as detailed in the *Prior Analytics*.[97] If common signs are associated with other signs, however (so that circumstances are taken into account), they can provide a correct argument in rhetorical context, that is, if, in addition to 'being pale', one takes other indices in order to convince that the woman has given birth.[98]

The reason why the invalid second-figure argument in *Prior Analytics* II, 27 (or in the *Sophistici Elenchi* 5 according to the commentary ascribed to Robert Kilwardby) would be sophistic, in addition to using a non-useful combination, is indeed quite tricky. As seen, it cannot be fallacious because the two terms of the major proposition ('Whoever having given birth is pale') would be only apparently convertible in such a way that the major proposition would be false, while its converse ('Whoever is pale has given birth') would be true, since it is the actual proposition of the sophistic syllogism which is true and the converse which is false.

The only reason why it can be described as fallacious is the following: supposing fallaciously that the two terms of the major proposition were convertible, then the whole invalid, second-figure argument with a true major could be turned into a perfect first-figure syllogism, by converting the major premise: 'a pale woman is a woman who has given birth, this woman is pale, so she has given birth'. In this case, the major premise of the valid syllogism obtained by conversion is false, and this is exactly the equivalent of the case taken as an example in the *De ortu scientiarum*. This means that when the middle term of the corresponding syllogism for a given type of enthymeme does not convert with the major term (or at least is not smaller that the major), you can either formulate a first-figure syllogism with a false major, which you should hide, as explained in the *De ortu scientiarum*, in order not to expose its falsity, or formulate an invalid second-figure argument with a converse true major, the major of which, again, you should hide, in order to conceal the fact that the argument is inconclusive. The argument can only, at best, be unsound and fallacious, although valid, in the first case, that is, if the major is replaced by its convert in a first-figure syllogism, playing on the apparent convertibility of terms thanks to a fallacy of the consequent. The only available combination left, that would be both sound and valid, namely 'a theft wanders around by night, he is a theft, therefore he wanders around by night', is useless since it takes as a premise ('he is a theft') the unestablished fact one wants to prove, or what is signified, instead of the sign.

By connecting the first-figure example in the *De ortu scientiarum* with the second-figure case in the *Prior Analytics* II, 27, we can see that an additional case is designed by Robert Kilwardby, with respect to the three cases listed in the *Prior Analytics*, that is, the case of a rhetorical enthymeme in the first figure where the non-formulation of the major premise is motivated by its falsity. The connection also helps understanding how the 'belief' (*fides*) in the enthymeme in the second figure could be grounded on the syllogism, as contended by Aristotle in *Prior Analytics* II, 23, despite the fact that the argument obtained by addition of a premise is just invalid. The enthymeme's being convincing thanks to its apparent syllogistic reduction is derived from the fallaciously presupposed convertibility of the terms in the major premise so that the second-figure syllogism would be itself grounded on the first-figure syllogism obtained by conversion of the major premise. The argument given by Aristotle in *Prior Analytics* II, 27 would be just a case of a fallacious enthymeme.

Understood in this way, we can analyse the second-figure invalid, fallacious argument of *Prior Analytics* II, 27 as a sort of 'not-even materially convertible into a valid argument' fallacy, as opposed to another case of invalid second-figure argument given by Aristotle in the *Posterior Analytics*, namely the 'Caeneus argument'. It is a second-figure argument with two affirmative premises so that it follows a useless combination, as in the case of the 'pale woman' argument in *Prior Analytics* II, 27. But the difference is that it can be reduced into a Barbara syllogism thanks to its matters, that is, because the terms of the major proposition do convert.[99] This example was indeed the one taken by Alexander of Aphrodisias in order to reject the idea that arguments without a formally obtained conclusion, but with a materially necessarily obtained conclusion would be syllogistic, under the sole justification that the middle term and the major term do convert.[100] At the turn of the twelfth century, the 'Caeneus argument' was typically the example taken by some Latin logicians in order to illustrate the case of formally defective arguments, when dealing with the classification of materially or formally defective arguments in commentaries on the *Sophistici Elenchi*.[101] The 'pale woman' argument in *Prior Analytics* II, 27 would then be both materially and formally defective, so a 'twice sophistic' version of the Caeneus argument, because following a non-useful combination only apparently reducible to a useful one by converting the terms. On the contrary, the 'Caeneus' argument is formally defective, but contains really convertible terms. When converted, the 'pale woman argument' just yields a false major.

This explanation is, however, just a likely reconstruction, since it is not articulated as such in our texts. Nothing significant is found on this topic in the commentary by Robert Kilwardby on the *Posterior Analytics* 78a1–2.[102] But Albert the Great provides an explanation that shows, once again, how a non-formalistic view is taken by many mediaeval logicians on syllogistic form. He says that, because of the scientific context, where major and middle terms convert (as opposed to dialectical context where no such thing can be presupposed), the Caeneus argument shows that one can demonstrate without syllogizing (according to the form defined in the *Prior Analytics*), or that one can syllogize 'thanks to the matter (*gratia materiae*)' (because of the convertibility of terms), although not according to the authorized figures and moods of the *Prior Analytics*. Even if not spelled out in this way by Albert, the explanation given when justifying how the Caeneus's argument does demonstrate consists in reformulating the argument in the corresponding first-figure syllogism by converting the terms of the major proposition. Albert says that Caeneus has syllogized (*sic syllogizavit*), for the major, in the following way: 'quidquid in multiplicata analogia se habet ad alterum, citius generatur' (where 'citus generatur' is the subject so that it yields a second-figure invalid argument). He further says that he should form the syllogism (*formandum est syllogismum*) with, for the major, 'velocis est generationis, quod in multiplicata analogia se habet ad alterum' (where 'velocis est generationis' is the predicate so that you get a first-figure syllogism). The Caeneus argument does syllogize, although it does not immediately seem to do so (*tamen non videtur*), if judged against the syllogistic form of the *Prior Analytics*[103] – as opposed to the 'pale woman' argument, which is 'really apparently' a syllogism (we would add).

4.3.2 The commentary on the *Prior Analytics*

4.3.2.1 *The enthymeme before book II, chapter 27*

Before turning to the specific treatment of the enthymeme in book II, chapter 27, some important clues are offered at the beginning of the commentary.

One of them comes from the prologue, where the division of logic according to invention and discovery is dealt with. A question is then raised, namely why it is so that judgement is not covered by rhetoric, a question also asked in the *De ortu scientiarum*, as just seen. The answer put forward by the latter, namely that the judgement is not performed by one of the adversaries, but by the judge, is deemed here insufficient.[104] The final answer consists in dividing judgement. On the one hand, there is a judgement focused on the 'figure' of the argument, a topic that transcends rhetoric and any science that proceeds by specialized disputation (*scientia disputans specialiter*): this is treated by logic or, more specifically, by the *Prior Analytics*. On the other hand, we have the judgement focused on the 'mood' of the argument, which is also of no concern for rhetoric, since the latter does not use arguments 'put in mood (*modificati*)', which are endowed with 'necessity', but 'enthymemes and signs, which produce inclination (*suspicio*)'.[105] Rhetoric is obviously not considered as a part of logic.

This solution means that for a syllogism to be put in figure (*figuratus*) and to be put in mood (*modificatus*) are not exactly put on the same plane. This is confirmed by the analysis of enthymemes as reducible to syllogisms when commenting on *Prior Analytics* II, 27. No premise is quantified in the examples given by Robert Kilwardby. This is not admitted for syllogisms strictly speaking, but it does not prevent at least the enthymeme in the first figure to be judged as a 'syllogism' all the same. The distinction could be reinforced by the fact that, more generally, in the beginning of the whole section, at *Prior Analytics* II, 23, Aristotle says that every argument (induction, example, abduction, objection, enthymeme) is reducible to syllogisms according to the 'three figures', without mentioning the mood.

The enthymeme is also dealt with when the definition of the syllogism is commented upon, according to three different interpretations. In a first one, the part of the definition saying that the conclusion is obtained necessarily 'from some things (*quibusdam*, *Prior Analytics* 24b18)'[106] is put in the definition in order to exclude enthymemes (because of the plural : it needs more than one premise). In the second interpretation, the definition of the syllogism is meant to target the syllogism as it can perfect all other types of argumentations (e.g. induction, enthymeme) so that the latter are not excluded.[107] Robert Kilwardby seems to accept, at least as a provisory position, both interpretations since he explicitly rejects only a third one, where every sophistic syllogism would be rejected by the definition of the syllogism. On the contrary, he makes it clear in that only the paralogisms from 'begging the question' and from 'the non-cause as a cause' are excluded by the definition,[108] all eleven other fallacies being fallacious, but syllogisms all the same, that is, not formally defective arguments.[109]

A puzzling fact is that neither Robert Kilwardby nor any of the previous commentators to which he alludes to seemed to have considered the option of rejecting the enthymeme because of that part of the definition in the syllogism which says 'because these [= the premises] are the case (*eo quae hec sunt*, *Prior Analytics* 24b19–21)': it is meant, according to Aristotle, to exclude an argument that would need an extra term in order to necessarily obtain the conclusion (*nullius extrinsecus termini indigere ut fiat necessarium*, 24b20–2). Rather, this portion of the definition is meant by Robert Kilwardby to exclude the fallacy of the 'non-cause as a cause' as a formally defective argument, because a non-useful (but apparently useful) premise is added to the already posited two premises: the non-redundancy clause is not respected.[110] Robert Kilwardby rather insists on the plural of the previously mentioned portion of the definition ('*quibusdam*'), which means that more than one premise is needed[111] – a defect that can be fixed in the case of the enthymeme by formulating the understated premise.

This means that, in addition to often displaying a non-formalistic understanding of syllogistic form, as previously seen, many mediaeval commentators saw the definition of the syllogism as not absolutely excluding one-premise arguments and as not absolutely excluding unexpressed premises. This is a clearly different position from the one defended by many contemporary scholars, as recently emphasized by Ana Maria Mora-Márquez, when dealing with mediaeval views on the definition of the syllogism in the *Topics* and with dialectical syllogisms as fully fledged syllogisms.[112]

Enthymemes are also analysed when the possibility of identifying conversions with enthymemes is considered. For a conversion to be identified with an enthymeme, which has three terms in the same manner as a syllogism, one would have to use a distinction between having terms 'in reality' (*secundum rem*) and having three terms 'according to reason' (*secundum rationem*): the conversion would have three terms according to reason, even though it has only two terms in reality, by reduplicating one of the two terms, in the same manner as in syllogisms from opposites.[113] In addition, in order to avoid circularity (the conversion is perfected by the syllogism while some syllogisms (not in the first figure) are perfected by conversion), one would have to distinguish between 'perfection of the necessity' for the enthymeme/conversion and 'perfection of the evidence' for the second- and third-figure syllogisms, which are perfected through conversion.[114] This solution can be judged unconvincing, according to Robert Kilwardby, because the conversion would need to have the perfection of the evidence in order to cause it in the perfected syllogism. But the master rejects this objection, saying that the conversion does not need to have the perfection of the evidence in order to communicate it to the perfected syllogism, but it can have something on a higher modality (*excellentiori modo*), in the same manner as the sun does not have to have heat as its essence to be the cause of heat on earth. Unfortunately, Kilwardby's reflection leaves open the option that enthymemes would share with second- and third-figure syllogisms the 'perfection of the consequence', but, as previously emphasized with Burnyeat (see Section 4.2.2), one would have to admit this theory if one wants to defend the idea that enthymemes and syllogisms are 'substantially' the same, as Robert Kilwardby will do later, commenting on *Prior Analytics* II, 27.

The whole argument of the conversion is eventually rejected as 'difficult': starting from a conversion to be perfected by a syllogism and ending with the conversion that perfects the syllogism, we would have a syllogism where the premises and the conclusion are identical.[115] Robert Kilwardby offers a 'safer' solution, where the conversion is a 'consequence' (*consequentia*) from one thing to another. It is not an argument but a property of terms.[116] This means that there is a clear-cut general difference between two types of consequences and that a syllogism is a consequence which is always an argument. The consequence-argument, being always reducible to a syllogism, as any kind of arguments, always involves three terms 'according to reality' or 'according to reason', with two premises and a conclusion different from the premises; the consequence from one thing to another which is not an argument; the conversion is in fact a consequence of one thing to itself in a different way (*eiusdem cum se ipso alterato*).[117]

The enthymeme is again under scrutiny when the possibility of having a one-premise argument is considered. What Aristotle says in *Prior Analytics* 34a16, namely that out of one (premise) nothing is necessarily obtained, seems to be false according to the commentator, since the enthymeme is a concluding argument, and the same goes for many arguments called 'topical inferences' where, from a topic and a maximal proposition, one conclusion is obtained necessarily from one premise.[118] Aristotle also says in the *Topics* VIII, 12 (162b1–2), as seen earlier, that a conclusion can be necessarily obtained if something is missing (i.e. if a very widely admitted premise is missing). Robert Kilwardby answers that there always must be a middle term and so two premises according to the two relationships the middle term has to each of the extremes. But one has to distinguish between premises 'according to reason (*prout sunt apud rationem*)' and 'according to discourse (*apud sermonem*)', a distinction which comes in addition to the one between terms 'according to reality' and 'according to reason', developed in the question related to conversion. The necessity of the consequence needs two premises according to reason, but the latter do not need to be expressed 'through a vocal sound (*per vocem*)', which is just a variation for 'according to the discourse': the other premise just needs to be obviously (*manifeste*) 'under-thought' (*subintellegitur*) by the speaker as well as by the hearer.[119] The concepts here at hand are mobilized again when commenting on book II, chapter 27, where a reference to this question is made.[120]

4.3.2.2 The theory of enthymeme in book II, chapter 27

Chapter 27 is the last chapter of a whole section begun in chapter 23. It is dedicated to various types of arguments, and Aristotle wants to show that not only dialectical and demonstrative syllogisms, but also rhetorical syllogisms and any belief (*fides*) in whatever art are produced according to the three previously studied figures (68b10–14).

As seen, the enthymeme is defined by Aristotle as 'a syllogism from a likelihood (*ikos*), or from a sign'. The enthymeme is then distinguished according to the three figures, two of them being from one acceptable premise, the first one from a necessary sign. In the latter case, the enthymeme is necessary, infallible: it can be reduced to a syllogism in the first figure where the connection between the middle term and the extremes is necessary, if the added premise is indeed true (*si vera sit propositio*). Here a syllogism similar to a Darii combination (with singular propositions) is given as an example by Robert Kilwardby. The sign is then a 'proof' (*progidium*). The sign can be acceptable and not infallible, if the middle term insufficiently connects the extremes, as a syllogism in the third figure with two affirmative singular propositions as premises and an indefinite conclusion: that Pittacus is a learned man and that Pittacus is wise, it does not follow that learned men are wise, although it can be the case. When the middle term is in the predicate position in both premises and each is affirmative, we always get an invalid argument in the second figure.

The first type of arguments dealt with in chapter 23 was induction. According to Robert Kilwardby, induction is considered in the *Prior Analytics* (as distinguished from the *Topics*, where it is considered not as 'in-figure') according to its being 'in-figure' (*figurata*) and 'in-mood' (*modificata*), because it is 'put in the definition of the act of syllogizing'.[121] Indeed, the syllogistic reconstruction of an induction gives as an example a Barbara syllogism.

This comes in contrast with the examples given for the enthymemes, where no proposition is correctly quantified. As already underlined, this is coherent with what the author had said in the prologue, namely that rhetorical syllogisms are 'in-figure' but not 'in-mood'. Even for the enthymeme from a necessary sign, transformed into a first-figure syllogism, we have the following example, where only the major premise is universal, the two other being singular, since with pronouns:

Every lactating woman has given birth
This [woman] is lactating
Therefore, she has given birth.[122]

Robert Kilwardby says that Aristotle in chapter 27 first shows the 'substance' of the enthymeme, then he shows the ways to discover 'the sign, which is the middle term in enthymeme', by which the commentator means the end of the chapter dedicated to physiognomic signs.[123] As specified when this topic will be dealt with, physiognomic signs are all *progidia*, necessary signs.[124]

Aristotle says only about the third figure that one premise is not expressed because it is obvious (70a19), namely that Pittacus is wise, but Robert Kilwardby considers that this applies to each case offered by Aristotle as examples in the first and in the third figure.[125] He makes Aristotle saying that the enthymeme is from a sign and has only one premise, whereas the syllogism in each figure is obtained by the formulation of the 'other (*altera*) proposition', commenting on *Prior Analytics* 70a25. He draws from this the idea that what is a sign in the enthymeme is the middle term in the corresponding syllogism.

He then announces Aristotle's 'examples (*exempla*)'. As we shall see later, those are really only examples for the commentator.

The example for the enthymeme in the first figure is one where the sign, or the middle, is convertible with the major term; in the example for the third figure, it is smaller (*minus*) with respect to the major, and in the second figure it is larger (*in plus*). Robert Kilwardby explicitly says that the 'enthymeme in the second figure' is 'sophistic'.[126]. The example is the 'pale woman argument':

> Whoever has given birth is pale
> This [one] is pale
> [She] has given birth.[127]

The commentator does not explain why it is fallacious. As seen when dealing with the example given in chapter 61 of the *De ortu scientiarum*, the major premise of this argument is true and its converse is false. As a consequence, it cannot be the case that it is fallacious because it fallaciously asserts the major. It is fallacious because it is formally defective (with two affirmative premises in the second figure) while it could appear as correct if the two terms of the major proposition were fallaciously considered as convertible: then the argument could be equivalent to a first-figure syllogism, but this time with a false major premise, as in the example of the *De ortu scientiarum*. As already mentioned, commenting on the same passage and following Robert Kilwardby's text, Albert the Great explicitly says that this argument contains a fallacy of the consequent:[128] it is fallaciously based upon the idea that it could be an equivalent to a correct argument, similar to Barbara syllogism, because of the apparent convertibility of the major and the middle term. We have suggested that the 'pale woman argument' being fallacious could be interpreted as the 'twice fallacious version' of the Caeneus argument, that is, an argument that is not even materially concluding by conversion of the terms, so that the example given by Aristotle would illustrate sophistic enthymemes. Beyond this example, there are non-sophistic rhetorical enthymemes and even non-rhetorical enthymemes.

4.3.3 Robert Kilwardby on the art of reducing enthymemes into syllogisms and on the art of discovering enthymemes

In the series of doubts, the author explains the reason why the enthymeme is rightfully dealt with in a treatise normally dedicated to the syllogism *simpliciter*, regardless of the different matters to which the latter applies: this is because the enthymeme is in itself 'common' to dialectical and demonstrative logicians. Enthymemes from necessary signs are used by demonstrative logicians, whereas enthymemes from acceptable premises are used by dialecticians and rhetoricians.[129] This means that rhetorical enthymemes are just one type of enthymemes.

This point is enlightened by the next doubt, which is concerned with the art of reducing every enthymeme of whatever figure into a syllogism. Here the reduction, by adding a premise, is done in a systematic way, depending on the subject/predicate position of the three terms in the original enthymeme, regardless of the middle term (or the sign) being convertible, larger or smaller than the major. On the contrary, it is clearly asserted that the premise should be formulated according to the 'possibility of the terms' and according to the 'inherence'. At least on one occasion, Robert Kilwardby even says that the addition of the premise must be done so that the latter (in this case, the added minor) would be 'true' (*secundum quod possunt facere minorem veram*).[130] This presupposes that we must fill up enthymemes so that a true conclusion is syllogistically obtained from true premises. When the enthymematic premise and the conclusion share a subject term, then you have to add a premise as a major and you obtain a first-figure syllogism or a second-figure syllogism[131]; if they share the predicate term, then you must add a minor and you obtain a first-figure syllogism or third-figure syllogism[132]; if the shared term is subject in the premise and predicate in the conclusion, you must add a minor and get a second-figure syllogism, if the other way around, you must add a major and you will get a third-figure syllogism.[133]

All these combinations are called 'syllogisms', and the choice between one figure or the other depends clearly on what allows to construct of an argument from true premises to a true conclusion. On the contrary, Robert Kilwardby has been very keen on never calling the two previous Aristotelian examples of invalid arguments 'syllogisms', but 'enthymemes': 'enthymemes from a sign in the second or the third figure'.[134] He has also explained that only in the enthymemes from a necessary sign, a *progidium*, you have a first-figure 'syllogism', as he explicitly calls it. This is because the sign, or middle term, really has the essence of a middle term (*ratio medii*), whereas in the two other cases, the sign does not have the essence of a middle term but that of the extremes (*rationes extremitatum*). Being 'larger' (than the major) or 'smaller' (than the minor), it cannot connect the extremes, since it is not in an intermediary position regarding the things signified by the terms or the extensions of the terms.[135]

The whole argument is confirmed by looking at the second part of the chapter dedicated to enthymemes, namely the 'discovery of the middle term' in physiognomonic, necessary signs (*progidia*). As should be the case in scientific contexts, only syllogisms in the first figure where the middle term converts with the major are considered.[136] Physiognomonic signs are said to be considered here by the logician, not because they are not used in science, since they are used by scientists (*demonstratores*) as much as by dialecticians, but because they are considered in this context in a logical way, that is, within a theory of enthymemes, according to general, second-order, common properties (like convertibility) and not mainly according to the nature of things, their existence and their principles, peculiar to each science.[137]

The last important point of the series of doubts is the comparison between enthymeme and syllogism. Robert Kilwardby makes it clear that they are 'the same substantially (*substantialiter idem*)', and this is because 'according to reality' and 'according to reason', they have not only three terms but also two propositions as premises, and this is enough to be considered a syllogism.[138]

The development about the art of reducing enthymemes into syllogisms has shown that there can be enthymemes turned into real syllogisms in the three figures, provided one chooses the right figure, according to the relationship the middle term does have to the extremes. It has also established that the two invalid arguments in the second and the third figures given by Aristotle are just two examples, connected to a rhetorical use of enthymemes, which represents only a part of the uses of enthymeme. As far as the second-figure enthymemes are concerned, it shows that Aristotle's example is even only a part of the use of enthymemes in rhetorical contexts, namely enthymemes which are only apparently so (and apparently syllogisms): they correspond to the sophistic enthymemes studied in *Rhetoric*. The reason why Robert Kilwardby does not feel compelled to answer the problem represented by some enthymemes that seem to be grounded in 'invalid, syllogistically-arranged arguments' or, worse, 'invalid syllogisms' is that there is no such thing as an 'invalid syllogisms' for him. The examples given by Aristotle are invalid arguments with no ground at all; their being valid or invalid is just judged against the correct arrangement according to the three figures, as for any other argument. In addition, the second-figure enthymeme given as an example is fallaciously grounded on the appearance that it follows a correct, second-figure syllogism or, more fundamentally (if a fallacy of the consequent is indeed understood by Robert Kilwardby, as very probably the case), on the appearance that, through conversion, it could fallaciously be turned into a first-figure syllogism.

The art of reducing enthymeme into syllogisms is based upon enthymemes whose premises and conclusions are supposed to be true so that the missing premise must be placed at the right place (as minor or as major), and with the terms in the right order (as predicate or a subject), in order to obtain an authentic syllogism with two true premises and a true conclusion. This seems to be exactly what mediaeval teachers (masters and bachelors in charge of the *lectio cursiva*) were doing on a regular basis in each class, when commenting the Aristotelian corpus. If we think about Boethius's paradigmatic example of an enthymeme which included *per se*, essential propositions, about the general agreement on the existence of necessary-sign enthymemes, and about the general recognition of a use of these enthymemes in dialectical and scientific contexts, we may be authorized to imagine that mediaeval authors such as Robert Kilwardby would probably have agreed to call these abbreviated non-rhetorical syllogisms 'enthymemes', provided that the premise omitted by Aristotle was 'well known' or 'self-evident' – not to the general public, as in rhetoric, but to the circle of initiated Aristotelian scholars, as was every student and masters at the time.

4.3.4 Enthymemes as syllogisms after *Rhetoric*: Giles of Rome and the wandering logic of enthymemes

Giles of Rome, the author of the first Latin commentary on Aristotle's *Rhetoric*,[139] worked with two Latin translations of Aristotle's treatise, the one from Arabic, the 'other text', and the new translation by William of Moerbeke. We can get an idea of his views on syllogisms, on the fallacy of the consequent or on sign demonstrations by reading his other logical commentaries, on the *Sophistici Elenchi* (1274) and on the *Posterior Analytics* (1285/1291). But we cannot compare his logical analysis of enthymemes as syllogisms with a commentary on the *Prior Analytics*, since the one previously ascribed to him has been now recognized as a work by Robert Kilwardby

– the one precisely studied in the previous section. The commentary on the *Rhetoric* was the first logical commentary he composed, so we cannot count on a systematic, detailed comparison with the enthymemes as dealt with elsewhere, although Aristotle's logical works are often referred to, especially *Prior Analytics* II, 27, which is the basis of the exegesis for *Rhetoric* I, 2.

The details of Giles of Rome's commentary about enthymemes as syllogisms from a sign or a likelihood in the *Rhetoric* have been fully explored in Marmo and Bellucci's forthcoming book on sign demonstrations. His strange interpretation of *Rhetoric* II, 2, where 'likelihood' (*ikos*) refers only to second-figure, invalid arguments, whereas third-figure arguments are from non-necessary signs that do not have a name of their own, probably stems from an anticipation of *Rhetoric* II, 25. As already mentioned, Aristotle distinguishes there four elements out of which enthymeme are composed, namely the example, the likelihood, the proof and the sign, which means that 'sign' is identical with neither likelihood nor proof, contrary to the broad sense of 'sign' read in *Rhetoric* I, 2 and in *Prior Analytics* II, 27.

The logical analysis of enthymemes as syllogisms is essentially contained in the commentary on the two first chapters of the first book of the *Rhetoric*. But the theory remains sketchy and somewhat not fully coherent.

About Aristotle's saying that the enthymeme is a 'sort of syllogism (*syllogismus quidam*) (1355a9)', Giles of Rome seems to understand that it is rather a syllogism 'of a sort', since it is said to be a 'defective syllogism (*defectivus syllogismus*)'.[140] When commenting on the idea that the enthymeme, as a syllogism of a sort, would have to be dealt with by dialectic or by rhetoric, he claims that the enthymeme is dealt with as such by rhetoric, whereas it is dealt with as a defective syllogism by dialectic, this being the task here (*i.e.* in the passage) envisaged by Aristotle.[141] Further on, he says that rhetoric is not properly subalternated to dialectic because what rhetoric properly deals with, namely enthymeme, is dealt with only 'by accident' by dialectic, namely as a defective syllogism.[142] The way of proceeding (*modus procedendi*) is not the same in each case, nor the cognitive state aimed at, that is, 'belief' (*fides*) for rhetoric and opinion for dialectic.

This passage is very important. It makes it clear that the enthymeme being a defective syllogism is incidental to its being the instrument of persuasion and the object of rhetoric. The approach adopted by Giles of Rome means that some enthymemes being reducible to invalid second- and third-figure arguments may not be an impediment to their being efficient rhetorical arguments. Conversely, it may also mean that some enthymemes being perfectly all-right first-figure syllogism could be considered, at least partially, as irrelevant too, as far as rhetoric is properly concerned. This approach is found again on several occasions in the commentary.

When commenting on the definition of the syllogism in *Rhet*. I, 2, 1356b15–20, the author does not emphasize the absence of the necessity clause, if compared to the definitions in the *Prior Analytics* and in the *Topics*. Furthermore, he understands the two possibilities for the conclusion to be obtained (universally/for the most part) to bear on the nature of the premises, not on the nature of the consequence.[143] Because he takes the verb 'turbare'[144] according to its negative meaning, that is, 'disturb', and not 'move', he understands Aristotle's text the other way around: he takes Aristotle to say that the example could be a better means of persuasion (instead of the enthymeme being more apt to move the audience).[145] We might think that this is because examples are shorter, so less demanding for common people (*vulgares*) or maybe easier to catch.[146] The superiority of the enthymeme as the most powerful means of persuasion seems to have been lost.

When commenting on the passage where Aristotle says that 'often' (*saepe*) the enthymeme is built with less premise than the syllogism, because the missing premise can be easily filled in, since well-known – which means that not every enthymeme does so – Giles of Rome just more or less repeats Aristotle's words, adding that this happens sometimes (*aliquando*). He additionally notices that 'from one [premise] nothing follows':[147] as for Robert Kilwardby, who quotes the same sentence, this comes from *Prior Analytics* 34a16. The fact that this passage is utterly at odds with the traditional theory of the enthymeme he endorses elsewhere seems to escape his attention. Maybe the enthymeme being defective or not as a syllogism appears to him as irrelevant, because, as previously established, this feature is incidental to the enthymeme properly considered by rhetoric – though not by dialectic.

The commentary on enthymemes from a sign or a likelihood (*Rhet.* I, 2, 1357a30–b22) is entirely conducted within the framework provided by *Prior Analytics* II, 27.[148] It organizes a tripartite division according to the three syllogistic figures – which are not mentioned in the *Rhetoric*. This is easy to understand since some examples in the *Rhetoric* are either identical to those in the *Prior Analytics*, as the lactating women, or quasi-identical, with 'Socrates' instead of 'Pittacus', or, again, similar, with 'having fever' and 'to be short of breath' instead of 'being pale' and 'having given birth'. Signs and likelihood are, in the same manner as in *Prior Analytics*, contrasted with necessary signs, proofs (*progidia*).[149] Giles of Rome takes 'Pittacus' together with 'Socrates' and introduces the example derived from the *Sophistici Elenchi* 5 and from *Rhetoric* II, 24, namely with 'thief' and 'wandering around by night'. As seen, he offers to call the sign in the second figure a likelihood (*ikos*) and says that the non-necessary sign in the third figure does not have a name of its own, although it admits that, in a broad sense, the latter is included in the likelihood. 'Sign' would only apply to a proof.

The logical theory displayed by Giles of Rome is somewhat incoherent. About signs in the second and in the third figures, he says that, from them, 'a syllogism would be formed (*formetur syllogismum*)',[150] with examples in each case, while, further on, repeating Aristotle's own word, he says that enthymemes from those signs are not syllogizable (*insillogizabilis*). If the premises are true and the conclusion also true, this would not be 'in virtue of the form (*gratia formae*)',[151] that is, the truth of the conclusion would not result from the truth of the premises.

The superficial treatment of the topic of the logic of enthymemes is confirmed by the way the author deals with enthymemes in *Rhetoric* II, 22–25.[152] When commentating on *Rhetoric* II, 22, Giles of Rome actually records Aristotle's words and even says that 'it *sometimes* suffices to argue from one of the premises, if the other is known, so that it is understated'.[153] He adds, about uneducated people being more persuasive than learned men, according to Aristotle, that 'one must not syllogize (*syllogizare*) and investigate what is proper to each topic'. He then uses 'enthymeme' and 'syllogism' as equivalent and deals with the art (*ars*) of finding them.[154] As was the case for the commentary on

Rhet. I, 2, he does not seem to be interested in the fact that the presence of 'sometimes' contradicts the definition of the enthymeme as an incomplete syllogism.

When commenting on the sophistic enthymeme from the fallacy of the consequent (II, 24), it does take as an example an argument which is in the second figure, but with a *conjunction* of signs ('being fancily dressed' *and* 'wandering around by night') as a predicate, as is indeed the case in the original text of *Rhetoric* 1401b20–5[155] (whereas one reads a disjunction in the *Sophistici Elenchi* 5). But he does not formulate the notion that this argument bears a syllogistic arrangement, nor does he comment on the conjunction of signs, nor, again, on the possible connection with the *Sophistici Elenchi*, maybe because he did not know this text very well yet. This is quite disappointing and prevents any reflection about enthymemes from a likelihood being problematically reduced not only to 'invalid syllogisms' but also, more precisely, to paralogisms based upon the rhetorical fallacy of the consequent.

Since he thinks, as previously seen, that enthymemes from a likelihood (*ikos*) are only concerned by the second-figure 'invalid syllogisms', so that enthymemes in the third figure are from non-necessary sign that do not have a name of their own, he gives a restricted interpretation to Aristotle's saying that 'a sign cannot yield a syllogism (*asillogizatum*)' in *Rhetoric* II, 25, 1403a5 : this applies only to likelihood and means just a repetition of what has been said about *Rhet.* I, 2.[156] As for the syllogism from a proof, it cannot be refuted showing that it would be 'defective according to the form' (*peccet in forma*), since this cannot be the case, but it must be shown to be defective 'according to the matter' (*peccat in materia*), that is, showing that one premise is false.[157]

After commenting on *Rhet.* I, 2, Giles of Rome offers a separate, independent discussion about the relationships between example, induction, enthymeme and syllogism. Regarding the enthymeme and the syllogism, he insists again on the notion that enthymemes are imperfect and even defective syllogisms. They are defective according to the matter (*quantum ad materia*), because their premises are only intended to look like truth (but are not), and they are defective according to the form (*quantum ad formam*), because the order (*ordo*) of the terms and propositions in figures and moods, which characterizes the form of the syllogism, is not completely preserved (*reservetur complete*):

> If one premise in known (*nota*), it is sufficient to put the other one, because the listener will add it [*i.e.* the 'known' premise] by himself. And since 'from one [premise] nothing follows' [=*Prior Analytics* 34a16], the enthymeme is deficient regarding the above-mentioned order.[158]

This text acknowledges once again, without caring much about it, that not every enthymeme has a missing premise, since this happens only when the latter is well known and can be easily fit in by the listener. As opposed to Robert Kilwardby's solution, based upon the distinction between the real and the vocal disposition of terms and propositions, the enthymeme is deemed a formally deficient syllogism because the possibility exists that one premise would not be expressed, which is entirely forbidden for a syllogism. On the other hand, the notion that most enthymemes (since very few are based upon necessary signs in rhetoric) would be reducible to 'invalid syllogisms' does not enter the picture as a problem of its own.

The paragraph ends on a general methodological reflection, where the consideration of the enthymeme as a syllogism, that is, as a defective syllogism, belongs to dialectic as a side topic (*obliquitas*), whereas the consideration of the enthymeme fully belongs to the rhetorician, but not as a syllogism.[159] This idea echoes what has been said when commenting on *Rhet.* I, 2, that is, the notion that being a defective syllogism is only incidental to the enthymeme as the object of rhetoric.

The general impression derived from the reading of the commentary on the *Rhetoric* is that the logic of the enthymeme offered by Giles of Rome is not entirely coherent: the enthymeme is defined as a 'defective' syllogism, of which a premise in missing only 'sometimes'; it is an argument that can, as far as second- and third-figures enthymemes are concerned, be both a 'syllogism' and an 'invalid' argument, deficient according to the form. Far from being only the result of a careless mind, or a lack of experience as a commentator on Aristotle's logic, this treatment can be explained on the principle, that is, because the logic of enthymeme is a topic that falls for Giles of Rome in between two disciplines, rhetoric and dialectic. It is fully treated neither by rhetoric, because the enthymeme being a (failed) syllogism is irrelevant to its being an enthymeme *per se*, nor by dialectic, because the description of the enthymeme against syllogistic standards is 'incidental' to the enthymeme, as well as a 'sideway' topic for the dialectician.

4.4 Conclusion

We have seen how Robert Kilwardby offered a robust theorization of the logic of enthymemes. The scientific role of necessary-sign enthymemes was fully recognized together with the idea of non-rhetorical types of enthymemes. The absurd idea that enthymemes would be grounded on third- and second-figure 'invalid syllogisms' was avoided, while the method for a systematic syllogistic reconstruction of enthymemes in every figure was described, a method which could perfectly match actual exegetical 'enthymematic' practices of the time recognized in scientific works by Aristotle. Robert Kilwardby also offered, in the *De ortu scientiarum*, clues for an explanation about the reason why, at least sometimes, it is the orator's best interest to hide the unformulated premise, that is, in order to conceal its being false or even its being sometimes not acceptable – but within a valid argument. Probably because his reflection developed before the full recovery of the text of the *Rhetoric*, on the side of rhetoric, and essentially in connection with the *Prior Analytics*, on the side of enthymemes, Robert Kilwardby could be confident in the syllogistic nature of enthymemes, where rhetorical enthymemes based upon invalid, non-syllogizable arguments are merely a part of the picture, not only for enthymemes at large but also for rhetorical enthymemes. There is no systematic connection between being a rhetorical enthymeme and being non-syllogizable, because based upon a non-necessary sign. The centrality of the syllogistic nature of enthymemes is motivated by the yet unchallenged belief in the syllogism being the ultimate foundation of any argument, as well as by the intrinsic legitimacy bestowed on the project of a properly logical analysis of enthymeme. The confidence in the syllogistic nature of enthymemes was based upon a non-formalistic description of syllogistic form, where the components of the latter (terms and propositions according to correct moods and figures) are checked 'according to reason' and not 'according to vocal terms'.

It is this very same non-formalistic approach to logical form which allowed Latin mediaeval commentators to see syllogisms everywhere in the Aristotelian corpus (and in other authoritative texts), even when unformulated. The practice of presenting syllogistically understated arguments as utterly unproblematic is even pictured as a trademark of 'philosophers' by Thomas Aquinas, who also reconstructs himself a lot of syllogisms in his biblical commentaries, especially in the commentary on the Epistle to the Corinthians. He justifies the fact that the definition of faith given by Saint Paul (*'fides est substantia sperandarum rerum, argumentum non apparentium'*, Heb. 11.1) would be ill-formed by the fact that is a good definition even though the exact 'mode of the definition' has been neglected by the author, 'in the same manner as the philosophers also have neglected it, and in the same manner as they omit the form of the syllogism when they put that out of which [i.e. the premises, the terms] a syllogism can be formed'.[160]

Giles of Rome's commentary on the *Rhetoric* is rather disappointing regarding the logical analysis of enthymemes: none of the new elements offered by Aristotle's text is accurately recorded, while the logic of enthymemes is somewhat carelessly touched upon. Beyond circumstantial explanations, we have seen that this superficial treatment is philosophically grounded. Giles of Rome, faced with the generally accepted theory of the enthymeme as an incomplete syllogism when he redacted the first Latin commentary on the treatise, reacted to this negative statement by claiming that being an incomplete or even a 'defective' syllogism is 'incidental' to the enthymeme. As a consequence, the very project of a logic of enthymeme falls outside the scope of both rhetoric and dialectic. The idea of a scientific, non-rhetorical use of enthymemes is also neglected. Ultimately, Giles of Rome's position is grounded on the fact that he does not accept Aristotle's idea that rhetoric would be 'a part' or a 'counterpart (*assecutiva*)' of dialectic, as formulated in the *Rhetoric*.[161] He lists a series of fundamental differences between rhetoric and dialectic and insists on the notion that rhetoric is deficient with regards to dialectic according to the degree of certainty, to the relationship to the intellect, which it moves by appetite (through persuasion), instead of being moved by itself, as in dialectic, and to the instruments of argumentation (examples and enthymemes). Rhetoric is not even properly speaking subalternated to dialectic. A bridge cannot be built between the two disciplines, which represents a condition for the logical analysis of enthymemes to be recognized as a central topic, according to the project delineated by Aristotle himself when he offered to logically (dialectically, upon his terms) reassess the discipline in the *Rhetoric*.

The subsequent story of the logical analysis of enthymeme can be read in the next Latin commentary on the *Rhetoric*, composed by John of Jandun in the 1310s. It displays a striking evolution that announces the end of the 'golden age' for Aristotelian syllogistic. Rhetoric is considered again as a part of dialectic[162] and highly valued.[163] As for the enthymeme, it is surprisingly never defined as an incomplete syllogism, probably because syllogistic is already in the process of being included in a general theory of consequence. It is split into two categories: on the one hand, the persuasive, rhetorical enthymeme, close to the dialectical argument by its being based upon 'common' terms and topics, and, on the other hand, the scientific enthymeme, based upon specialized terms and topics. The existence of enthymemes in sciences is so much considered as obvious that a question (question I/11) is even devoted to the difference between the two types of enthymemes: 'are rhetorical enthymemes different from enthymemes in other sciences? (*utrum entimema rhetorica differant ab entimematibus aliarum scientiarum*)'. The whole impression derived from the treatment of persuasive and scientific enthymemes is that an argument being explicitly syllogistically formulated, according to moods and figures, or being potentially so, is no longer under focus, while the main logical difference lies in the nature of the types of topics (common vs. specialized) that warrant inferences within each field of knowledge.[164]

Acknowledgement

I would like to deeply thank Barbara Bartocci for her careful reading of this text. She has offered many precious corrections and suggestions which have helped considerably to improve the chapter.

Notes

1 For an overview about rhetoric in the thirteenth century, see Rosier-Catach 1998, pp. 87–110; J. Ward 1996, Vol. LIV, pp. 159–231.
2 See J. Brumberg-Chaumont 2015. For the syllogistic form, see Thom 2015; *id.* 2013; J. Brumberg-Chaumont 2017a; *ead.* 2017b; *ead.* 2022.
3 See I. Rosier-Catach 1998; G. Dahan 1998, p. 65. The translation, preserved in two manuscripts, is not edited. It includes some glosses by Avicenna and Averroes in places where Aristotle's text was judged too obscure. It was poorly known, although referred to by Roger Bacon, as recorded by Rosier-Catach (Rosier-Catach 1998). It is quoted by Giles of Rome, as shown in details by Costantino Marmo, who has offered some excerpts from the Arabic translation (C. Marmo 1998, pp. 111–34). See also *Rhetorica, Aristoteles Latinus,* 1978, (XXXI I-2) pp. IX–X and pp. 339–43, for the transcription of some extracts. A transcription of the prologue of the translator, where Averroes's commentary is explicitly quoted, and of the *explicit* of the translation is found in *Aristoteles Latinus* (1939), *Codices* I, pp. 211–12. Hermann Allemannus makes it clear that rhetoric, in the same manner as poetics, belongs to logic as a 'rational science', as opposed to Cicero, who includes it in civil science, and to Horace, who includes it in grammar (p. 211), and that great Arabic commentators, namely Alfarabi (whose *Didascalia* he also translated), Avicenna and Averroes, are to be followed on that account. Some significant passages of the translations are transcribed by Gilbert Dahan at the end of his paper (G. Dahan 1998). The prologue can also be read in Boggess 1971, pp. 227–50.
4 After another first, anonymous translation that remained almost unnoticed during the Middle Ages.

5 See Alexander, *In Top*, CAG 2.2, p. 62, 9–13 (quoted by M. F. Burnyeat 1994, p. 7); Ps-Philoponus, *In APr* 13.2, p. 33, 10–13, *In Apo*, 52, 19–25 (quoted by M. F. Burnyeat 1994, p. 6 as Philoponus).
6 In *Ciceronis Topica*, PL 64, 1050B; *De differentiis topicis*, PL 64, 1184B-C; 1206C. The *De Differentiis topicis* was an extremely influential text in the Middle Ages, either directly, till the thirteenth century, or indirectly, later on. We shall quote these texts later.
7 Quintilian, *Institutiones* V, 10 (*imperfectus syllogismus*). The reference was made by M. F. Burnyeat 1994, p. 39.
8 M. F. Burnyeat 1994, pp. 3–55. For Arabic authors see Black 1990; M. Aouad 2002, pp. 95 *sqq*.; *id.* 1992, pp. 133–90. For a general overview on Greek, Arabic and Latin traditions see C. Marmo and F. Bellucci forthcoming.
9 Some differences in the topics are the foundation of demonstrative syllogisms, that is, those from definition, genus, difference and cause: 'sed ea [= differentiae] quidem quae **ex diffinitione, vel genere, vel differentia, vel causis argumenta** ducuntur, **demonstrativis** maxime syllogismis **vires atque ordinem subministrant**, reliqua verisimilibus ac dialecticis. Atque hi loci qui maxime in eorum substantia sunt de quibus in quaestione dubitatur, ad praedicativos ac simplices, reliqui vero ad hypotheticos et conditionales respiciunt syllogismos', *De differentiis topicis*, PL 64, **1195B-1196A**.
10 See later, our conclusion.
11 M. F. Burnyeat 1994, p. 38. He adds in a footnote (38) that the 'subsequent rhetorical tradition is for the most part no better' and makes an exception for Quintilian (see Section 4.3.1.2, footnote 97).
12 More on this topic in Section 4.2.1.
13 Some other masters from the thirteenth century are very briefly mentioned, following the material offered by C. Marmo and F. Bellucci in their forthcoming book (*Demonstrationes per signa*). Albert the Great, because of his very strong dependence on Robert Kilwardby in the logical analysis of enthymeme, is not dealt with in this contribution, except for few remarks. Many late-thirteenth-century authors were influenced by Robert Kilwardby's ideas through Albert's logical commentaries.
14 The coherence between the theories developed in the *De ortu scientiarum*, an encyclopaedia composed at Oxford around 1250 as a Dominican teacher, and the logical commentaries, composed at Paris as a Master of Arts in the 1240s, is a vexing issue in mediaeval scholarship. This problem is left aside in the present contribution.
15 'Qui vero secundum consequens est elenchis eo quod putent converti consequentiam . . . Hoc autem non est necessarium. **Et in rhetoricis** quae secundum signum sunt demonstrationes **ex adiunctis** sunt. Volentes enim ostendere quoniam adulter, quod adiunctum est accipiunt, quoniam compositus **aut** quoniam in nocte videtur errabundus. Pluribus autel haec quidem insunt, pradicatum vero non inest. Similiter autem in syllogisticis', *Sophistici Elenchi* 167b7-13, *Aristoteles Latinus* VI-1-3 (1975), p. 11.
16 C. Marmo and F. Bellucci forthcoming, § 6.2.1.
17 'Et quoniam comptus **et** nocte vagatur, adulterer, quia et adulteri tales', *Rhetorica*, *Aristoteles Latinus* XXXI I-2, p. 276.
18 See C. Marmo and F. Bellucci, forthcoming, §6.2.
19 The Latin version of the text corresponds to the prologue and the very beginning of a long commentary by Alfarabi; see Alfarabi 1971.

20 For a synthesis, see G. Dahan 1998. For detailed discussions, see the contributions in J. Brumberg-Chaumont (ed.) 2013.
21 See D. Black 1990; D. Black 1997, pp. 233–54.
22 Hugh of Saint Victor's *Didascalicon* I, 11, Buttimer pp. 20–1; as we shall see later, this *trivium* identified to logic will be met again in Robert Kilwardby's *De ortu scientiarum* (Section 4.3.1.1).
23 On the Latin long *Organon* as connected to the trivial arts, to the multi-location of rhetoric and poetic and to a non-Arabic version of the long *Organon* (i.e. where the different parts of logic are not material variations of the syllogism), see J. Brumberg-Chaumont 2013. For the synthetic, somewhat confusing presentation by Dominicus Gundissalinus, see J.-M. Mandosio 2013, especially p. 301 and conclusion.
24 See C. Marmo 1990, pp. 145–98; J. Brumberg-Chaumont 2013; C. Marmo and F. Bellucci forthcoming.
25 See *Rhetoric* I, 2, 1357a32-33 (also 1359a7-10). In book II, chapter 25, Aristotle distinguishes four elements out of which enthymemes are composed, the example, the likelihood, the proof and the sign, which means that 'sign' is identified with neither likelihood nor proof, contrary to the broad sense of 'sign' we can read elsewhere in *Rhetoric* (I, 2) and in *Prior Analytics* II, 27. Aristotle explains in this chapter that 'a sign cannot yield a syllogism (*asillogizatum*)' (*Rhet* II, 25, 1403a5).
26 About this passage, Miles Burnyeat thinks that the enthymeme is not a kind of syllogism but a 'syllogisms of a kind', where the conclusion is not always necessarily obtained, where 'syllogism' does not have its technical, syllogistic meaning, only differentiated by the kind of premises it contains. He denies that 'a syllogisms from a sign/likelihood' is the definition of the enthymeme; see M. F. Burnyeat 1994, pp. 9 *sqq*.
27 See *Rhetorica*, *Aristoteles Latinus* XXXI I-2, p. 161, for the Latin text.
28 M. F. Burnyeat 1994, p. 20.
29 *Rhetoric* 1357b15-17, *Aristoteles Latinus* XXXI I-2, p. 190.
30 A common point emphasized by Gilles of Rome in his commentary on *Rhetoric* (I, 6, fol. 9ra).
31 *Analytica Priora*, *Aristoteles Latinus* III/1-3, 1962, p. 189.
32 *Analytica Posteriora*, *Aristoteles Latinus* IV/1-3, 1968, p. 19.
33 See C. Marmo and F. Bellucci forthcoming.
34 See C. Marmo and F. Bellucci forthcoming.
35 See M. F. Burnyeat 1994, p. 49, note 130.
36 See M. F. Burnyeat 1994, p. 6 *sqq*.
37 The conclusion is obtained either universally or 'for the most part', while the 'necessity' clause is not formulated in the *Rhetoric*'s version of the definition of the syllogism; see M. F. Burnyeat 1994, pp. 15 *sqq*., p. 20.
38 See M. F. Burnyeat 1994, pp. 31 *sqq*., about the Solmsen/Barnes's hypothesis and the non-technical sense (i.e. not referred to moods and figures) of 'syllogism' which is not defined by correct combinations (*schemata*).
39 See M. F. Burnyeat 1994, p. 15.
40 Robert Kilwardby does not say which part of the syllogism corresponds to the form of the syllogism, while he records the opinion of those who says that 'from the things that have been posited (*positis*)' corresponds to the figure and mood; Robert Kilwardby, *Notule libri priorum*, 2015, t. I, p. 82.
41 *Immodificatus* translates once *asyllogizatos* in the Latin version of the *Sophistici Elenchi* (168a21, AL, p. 15) and then served in the tradition to deal with the fact

that an argument can be arranged according to moods and figures, without being necessarily a syllogism for that, see J. Brumberg-Chaumont 2017b, p. 107 (for Robert Kilwardby in the *De ortu scientiarum*) and pp. 155–16 (for Albert as a commentator of the *Sophistici Elenchi*). The distinction is connected to the idea of a syllogistic arrangement (*dispositio*) according to the vocal sound only, or according to the reality also, by which he does not mean the external reality but the logical reality of the argument, that is, connected to some aspects of its semantic content. Here *immodificatus* includes figure, while *modificatus* is sometimes used just for mood, in association with *figuratus*, as we shall see later (Section 4.3.1.1).

42 For this complex story and the origins of the notion of *immodificatus* in the Latin translation of the *Sophistici Elenchi* (for asyllogizon), see J. Brumberg-Chaumont 2015.

43 See Alexander of Aphrodisias, *In APr* pp. 21, 25–28, on the definition of the syllogism (quoted by Burnyeat, 'Enthymeme: Aristotle', p. 47) where one-premise arguments are excluded by this part of the definition which says that the conclusion is obtained 'because of them/by virtue of the things being the case'. 'One-premise argument', from Stoic origins, is obviously identified with enthymemes. Alexander indeed says that they 'need for their conclusion an extra term, or premise' (which is forbidden for a syllogism according to its definition); the premise is supplied by 'the person to whom the argument is addressed because it is familiar'. This means that enthymemes as they stand are not syllogisms, because they are incomplete syllogisms, but that they can instantly be turned into syllogisms by adding the obvious, missing premise. As underlined by Burnyeat, Alexander would not allow for 'invalid syllogisms' (p. 47). A similar doctrine is read in Ammonius, who, when reflecting on the definition of the syllogism, explicitly refers to 'incomplete one-premise syllogisms', identifies them to 'enthymemes' and to the arguments used by orator (see *In Porph*, pp. 8, 5–9, quoted by M. F. Burnyeat 1994, p. 49).

44 The necessary sign is the one out of which a syllogism can be constructed, while, on the contrary, the enthymeme from a non-necessary sign is described as *asyllogiston/insillogizabile*, with an example that is almost the same as the one in the third figure taken in the *Prior Analytics* ('Socrates' in the *Rhetoric*, 'Pittacus' in the *Prior Analytics*); see *Rhetorica, Aristoteles Latinus* XXXI, I-2, p. 167; the same difference is repeated in 1357b22–5 with an explicit reference to the *Prior Analytics* (*sillogizabilia* vs. *insillogizabilia*, p. 168). The problem raised by this reference can be evaded by a 'Solmsen/Barnes chronology' of Aristotle's logical works, where the *Rhetoric* was written before the discovery of the theory of the syllogism in the *Prior Analytics* so that some passages of the *Rhetoric* where the *Prior Analytics* are alluded to are considered as later additions; see M. F. Burnyeat 1994, pp. 31 *sqq*. This solution was obviously not available to mediaeval commentators.

45 We also have 'liberal' instead of 'learned' and 'ambitious' instead of 'wise'.

46 *Analytica Priora, Aristoteles Latinus* III/1-3, p. 190 (70a35-36).

47 *In An.pr*, pp. 481, 28–9; 482, 10–11, quoted by M. F. Burnyeat 1994.

48 See M. F. Burnyeat 1994, p. 48.

49 See the references given in note 8.

50 As shown by Burnyeat, David has envisaged concealing the falsity of the missing premise among the motivations for not formulating it (M. F. Burnyeat 1994, p. 6, note 10).

51 See D. Black 1990; M. Aouad, 2002, pp. 95–6; *id*. 1992, p. 153.

52 See Alfarabi (1971), p. 164.

53 *Analytica Priora, Aristoteles Latinus* III/1-3, p. 369.
54 Albert the Great, *Libri priorum analyticorum, Opera omnia* I, ed. A. Borgnet, Paris, 1890, p. 620A.
55 Alfarabi 1971, p. 68.
56 *In Ciceronis Topica*, PL 64, 1050B : 'Enthymema vero est imperfectus syllogismus, cujus aliquae partes, vel propter **brevitatem**, vel propter **notitiam**, praetermissae sunt'; *De differentiis topicis*, PL 64, 1206C: 'Dialectica perfectis utitur syllogismis. Rhetorica enthymematum brevitate contenta est'.
57 *De differentiis topicis*, PL 64, 1184B-C: 'Enthymema quippe est **imperfectus syllogismus**, id est oratio in qua non omnibus antea propositionibus constitutis infertur **festinata** conclusio, ut si quis ita dicat: **homo animal est, substantia igitur est**. Praetermisit enim alteram propositionem qua proponitur, **omne animal est substantia**. Ergo quoniam enthymema ab universalibus ad particularia probanda contendit **quasi simile syllogismo** est ; quod vero non omnibus quae conveniunt syllogismo utitur propositionibus, a syllogismi ratione discedit, atque ideo **imperfectus** vocatus est syllogismus.'
58 Quoted Marmo and Bellucci forthcoming, § 6.1.3, extracts edited in Appendix D. As shown by C. Marmo and F. Bellucci, the author is actually commenting on an interpolated passage of the *Tractatus*.
59 As shown by C. Marmo and F. Bellucci, a different position is found in Simon of Faversham's commentary on the *Prior Analytics*, where enthymemes, notwithstanding the fact that they are syllogisms according to the concept (*quantum ad esse intellectum*), are not obviously syllogisms and are deemed defective according to the matter and the form; their being not fully syllogistically disposed according to the vocal sound prevents them from being used in scientific demonstrations (C. Marmo and F. Bellucci forthcoming, §3.1.3 and Appendix E). Maybe the influence of Giles of Rome can be identified here.
60 For Mendicant schools of logic and philosophy see A. Maierù 1994; M. Mulchahey 1998; B. Roest 2000; N. Şenocak 2012; Vv. Aa. 1978; Vv. Aa. 2002; Vv. Aa. 2012. For a recent study focused on logic in thirteenth-century Dominican and Franciscan *studia*, see J. Brumberg-Chaumont (in print).
61 See also *Topics* 104a33-34, 105b1.
62 See J. Barnes 1981; J. Lennox 2001, pp. 4–6; D. Bronstein 2016.
63 See for instance *Topics* I, 8, 103b7 *sqq*.
64 The practices of completing understated syllogisms would not have been considered as enthymematic by Averroes, who thinks that enthymemes are rhetorical arguments and incorrect syllogisms. As seen, Alfarabi explicitly says that abbreviated syllogisms in exchanges and letters are not to be considered as enthymemes, since the premise is just understated, since self-evident, not hidden for sake of persuasion. Even though never described that way by Latin authors, we can gather a bundle of evidence that they would readily consider Aristotle's abbreviated syllogisms as enthymemes. As we shall see with Robert Kilwardby, this is because there are necessary-sign enthymemes, in a scientific use of enthymeme, a method for reconstructing every enthyeme into a syllogism according to the three figures (as opposed to examples with invalid argument given by Aristotle in *Prior Analytics* II, 27) so that a true, appropriated premise is filled in – a series of indications which is reinforced by Boethius's examples of enthymemes with *per se* universal necessary propositions.
65 J. Murdoch 1989, pp. 4–5.

66 For more on the 'exegetical practices' and the syllogization of Aristotle, see J. Brumberg-Chaumont, forthcoming, Part 4; *ead.* 2021.
67 See, for instance, the very beginning of his commentary on the *De anima*, where he finds a 'categorical syllogism' in Aristotle's text: 'Et sermo eius est in forma sillogismi categorici', Averroes 1953, p. 4.
68 See, for instance, this extract of Adam's commentary on the *De memoria*, explaining Aristotle's demonstration that memory, even of the intelligible, of which it is by accident, belongs to the sensitive faculty [= object of the main syllogism] because it always comes with phantasm, while our thinking cannot be without a phantasm, since it always comes with continuity and time [= object of the pro-syllogism, of which only the minor is formulated and proven]; *De memoria* 450a1-10: 'First, he presents the proposition that he intends to prove, saying that our thinking is never without a phantasm. This is in the passage: SINCE. Then he proves it by the following reasoning [= **a first-figure syllogism**]: "a cognition that comes with continuity and time comes with a phantasm. Now all our thinking comes with continuity and time. Therefore [our thinking comes with a phantasm]". He does not present the **major premise** of this reasoning, but, **since it is self-evident** (*manifesta est de se*), he immediately puts forward the **conclusion**. Accordingly, he only proves the **minor premise**, and first the first part of it, and then the second: Now SIZE. Therefore, he proves the first part by means of a **comparison**, as follows [. . .] It is therefore established in this way that our thinking comes with continuity. He then explains that it comes with time as follows: size, movement, and time are cognized by the same faculty. This is why we think not only with size, but we think with time. **The minor of this reasoning** has been proven before, so he adds only the **major**. This is in the passage: NOW SIZE. He then shows his point as follows [= **a first-figure syllogism**]: any cognition that comes with a phantasm is in the first sensitive faculty – that is to say, in the common sense. But there is no memory of either sensible or intelligible things without a phantasm. That is why memory is an affection of the common sense in itself, and of the intellect only by accident. **He first explains the major premise** of this reasoning as follows: imagination is in itself an affection of the common sense. Therefore, a cognition that comes with a phantasm also belongs to the common sense. First, he presents the **premise**: Now IMAGINATION. Secondly, he draws the **conclusion, which is the major premise of the main reasoning:** THAT IS WHY IT IS CLEAR. Thirdly he presents the **minor premise** of the **main reasoning**: Now MEMORY [. . .] Finally, he draws the main conclusion of his reasoning. This is in the passage: THUS TO THE INTELLECT', Adam of Bockenfield 2022. We also find elsewhere, about an unformulated premise : 'it is self-evident (*patet de se*)', l.195.
69 See, for instance, Robert Kilwardby 1976, p. 160.
70 The commentary on the *Categories* was read in the provisory edition professor Alessandro Conti was kind enough to give access to. For the commentary on the *Posterior Analytics*, see, for instance, at the beginning of the commentary, Cannone 2003–2004, p. 24, p. 34, p. 47, p. 58, etc. For the commentary on the *Prior Analytics*, see, for instance, Robert Kilwardby 2015, t. I, pp. 56, 142, 264, etc.
71 Robert Kilwardby, 2015, t. II, p. 1566.
72 Robert Kilwardby 1976, pp. 161–2.
73 Robert Kilwardby 1976, pp. 146 *sqq.*
74 The same idea occurs p. 147 and is repeated p. 195.
75 Robert Kilwardby 1976, p. 167.

76 See *Analytica Priora*, *Aristoteles Latinus* III/1-3, pp. 133-4: 'Quoniam autem non solum dialectici et demonstrativi syllogismi per praedictas fiunt figuras, sed et rhetoricis et simpliciter quaecumque fides et secundum quam artem, nunc erit dicendum.'
77 Robert Kilwardby 1976, p. 168.
78 Robert Kilwardby 1976p. 170.
79 'Necessitas et sufficienta in logica', Robert Kilwardby 1976*arum*, p. 173.
80 Robert Kilwardby 1976, p. 177.
81 'Sermocinalis scientia ratiocinativa', Robert Kilwardby 1976, p. 204.
82 'Questio civilis', Robert Kilwardby 1976, pp. 202, 203.
83 Robert Kilwardby 1976, p. 204.
84 Robert Kilwardby 1976, p. 205.
85 Robert Kilwardby 1976, pp. 205-6.
86 Dominicus Gundissalinus 1903, pp. 75-6.
87 Robert Kilwardby 1976, p. 209.
88 Robert Kilwardby 1976, p. 209.
89 Robert Kilwardby 1976, p. 210.
90 Where answers and interrogations are interwoven, Robert Kilwardby 1976, pp. 210-11.
91 Robert Kilwardby 1976, p. 209 (our reconstruction, but following precisely the text).
92 See Robert Kilwardby 2015, t. II, p. 1570.
93 Albert the Great 1890, p. 805b.
94 Even though probable, because non-necessary according to the commentator, see C. Marmo and F. Bellucci forthcoming, Appendix H, second doubt.
95 See C. Marmo and F. Bellucci forthcoming, Appendix H.
96 Same doctrine about the first figure in Albert the Great 1890, p. 586A-B, but with the idea that some women may have milk without having given birth, as he says in his *De animalibus*, and with a strange identification of these signs with *ikota*; see C. Marmo and F. Bellucci forthcoming, §6.2.2.
97 See C. Marmo and F. Bellucci forthcoming, Appendix H, answer to the third doubt. Similar argument in Radulphus Brito's commentary on the *Sophistici Elenchi*; see C. Marmo and F. Bellucci forthcoming, §6.2.2, text in Appendix I.
98 This 'probabilistic' approach (as labelled by Marmo and Bellucci) is also found in *The Dialectica monacensis*, in Nicholas of Paris's commentary on the *De differentiis topicis* (where *suspicio* is obtained by multiples signs), in Albert the Great's paraphrase on the *Sophistici Elenchi*, who explicitly says that arguments with signs taken in conjunction are used in physiognomonic and in other sciences where you have a demonstration from a sign, in Master Simon (Simon of Faversham?)'s commentary on the *Tractatus*, which depends on Albert's analysis, and in Radulphus's Brito's commentary on the *Sophistici Elenchi* (but with topics, rather than signs, mentioned); see Marmo and Bellucci, *Demonstrationes per signa*, § 6.2.1, 6.2.2. It should be noted that the addition of several too large signs as a solution for turning a deficient argument into an acceptable one in rhetoric was already the solution suggested by Quintilian V, 10 ('etsi ad tollendam dubitationem sola non sufficiunt, tamen adjunctis ceteris, plurimum valent'). This point has been emphasized by M. F. Burnyeat 1994, p. 38.
99 'Caeneus argument': 'Everything that consists in multiple proportion develops quickly, fire develops quickly, fire consists in multiple proportion' (*Anal po* 78 a 1-2, *Analytica posteriora*, *Aristoteles Latinus* IV/1-3, p. 128). If one puts 'everything that develops quickly consists in multiple proportion', one gets a first-figure syllogism.

100 'And it is ridiculous to think that he [Aristotle] says "sometimes" because the conclusion of such a combination is necessary in the case of certain material terms. For on this way "of looking things", nothing would prevent one from saying that even non-syllogistic combinations are syllogistic "sometimes", for they will be found to yield a conclusion in the case of certain material terms [*Here Caeneus argument is taken as an example of a materially conclusive argument: the major converts because of the matter*]', Alexander of Aphrodisias, 1883, pp. 125, 15–24; *id.*1991, p. 60.
101 See J. Brumberg-Chaumont (2017a), pp. 191 *sqq*.
102 See D. Cannone, 2002, pp. 161–2.
103 'In demonstrativis sive doctrinalibus contingit quosdam **demonstratores non syllogizare**, hoc est, **non secundum formam generalem syllogismi in Prioribus determinatam**: eo quod in demonstrativis **contingit** in terminis convertibilibus in secunda figura ex affirmativis **syllogizare, quod est contra formam syllogismi** in dialecticis determinatam, quando scilicet accipiunt media utrisque extremitatibus convertibiliter inhaerentia: sic enim fit dispositio secundae figurae in qua medium bis praedicatur. Hoc autem in dialecticis non contingit. Hunc modum Caeneus Philosophus fecit in syllogizando: volens enim probare Caeneus, quod ignis ut formale elementum est facilis generationis, et ideo primum elementorum immediate a motu orbis generatum, **sic syllogizavit**: quidquid in multiplicata analogia se habet ad alterum, citius generatur: ignis in multiplicata analogia se habet ad quodlibet elementum: ergo facilis est generationis et citius generatur. Et sic **formandus est syllogismus**: velocis est generationis, quod in multiplicata analogia se habet ad alterum: ignis in multiplicata analogia se habet ad quodlibet alterum: ergo cito generatur sive velocis generationis est [= first-figure syllogism]. Dicitur autem in multiplicata analogia ignis se habere ad alterum: quia ex uno pugillo terrae multi pugilli fiunt aquae, et ex uno pugillo aquae multi pugilli fiunt aeris, et ex uno pugillo aeris multi pugilli fiunt ignis: et sic ignis formalior est omnibus aliis: et quanto aliquid formalius est, tanto est velocioris generationis: in multiplicata analogia sic esse aliquid, convertitur cum eo quod est esse facilis generationis. Propter **quod gratia materia et in secunda figura aliquando syllogizatur ex talibus**: quoniam medium est causa majoris extremitatis et minor extremitas continetur sub majori: et ideo per tale medium concluditur de ipsa, sicut patet in syllogismo inducto. Ex sic ergo acceptis in terminis convertibilibus aliquando syllogizare contingit: sed **tamen non videtur**, eo quod **forma syllogizandi non servatur**'; Albert the Great 1890, p. 80A-B.
104 Robert Kilwardby 2015, t. I, p. 22.
105 Robert Kilwardby 2015, t. I, p. 24.
106 Aristotle 1978, III 1-3, p. 6.
107 Robert Kilwardby 2015, t. I, pp. 78–80.
108 Robert Kilwardby 2015, t. I, p. 80.
109 This contradicts the position taken in the *De ortu scientiarum*, as well as the position adopted by a majority of logicians during the thirteenth century, where all thirteen fallacies of the *Sophistici Elenchi* are deemed formally deficient, even when apparently respecting the correct moods and figures, such as the fallacious Barbaras (see J. Brumberg-Chaumont 2017a; *ead*. 2017b).
110 Robert Kilwardby 2015, t. I, p. 78.
111 The *Anonymus Aurelianensis* III (an incomplete commentary from the end of the twelfth century) indeed has this comment, where the enthymeme is explicitly referred to; it also seems to potentially exclude the enthymeme with the portion

of the definition *nullius extrinsecus termini indigere ut fiat necessarium*, where arguments with something less (*habens minus*) are excluded (see *Anonymus* 2014, *ad loc.*).

112. Mora-Márquez 2021, pp. 175–6. Her position is that what is required according to Aristotle is that the conclusion is established through the relevant and explicitly introduced mediating term, so that one-premise arguments, with one unexpressed premise, can be accepted – hence, we would add, enthymeme also (enthymemes are not addressed here by Mora-Márquez). Marko Malink is especially bound to adopt the opposite view, with his idea that what is specific to the syllogistic developed in the *Prior Analytics* is that it aims at 'gapless deductions in which no premise is missing'; see M. Malink 2015, p. 272.
113. Robert Kilwardby 2015, t. I, pp. 112–14.
114. Robert Kilwardby 2015, t. I, pp. 114–16.
115. Robert Kilwardby 2015, t. I, p. 118.
116. Robert Kilwardby 2015, t. I, pp. 116–18.
117. Robert Kilwardby 2015, t. I, pp. 118–20.
118. Robert Kilwardby 2015, t. I, p. 454.
119. Robert Kilwardby 2015, t. I, pp. 454–6.
120. Robert Kilwardby 2015, t. II, p. 1580.
121. Robert Kilwardby 2015, t. II, pp. 1520–2.
122. Robert Kilwardby 2015, t. II, p. 1570.
123. Robert Kilwardby 2015, t. II, p. 1566.
124. Robert Kilwardby 2015, t. II, p. 1582. Physiognomonic enthymemes are also considered by Albert the Great; see *Analytica Priora*, p. 807a. See C. Marmo and F. Bellucci forthcoming, § 6.1.4. The authors show how Radulphus Brito's questions on physiognomy make it clear that this discipline cannot be strictly speaking a science, since it does not demonstrate by the causes (but by signs).
125. Robert Kilwardby 2015, t. II, p. 1572.
126. Robert Kilwardby 2015, t. II, p. 1572.
127. Robert Kilwardby 2015, t. II, p. 1570.
128. Albert the Great 1890, p. 805b.
129. Robert Kilwardby 2015, t. II, p. 1574.
130. Robert Kilwardby 2015, t. II, p. 1576.
131. Robert Kilwardby does not spell it, but we can reconstruct that it depends on the location of the middle term in the added major premise: as a subject = first figure; as a predicate = second figure.
132. Middle term as predicate = first figure; as subject = third figure.
133. Robert Kilwardby 2015, t. II, pp. 1574–6.
134. Robert Kilwardby 2015, t. II, p. 1570.
135. Robert Kilwardby 2015, t. II, p. 1572.
136. Robert Kilwardby 2015, t. II, p. 1588.
137. Robert Kilwardby 2015, t. II, pp. 1590–2.
138. Robert Kilwardby 2015, t. II, p. 1578.
139. For a general study of rhetoric within the scope of a logical reflection according to Giles of Rome, see C. Marmo 1990, pp. 187 *sqq*.
140. Giles of Rome, *Super libros Rhetoricorum*, Venetiis, 1515, fol. 4rb.
141. *Super libros Rhetoricorum*, fol. 5ra.
142. *Super libros Rhetoricorum*, fol. 7vb.
143. *Super libros Rhetoricorum*, fol. 8rb.

144 *Rhet.* 1356b20-24; *Rhetorica, Aristoteles Latinus*, p. 165.
145 *Super libros Rhetoricorum*, fol.8rb.
146 Same valuation of examples with regard to enthymemes in Averroes's commentary on *Rhetoric*, because they are deemed more 'manifest'; see M. Aouad, 2002, tome 1, p. 89.
147 *Super libros Rhetoricorum*, fol. 9ra.
148 *Super libros Rhetoricorum*, fol. 9va-10ra. This passage can be read in the provisory edition prepared by C. Marmo and F. Bellucci, forthcoming, Appendix C.
149 Also called 'retinerium'. On the origins of this words in William of Moerbeke's manuscript, see C. Marmo and F. Bellucci forthcoming, § 6.21.
150 Same verbal form (*formetur*) for the first figure, which means that it is not significant.
151 *Super libros Rhetoricorum*, fol. 10ra.
152 After the comment on *Rhet.* I, 2, Giles offers also a very long development about rhetoric and dialectic, necessary and probable matters, arguments from the form and from the matter, all triggered by the fact that instead of a 'refutative (elenchus) enthymeme', as written in the *Moerbekiana*, the Arabic translation speaks about an enthymeme which 'would lead to the impossible (*ducendo ad impossibile*)'. For Giles, you cannot have an impossible matter when dealing with probable matters as rhetoric does, except if you accept 'impossible' in a large sense (see *Super libros Rhetoricorum*, fol. 79ra-rb).
153 'Sufficit **aliquando** aguere ex una premissarum si altera sit nota ideo subditur', *Super libros Rhetoricorum*, fol. 77va.
154 *Super libros Rhetoricorum*, 77vb ('De quo debet fieri syllogismus et enthymemata').
155 'Computus **et** nocte vagatur', *Super libros Rhetoricorum*, fol. 87vb.
156 *Super libros Rhetoricorum*, fol. 89vb.
157 *Super libros Rhetoricorum*, fol. 90 ra.
158 *Super libros Rhetoricorum*, fol. 10vb.
159 *Super libros Rhetoricorum*, fol. 10vb-11ra.
160 'Et etiam philosophi, neglexerunt, sicut etiam et **formam syllogismi praetermittunt** ponentes ea ex quibus syllogismus formari potest', Thomas Aquinas, commentary on the *Sentences* III, d. 23 q. 2 a. 1.
161 On this topic, see C. Marmo, 1990, pp. 188–90.
162 At least as focused on persuasive enthymemes (as opposed to passions), where premises are probable in the same manner as in dialectic (*Question* I, 9: 'Utrum rhetorica sit pars dialectica'). John of Jandun nonetheless lists a series of aspects of rhetoric by which it is imperfect with regard to dialectic, and he says that the 'dialectical syllogism' is 'more perfect' than the enthymeme, without further comments in the prologue. The text has been read in the unpublished provisory edition by B. Preben-Hansen (with some passage by S. Ebbesen).
163 See E. Beltran 1998 (see pp. 156–7 for the list of questions).
164 In *Question* I, 11, John of Jandun says that rhetorical enthymemes are composed of common terms and common topics, like 'opposite', 'bigger', smaller' and so on, which can be applied to several sorts of objects (although not every sort, as is dialectic). He takes as an example for scientific enthymemes a one-premise inference with scientific, specialized terms ('white', 'black', 'dissociating the vision' (*disgregativus visus*); see *Met.* 1057b10). It is based upon a 'scientific topic', the 'topic of the white' or 'the topic of the opposition of white and black' so that from white being dissociating vision, you can conclude that black is not dissociating vision. In *Question* I, 10, dedicated to the reduction of every proof (*ostensio*) to syllogism and induction, the

reduction of enthymemes to syllogism is never addressed, while the relationship between induction and syllogism does not touch upon the technicalities of syllogistic reduction, but on epistemic matters, namely the relationship between principles, established by induction, and conclusions, established by syllogism. Figures, moods, middle terms and premises, that is, all the technicalities of syllogistic, are utterly absent from the commentary.

Bibliography

Adam of Bockenfield (2022), 'Commentary "In precedenti libro"', in *Adam of Bockenfield and his circle in the De memoria and reminiscentia*, J. Brumberg-Chaumont and D. Poirel (eds), Auctores Britannici Medii Aevi 37, Oxford, Oxford University Press/British Academy, l, pp. 87–143.

Albert the Great (1890), *Libri posteriora, Opera omnia I*, A. Borgnet (ed.), Paris, Vives.

Albert the Great (1890), *Libri priorum analyticorum, Opera omnia I*, A. Borgnet (ed.), Paris, Vives.

Alexander of Aphrodisias (1883), *In Topica, Commentaria in Aristotelem Graeca (CAG)*, M. Wallies (ed.), Berlin, Reimer.

Alexander of Aphrodisias (1991), *On Aristotle's Prior Analytics* 1, 1–7, J. Barnes, S. Bobzien, K. Flannery, K. Ierodiakonou (trans.), Ithaca/New York, Cornell University Press.

Alfarabi (1971), *Deux ouvrages inédits sur la Rhétorique. I. Kitab al-Hataba. II. Disdascalia in Rhetoricam Aristotelis ex Glosa Alpharabi*, J. Langhade and M. Grignaschi (eds), Beyrouth, Dar el-Machreq.

Anonymus (2014) '*Anonymus Aurelianensis III*' in *Aristotelis Analytica Priora*, C. Thomsen Thörnqvist (ed.), Leiden,. Brill

Aouad, M. (1992), 'Les fondements de la rhétorique reconsidérés par Alfarabi ou le concept de point de vue commun immédiat', *Arabic Sciences and Philosophy* 2, pp. 133-180.

Aouad, M. (2002), *Commentaire moyen à la Rhétorique d'Averroes*, vol. 1, Paris, Vrin.

Aristote (1939), *Aristoteles Latinus, Codices I*, G. Lacombe (ed.), Rome, La Libreria dello Stato, pp. 211–12.

Aristote (1975), *Sophistici Elenchi, Aristoteles Latinus VI.1-3*, B. G. Dod (ed.), Leiden/Brussels, Brill.

Aristote (1978), *Rhetorica, Aristoteles Latinus, XXXI I-2*, B. Schneider (ed.), Leiden, Brill.

Averroes (1953), *Averroes Commentarium Magnum de Anima*, F. S. Crawford (ed.), Cambridge, MA, Mediaeval Academy of America.

Barnes, J. (1981), 'Proof and the Syllogism', in *Aristotle on Science and the 'Posterior Analytics'*, E. Berti (ed.), Padova, Antenore, pp. 17–59.

Beltran, E. (1998), 'Les Questions sur la *Rhétorique* de Jean de Jandun', in *La Rhétorique d'Aristote, traditions et commentaires de l'Antiquité au XVIIe siècle*, I. Rosier-Catach and G. Dahan (eds), Paris, Vrin, pp. 153–68.

Black, D. (1990), *Logic and Aristotle's Rhetoric and Poetic in Medieval Arabic Philosophy*, Leiden, Brill.

Black, D. (1997), 'Tradition and Transformations in the Medieval Approach to Rhetoric and Related Linguistic Arts', in *L'Enseignement de la philosophie au XIIIe siècle. Autour* du *'Guide de l'Étudiant' du ms. Ripoll 109*, Cl. Lafleur and J. Carrier (eds), Turnhout, Brepols, pp. 233–54.

Boggess, W. F. (1971), 'Hermannus Allemannus's Rhetorical Translations', *Viator* 2, pp. 227–50.

Bronstein, D. (2016), *Aristotle on Knowledge and Learning. The Posterior Analytics*, Oxford, Oxford University Press.

Brumberg-Chaumont, J. (2013), 'Les divisions de la logique selon Albert le Grand', in *'Ad notitiam ignoti' L'Organon dans la translation studiorum à l'époque d'Albert le Grand*, J. Brumberg-Chaumont (ed.), Turnhout, Brepols, pp. 335–416.

Brumberg-Chaumont, J. (2015), 'Universal Logic and Aristotelian Logic: Formality and Essence of Logic', *Logica Universalis* 9 (2), pp. 263–78.

Brumberg-Chaumont, J. (2017a), 'Form and Matter of the Syllogism in the Anonymus Cantabrigiensis', in *The Aristotelian Tradition, Aristotle's woks on Logic and Metaphysics and their Reception in the Middle Ages*, C. Thomsen Thönrvisq and B. Byden (eds), Toronto, University of Toronto Press, pp. 188–213.

Brumberg-Chaumont, J. (2017b), 'La forme syllogistique et le problème des syllogismes sophistiques chez Robert Kilwardby', in *Formal Approaches and Natural Languages in Medieval Logic*, L. Cesalli, F. Goubier, and A. de Libera (eds), Barcelona/Roma, Brepols, pp. 93–116.

Brumberg-Chaumont, J. (2020), '"Logica hominis in via": anthropologie, philosophie et pratiques de la logique chez Gilles de Rome', *Quaestio* 20, pp. 3–28.

Brumberg-Chaumont, J. (in print), 'Les débuts de l'enseignement de la logique dans les studia dominicains et franciscains en Italie : une organisation précoce et innovante', in *Les savoirs dans les ordres mendiants (XIIIe-XVe s)*, J. Chandelier and A. Robert (eds), Roma, École française de Rome, pp. 29–113.

Brumberg-Chaumont, J. (2021), 'The Rise of Logical Skills and the 13th Century Origins of the Logical Man', in *Logical Skills. Social-Historical Perspectives*, J. Brumberg-Chaumont and Cl. Rosental (eds), Basel, Springer, 2021, pp. 91–120.

Brumberg-Chaumont, J. (2022), 'Logical Hylomorphism in the Thirteenth Century', in *Logic in Question - Talks from the Annual Sorbonne Logic Workshop (2011–2019)*, J.-Y. Béziau, J.-P. Desclés, A. Moktefi and A. C. Pascu (eds), Basel, Birkhäuser, pp. 17–34.

Brumberg-Chaumont, J. (forthcoming), *À l'école de la logique. L'essor d'une norme intellectuelle, sociale et anthropologique au XIIIe siècle*, Paris, Classiques Garnier.

Burnyeat, M. F. (1994), 'Enthymeme: Aristotle on the Logic of Persuasion', in *Aristotle's "Rhetoric": Philosophical Essays*, A. Nehamas and D. J. Furley (eds), Princeton, NJ, Princeton University Press, pp. 3–56.

Boethius, Severinus, 'De differentiis topicis', in *Patrologia Latina,* 64, J.-P. Migne (ed.), Paris, Garnier, 1844–1855,.

Cannone, D. (2002), 'Le "Notule Libri Posteriorum" di Robert Kilwardby: il commento ad Analitici posteriori I, 4, 73a34-b24', *Documenti e studi sulla tradizione filosofica medievale* 13, pp. 71–136.

Cicero, Marcus Tullius, 'Topica', in *Patrologia Latina,* 64, J.-P. Migne (ed.), Paris, Garnier, 1844–1855.

Dahan, G. (1998), 'L'entrée de la Rhétorique d'Aristote dans le monde latin, entre 1240 et 1270', in *La Rhétorique d'Aristote. Traditions et commentaires de l'Antiquité au XVIIe siècle*, I. Rosier-Catach and G. Dahan (eds), Paris, Vrin, pp. 65–86.

Dominicus Gundissalinus (1903), *De Divisione philosophiae*, L. Baur (ed.), Münster, Aschendorff.

Giles of Rome, *Rhetoricorum*, Venetiis, 1515.
Hugh of Saint Victor (1939), *Didascalicon*, I, 11, E. Buttimer (ed.), Washington, The Catholic University Press.
Lennox, J. (2001), *Aristotle's Philosophy of Biology. Studies in the Origins of Life Science*, Cambridge, Cambridge University Press.
Maierù, A. (1994), *University Training in Medieval Europe*, D. N. Pryds (trans.), Leiden/New York/Köln, Brill.
Malink, M. (2015), 'The Beginnings of Formal Logic: Deduction in Aristotle's *Topics* vs. *Prior Analytics*', *Phronesis* 60, pp. 267–309.
Mandosio, J.-M. (2013), 'La place de la logique et ses subdivisions dans l'Énumération des sciences d'al-Farabi et chez Dominicus Gundissalinus', in J. Brumberg-Chaumont (ed.), *Ad notitiam ignoti'. L'Organon dans la translatio studiorum à l'époque d'Albert le Grand*, Turnhout, Brepols, pp. 285–310.
Marmo, C. (1990), '*Suspicio*: A Key Word to the Significance of Aristotle's Rhetoric in Thirteenth Century Scholasticism', *Cahiers de l'Institut du Moyen-Âge Grec et Latin* 60, pp. 145–98.
Marmo, C. and Bellucci, F. (forthcoming), *Demonstrationes per signa. Signs and Demonstrations from Aristotle to Radulphus Brito*.
Marmo, C. (1998), 'L'utilizzazione delle traduzioni latine della Retorica nel commento di Egidio Romano (1272–1273)', in *La Rhétorique d'Aristote. Traditions et commentaires de l'Antiquité au XVIIe siècle, I*. Rosier-Catach and G. Dahan (eds), Paris, Vrin, pp. 111–34.
Mora-Márquez, A. M. (2021), 'Elements of (Dialectical) Argumentation Theory in Aristotle's Topics', *Le Langage. Lectures d'Aristote*, L. Gazziero (ed.), Peeters, Louvain-la-Neuve, pp. 173–200.
Mulchahey, M. (1998), *'First the Bow is Bent in Study'. Dominican Education before 1350*, Toronto, Pontifical Institute of Medieval Studies.
Murdoch, J. (1989), 'The Involvement of Logic in Late Medieval Natural Philosophy', in *Studies in Medieval Natural Philosophy*, S. Caroti (ed.), Firenze, Olschki, pp. 3–28.
Quintilian (2002), *Institutio oratoria*, D. A. Russell (ed.), Cambridge, MA, Harvard University Press.
Robert Kilwardby (1976), *De ortu scientiarum*, A. Judy (ed.), Toronto, Pont. Inst. of Medieval Studies.
Robert Kilwardby (2015), *Notule libri priorum*, J. Scott and P. Thom (eds), Oxford, University Press, t. I.
Roest, B. (2000), *A History of Franciscan Education (c. 1210–1517)*, Leiden/Boston, Brill.
Rosier-Catach, I. (1998), 'Roger Bacon, Al-Farabi et Augustin. Rhétorique, logique et philosophie morale', in *La Rhétorique d'Aristote. Traditions et commentaires de l'Antiquité au XVIIe siècle*, I. Rosier-Catach and G. Dahan (eds), Paris, Vrin, pp. 87–110.
Şenocak, N. (2012), *The Poor and the Perfect, The Rise of Learning in the Franciscan Order, 1209–1310*, Ithaca, NY, Cornell University Press.
Thom, P. (2013), 'Robert Kilwardby on Syllogistic Form', in *The Cambridge Companion to Robert Kilwardby*, P. Thom. and H. Lagerlund (eds), Leiden/Boston, Brill, pp. 131–63.
Thom, P. (2015), 'Logical Form', in *The Oxford Handbook of Medieval Philosophy*, J. Marenbon (ed.), Oxford, Oxford University Press, pp. 271–88.
Vv. Aa. (1978), *Le Scuole degli Ordini Medicanti (secoli XIII-XIV)*, Spoleto, Centro Italiano di Studi sull'Alto Medioevo.

Vv. Aa. (2002), *Studio et studia: le scuole degli ordini mendicanti tra XIII e XIV secolo*, Spoleto, Centro Italiano di Studi sull'Alto Medioevo.

Vv. Aa. (2012), *Philosophy and Theology in the Studia of the Religious Orders and at the Papal and Royal Courts*, Courtenay et al. (eds), Turnhout, Brepols.

Ward, J. O. (1996) 'Rhetoric in the Faculty of Arts at the Universities of Paris and Oxford in the Middle Ages: A Summary of the Evidence', *Archivum Latinitatis Medii Aevi, Bulletin du Cange* LIV, pp. 159–231.

5

Inference and enthymeme in Ockham

Paola Müller

5.1 Introduction

The characteristics of simplicity and immediacy attributed by Aristotle to the enthymeme urged to express the syllogism in the most synthetic form possible, in an abbreviated form.[1]

Traditional mediaeval exegesis of the passage from Aristotle's *Rhetorica*[2] focuses on the absence of one of the two premises, making this the distinguishing feature of the enthymeme from the syllogism. Thanks to the influence of Boethius,[3] the enthymeme becomes the imperfect, mutilated syllogism, in that it is not explicit in all parts of the syllogism. In the thirteenth century, Peter of Spain[4] further entrenches this meaning by studying topics using enthymemes as incomplete syllogisms, endowed with three terms but only two utterances. Thanks to the development of topics and its gradual absorption into the doctrine of consequences, enthymemes' treatment will change. William of Ockham (c. 1289–1347) is placed in this new context, in which elements of the tradition and innovations of terminist logic come together.

Since Ockham speaks of enthymemes or argumentation in an enthymematic way within the treatment of consequences and topics, we will begin with a quick overview highlighting the link between topical logic, consequence theory and enthymemes (Section 5.2). We will then investigate the application of hylomorphic language to the doctrine of propositional inference, which leads Ockham to distinguish between material and formal consequences (Section 5.3) based on whether an intrinsic mean or an extrinsic mean is used. Enthymemes fall under formal consequences valid by an intrinsic mean. It will be seen how Ockham's elaboration keeps together semantic and syntactic characters. The talk will finally open up to the enthymeme's role in treating fallacies (Section 5.4).

5.2 Enthymeme, topicals and consequences

In the first half of the fourteenth century, several masters devoted separate treatises or sections within *summae* to consequences, very similar to what modern logic calls the doctrine of inference. In the former, there emerges an approach to logical relations between propositions based on both terms and propositions; in the latter, the consequences' study is with arguments, not with propositions. The masters rarely used synonymously the terms 'conditional' and 'consequences'.

Today we would say that inference is a performance in that it does not state a state of affairs; instead, conditional propositions state to obtain a consequent and antecedent relation. The latter belong to object language, the former to metalanguage, although mediaeval logic does not distinguish between object language and metalanguage.

Moreover, while conditional propositions are true or false, consequences, as arguments, are valid or invalid, hold or do not hold. An antecedent and a consequent form both conditional propositions and consequences: in the former, they correspond to *prodosis* and *apodosis*, in the latter to what comes before and what comes after.

The argument holds when the premises are right and the inference is valid. In other words: inference such as A $\vdash$ B, where A denotes a proposition serving as an antecedent and B a proposition serving as a consequent, A's truth guarantees B's truth either by terms' meaning in each proposition or by the form of A and B. The rules ensure the transition from the premise (or set of premises) A to the conclusion.

Mediaeval masters used the topical logic to explain valid inference,[5] as is evident from the gradual absorption of topicals into consequence theory around the fourteenth century.[6]

The enthymeme falls under topical logic, which is attentive to the validity or inclusiveness of the argument.

The traditional doctrine of the enthymeme is elaborated around the second century by authors such as Galen (*c.* 129–201)[7] and Alexander of Aphrodisias (second century AD),[8] influenced by the principles of Stoic and Peripatetic logic,[9] of a strictly syntactic-formal nature. Galen insists on the semantic aspects of the problem.

It will be taken up later by Ammonius (*c.* 174–242)[10] and John Philoponus (†*c.* 567)[11] and transmitted by Boethius (*c.* 480–525).[12] What prevails is the understanding of enthymeme as a syllogism lacking completeness. Therefore, it is necessary to complete the enthymematic argument, that is, to lead it back to the syllogistic form and justify it.

The starting point for the mediaeval treatment is Boethius, for whom, in order to demonstrate the validity of an enthymeme, it is necessary to go back to the principles that underlie it. This process takes place in stages. In the first instance, it is necessary to complete the argument with the universal proposition on which it depends. It is then necessary to indicate the inferential scheme based on the validity of the argument thus completed. It is necessary to identify what Boethius calls *maxima propositio*, whose specific quality is to be *known for itself*, and *differentia maximae propositionis*.

> Maximal propositions have two functions in *De top. diff.* First, they are general premises essential to the validity of certain dialectical arguments, though they are not always an explicit part of the argument. Secondly, they help find arguments because, in Boethius's view, they are the principles that give arguments their force and the generalizations on which arguments depend. [. . .] *Differentiae* must function to find argument by aiding in the discovery of such intermediates.[13]

Let us take the enthymeme 'a man runs; therefore, an animal runs' and proceed according to Boethius's instructions: 'every man is an animal' constitutes the topical difference; 'everything that is predicated of the species is predicated of the genus' represents the *maxima topica*. From this, it follows that the enthymeme 'a man runs; therefore, an animal runs' is a valid consequence. By identifying the maxim and the difference, it was possible to verify the validity of the propositional inference, which can be traced back to the syllogism 'every man is an animal, a man runs; therefore, an animal runs'.

The rediscovery of the *Second Analytics*[14] emphasizes the categorical syllogism as the foundation of inference, combined with the influence of terminist logic from the mid-thirteenth century onwards, leading to the development of a new consideration of the relationship between topical principles and syllogism.[15]

Topical principles, considered as rules of inference, are discussed in the context of consequences.

Ockham returns topical analysis to an inferential form formulated in object language, moving away from a metalinguistic explanation of the subject.[16]

That the enthymeme is an 'incomplete' syllogism, a *syllogismus imperfectus*, is an idea that is conveyed by many of Aristotle's commentators[17] and that we also find in Ockham, who wishes 'to subsume enthymemes under the rubric of formal inferences by indicating how they can be reduced to syllogism'.[18]

5.3 Formal consequence and material consequence

The use of hylomorphic terminology in logic can be found well before the Latin translations of Aristotle. It is already found in Alexander of Aphrodisias's syllogisms, which makes the form correspond to the mode and not to the figure. Such terminology not only emphasizes the relational character of consequences but also concerns the classification of enthymemes.[19]

Ockham makes use of hylomorphic language in the subdivision of consequences.[20] He proposes nine subdivisions within consequences,[21] the most important of which, concerning our discourse, are those between absolute consequence (*simplex*) and factual or as-of-now consequence (*ut nunc*), between consequence that holds in virtue of an intrinsic mean and consequence that holds in virtue of an extrinsic mean and that between formal consequence and material consequence.[22]

The factual or as-of-now consequence is valid in a one-time frame, while it may be invalid in another. For example, the consequence 'Every animal runs; therefore, Socrates runs' is valid if Socrates exists and for the time of Socrates's existence. On the other hand, if Socrates does not exist, the antecedent may be true but the consequent false.[23] An absolute consequence is instead always valid, regardless of any temporal connotation. In this case, the antecedent can never be valid without the consequent also being true. For example, 'No animal runs; therefore, no man runs' is a *simplex* consequence because the antecedent cannot be true without the consequent being true.[24]

Consequences can also be distinguished based on the mean by which they are valid. This medium can be intrinsic or extrinsic. The consequences that hold in virtue of an intrinsic mean imply for their validity a proposition formed by the same terms present in the antecedent and consequent of the consequence. For example, the consequence 'Socrates does not run; therefore, a man does not run' holds on the intrinsic mean 'Socrates is a man'.[25] Consequences that hold in virtue of an extrinsic mean imply a general rule concerning the form of propositions and imply a proposition that does not contain the terms that form antecedent and consequent. For example, the consequence 'The only man is an ass; therefore, every ass is a man' holds by the rule which affirms the permissibility of converting[26] exclusive and affirmative universal propositions – not by a proposition composed of the terms present in the extremes.[27] These conditions are not mutually exclusive but can indeed be present both. To sum up: the passage from the antecedent to the consequent of a conditional proposition is valid either through an intrinsic mean or an extrinsic mean or both.

The distinction between formal and material consequence is one that directly involves the discussion about the enthymeme.

Ockham calls 'formal' the consequence valid by a logical rule concerning the structure of the propositions that compose it. In the *Summa Logicae* he distinguishes two formal consequences according to the medium that makes them valid. The first type is valid by an extrinsic mean; that is, it holds by rules concerning the proposition's form.[28] For example, the consequence 'The only man is an ass; therefore, every ass is a man' refers to a general rule concerning the conversion of universal exclusive and affirmative propositions, according to which an exclusive affirmative proposition converts into a universal affirmative one.[29]

The second type of formal consequence can be valid due to the concurrence of an intrinsic mean and an extrinsic mean. This extrinsic mean concerns the 'general conditions' of the propositions, their form, 'not their truth or falsity, nor their necessity or impossibility'.[30] The consequence 'Socrates does not run; therefore a man does not run' is immediately valid by an intrinsic mean, that is, it holds thanks to the proposition 'Socrates is a man', which allows the formal consequence to be transformed into a syllogism: 'Socrates is a man; Socrates does not run; therefore, a man does not run'. This consequence turns out to be valid if and only if the intrinsic mean ('Socrates is a man') is true, that is, if 'Socrates' and 'man' assume for the same individual. If Socrates assumed for a donkey or a plant, the consequence would not hold. This consequence also holds mediately thanks to an extrinsic mean, namely the general rule that states that 'from singular to indefinite and from lower to higher with a negation placed after it is a good consequence'. Ockham here composes together two rules[31] presented among those that 'serve enthymemes arising from particular and indefinite propositions', specifying that these rules apply if the terms are taken according to their personal or significant supposition.[32] This specification is consistent with what was stated earlier: if the term Socrates was not assumed in a meaningful sense, that is, indicating a particular individual, but according to its material supposition, that is, because of its material structure or grammatical function, the intrinsic mean could not be true. Such rules are enumerated among those proper to the consequences that hold in virtue of the intrinsic mean.[33]

Thus, we have two types of formal consequences:

(a) the formal consequence that holds by an extrinsic mean, and
(b) the formal consequence that holds immediately thanks to an intrinsic mean and mediately thanks to an extrinsic mean.

In both cases, the extrinsic mean is present; in no case is a formal consequence given that it is valid only by the intrinsic mean. In the first case (a), the extrinsic mean is related to the proposition's form and syncategorematic terms' arrangement – in this case, '*tantum*'. In the second case (b), on the other hand, the extrinsic mean relates to the categorical terms (Socrates, man) and their semantic relation (between lower and higher, between part and whole, between defined and definition) that holds the terms together.[34]

It should be noted that to clarify the role of an extrinsic mean, consisting of a true general proposition, Ockham uses the *superior–inferior* relation rather than the *genus–species* relation. This use allows him to take the utterance's propositional content according to the personal and meaningful supposition, thus making a *descensus*[35] from the general to the particular, and not according to the simple supposition, which is conceptual in nature.[36]

To clarify this point, two other Ockham's texts can help us: the *Ordinatio* and the *Expositio super libros elenchorum*.

In q. 1 of d. 4 of the first book of the *Commentary on the Sentences*,[37] Ockham explicitly introduces a twofold distinction between formal consequences, suggesting that the second type of formal consequence includes enthymemes.

Here the *Venerabilis Inceptor* distinguishes formal consequences according to the reason for which they are valid. We will therefore have:

(A) the formal consequence that holds *ratione complexorum* and corresponds to the syllogism, and
(B) the formal consequence that holds *ratione terminorum*, as the terms are placed in relation to each other in a certain way.

Characterizing the first (A), Ockham refers to two rules concerning propositions: 'From exclusive to universal with transposed terms is a good consequence'[38] and 'from a copulative to a part of it is a good consequence'.[39] The first rule states that it is licit to pass from an exclusive proposition ('Only Socrates is a philosopher') to the corresponding universal proposition, after exchanging the order of the terms that act as subject and predicate ('every philosopher is Socrates'). The second rule states that it is permissible to pass from a copulative proposition, that is, from a proposition formed by two or more categorical statements joined by the preposition '*et*' ('Socrates runs and Plato disputes'), to one of its parts ('therefore Socrates runs' or 'therefore Plato disputes'). This formal consequence (A) thus refers to the first formulation (a) we found in the *Summa Logicae*.

The second formal consequence (B) does hold by a rule ('from the universal to the particular is a good consequence'), but Ockham stresses the importance of reference to the meaning of the terms in the propositions. The consequence 'every man runs; therefore, this man runs' is valid if it points to (*demonstrat*) Socrates, who is really a man, and not an ass. Therefore, the extrinsic mean is also flanked by an intrinsic mean, by which one term is affirmed or denied by the other. This intrinsic mean, not made explicit by Ockham, should therefore be 'this man is a man'. Such a mean guarantees truth and 'establishes a semantic relation between "this man" and "man"'.[40] Surprisingly, Ockham does not mention supposition doctrine to explicate further and clarify this distinction. The term 'man' has in both propositions a personal supposition.[41] However, in the proposition 'every man runs' it has a common supposition,[42] characterized by logical descent to disjunction, since it is possible to infer from the initial proposition containing the common term 'man', at the conjunction of the corresponding singulars ('therefore this man and that man and that other man, etc.'), indicating all the individuals included in the common term. In the proposition 'this man runs', the term 'man' has a discrete supposition instead,[43] since the term 'man' is singularized. The supposition implies semantic and syntactic relations.[44] Semantic, in that the term supposes for one or more realities whose place it holds. Syntactic, because it takes place in a proposition and uses the idea of predication. This formal consequence (B) thus recalls the second form (b) we found in the *Summa Logicae*, in that there is recourse to a double factor.

Since (B) can be reduced to a syllogism, it corresponds to the enthymeme.

In the *Expositio in libros elenchorum*, dealing with fallacies, Ockham proposes a distinction within the formal consequence using elements present in both the *Summa* and *Ordinatio*; in fact, he distinguishes formal consequences based on whether they hold by complex or incomplex elements, thanks to an intrinsic mean or an extrinsic mean.[45] It recognizes:

(*a*) formal consequences that hold for the incomplexes and an intrinsic mean, and
(*b*) formal consequences that hold for complexes and an extrinsic mean.

The example given for the first type (*a*) corresponds to that given in the *Ordinatio* for (B): 'Every man runs, therefore Socrates runs'. This consequence holds for the fact that Socrates is a man, and therefore the intrinsic mean is true. For the second type (*b*) he proposes the consequence 'Only Socrates is a man; therefore, every man is Socrates' which holds by the general rule (which serves as the extrinsic mean) that 'from an exclusive proposition to a universal one from the transposed terms is a good consequence', as we saw earlier.

We can say that Ockham means by 'complex' the propositions and by 'incomplex' the categorical terms, without identifying them respectively with extrinsic mean and intrinsic mean, since 'complex' and 'incomplex' refer to a state of fact of the structure of the proposition, while 'intrinsic mean' and 'extrinsic mean' refer to a statement concerning the relationship between the constituents of the consequence.[46]

Putting together the characterizations of formal consequences found in the three works, we can distinguish between formal consequences that hold in virtue of the relations there are between the propositions that constitute them (antecedent and consequent); relations that refer to rules; and formal consequences that hold in virtue of the semantic relations between the terms that constitute the propositions of the consequence itself.

Instead, a consequence is said to be material[47] when it holds up exclusively because of the terms that constitute it.

The propositional material is the categorical term. The qualification of material given to conditional implication indicates that it is a kind of implication related to the material consideration of truth values, prescinding from the connections related to meanings. In other words: while with the term 'implication', we commonly mean a consequence that logically connects a consequent to an antecedent, the material implication proper to the conditional calculus indicates the presence of the truth values established by the conditional implication.

In this regard, Ockham gives two paradoxical examples: 'A man runs, therefore God exists', and 'Man is an ass; therefore, God does not exist'. In the first example, the consequent is a necessary proposition, but it has an irrelevant connection to the antecedent. In the second example, the antecedent is an impossible proposition, from which a false consequent follows. Ockham uses a procedure that makes use of the assumption of a necessary conclusion ('therefore God exists')[48] or of an impossible premise ('man is an ass').

According to the corrections proposed by F. Schupp[49] to the critical edition of the *Summa Logicae* edited by Buytaert, even the material consequence would have an extrinsic medium of reference. This theory would be consistent with the interpretation of the two examples proposed by Ockham. Both examples refer to two rules of the derivation of the school of Parvipontani[50] and rest on the *locus a minori*. The former holds based on the rule 'what is necessary follows from anything', while the latter holds for the rule that 'from the impossible anything follows'.[51] The qualification of necessary and impossible attributed to the utterances derives from the meaning of the categorical terms (man, donkey, God) contained in the propositions. Again, rules belonging to propositional logic are relocatable within the framework of the logic of terms. In both examples, the antecedent (man, donkey) categorical term does not appear in the consequent, where instead, the term 'God' is always present. The terms of the antecedent and the consequent are therefore unrelated. There is, therefore, no semantic relation between the propositions which constitute the consequent.

We might say that formal consequences hold in virtue of some relation between antecedent and consequent, whereas material consequences hold in virtue of some relationships within their antecedent or consequent. According to this understanding, material consequences do not give rise to enthymemes since they cannot be traced to a syllogism. Instead, it is the formal consequences that hold for an intrinsic mean that are enthymematic since they have a missing premise and can be traced back to a syllogism. Thus, it is the presence of the intrinsic mean that primarily characterizes an enthymematic consequence. Ockham himself states that the extrinsic mean, even if it is added to the antecedent, does not form a syllogism. The consequence, 'Only Socrates is a man; therefore, every man is Socrates', cannot be resolved in a syllogism, but only in the concatenation, 'Only Socrates is a man; from the exclusive to the universal with the transposed terms is a good consequence; therefore, every man is Socrates', which is undoubtedly not a syllogism.[52]

However, we have seen that for Ockham, no formal consequence holds only by an intrinsic mean. It is, therefore, necessary also an extrinsic mean on which the formal consequence rests mediately. This extrinsic mean that is the general rule can be applied only thanks to the intrinsic mean, making the argument valid more immediately and completely.[53]

The double reference to intrinsic mean and extrinsic mean may indicate that topical logic, understood as 'logic of arguments or consequences' whose validity depends on a semantic relation between their terms endowed with meaning, constitutes the most extensive part of Ockham's treatise on consequences.[54]

Ockham seems to oscillate between a syntactic and a semantic notion of logical consequence. He tries to bring back the validity of all consequences 'to a true-functional property of inference', referring as the ultimate criterion to an extrinsic mean, that is, to a principle based on the form of the proposition by 'rules that [allow] its syntactic transformation'.[55] The tracing of material consequences to an extrinsic mean, and the consequent connection to a true-functional property, occurs through an intrinsic mean that depends on a semantic relation between its terms. This relates the extrinsic mean to 'general conditions of propositions such as truth or falsity, necessity or impossibility'.[56] Such conditions are also semantic in nature.

Likewise, formal consequences that are[57] valid according to a true-functional criterion are also valid material consequences but not vice versa; moreover, 'any valid material consequence, that is, according to the criterion of relevance, can be transformed into a valid formal consequence, but not vice versa'.[58] The two different conceptions of logical consequence's validity remain distinct, despite Ockham's proposal to trace the validity of all consequences to an extrinsic mean.

5.4 Enthymeme and fallacy

To get a fuller picture of Ockham's position about enthymemes, it is worth seeing what he writes about them in dealing with fallacies (*fallaciae*), that is, those captious arguments that do not guarantee the truthfulness of conclusions according to Aristotelian dictates, even though they stand as a 'justified claim'.[59]

Ockham applies the terminology of *loci* theory, derived from Boethian terminology, to the theory of fallacies.[60] This application allows us to speak of the thirteen Aristotelian classes of fallacies as the same number of *sophistic loci*. It also allows one to identify 'the relevant Maxima, that is, the general, erroneous, but a plausible rule that gives strength to the captious argument'.[61]

Ockham distinguishes the fallacies that depend on linguistic expression (*in dictione*) from those that do not depend on linguistic expression (*extra dictionem*). Taking up the division proposed by Aristotle, Ockham states that there are thirteen fallacies: six depend on linguistic expression, and seven do not depend on it.[62]

The six classes of fallacies that depend on linguistic expression are due to ambiguity, the pitfalls of which can be neutralized (or accentuated) by resorting to the distinctive features of linguistic expressions, such as pronunciation. Unlike those *in dictione*, Aristotle does not collect fallacies not depending on linguistic expression under a common category; instead, this seems to be of a 'residual classification'[63] into which fallacies are placed to the distinctive features of linguistic expression that is not relevant.

Reference to the enthymeme or an enthymematic procedure appears in the case of three fallacies: the fallacy *figura dictionis, secundum quid et simpliciter, consequentis*.

The source of confusion of the fallacy of the form of expression (*figura dictionis*) is occasioned by the morphological similarity of some terms, although they have different meanings and belong to different grammatical or semantic categories – for example, exchanging the neuter gender for the masculine because of the desinence.

Using a classification that can be traced back to the Aristotelian treatment that has become current since the second half of the twelfth century, Ockham proposes a tripartition of the fallacy due to linguistic expression,[64] depending on whether one refers to the difference of grammatical accidences (which frequently leads to solecism),[65] to the diversity of meanings[66] and to the different modes of meaning.[67] The latter group can be further subdivided according to the use of terms with a different supposition,[68] or a categorical exchange, the presence of a syncategorem,[69] the tense[70] or the verb's mode.[71]

At the end of this fallacy's analytical exposition, the *Venerabilis Inceptor* adds that this fallacy can also occur in consequences and enthymemes since it does not depend only on one predication being changed into another. It also depends on the significant value of the terms occurring in utterances that signify all their meanings, without referring to something in a principal way and something else in a secondary way, without signifying something in a direct case and something else in an oblique one, something in an affirmative way and something else in a negative way.[72] This is the case of the consequences: 'a man was an animal; therefore an animal was a man' or 'whiteness can be a color; therefore a color can be whiteness'. In both, there is a term of the genus of the substance or an abstract term in the genus of the quality corresponding concrete ones supposing for distinct realities different from the one to which the abstract counterparts refer.[73]

The enthymematic form also appears about the fallacy in an absolute sense or for a specific aspect (*secundum quid et simpliciter*). This fallacy is related to semantic considerations: it occurs when one argues from something taken with a determination (*secundum quid*) to something taken per se (*simpliciter*), thinking that the two elements are similar to each other, although, in reality, they are different.[74] In order to assess the validity of these enthymemes, Ockham states that one must understand whether the added intrinsic mean is necessary or not.

For example, the enthymeme 'Ethiopian is white by the teeth; therefore, Ethiopian is white', to be traced back to a categorical syllogism, should have as its middle: 'everything white by the teeth is white'. However, such an utterance is not necessary, so the fallacy occurs.[75] The enthymeme 'Socrates is white; therefore, Socrates is' can be reduced to a hypothetical syllogism by adding the premise: 'if something is white, it is'. A premise that is necessary and makes the syllogism valid. Only if the middle is not necessary does one have the fallacy *secundum quid et simpliciter*.[76]

Ockham also uses a hylomorphic terminology, distinguishing between defective syllogisms from a material point of view (*peccantes in materia*) and a formal point of view (*peccantes in forma*). The *materia* is the specific statements that serve as premises;

the *forma* is the syllogistic structure, which disregards the individual terms used from time to time to establish general rules that are always valid. The first ones are formally valid syllogisms, which contain at least one false premise; the second ones are invalid syllogisms because a formal defect vitiates them.

The inference 'Ethiopian is white by the teeth; therefore, Ethiopian is white' is defective from a material point of view, since, when reduced to a syllogism, it has a false premise ('everything white by the teeth is white').[77] To have a fallacy *secundum quid et simpliciter* the falsity of the mean by which the syllogism holds must not occur simultaneously (*simul*) of what is predicated of both extremes.[78]

However, the enthymeme can be resolved by transforming the antecedent into a proposition of equal meaning, that is, transforming 'the Ethiopian is white by the teeth' into 'the Ethiopian has white teeth'. This transformation makes it easy to deduce the incorrectness of the reasoning. It is not permissible to argue: 'the Ethiopian has white teeth; therefore, the Ethiopian is white'.[79]

The fallacy of consequent (*consequens*) consists in the error of considering convertible the implication's link leading from antecedent's truth to that of the consequent, as when we say, 'the earth is wet; therefore, it rained'.[80] This fallacy is frequently found in enthymematic arguments.[81] In this regard, Ockham provides special rules that one must know to not fall into this fallacy. Such rules act as extrinsic mediums of inferences. It is necessary to know all the rules of propositional inferences and all those that can be used for enthymemes to recognize and resolve this kind of fallacy.[82]

Again, the reduction of the enthymeme 'every man runs, therefore every animal runs' to the syllogism 'every man runs, every animal is man; therefore, every animal runs' involves a defect from a material point of view since the added premise ('every animal is man') is false.[83]

The enthymematic procedure thus turns out to be necessary to distinguish the fallacy of the consequent. For, in this case, it is necessary to reduce the syllogism to two enthymemes and see that the conclusion cannot be inferred from the premises, although the premises can be inferred from the conclusion. For example, the syllogism 'man is an animal; the donkey is an animal; therefore, donkey is a man' must be hived off into 'man is an animal; therefore, donkey is a man' and into 'donkey is an animal; therefore, donkey is a man'. The conclusion ('donkey is a man') is not derived from either premise. However, from the conclusion, it is possible to infer the premises: 'the donkey is a man; therefore, the man is an animal'; 'the donkey is a man, therefore the donkey is an animal'.[84]

Therefore, Ockham does not elaborate a specific doctrine of enthymemes but deals with them to treat consequences and fallacies. From his texts emerges an attempt to keep united the semantic approach with the syntactic one, as in the logical consequence. The terminology used refers to both aspects: complex and incomplex, terms and utterances. Thanks to the distinction between intrinsic mean, related to semantic rules that relate terms to each other, and extrinsic mean, which is a general rule of syntactic character, Ockham distinguishes formal consequence from material consequence. The enthymeme is among the formal consequences that hold thanks to an intrinsic mean since it can lead the enthymeme back to the syllogism. The extrinsic mean is a necessary condition but not sufficient: it is also a necessary general rule, the extrinsic mean, thanks to which the reasoning holds, albeit in a mediated way.

Ockham takes up the previous tradition, particularly the Boethian one, with inlays of originality, opening the way for subsequent treatises.

Notes

1 Sprute 1982; Zanatta 2004.
2 *Rhetorica* 1357a 13–19. Burnyeat 1996; Piazza 2000.
3 Boethius, *De topicis differentiis*, PL LXIV, 1184, B: 'Enthymema quippe est imperfectus syllogismus, id est oratio in qua non omnibus propositionibus constitutis infertur festinata conclusio, ut si quis dicat: "Homo animal est, substantia igitur est"', *In Topicis Ciceronis Libri VI*, PL LXIV, 1050 B-C: 'Enthymema vero est imperfectus syllogismus, cuius aliquae partes, vel propter brevitatem, vel propter notitiam, praetermissae sunt', *De syllogismo categorico*, PL LXIV, 821 B: 'Sunt enim qui putantur esse huiusmodi syllogismi, in quidem tantum una propositio est et una conclusio. Qualis est hic: "Vides, vivis igitur"; "homo es; animal igitur es", et alia huiusmodi, quos scilicet veteres in syllogismis non acceperunt, syllogismus enim est aliquorum collectio. At vero collectio non nisi plurimorum est, et quicumque unam posuit propositionem, ille non colligit. Nullum igitur faciet syllogismum. Debet enim syllogismus, ut angustissimus sit, duabus propositionibus comprobari.'
4 Peter of Spain, *Summaries of Logic*, V. 3, p. 198: 'Entimema est sillogismus imperfectus – idest oratio in qua non omnibus antea positis propositionibus infertur festinata conclusio, ut Omne animal currit; ergo omnis homo currit. In hac enim dicta argumentatione subintelligitur hec propositio – scilicet omnis homo est animal – et non apponitur ibi, quia si apponeretur ibi, perfectus esset sillogismus. Sciendum autem quod omne entimema debet reduci ad sillogismum. Ergo in quolibet entimemate sunt tres termini, sicut in sillogismo. Quorum terminorum duo ponuntur in conclusione et sunt extremitates, et alius est medium et numquam ponitur in conclusione. Illarum autem extremitatum altera est sumpta bis in entimemate, altera semel.'
5 Bird 1962; Green-Pedersen 1984, 1987.
6 Stump 1982; Biard & Mariani Zini 2009; Klima 2016; Archambault 2018.
7 Barnes 2003; Morison 2008a, 2008b; Chiaradonna 2008.
8 Grimaldi 1988; Flannery 1995; Moraux 2001; Frede 2007.
9 Müller 1969; Bobzien 2003.
10 Burnyeat 1994.
11 Sorabji 1988; Fortenbaugh 2000; Kraus 2012.
12 Magnano 2014.
13 Stump 1981, p. 250.
14 Bianchi 2011; Bydén and Thomsen Thörnqvist 2017; de Haas, Leunissen, and Martijn 2020.
15 Jacobi 1993; King 2001.
16 Stump 1989; Dutilh Novaes 2008.
17 Green 1995; Kraus 2012; Fredal 2018.
18 M. Mc Cord Adams 1987, vol. 1 p. 459.
19 Crimi 2018.

20 Read 1993; Spruyt 2003; Dutilh Novaes 2012.
21 Pinzani 2005; Crimi 2014.
22 Further distinctions within consequences can be traced to the logical functions of the constituent terms or their grammatical characters: different consequences are depending on whether the subject supposes in a significant way or simply or materially, whether the antecedent is affirmative or negative and so on. Ockham, *Summa Logicae,* III-3, c. 1, pp. 590 59–80.
23 Ockham, *Summa Logicae*, III-3 c. 1 pp. 587–8 11–18: 'Consequentia "ut nunc" est quando antecedens pro aliquo tempore potest esse verum sine consequente sed non pro isto tempore. Sicut ista consequentia est ut nunc solum "omne animal currit, igitur Sortes currit", quia pro isto tempore pro quo Sortes est animal, non potest antecedens esse verum sine consequente; et tamen pro aliquo tempore poterit antecedens esse verum sine consequente, quia quando Sortes erit mortuus, poterit antecedens esse verum consequente exsistente falso.'
24 Ockham, *Summa Logicae*, III-3 c. 1 pp. 588 18–22: 'Consequentia simplex est quando pro nullo tempore poterit antecedens esse verum sine consequente. Sicut ista consequentia est simplex "nullum animal currit, ergo nullus homo currit", quia numquam poterit haec est vera "nullum animal currit" nisi ista sit vera "nullus homo currit", si formetur.'
25 Ockham, *Summa Logicae*, III-3 c. 1 pp. 589 23–8: 'Alia distinctio est quod aliquando consequentia tenet per medium extrinsecum, aliquando per medium intrinsecum. Illa consequentia tenet per medium intrinsecum quando tenet virtute alicuius propositionis formatae ex eisdem terminis. Sicut ista "Sortes non currit, igitur homo non currit" tenet virtute istius medii "Sortes est homo"; unde nisi haec esset vera "Sortes est homo", non valeret consequentia.'
26 According to the Aristotelian tradition of the *Analitici Primi* (I c. 2 25a 1–26), Ockham dedicates some chapters of the second part of the *Summa Logicae* (cc. 21–9) to the analysis of the conversion of the propositions, then used in the third part to lead back the syllogisms of second and third figure to the syllogisms of first figure. The conversion of propositions is the operation by which from an utterance one derives another, considered equivalent, through the exchange of the respective positions of the terms that act as subject and predicate, without changing the form of the proposition or altering the truth. Müller 2012, pp. 145–51.
27 Ockham, *Summa Logicae*, III-3 c. 1 pp. 588 28–34: 'Consequentia autem quae tenet per medium extrinsecum est quando tenet per aliquam regulam generalem quae non plus respicit illos terminos quam alios. Sicut ista consequentia "tantum homo est asinus, igitur omnis asinus est homo" non tenet per aliquam propositionem veram formatam ex istis terminis "homo" et "asinus", sed per istam regulam generalem "exclusiva et universalis de terminis transpositis idem significant et convertuntur".'
28 Ockham, *Summa Logicae*, III-3 c. 1 pp. 589 46–50: 'Consequentia formalis est duplex, quia quaedam tenet per medium extrinsecum, quod respicit formam propositionis. Sicut sunt tales regulae "ab exclusiva ad universalem de terminis transpositis est bona consequentia"; "ex maiore de necessario et minore de inesse sequitur conclusione de necessario".'
29 Ockham, *Summa Logicae*, II c. 23 pp. 326 28–33: 'Circa conversionem propositionum exclusivarum est sciendum quod exclusiva non convertitur in exclusivam. Non enim sequitur "tantum animal est homo, igitur tantum homo est animal", sed ipsa convertitur in universalem, sicut sequitur "tantum animal est homo, igitur omnis

homo est animal". Similiter sequitur "tantum homo non currit, igitur omne non currens est homo".

30 Ockham, *Summa Logicae*, III-3 c. 1 pp. 589 51-4: 'Quaedam tenet per medium intrinsecum immediate, et mediate per medium extrinsecum respiciens generales condiciones propositionum, non veritatem vel falsitatem, nec necessitatem vel impossibilitatem, cuiusmodi est ista "Sortes non currit, igitur homo non currit".

31 Ockham, *Summa Logicae*, III-3 c. 6 pp. 600 24-6: 'Alia regula: ab inferiori ad superius postposita negatione est bona consequentia, sed non simplex, nisi quando praedicatio superioris de inferiori est necessaria.'

32 Ockham, *Summa Logicae*, III-3 c. 6 pp. 600 6-10: 'Et quia, [. . .] particularis et indefinita convertuntur semper quando termini supponunt personaliter et significative, et quia omnes fere regulae quae deserviunt enthymematibus ex particularibus et indefinitis deserviunt etiam consequentiis ex singularibus, ideo dicendum est de eis communiter.' *Expositio in librum Perihermeneias Aristotelis*, OPh II, c. 18 § 2, pp. 323 48-53: 'Et ideo omnes tales regulae "ab inferiori ad superius est bona consequentia", "a negatione superioris ad negationem inferioris est bona consequentia" et "prius est illud a quo non convertitur consequentia" debent intelligi quando in talibus consequentiis exercitis termini omnes supponunt personaliter et significative".

33 Ockham, *Summa Logicae*, III-3 c. 6 pp. 600 12-13: 'Est autem primo dicendum de illis quae tenent per medium intrinsecum.'

34 Crimi 2018.

35 The *descensus ad inferiora* is a logical procedure for establishing the truth or falsity of propositions. Ockham distinguishes various types of logical descent to the singular, according to the possibility of inferring from a given proposition containing a common term the disjunction of the corresponding propositions, concerning the individuals included in the common term; the conjunction of the relevant corresponding singulars; a proposition containing a predicate given by the disjunction of the individual terms.

36 Buzzetti 2019, p. 1024.

37 Ockham, *Ordinatio*, I d. 4 q. 1 p. 15: 'Dico quod consequentia formalis est duplex. Aliquando tenet ratione complexorum, et talis consequentia est syllogismus, quia ubicumque et ex quibuscumque terminis fiat syllogismus habens tales praemissas sic dispositas, ibi est bonus syllogismus. Similiter ab exclusiva ad universalem de terminis transpositis est bona consequentia. Similiter a copulativa ad alteram partem est bona consequentia, quaecumque pars accipiatur. Et talis consequentia tenet in omnibus terminis. Aliquando consequentia est formalis praecise ratione terminorum, quia scilicet termini ipsi se habent sic ad invicem vel sic. Et isto modo ab universali ad singularem est bona consequentia, non ad quamcumque, sed quia terminus unus continetur sub alio. Unde bene sequitur "omnis homo currit, igitur iste homo currit", demonstrando Sortem qui vere est homo. Sed non sequitur "omnis homo currit, igitur iste homo currit", demonstrando asinum. Et ratio est quia omnis consequentia tenet per medium unum intrinsecum in quo unus terminus verificatur vel negatur ab alio. Et ideo quando talis propositio per quam consequentia deberet reduci in syllogismum est vera, tunc est bona consequentia, et quando non est vera, tunc non valet.'

38 Ockham, *Summa Logicae*, II c. 17 pp. 305 268-76: 'Una est quod ab exclusiva ad universalem de terminis transpositis est bona consequentia et e converso, quia semper exclusiva et universalis de terminis transpositis convertuntur, et est ista regula intelligenda quando praeiacens exclusivae et similiter universalis de terminis

transpositis sunt convertibiles, ita quod utraque possit proprie converti. Vel si praeiacens exclusivae sit semper convertibilis, nulla mutatione facta circa terminos praeter solam transpositionem vel aliqua mutatione, tunc debet consimilis universalis accipi, cum qua convertatur exclusiva.'

39 Ockham, *Summa Logicae*, II c. 32 pp. 348-9 29-35: 'Oportet autem scire quod semper a copulative ad utramque partem est consequentia bona sicut sequitur "Sortes non currit et Plato disputat, ergo Plato disputat"; sed e converso est fallacia consequentis. Tamen sciendum est quod quandoque ab altera parte copulativae ad copulativam potest esse consequentia bona gratia materiae, puta si una pars copulativae inferat aliam, tunc ab illa parte ad totam copulativam consequentia bona.'

40 Crimi 2018, p. 263.

41 A term has a personal supposition when it is used in the meaningful function that is proper to it by nature or convention – that is, when it designates the concrete individuals whose place it holds in the proposition.

42 A term has common personal supposition when it is a common name that stands in place of the individuals included in it. It is proper to the subject of universal affirmative propositions.

43 A term has a discrete personal supposition when it designates only one individual, and the proposition in which it occurs is singular, that is, when the supposing term is a proper name, or a demonstrative pronoun taken significantly, or a common term accompanied by a demonstrative adjective.

44 Biard 1989, pp. 82-4.

45 Ockham, *Expositio super libros Elenchrorum*, II c. 7 § 8, pp. 204-5 125-35: 'Dicendum est quod sicut aliquae consequentiae sunt formales ratione complexorum, et aliquae ratione incomplexorum; hoc est aliquae tenent per medium intrisecum et aliquae per medium extrinsecum. Nam ista consequentia "omnis homo currit; igitur Sortes currit" non tenet ratione complexorum quia tunc: quandocumque antecedens esset universalis et consequens esset una singularis, esset bona consequentia; et ita ista consequentia esset bona: "omne animal est substantia; igitur haec albedo est substantia". Et ideo consequentia non tenet ratione complexorum nec per medium extrinsecum, sed tenet ratione incomplexorum et per medium intrinsecum, quia enim Sortes est homo, ita quod hoc medium est verum "Sortes est homo", ideo praedicta consequentia est bona [. . .]. Sed aliquae consequentiae tenent ratione complexorum et per medium extrinsecum. Sicut ista consequentia est bona: "tantum Sortes est homo; igitur omnis homo est Sortes". Et tenet ratione complexorum, ex hoc scilicet quod arguitur ab exclusiva ad universalem de terminis transpositis. Et tenet per medium extrinsecum, per hoc scilicet quod "ab exclusiva ad universalem de terminis transpositis est bona consequentia" [. . .]. Et ita aliquae consequentiae sunt formales ratione complexorum et per medium extrinsecum, aliquae sunt formales ratione incomplexorum et per medium intrinsecum.'

46 Crimi 2018, p. 267.

47 Kaufmann 1993.

48 Ockham specifies that an utterance is necessary not because it is always true but instead because if it is, it is true and cannot be false. The proposition 'God exists' is necessary, not because it is always true (if no one formulates it or if no one knows it, it is not true) but because at the moment it is uttered or known, it cannot be false, except because of the change in the meaning of the terms composing it. Ockham, *Summa Logicae,* II, c. 9 pp. 275 72-9.

49 Schupp 1993.

50 Iwakuma 1993; Spruyt 1993.
51 Ockham specifies the scope of these two rules, which are based on the definition of consequence's validity, in this case, given by the relationship of truth between the constituent parts. Ockham, *Summa Logicae*, III-3 c. 38 pp. 730–1 88–92: 'Aliae regulae dantur, quod "ex impossibili sequitur quodllibet" et quod "necessarium sequitur ad quodlibet"; ideo sequitur "tu es asinus, igitur tu es Deus", et sequitur "tu es albus, igitur Deus est trinus et unus". Sed tales consequentiae non sunt formales, et ideo istae regulae non sunt multum usitatae.' Normore 2015.
52 Ockham, *Expositio super Libros Elenchorum*, c. 7 § 8, pp. 205 148–51: 'Dicitur autem "medium estrinsecun" quia, isto adiuncto antecedent, non fit syllogismus. Hic enim nulla est forma syllogistica: "tantum Sortes est homo; ab exclusiva ad universalem de terminis transpositis est bona consequentia; igitur omnis homo est Sortes".'
53 Ockham, *Summa Logicae*, III-3, c. 1 pp. 588–9 40–4: 'Dicendum est quod tenet per istud medium extrinsecum remote et mediate et insufficienter, quia praeter istam regulam generalem requiritur plus, scilicet quod Sortes sit homo; et ideo magis immediate et magis sufficienter tenet per istud medium "Sortes est homo", quod est medium intrinsecum.'
54 Bird 1962, pp. 321–2.
55 Buzzetti 2019, p. 1024.
56 Ockham, *Summa Logicae*, III-3, c. 1 pp. 589 52–3.
57 The formal consequences which maybe those (1) which hold in virtue of an extrinsic mean, concerning proposition's form, or those (2) which hold immediately in virtue of an intrinsic mean and mediately thanks to an extrinsic mean, concerning propositions' general conditions.
58 Buzzetti 2019, p. 1025.
59 Ebbesen 1981, 1987; Tabarroni 2002.
60 Every argument is based on a general principle or rule (*maxima propositio*) that constitutes its justification and gives it argumentative force. Such dialectical rules can be classified through the *differentia maximae*, which names a dialectical locus and defines a class of arguments that are warranted by the maxims sharing the same *differentia*. Ebbesen 1993.
61 Tabarroni 2002, p. 19.
62 Ockham, *Summa Logicae*, III-4 c. 1 pp. 749 3–5: 'Huiusmodi autem defectus vocantur fallaciae, penes quas peccant argumenta falsa'. 17–19: 'Secundo sciendum quod istarum fallaciarum quaedam ponuntur in dictione, quaedam extra dictionem. Sex autem fallaciae ponuntur in dictione et septem extra dictionem.'
63 Tabarroni 2002, p. 8.
64 Ockham, *Summa Logicae*, III-4 c. 10, pp. 792 27–31: 'Unde generaliter quandocumque est fallacia figurae dictionis, contingit invenire consimilem modum arguendi bonum ex aliis terminis, et hoc propter diversitatem accidentium grammaticalium vel modorum significandi vel propter diversitatem significatorum, largissime accipiendo "significata".'
65 Ockham, *Summa Logicae*, III-4 c. 10, pp. 792 32–5: 'Iuxta praedicta possunt accipi tres modi istius fallaciae. Quorum primus est quando accidit defectus in arguendo propter diversitatem accidentium grammaticalium diversarum dictionum. Et talis modus arguendi sophisticus vel semper vel frequenter ducit ad soloecismum.'
66 Ockham, *Summa Logicae*, III-4 c. 10, pp. 793 50–6: 'Secundus modus principalis istius fallaciae accipitur ex diversitate significatorum diversarum dictionum. Verumtamen aliqua diversitas talis est sufficiens ad istam fallaciam in aliquo modo arguendo

et aliqua non sufficit. Sed ad sciendum in speciali quando sufficit et quando non sufficit, per logicam sciri non potest, sicut nec per logicam sciri potest in speciali de qualibet dictione an sit aequivoca vel non sit aequivoca, sed hoc debet sciri per speciales scientias.'

67 Ockham, *Summa Logicae*, III-4 c. 10, pp. 798 188–91: 'Tertius modus principalis figurae dictionis est habens ortum ex diversitate modorum significandi diversarum dictionum quae videntur similes inter se, propter quod quandoque deceptus credit quod similiter est arguendum ex una dictione et ex alia.'

68 Ockham, *Summa Logicae*, III-4 c. 10, pp. 799 209–14: 'Et secundum praedicta sub isto tertio modo principali possunt accipi tres modi speciales istius fallaciae. Primus modus potest esse secundum dictiones quae habent finitas significationes et quae non habent finitas significationes. Et penes istum modum peccant consequentiae in quibus commutator unus modus supponendi in alium; sicut si arguatur sic "omnis homo est animal, ergo animal est omnis homo". Dutilh Novaes 2007.

69 Ockham, *Summa Logicae*, III-4 c. 10, pp. 801 268–71: 'Non solum autem tertius modus accidit ex vario modo significandi, qui frequenter accidit ex modo significandi termini categorematici et syncategorematici, sed etiam accidit ex diversis modis significandi incomplexorum in diversis praedicamentis.'

70 Ockham, *Summa Logicae,* III-4 c. 10, pp. 807 463–8: 'Aliter peccat talis modus arguendo penes fallaciam figurae dictionis, arguendo ex propositionibus de praeterito et de futuro, et hoc vel arguendo ex omnibus de praeterito vel ex una de praeterito et una de praesenti. Et eodem modo, proportionaliter, dicendum est de illis de futuro.'

71 Ockham, *Summa Logicae*, III-4 c. 10, pp. 809 513–15: 'Aliter contingit fallacia figurae dictionis ex diversitate praedicamentorum in propositionibus modalibus.'

72 Ockham, *Summa Logicae*, III-4 c. 10 pp. 809–10 542–52: 'Oportet scire quod non solum iste modus fallaciae figurae dictionis est in talibus discursibus compositis ex pluribus praemissis, sed etiam accidit in consequentiis et enthymematibus; quia iste modus non est tantum ex hoc quod unum praedicamentum commutatur in aliud, hoc est ex hoc quod primo in maiore accipitur signum distributivum correspondens uni praedicamento et postea accipitur sub incomplexum alterius praedicamenti. Quia numquam dicit Philosophus quod figura dictionis est ex commutatione unius praedicamenti in aliud, sed dicit quod est ex quod diversa sunt praedicamenta et easdem res diversimode significant, ideo frequenter non valent consequentiae ex incomplexis aliquorum praedicamentorum.'

73 Ockham, *Summa Logicae*, III-4 c. 10 pp. 810 559–63: 'Quae ideo bonae consequentiae sunt quia termini ex quibus componuntur non significant aliquid in recto et aliquid in obliquo, nec significant aliquid primo et principaliter et aliquid secundario, nec significant aliquid affirmative et aliquid negative, sed eodem modo significant omnia sua significata.'

74 Ockham, *Summa Logicae*, III-4 c. 13 pp. 831 2–4: 'Sequitur videre de fallacia secundum quid et simpliciter, quae est quando arguitur sophistice ab aliquo sumpto cum determinatione ad aliquid per se sumptum, vel e converso.'

75 Ockham, *Summa Logicae*, III-4 c. 13 pp. 837 188–96: 'Verbi gratia si arguatur sic "Sortes est albus secundum pedem, igitur Sortes est albus" addenda est ista propositio "omnem album secundum pedem est album", qua expressa completur forma syllogistica, sic arguendo "omne album secundum pedem est album; Sortes est albus secundum pedem; igitur Sortes est albus". Et si ista propositio, vel ista condicionalis, "si aliquid est album secundum pedem, ipsum est album" sit necessaria, prima

consequentia erit bona. Sed quia neutra illarum propositionum est necessaria, ideo est ibi fallacia secundum quid et simpliciter.'

76 Ockham, *Expositio super Libros elenchorum*, II, c. 10 § 2, pp. 264 57–63: 'Ad cuius intellectum sciendum quod ad cognoscendum quando in tali modo arguendi est fallacia secundum quid et simpliciter et quando non, talis consequentia est reducenda in syllogismum categoricum vel hypotheticum. In quo syllogismo si medium additum, virtute cuius deberet tenere consequentia, sit necessarium, non est ibi fallacia secundum quid et simpliciter; si autem non sit necessarium, est fallacia secundum quid et simpliciter.'

77 Ockham, *Expositio super Libros elenchorum*, II, c. 10 § 2, pp. 264 40–6: 'Illi syllogismi essent veri elenchi non peccantes in forma, quamvis peccarent in materia. Sicut hic est fallacia secundum quid et simpliciter "Aethiops est albus secundum dentes; igitur Aethiops est albus", et deberet sic reduci in syllogismum "omne album secundum dentes est album; Aethiops est albus secundum detes; igitur Aethiops est albus", ubi non est aliqua fallacia, quamvis maior sit falsa.'

78 Ockham, *Expositio super Libros elenchorum*, II, c. 10 § 12, pp. 274 48–53: "Et ideo, quando fit tale enthymeme, reducendum est in syllogismum. Et si medium per quod tenet non possit esse falsum simul cum hoc quod esse praedicetur de utroque, tunc non est fallacia secundum quid et simpliciter; si autem possit esse falsum cum hoc quod de utroque verificetur esse, tunc est fallacia secundum quid et simpliciter."

79 Ockham, *Summa Logicae*, III-4 c. 13 pp. 835–36 144–52: 'Ad sciendum autem quando est talis fallacia et quando non in tali modo arguendi, utile est resolvere propositiones in propositiones priores, quantum possibile est, vel exprimendo definitiones exprimentes quid nominis terminorum, vel aliquo alio convenienti modo, et videre an ex propositionibus in quas fit resolutio valeat talis modus arguendi. Verbi gratia ista propositio "Aethiops est albus secundum dentes" aequivaleat isti "Aethiops habet dentes albos"; et ideo sicut manifestum est quod non sequitur "Aethiops habet albos dentes, igitur est albus", ita non sequitur "Aethiops est albus secundum dentes, igitur est albus"'.

80 Ockham, *Summa Logicae*, III-4 c. 12 pp. 826 5–6: 'Et est fallacia consequentis quando creditor antecedens sequi ad consequens sicut consequens sequitur ad antecedens.'

81 Ockham, *Summa Logicae*, III-4 c. 12 pp. 827 32–5: 'Et universaliter quando est fallacia consequentis etiam in enthymemate, et illa consequentia reducitur in figuram debitam, si remaneat fallacia consequentis in illo discursu composito ex propositionibus dispositis in figura, erit non solum fallacia consequentis, sed etiam erit fallacia accidentis.' 47–49: 'Videndum est ergo de fallacia consequentis arguendo enthymematice, quo viso scietur faciliter quando generaliter est fallacia consequentis, sive arguatur ex pluribus praemissis sive non.'

82 Ockham, *Summa Logicae*, III-4 c. 12 pp. 830–1 141–7: 'Multae aliae regulae possent dari deservientes isti fallaciae. Sed sciendum est quod ad sciendum generaliter quando est fallacia consequentis et quando non, oportet scire omnes regulas, datas prius, deservientes consequentiis, et universaliter omnes quae possunt deservire cuicumque enthymemati. Et ideo nisi sciantur omnes regulae consequentiarum non potest universaliter sciri quando est ista fallacia et quando non accidit huiusmodi fallacia.'

83 Ockham, *Expositio super Libros elenchorum*, II, c. 10 § 2, pp. 264 29–38: 'Unde pro intentione Philosophi est sciendum quod fallacia aliquando est in oratione habente plures praemissas, aliquando est in enthymemate; quod enthymema si reduceretur in syllogismum, non esset fallacia aliqua in illo syllogismo, sed tantum ille

syllogismus peccaret in materia et non in forma. Sicut in isto enthymemate est fallacia consequentis "omnis homo currit; igitur omne animal currit"; et si deberet reduce in syllogismum, deberet sic reduci "omnis homo currit; omne animal est homo; igitur omne animal currit", in quo non est aliqua fallacia, sed accipit minorem falsam.'

84 Ockham, *Expositio super Libros elenchorum*, II, c. 13 § 3 pp. 286 75–80: 'Sed ad hoc quod in discursu tali sit fallacia consequentis, oportet quod utraque praemissarum sequatur enthymematice ex conclusione, et non e converso. Et ideo hic est fallacia consequentis "homo est animal; asinus est animal, igitur asinus est homo", nam neutra praemissarum infert conclusionem, et tamen utraque sequitur ex conclusione, sicut evidenter patet.'

Bibliography

Adams, Marilyn McCord (1987), *William Ockham*, Notre Dame, University of Notre Dame Press, 2 vols.

Archambault J. (ed.) (2018), 'Introduction: Consequences in Medieval Logic', *Vivarium* 56-3 (4), pp. 201–21.

Barnes, J. (2003), 'Proofs and Syllogism in Galen', in *Galien et la philosophie*, Barnes et alii (ed.), Eight presentations followed by discussions by J. Barnes, R. J. Hankinson, M. Frede, T. Tielman, D. Manetti, J. Jouanna, V. Boudon, G. Strohmaier, Geneva, Fondation Hardt, Entretiens sur l'antiquité classique, Tome XLIX, pp. 1–24.

Bianchi, L. (ed.) (2011), *Christian Readings of Aristotle from the Middle Ages to the Renaissance, (Studia Artistarum 29)*, Turnhout, Brepols.

Biard, J. (1989), *Logique et théorie du signe au XIVe siècle*, Paris, Vrin.

Biard, J. and Mariani Zini, F. (eds) (2009), *Les lieux de l'argumentation. Histoire du syllogisme topique d'Aristote à Leibniz, (Studia Artistarum 22)*, Turnhout, Brepols.

Bird, O. (1962), 'The Tradition of the Logical Topics: Aristotle to Ockham', *Journal of the History of Ideas* 23 (3), pp. 307–23.

Bobzien, S. (2003), 'Logic', in B. Inwood (ed.), *The Cambridge Companion to the Stoics*, Cambridge, Cambridge University Press, pp. 85–123.

Boethius, Severinus (1847), *Manlii Severini Boetii opera omnia: Patrologiae latinae tomus 64*, J.-P. Migne (ed.) (rpt 1997), Paris, Garnier.

Boethius, Severinus (1978), *Boethius's De topicis differentiis*, E. Stump (ed. and trans.), Ithaca, NY, Cornell University Press.

Bydén, B. and Thomsen Thörnqvist, C. (eds) (2017), *The Aristotelian Tradition: Aristotle's Works on Logic and Metaphysics and Their Reception in the Middle Ages*, (Papers in Mediaeval Studies 28), Turnhout, Brepols.

Burnyeat, M. F. (1994), 'Aristotle on the Logic of Persuasion', in *Aristotle's Rhetoric: Philosophical Essays*, D. J. Furley and A. Nehamas (eds), Princeton, NJ, Princeton University Press, pp. 3–55.

Burnyeat, M. F. (1996), 'Enthymeme: Aristotle on the Rationality of Rhetoric', in A. Oksenberg Rorty, (ed.), *Essays on Aristotle's Rhetoric*, Berkeley, CA, California University Press, pp. 88–115.

Buzzetti, D. (2019), 'Parafrasando Vignaux: Il posto della logica nella storia del pensiero medievale', in *Tra antichità e modernità: Studi di storia della filosofia medievale e rinascimentale, 'Quaderni di Noctua'*, F. Amerini, S. Fellina and A. Strazzoni (eds), vol. 5, pp. 974–1044.

Chiaradonna, R. (2008), 'Scienza e contingenza in Galeno', in *Conoscenza e contingenza nella tradizione aristotelica medievale*, S. Perfetti (ed.), Pisa, Ets, pp. 13–30.
Crimi, M. (2014), 'Significant Supposition and Ockham's Rule', *Vivarium* 52 (1/2), pp. 72–101.
Crimi, M. (2018), 'Formal and Material Consequences in Ockham and Buridan', *Vivarium* 56 (3/4), pp. 241–71.
de Haas F.A.J., Leunissen, M. and Martijn, M. (2020), *Interpreting Aristotle's Posterior Analytics in Late Antiquity and Beyond*, Leiden, Brill.
Duthil Novaes, C. (2007), 'Theory of Supposition vs. Theory of Fallacies in Ockham', *Vivarium* 45 (2), pp. 343–59.
Duthil Novaes, C. (2008), 'An Intensional Interpretation of Ockham's Theory of Supposition', *Journal of the History of Philosophy* 46 (3), pp. 365–93.
Duthil Novaes, C. (2012), 'Form and Matter in Later Latin Medieval Logic: The Cases of Suppositio and Consequentia', *Journal of the History of Philosophy* 50 (3), pp. 339–64.
Ebbesen, S. (1981), *Commentators and Commentaries on Aristotle's Sophistici elenchi. A Study of Post-Aristotelian Ancient and Medieval Writings on Fallacies*, Turnhout, Brepols, 3 vols.
Ebbesen, S. (1987), 'The Way Fallacies were Treated in Scholastic Logic', *Cahiers de l'Institut du Moyen Age Grec et Latin* 55, pp. 107–34.
Ebbesen, S. (1993), 'The Theory of Loci in Antiquity and the Middle Ages', in K. Jacobi (1993), Leiden, Brill, pp. 15–39.
Flannery, K. L. (1995), *Ways Into the Logic of Alexander of Aphrodisias*, Leiden/New York/Köln, Brill.
Fortenbaugh, W. (2000), 'Theophrastus of Eresus: Rhetorical Argumentation and Hypothetical Syllogistics', *Aevum* 74, pp. 65–79.
Fredal, J. (2018), 'Is the Enthymeme a Syllogism?', *Philosophy & Rhetoric* 51 (1), pp. 24–49.
Frede, D. (2007), 'Alexander of Aphrodisias', *The Stanford Encyclopaedia of Philosophy*, first published: 2003; substantive revision: 2007.
Green, L. D. (1995), 'Aristotle's Enthymeme and the Imperfect Syllogism', in W. B. Horner, M. Leff, R. Gaines, J. Dietz Moss, B. S. Bennett (eds), *Rhetoric and Pedagogy*, London, Routledge, pp. 19–41.
Green-Pedersen, N.J. (1984), *The Tradition of the Topics in the Middle Ages*, München, Philosophia Verlag.
Green-Pedersen, N.J. (1987), 'The Topics in Medieval Logic', *Argumentation* 1, pp. 407–17.
Grimaldi, W. M. A. (ed.) (1988), *Aristotle, Rhetoric I. A Commentary*, New York, Fordham University Press.
Guillelmus de Ockham (= Wilhelm of Ockham=Ockham) (1974), *Opera Philosophica*. Vol. I: *Summa Logicae*, ed. by Ph. Boehner, O.F.M; revised and completed by G. Gál, O.F.M. & S. F. Brown. St. Bonaventure, NY, The Franciscan Institute.
Guillelmus de Ockham (1977), *Opera Theologica*. Vol. III: *Scriptum in Librum Primum Sententiarum. Ordinatio (Dist. IV-VIII)*, G. Etzkorn (ed.), St. Bonaventure, NY, The Franciscan Institute.
Guillelmus de Ockham (1978), 'Opera Philosophica', in *Vol. II: Expositionis in Libros Artis Logicae Prooemium et Expositio in Librum Porphyrii de Praedicabilibus*, ed. E.A. Moody, St. Bonaventure, NY, The Franciscan Institute.
Guillelmus de Ockham (1985), *Opera Philosophica. Vol. III: Expositio super Libros Elenchorum Aristotelis*, F. Dal Punta (ed.), St. Bonaventure, NY, The Franciscan Institute.

Iwakuma, Y. (1993), Parvipontani's Thesis ex impossibili quidlibet sequitur: Comments on the Sources of the Thesis from the Twelfth Century, in K. Jacobi (1993), pp. 123–52.

Jacobi, K. (ed.) (1993), Argumentationstheorie. *Scholastische Forschungen zu den logischen und semantischen Regeln korrekten Folgerns*, (Studien und Texte zur Geistesgeschichte des Mittelalters, 38), Leiden, Brill.

Kaufmann, M. (1993), *Nochmals: Ockhams consequentiae und die materiale Implikation*, in K. Jacobi (1993), pp. 223–32.

King P. (2001), 'Consequence as Inference: Mediaeval Proof Theory 1300–1350', in *Medieval Formal Logic. The New Synthese Historical Library* (Texts and Studies in the History of Philosophy, 49), M. Yrjönsuuri (ed.), Dordrecht, Springer, pp. 117–45.

Klima, G. (2016), 'Consequence', in *The Cambridge Companion to Medieval Logic (Cambridge Companions to Philosophy)*, C. Dutilh Novaes and S. Read (eds), Cambridge, Cambridge University Press, pp. 316–41.

Kraus, M. (2012), 'Theories of "Entimema" in Antiquity', *Pan* 1, pp. 17–30.

Magnano, F. (2014), *Il De topicis differentiis di Severino Boezio*, Palermo, Officina di Studi Medievali.

Morison, B. (2008a), 'Logic', in R. Hankinson (ed.), *The Cambridge Companion to Galen*, Cambridge, Cambridge University Press, pp. 66–115.

Morison, B. (2008b), 'Language', in R. Hankinson (ed.), *The Cambridge Companion to Galen*, Cambridge, Cambridge University Press, pp. 116–56.

Moraux, P. (2001), 'Aristotelianism Among the Greeks. From Andronikos to Alexander of Aphrodisias', *Dritter Band: Alexander von Aphrodisias*, Berlin/New York, de Gruyter.

Müller, I. (1969), 'Stoic and Peripatetic Logic', *Archiv für Geschichte der Philosophie* 51, pp. 173–87.

Müller, P. (2012), *La logica di Ockham*, Milano, Vita e Pensiero.

Normore, C. G. (2015), 'Ex impossibili quodlibet sequitur (Angel d'Ors)', *Vivarium* 53 (2/4), pp. 353–71.

Peter of Spain (2014), *Peter of Spain: Summaries of Logic - Text, Translation, Introduction, and Notes*, B. P. Copenhaver, C. Normore, T. Parsons (eds), Oxford, Oxford University Press.

Piazza, F. (2000), *Il corpo della persuasione. L'entimema nella retorica greca*, Palermo, Novecento.

Pinzani, R. (2005), *Le conseguenze di Ockham. Appunti e proposte interpretative*, Roma, Aracne.

Read, S. (1993), *Formal and Material Consequence, Disjunctive Syllogism and Gamma*, in K. Jacobi (1993), pp. 233–62.

Schupp, F. (1993), *On the Textual Reconstruction of Formal and Material Inference in the Critical Ockham Edition*, in K. Jacobi (1993), pp. 213–21.

Sorabji, R. R. K. (1988), 'Johannes Philoponos', *TRE* 17, pp. 144–50.

Sprute, J. (1982), *Die Enthymemtheorie der aristotelischen Rhetorik*, Göttingen, Vandenhoeck and Ruprecht.

Spruyt, J. (1993), *Thirteenth-Century Positions on the Rule 'Ex Impossibili Sequitur Quidlibet'*, in K. Jacobi (1993), pp. 195–212.

Spruyt, J. (2003), 'The "Forma-Materia" Device in Thirteenth-Century Logic and Semantics', *Vivarium* 41 (1), pp. 1–46.

Stump, E. (1981), 'Boethius's Theory of Topics and Its Place in Early Scholastic Logic', in L. Obertello (ed.), *Atti del Congresso internazionale di studi boeziani (Pavia, 5–8 Ottobre 1980)*, Genova, Accademia Ligure di Scienze e Lettere, pp. 249–62.

Stump, E. (1982), 'Topics: Their Development and Absorption into Consequences', in *The Cambridge History of Later Medieval Philosophy: From the Rediscovery of Aristotle to the Disintegration of Scholasticism, 1100–1600*, N. Kretzmann, A. Kenny, J. Pinborg and E. Stump (eds), Cambridge, Cambridge University Press, pp. 271–99.

Stump, E. (1989), *Topics, Consequences, and Obligations in Ockham's Summa logicae*, in Ead., *Dialectic and Its Place in the Development of Medieval Logic*, Ithaca, NY, Cornell University Press, pp. 251–70.

Tabarroni, A. (2002), 'Fantastiche argomentazioni: lo studio logico delle fallacie da Aristotele a Whately', in *Quando il pensiero sbaglia. La fallacia tra psicologia e scienza*, G. Mucciarelli & G. Celani (eds), Turin, UTET, pp. 3–38.

Zanatta, M. (ed.) (2004), *Aristotele, Retorica e Poetica*, Torino, UTET.

6

Enthymematic inferences in John Buridan

Barbara Bartocci

6.1 Introduction

The concept of enthymeme is historically and philosophically problematic. In the *Prior Analytics* (II.27, 70a10), Aristotle defines an enthymeme as 'a *syllogism* from likelihoods or signs'. Apparently, the interpolation of the short word 'incomplete' (*atelēs, imperfectus*) immediately after 'syllogism', which seems to have occurred in antiquity, has strongly influenced the reception and interpretation of Aristotle's genuine theory of enthymeme from ancient to modern times. Although this misleading interpolation does not appear in Boethius's Latin translation of Aristotle's *Prior Analytics*, the standard, prevailing definition of enthymeme in the Western philosophical tradition takes it to be an incomplete or shortened syllogism (*syllogismus imperfectus* or *truncatus*).[1] This characterization of enthymematic consequences is already found in late antiquity and still appears today in some logic textbooks and essays, where enthymemes are described as arguments with at least one missing (or, in a more pragmatic vein, unstated) component, usually a premise, and which are generally considered as deductively invalid arguments.[2]

Whether an enthymeme should be defined as an incomplete and/or an invalid argument is by no means an irrelevant or an unproblematic issue. It is not irrelevant because through the proper features of the concept of enthymemes it is possible to determine its extension and solve the demarcation problem. Indeed, by establishing the necessary and sufficient conditions of enthymematicity it is possible to distinguish enthymemes from mere non sequiturs, on the one hand, and from formally valid arguments, on the other hand, with which logic is usually considered to be concerned. It is not an unproblematic issue for if an enthymeme is an incomplete argument, then one should also specify what counts as a complete argument and, more generally, what are the criteria of completeness relative to which an argument is appraised. And if enthymemes lack at least one component which the 'complete' argument ought to have, then it should be specified what this missing element is, for example, is it an inference claim, one premise or more, the conclusion? If it is a premise, then one should specify its features and the procedures for filling in the missing premise(s). If incompleteness and invalidity are coupled to define enthymeme, then other problems arise, as for example that raised by Sorensen concerning whether the following argument can be considered an enthymeme or not: 'All arguments missing a premise are enthymemes; this argument is an enthymeme.'³

John Buridan followed the crowd and defined enthymemes as 'imperfect syllogisms'. Starting from his writings on logic we can reconstruct his theory of enthymeme, which can teach us something not only concerning his understanding of enthymematic consequences but also, more generally, about his view on arguments that are formally invalid and yet have some value and are used in everyday discussions as well as in disciplines which do not aim to achieve absolutely certain conclusions. This, in turn, will show that Buridan had an inclusive notion of logic that is not limited to the study of formal consequences but finds room for a discipline like rhetoric.

In Section 6.2 I will analyse Buridan's notion of enthymeme, which tries to put together the traditional Aristotelian syllogistic and the doctrine of consequences, which is an original development in mediaeval logic. In Section 6.3, I will consider the relation between material consequences, *a fortiori* enthymemes, and topical rules of inference. In Section 6.4 I will focus on some of Buridan's examples of enthymemes and how he expands them to produce a complete syllogism (*reductio ad syllogismus*), where 'syllogism' has to be understood broadly as including categorical and hypothetical syllogisms. In Section 6.5, I will consider the epistemic side of enthymemes, namely enthymemes as dialectical argumentations.

6.2 The definition(s) of enthymeme

John Buridan deals with enthymemes in all his logical works, from the commentaries on Aristotle's *Organon* to his *Summulae de Dialectica* and *Treatise on Consequences*. At the very end of his commentary on the *Prior Analytics*, Buridan considers the question whether Aristotle's definition of enthymeme as '<a syllogism> from likelihoods and signs' is a good one.[4] According to Buridan, strictly speaking, this is neither a good definition nor a suitable description of the enthymeme for two reasons. First, because a syllogism has two premises while an enthymeme has only one and so it is an incomplete syllogism (*enthymema est syllogismus truncatus*).[5] Second, because a syllogism is a formally valid argument (*est consequentia necessaria gratia formae*), unlike the enthymeme which is either materially valid (*concludit gratia materiae*) or is a merely probable argument.[6] If we put both reasons in a positive form, we have the two conditions an argument should meet to belong to the class of arguments called enthymemes: it is sufficient that it is a one-premise argument and it is necessary that the conclusion does not follow formally from the premise. Both claims need to be unpacked. We shall start with the first concerning enthymemes' premises.

In Buridan's logic, Aristotelian syllogistic and its rules are subsumed under the doctrine of consequences. For Buridan, a consequence (*consequentia*) is a molecular proposition[7] consisting of at least one premise and a conclusion. A syllogism is a type of consequence, specifically it is a formal consequence having a conjunctive antecedent whose conjuncts are the asserted premises of the syllogism: 'we want to understand by "syllogism" . . . only a formal consequence to a single-subject predicate conclusion by a middle [term] different from each of the extremes in the conclusion.'[8] Among the other types of consequences he lists rules of conversion, equivalences, inductions, examples and, obviously, enthymemes. An enthymeme is an incomplete syllogism; since Buridan defines syllogisms in terms of consequences, he defines enthymemes in the same way as a consequence whose only premise is one of the two premises a syllogism ought to have, usually the minor premise:

> When we say that 'an enthymeme is a syllogism', we take this proposition in place of another, namely 'an enthymeme is an incomplete syllogism', that is *'an enthymeme is a consequence from one premise and the conclusion of a syllogism, leaving out the other premise'.*[9]

This definition does not specify what type one-premise enthymemes are made of nor the kind of consequence they are; being so vague on these two crucial issues, that definition is not helpful for demarcating enthymemes from other consequences. Buridan provides many examples of enthymeme, the majority of which have as their one premise a simple subject-predicate proposition, as in the standard example 'A man is running, therefore an animal is running'. However, enthymemes are not the only consequences with one simple subject-predicate antecedent, for this feature is shared also by equivalences, subalternations, conversions, examples and inductions. Are these enthymemes as well? Yes, but only in a weak sense of the term: 'broadly speaking, they can be called enthymemes, if we wish to call all consequences from one simple subject-predicate [proposition] to another enthymemes.'[10] Moreover, Buridan seems also to admit enthymemes stated with a molecular premise, like 'A is an animal and is not rational, therefore it is irrational'.[11] But if an enthymeme can be a consequence with a conjunctive antecedent, on what basis can we differentiate it from a syllogism? Thus, to be a one-premise consequence seems to be sufficient but not necessary for being an enthymeme. The necessary condition of enthymematicity is non-formal validity, for enthymemes are characterized by the fact that their conclusion does not formally follow from the premise:

> Not every consequence from one simple subject-predicate proposition to another is to be called an enthymeme [*sc.* properly speaking]. For an enthymeme is an incomplete syllogism *because it is not valid formally (gratia formae)* until by the addition of the other premise it is turned into a complete syllogism.[12]

For Buridan, all consequences are valid consequences by definition, which means that the premise and the conclusion are linked by a relation of consequence only if it is impossible that in whatever way the premise signifies things to be the case it is not in whatever way the conclusion signifies things to be the case – or, to speak loosely, in terms of truth preservation, it is impossible for the premise to be true and conclusion to be false.[13] Defined in such modal terms, validity is a general criterion that all consequences should meet.

As is well known, Buridan admits of two types of consequences, material and formal. Formal consequences are those which are valid under every uniform substitution on the consequence's non-logical terms (viz subject and predicate for simple subject-predicate propositions): 'A consequence is called formal if it is valid in all terms retaining a similar form',[14] for example, syllogisms and one-premise consequences like conversions, equipollences and subalternations. Material consequences are those in which not every equiform consequence is a valid consequence: a material consequence 'does not hold in all terms retaining the same forms',[15] as happens with inductions, examples and enthymemes – taking enthymeme in the stricter sense. Since validity is a necessary condition for both kinds of consequence, it is a wider notion than formal validity, which is a special case of validity and delimits a subclass of consequences. Or, to put it differently, all formally valid consequences are also materially valid consequences, while not all materially valid consequence are also formally valid ones, although they can be turned into a formal consequence by adding a suitable proposition (or more than one) to their premises.

Thus the difference between these two types of consequences does not depend on some logical property present in formal consequences and not in material ones. As Dutilh Novaes and Bosman (2017) have convincingly argued, the difference between them is epistemic and concerns the degree of evidentness (*evidentia*) with which the consequence relation between a consequence's premise and conclusion appears to the agent to hold. In the case of material consequences, their validity does not and cannot appear with the highest degree of evidentness, which is proper only to formal consequences, so the validity of material consequences needs to be proved: 'It seems to me that no material consequence is *evident* in inference except by its reduction to a formal one . . . everyone arguing enthymematically endeavours to *prove* his consequences . . . if they are not formal.'[16] From an epistemic perspective, the reduction of material to formal consequences that is obtained by adding an appropriate premise amounts to a procedure for evaluating whether a consequence is valid or not. And to say that an enthymeme is an imperfect syllogism means that it is not evidently valid and so needs to be expanded for proving its validity:

> An enthymeme is valid if by the addition of a necessary proposition it can be completed into a formally valid syllogism – for it is by such additions that we usually *prove* our enthymemes. For example, we say that this is a valid consequence: 'A donkey flies; therefore, a donkey has wings', for this is necessary: 'Everything flying has wings', and if we add this as the major, then we get a valid syllogism in the third mode of the first figure.[17]

Being a material consequence, an enthymeme only needs to satisfy the general validity condition that 'it is impossible for things to be altogether as [the premise] signifies unless they are altogether as the [conclusion] signifies when they are proposed together'[18] or, in looser terms, that given the signification of the premise and of the conclusion, it is impossible for the premise to be true and the conclusion to be false. This validity condition places a specific restriction upon the consequence's premise and conclusion, namely that they should be suitably connected in signification, explicitly or implicitly. If the premises were not so connected, we would have sophistical fallacies, and if they were not relevant and did not provide support to the conclusions, we would have mere non sequiturs.

6.3 Material validity, topical rules and enthymemes

For Buridan propositional signification depends on the terms constituting a proposition, both the logical terms, like quantifiers, copula(s), negations and word order and so on, as well, and mostly, as the non-logical terms such as subject and predicate. Unlike logical terms, non-logical terms signify different features of the world like objects, qualities, events and so on, and, in Buridan's token-based semantics, their meaning is defined extensionally as the set (or category, for ontological realists) of all the things signified by a term (its *significata*). Accordingly, to say that material validity requires a relation of signification is to say that the premise and conclusion of a consequence should share, explicitly or implicitly, at least one non-logical term and, more generally, that there should be a relation (*habitudo*) between the sets to which the items signified by their non-logical terms belong. The relations existing between sets – specifically between sets of terms of second intention like genus and species, cause and effects, parts and whole – are captured by the different topics. Following the Boethian tradition of the topics, Buridan metaphorically describes a topic (*locus*) as the 'seat (*sedes*) of an argument' (see Section 6.5). Metaphor aside, we can describe a topic as a generalization (*maxima*), which can be either absolute or defeasible[19] and which spells out various types of relations in virtue of which the consequence relation obtains:

> [A] maxim contains universally the whole power of the argument, and again, the terms of th[e] *maxima*, on account of their relation (*habitudo*) to one another, contain virtually the *maxima* itself; indeed, the *maxima* is but a certain exemplification of the relation (*explanatio illius habitudinis*) that the terms have to one another, on account of which the whole argument has its power and efficacy.[20]

Accordingly, a topic seems to play the role of an implicitly assumed inference rule that secures the inferential move from the premise to the conclusion in enthymematic consequences and, moreover, specifies which are the substitutions of the non-logical terms of a consequence that yield true or false conclusions.

Some examples might help clarifying things:[21]

Topic from the species to the genus. In the *Summulae de Dialectica* 6.3.5, Buridan considers the standard example of a material consequence mentioned earlier, namely [*cons. 1*] 'A man is running, therefore an animal is running' and says that it is valid in virtue of the topic from the species to the genus which is expressed by the inference rule 'Whatever is truly affirmed of the species is truly affirmed of its genus', which can be generalized as 'For every (term) x, if x is truly affirmed of the species, x is truly affirmed of the genus'. The non-logical terms of [*cons. 1*] are the subjects 'man' and 'animal', which stand to each other in a species–genus relation, and the common predicate 'running'. In the *Treatise on Consequences* 1.4, Buridan considers [*cons. 1*] and says that it is a material consequence, for the equiform consequence '<Some> horse walks, so <some> wood walks' is not valid. We can note that in the latter example, the substitution on the predicate is correct since both 'run' and 'walk' are members of the set 'movement', while the replacement of the subjects is wrong because the subject of the conclusion 'wood' is not the genus of the species 'horse' and is not even an animate being!

Topic from contraries: This topic spells out the relation of contrariety in terms of predication of two contrary predicates with respect to the same subject: 'Of whatever one of the contraries is truly affirmed, of the same the other is truly denied.'[22] Buridan specifies that this rule applies only to assertoric propositions in the present tense and that it should be used only for inferring a negative proposition, unless the contraries are immediate ones like healthy and sick. This rule supplies the backing for material consequences like [*cons.* 2] 'Socrates is black, therefore Socrates is not white',[23] and [*cons.* 3] 'Socrates is white, therefore he is not black',[24] [*cons.* 4] 'A is white, therefore A is not black';[25] or [*cons.* 5] 'Every man is sick, therefore no man is healthy' which, Buridan says, follows because it is impossible that the same person is sick and healthy at the same time.[26] Consider a dialectical situation in which someone asks the question: Is Socrates white or not? One of the participants to the discussion, say the opponent, wants to show that Socrates is not white. If the opponent knows that 'white' is mutually exclusive of 'black', she can resort to the topic from contraries, which spells out such a relation, and argue [*cons.* 2] 'Socrates is black, therefore Socrates is not white'. For, 'it is clear that the argument, the locus, and the maxim are drawn from the term "black" on account of the relation it bears, on the basis of its signification, to the term "white" posited in the question, namely, the relation of contrariety'.[27]

What emerges from these examples, namely that topics are inference rules implicitly assumed in virtue of which the conclusion follows from the premises in materially valid consequences like enthymemes, is clearly stated by Buridan himself:

> [The *maxima*] is the self-evident proposition that confirms the argument, and that need not be composed of the terms placed in the argument but [may be composed] of terms of second imposition suppositing for the terms whose relation to one another is what accounts for the validity of the argument . . . In the case of demonstrations, which are syllogisms consisting of self-evident premises or of premises sufficiently proved by other syllogisms, it is not necessary to look for *maximae*, but only for the premises of those other syllogisms. For they conclude of themselves formally (*gratia formae*); therefore, they do not need another proof by virtue of which the consequence is valid (*probatione virtute cuius valeat consequentia*).[28]

Topical inference rules can play this role because they are self-evident propositions, like scientific principles, namely they are not derived from previous deductions but are merely assumed and are known in virtue of the terms of which they are made. So, they are readily accepted on semantic grounds (*non concludunt gratia formae*) and are called assumptions (*suppositiones*).

6.4 Proving enthymemes: The 'reduction' of material consequences to formal consequences

As mentioned before, the proof for establishing the validity of a material consequence such as an enthymeme consists in converting it into a formal consequence, namely a syllogism, by adding a suitable premise to the enthymeme's single premise, which thus becomes the minor premise of the syllogism. Indeed usually, the missing premise is the major premise of the syllogism and can be produced almost mechanically; it is sufficient to know the syllogistic modes and figures and to identify the middle term which, as Buridan says in his own definition of enthymeme, is found in the single premise: 'An enthymeme is a consequence from one proposition to another by means of a middle term <which is> general and different from each extreme [*sc.* subject and predicate] of the conclusion.'[29] It is commonly assumed that enthymemes are expanded into categorical syllogism by adding one true proposition (or more, if needed) to the enthymeme's single premise.

In the cases considered above, Buridan expands the material consequences as follows:

[*cons.* 1] 'A man is running, therefore an animal is running' can be *proved* by adding to it the A-proposition 'Every man is an animal' to produce a syllogism in the third figure in Datisi;[30]

[*cons.* 2] 'Socrates is black, therefore Socrates is not white'[31] is expanded by adding the E-proposition 'Nothing black is white', thus obtaining the valid second-figure syllogism in Cesare 'Nothing black is white, Socrates is black, therefore Socrates is not white';

[*cons.* 3] 'Socrates is white, therefore he is not black'[32] and [*cons.* 4] 'A is white, therefore A is not black' can be expanded by adding the E-proposition, 'Nothing white is black'.

As was said earlier, the aim of the formalization of material consequences is that of testing their validity and to show with the highest possible degree of evidentness that the consequence relation between the premise and conclusion holds. In Buridan's philosophy, evidentness has an ineliminable subjective dimension for it depends on the agent's belief state. Thus, even if the formalization is correctly performed from a 'logical' viewpoint, it might fail to prove the consequence's validity to someone. This issue is tackled by Buridan himself in his *Questions* on Aristotle's *Topics*. Here Buridan asks if the same syllogism can be both dialectical and demonstrative. Demonstration and dialectical syllogism are equiform arguments which differ in that the premises of a demonstration (*demonstratio*) are necessary truths, while dialectical syllogisms start from probable premises, namely premises that *appear* (intuitively) true and thus are accepted by everybody, the majority or just the wiser people. Buridan replies affirmatively to the question; the reason is that the truth of the premises and/or the validity of the consequence relation might be perceived with different degrees of evidentness by either two different agents at the same time or by the same agent at different times, like a student before and after taking a course in logic. For example, the syllogism 'All rational mortal animals are risible; all men are rational mortal animals; all men are risible' is reckoned as demonstrative by the agent capable of seeing both the truth of the premises and that the consequence relation holds necessarily in virtue of well-formed premises that are properly arranged and of the *dici de omni*. However, that same syllogism is dialectical for the agent who fails to recognize the truth of the premises and/or their necessary relation and who therefore thinks that the conclusion follows from the premises only in virtue of a meaning relation, like that captured by the topic from definition and the corresponding dialectical inference rule (*maxima*): 'Whatever is predicated of the definiens is predicated of the definiendum.'[33]

Although the majority of enthymemes are proved by expanding them into a categorical syllogism by adding one premise, or more, Buridan says that some of them need to be proved in other ways, for example, by reductions to syllogisms with oblique terms, to syllogisms that do not fit the syllogistic figures or to syllogisms from a hypothesis. For Buridan the term 'syllogism from a hypothesis' refers to both hypothetical syllogisms, namely syllogisms whose premises and conclusion are wholly molecular propositions, and syllogisms with a molecular premise.[34] In the *Organon*, Aristotle does not delineate a fully fledged doctrine of the syllogism from a hypothesis, which comprises syllogisms through an impossibility, syllogisms by substitution and by quality; all of them are briefly dealt with in the *Prior Analytics* (book 1, chaps 23, 29, 44) and are mentioned in the *Topics* (book 1, ch. 18, and book 3, ch. 6). The peculiarity of syllogisms from a hypothesis is that they start from an agreed stipulation, that is, hypothesis or assumption, for it is unproved and unprovable, namely not reducible to any syllogistic figure. In these syllogisms the conclusion is deduced from the premises in virtue of the hypothesis.[35] Buridan analyses such syllogisms in the opening question of his commentary on the second book of the *Prior Analytics*, where he asks if all syllogisms are from a hypothesis. Here he explains that in ostensive, namely categorical, syllogisms the main conclusion is inferred necessarily (*necessaria et formalis illatio*) on the basis of syllogistic rules and principles, like the *dici de omni*, and no extra assumption is needed. While syllogisms from a hypothesis necessarily infer their main conclusion only in virtue of an extra implicit assumption, namely the topical inference rule (*istae suppositiones [vel hypotheses] sunt valde multiplices, secundum diversas maximas dialecticas*). After explaining the functioning of syllogisms *ad impossibile*, Buridan clarifies how to produce syllogisms by substitutions which, as the name says, are based on a replacement of the conclusion to be proved. Suppose the main conclusion we want to prove is $concl_0$; looking at the topical features of the non-logical terms of $concl_0$, we find a proposition that is topically related to it and which becomes the secondary conclusion to prove, call it $concl_1$. Then, we find the fitting premises for generating a categorical syllogism that yields $concl_1$ which, being the conclusion of a categorical syllogism, is a true proposition. Having proved $concl_1$, we can now infer $concl_0$ and this inferential move is grounded on an implicitly assumed topical rule of inference, more specifically on a necessary topical rule, which we can describe as an absolute universal generalization – if the inference was grounded on a merely probable topical rule (viz. defeasible generalization), the conclusion would not result necessarily. The necessity of topical rules depends on their non-logical terms: a *locus* is *necessarius* if the sets to which its non-logical terms belong are extensionally equivalent or if the one is a subset of the other. Buridan does not explain how such rules back the inference, a plausible explanation being that we can build a conditional proposition of the form $concl_1 concl_0$ which is an instantiation of the rule and contains the non-logical terms of both $concl_0$ and $concl_1$. If that is correct, the syllogism from a hypothesis amounts to a modus ponendo ponens or modus tollendo tollens. A few examples might help elucidate how this proof works.[36]

Suppose we want to prove $concl_0$ 'Every man is able to learn'; by resorting to the list of topics, we notice that among the many topical features of the subject 'man', there is that of being a definiendum; we then find its definiens, namely 'mortal rational animal', and replace 'man' by its definiens, thus obtaining $concl_1$ 'Every mortal rational animal is able to learn'. Then, we should prove it through a categorical syllogism, like 'Every individual intellectual substance is able to learn, every mortal rational animal is an individual substance, therefore every mortal rational animal is able to learn'. Having proved $concl_1$ we can conclude $concl_0$ 'Every man is able to learn' in virtue of the inference rule (*maxima*): 'Whatever is predicated of the definiens, is predicated of the definiendum', also expressible as an absolute generalization 'For every x, if x is predicated of the definiens, then x is predicated of the definiendum', from which we derive the conditional premise of the syllogism from a hypothesis, namely 'If every mortal rational animal is able to learn, then every man is able to learn'. And now we have all the elements for the syllogism: 'If every mortal rational animal is able to learn, then every man is capable to learn, but every mortal rational animal is able to learn, therefore every man is able to learn.'

If we want to prove $concl_0$ 'The king can take this castle', we know that the king's subjects are placed in an inferior position, thus we can resort to the topic from the minor. In the *Summulae de Dialectica* 6.5.6 Buridan makes it clear that 'minor' should be understood in semantic terms as meaning 'the lesser *appearance* that the predicate . . . is truly affirmed of the [subject]'; and he expresses the topical rule accordingly: 'if [the predicate] inheres in that in which it appears less greatly to inhere, then it inheres in that in which it more greatly appears [to inhere].' Then, we have to make a categorical syllogism having as conclusion $concl_1$ 'The count can take this castle'. Having proved that, and having derived the conditional premise, we can produce the syllogism from a hypothesis 'If the count can take this castle, then the king can take this castle, but the count can take this castle, therefore the king can take this castle'.

6.5 Probable arguments and dialectic

What about the reduction of material consequences to syllogisms that do not fit the syllogistic figures? Buridan leaves unsaid how this is supposed to work and to which type of material consequences this expansion applies. A hint might come from a passage in the aforementioned question on the definition of enthymemes in his commentary on the *Prior Analytics*, where Buridan claims that 'at times, an enthymeme does not imply necessarily its conclusion, either formally or materially (*nec gratia formae nec gratia materiae concludit de necessitate*), like enthymemes in the second figure'.[37] Here Buridan alludes to the three figures of enthymemes from signs (*semeia*) mentioned by Aristotle in *Prior Analytics* II, ch. 27. The second figure is characterized by the fact of being always defeasible (*solubilis*), namely that the consequence relation underpinning it is always probable and never necessary. These are the subclass of material consequences that Buridan calls *consequentiae probabiles* which, even if all restrictions are respected, are truth-preserving only in most cases and which hold in virtue of probable topics (*loci probabiles*). A probable topical rule can be understood as a defeasible generalization, namely subject to exceptions. Its defeasibility results from the fact that the sets to which the non-logical terms of the topical rule belong are intersecting but not coextensive, so only the great majority of, not all, the substitutions make both the premises and the conclusion true. In his commentary on Aristotle's *Rhetoric*, and briefly in the *Questions* on the *Prior Analytics* book 2, question 22, Buridan gives a nice example of a *consequentia probabilis* in which the conclusion does not always follow but only in most cases (*ut in pluribus*):

> Suppose that Socrates, who is a dice player and usually wanders at night, was at Plato's house and inspected a pack <of his> which was then stolen away, and <suppose> that on the following day that pack is found at Socrates' house, the door locked and the key kept by Socrates. One would plausibly (*probabiliter*) infer that Socrates stole the pack [$cons._6$ 'Socrates wanders abroad at night, therefore he is a thief']. For the premise, detailed in that way, being true, the conclusion would be true in most cases (*ut in pluribus*); thus, the plausibility (*probabilitas*) of this argument would be so great that a judge would put Socrates in prison. However, it is possible that that night Socrates slept at Robert's house and on the following morning was found in bed and <it is possible> that the door of <Socrates'> house was closed so that Socrates himself could not open it. From that one can plausibly (*probabiliter*) conclude that Socrates did not steal the pack.[38]

The second-figure enthymeme $cons._6$ 'Socrates wanders abroad at night, therefore he is a thief' is based on the probable topic from accidents contingently co-occurring in most cases (*Summulae de Dialectica*, chapter 6.4.17); obviously, the conclusion follows from the premises often but not always, as in the present case. This enthymeme can be expanded by adding the false A-premise 'Every thief wanders abroad at night' to produce a syllogism which is invalid since the middle term is undistributed. This kind of enthymemes that do not infer their conclusion necessarily, either formally or materially, have the merit of producing some belief in the agent and to persuade her, therefore they are better appraised by a dialectical rather than by a deductive standard.

In the Middle Ages the word 'dialectic' had a broader and a narrower meaning. In its broad sense, it was a synonym of logic, the art (or science, depending on the author's viewpoint) that studied the rules for reasoning correctly and discerning truth from falsehood. In its proper sense, dialectic was the part of logic dealing with topical rules and probable reasoning. For Buridan dialectic was the discipline concerned with establishing the epistemic norms for producing 'weak knowledge', namely justified likely true beliefs,[39] and with providing a reliable, though fallible belief-forming method which yields mostly true beliefs and could be used in those disciplines that deal with contingent subject matters and so cannot achieve 'strong knowledge' and absolute certainty. Taking on the minoritarian tradition of the 'Long Organon' rooted in Arabic logic, Buridan included rhetoric (and also poetic) in his logic, as the subdiscipline of dialectic dealing with human actions:

> Dialectic ... is divided insofar as the propositions entering dialectical arguments can consider the intellect in itself or can consider the intellect in relation to desire... The former and principal part of dialectic takes into account accepted propositions (*probabilia*) insofar as they consider the intellect in itself, the latter part insofar as they consider the intellect as related to desire. The first part is transmitted by Aristotle's *Topics* and *Sophistical Refutations* and can be called principal dialectic and is at the service of the first and most principal sciences, namely speculative <sciences> ... The second part is transmitted by the *Rhetoric* and can be named moral dialectic because it is at the service of the moral sciences, in which desire naturally moves the intellect. So, it is clear that rhetoric is a part of dialectic.[40]

This expanded conception of dialectic led Buridan to take dialectical argument, and not dialectical syllogism (as all his predecessors did), as both the subject matter of dialectic and the cornerstone of dialectical method. A dialectical argument is an ampliative inference, underpinned by a necessary or probable consequence, which produces an imperfect belief in the agent, called opinion (*considerat communiter de illis argumentationibus, quae fidem faciunt non perfectam, sed cum formidine ad oppositum*). Buridan defines arguments in general (viz. scientific and dialectical proof) as inferences that provide justification for assenting to the conclusion and believing a proposition that was unknown or doubted: 'an argument is a process in the mind whereby the mind, on account of the mental *premises* known to it, is compelled to concede a conclusion previously not known or doubted.'[41] From these words it seems that arguments are not enthymemes for they have more than one premise. Arguments can be expressed publicly, in speech or in writing, by means of argumentations; Buridan does not specify if there should be a structural correspondence between arguments and their expressions. This leaves open the possibility that a mental syllogism is expressed in enthymematic form. And a speaker might have various reasons for preferring enthymemes over syllogisms. She might think that it is the most fitting form of reasoning in 'scientific' contexts that require less strict standards, as in disciplines that do not or cannot reach mathematical certainty and accuracy but are satisfied with 'weak knowledge'. Or in public contexts with an audience formed of non-specialists, in which the speaker's aim is to produce justified persuasion: here, she would do better to use enthymemes, because the syllogistic general premise could be common knowledge and its presence would be redundant, or it might be a defeasible generalization that could weaken rather than strengthen her argument, if someone found an exception:

> One should use syllogisms more rarely than enthymemes... because commonly the audience has similar presuppositions and is unable to grasp many presuppositions joined together in the same argument nor it is able to understand the perfect connections of the extreme terms through the middle term, which are shown by the syllogism. Moreover, in a perfect syllogism one of the premises is a universal proposition, *viz.* the principle of a law. And if the hearer is a judge and he is good enough, he should already know <that legal principle> ... and the speaker should not express verbally that which the hearer is supposed to know, for this would only bother him as redundant, because by suppling the universal premise the

speaker would seem to give himself the role of judge and consider the latter to be ignorant, namely unable to supply <the legal principle> by himself. Moreover, usually one does not make universal propositions about actions, where there are many easy counterexamples . . . for if such a universal proposition of a syllogism was put forward and there was a counterexample, no one would be persuaded <by that syllogism> . . . Moreover, unlearned people usually grasp consequences by experience and do not know the causes, and such consequences are enthymematic and not syllogistic.[42]

Dialectical arguments are grounded on topical inference rules, which are defined as the 'seat of the argument'. From the logical viewpoint, a dialectical argument can be indifferently supported by a necessary or probable consequence, and the conclusion can result necessarily or in most cases.[43] Thus, not only syllogisms but also enthymemes, inductions and examples are equally dialectical argumentations.

From the epistemic viewpoint, a dialectical argument is a proof whose premises should meet two requirements: (1) they should be better known, either by experience or intellectual knowledge, and more certain than the conclusion, otherwise there would be epistemic circularity; and (2) they can be indifferently true and universal, universal or singular (then the conclusion will be singular) and accepted (*probabilia*, viz. propositions accepted by all or the majority or the wisest people).[44] The logical and epistemic requirements for dialectical proofs are therefore more relaxed than the high, almost ideal, standards required for scientific proofs (*demonstrationes*), for to have a good dialectical argument it is sufficient that the premises provide a sufficient support and justification for believing the conclusion. Consequently, insofar as it is a dialectical argumentation, an enthymeme does not need to be expanded into a formally valid argument, just like induction and examples: 'Although in the domain of argumentation in general these three <forms of argumentation> are correctly reduced to the syllogism as something imperfect to something perfect, yet not in the domain of dialectical argumentation. Thus, all these four argumentations, syllogism, induction etc, are equally perfect dialectical argumentations'.[45] These types of argument can be used in practical disciplines, like ethics and law, and theoretical sciences, like natural philosophy, which cannot achieve 'strong knowledge' but only 'weak knowledge'.[46] An illuminating example is found in Buridan's *Questions on the Heavens* of Aristotle. At the beginning of book 2, Aristotle wants to explain why there are different celestial bodies each moving with its own motion. Buridan devotes question nine to ascertain whether Aristotle argued soundly by basing his argumentation on God, the first mover. To show that he did argue correctly, Buridan reconstructs what he takes to be the implicit long chain of reasoning underpinning Aristotle's text and makes explicit all its steps, namely the consequences, their meaning relations and their grounding (*tunc videamus quo modo et quare teneant istae consequentiae*). For Buridan, the starting point of Aristotle's chain is the assumption that God exists, from which seven enchained consequences follow:

<1> 'God exists, therefore it is necessary that the heavens are moved eternally': 'If someone asks about this first consequence: From what topic (*unde locus*)? I reply that it is from the efficient cause to its effect, for when the efficient cause

is posited and there is no impediment, the effect must follow.' In the *Summulae de Dialectica*, chapter 6.4.10, Buridan deals with this topic and specifies all the assumptions and conditions (*circumstantiae*) under which the topical rule is necessary, for 'it is not valid for many predicates', and those under which it is merely probable. From follows:

<2> 'If the heavens are moved eternally, it is necessary that the <element> earth rests always in their middle': this inference is the object of question 22; from follows:

<3> 'If it is necessary that earth exists, it is necessary that fire exists': Buridan lists the three topics in virtue of which this inference can hold; why does he offer more than one topic? Because the objects signified by terms have different topical features, accordingly each of these can be used for producing a material consequence. In the present case, consequence can hold in virtue of the topic (i) from the minor; (ii) from the effect to its <material> cause; (iii) from the material cause to its effect: earth and fire have contrary qualities, contraries come naturally together in matter, in which one contrary exists actually and the other exists in potency, therefore if the earth exists <actually>, fire exists <in potency>. From follows:

<4> 'If it is necessary that earth and fire exist, it is necessary that water and air exist': this consequence holds in virtue of the topic from the material cause to its effect: contraries come together in matter, if fire and earth are naturally dry, they are not contrary under that respect, since dry is contrary to wet, therefore there should be other elements that are naturally wet, like air and water; from follows:

<5> 'If it is necessary that these four elements exist, it is necessary that there are generation and corruption in subcelestial bodies': this consequence can hold in virtue of the topic from efficient cause, insofar as each contrary acts and is acted upon by the other, or in virtue of the topic from the material cause, since when a contrary exists actually, the other exists in potency and potency cannot remain unactualized. From <5> follows

<6> 'If it is necessary that generation and corruption exist, it is necessary that there are multiple celestial motions': question 10 is devoted to this inference.

<7> Therefore, concluding from first to last: 'If god exists, it is necessary that there are multiple celestial motions': this consequence holds in virtue of the topic from the conclusion to the premise whose rule is 'whatever follows from the conclusion, follows from the premise'. Here Buridan makes an interesting remark: although this topic is not listed in the *Summulae de Dialectica* or in Peter of Spain's treatise, on which the *Summulae* are a commentary, for Buridan it is a valid inference rule 'because the terms "premise" and "conclusion" are notions (*intentiones*) related to each other just as "genus" and "species", "whole" and "part", "cause" and "effect" and so on."[47]

6.6 Conclusion

The originality of Buridan's concept of enthymeme can be fully appreciated if it is contextualized within his rich and inclusive view of logic and against the background of his subdivision of sciences. For Buridan, logic is not limited to formal logic, consequences and their rules but includes what we would call informal logic; accordingly, Buridan allows some merit, more precisely epistemic merit, also to arguments that, being grounded on probable consequence, have illative defects like dialectic and rhetorical enthymeme. Thus, for Buridan the goodness of enthymemes is both a logical and an epistemological matter. A logically good enthymeme is a consequence in which the conclusion follows from the single premise not formally but materially, that is, in virtue of a meaning connection between the non-logical terms entering the premise and conclusion. The various legitimate meaning connections are captured by the different topics and are spelt out by the topical *maximae*, which are semantic rules of inference. If it is appraised by epistemic standards, an enthymeme is a good dialectical argumentation if, by means of justifiably believed premises, it produces a justified likely true belief (*opinio*) in its conclusion. Enthymemes, as well as other dialectical argumentations, find broad application in many practical and theoretical disciplines, such as ethics, law or physics, which Buridan calls sciences in a broader sense (*communiter* and *large*) for they do not aspire to achieve *scientia* strictly speaking.

Acknowledgement

The preparation of this chapter was supported by the project *Filling the Gap: Medieval Aristotelian Logic 1240–1360*, funded by the Swedish Research Council (VR).

Notes

1 'Enthymema est syllogismus ex verisimilibus vel (*or* ikotibus et) signis' (Aristoteles 1962). For the textual interpolation of 'imperfect' see M. F. Burnyeat M. F. 1994. For the 'syllogismus truncatus' see C. Rapp 2002 vol. 2, pp. 187–9.
2 For example, A. R. Anderson and N. D. Belnap 1961, pp. 713–23.
3 R. A. Sorensen 1988, pp. 155–9, here p. 155; on the concept of enthymeme and related problems see: R. George 1972, pp. 113–16; D. Hitchcock 1985, pp. 83–97; D. Walton and C. A. Reed 2005, pp. 339–70.
4 J. Buridanus, *Quaestiones in Analytica Priora*, book 2, q. 22 'Utrum definitio enthymematis sit bona in qua dicitur enthymema est ex icotibus et signis'; all English translations are mine; all Latin citations are taken from the text prepared by H. Hubien available online at: http://www.logicmuseum.com/wiki/Authors/Buridan/Quaestiones_in_analytica_priora/Liber_2/Q22.
5 This definition is found in Buridanus, *Quaestiones in Analytica Priora*, book 2, q.22, and in the sixth treatise, *On topics* (*De Lociis*) of Buridan's *Summulae de Dialectica*, 6.1.4.
6 'Primo enim dicendum est quod enthymema non est syllogismus: quia est ex unica praemissa et syllogismus debet esse ex duabus praemissis, et quia syllogismus, simpliciter loquendo, est consequentia necessaria gratia formae, et tamen enthymema non est sic; immo aliquando enthymema nec gratia formae nec gratia materiae concludit de necessitate' (J. Buridanus, *Quaestiones in Analytica Priora*, book 2, q.22).
7 Throughout this chapter I will use the term 'proposition' in its mediaeval acceptation of 'token sentence'.

8   J. Buridanus, 2015, part 3, ch.1; all English citations are taken from J. Buridan 2015, p. 115; all Latin citations are taken from the critical edition made by H. Hubien 1976, here p. 81. The definition of consequence is given in the *Tractatus de Consequentiis* 1.3.
9   'Cum ... dicimus "enthymema est syllogismus", utimur hac propositione pro alia, scilicet pro ista "enthymema est syllogismus truncatus", id est "*enthymema est consequentia ex una praemissa syllogismi et conclusione, relinquendo aliam praemissam*"' (Buridanus, *Quaestiones in Analytica Priora*, book 2, q.22, *In corpore*; emphasis is added). An almost identical definition is found in Buridanus 2015, 3.1: 'Enthymema debet esse ex praemissa una ad conclusionem, quae quidem conclusio ex illa praemissa et alia sibi addita est innate sequi syllogistice'.
10 Buridan 2015, 3.1, p. 113; Buridanus 2015, p. 79.
11 Buridanus 2013, 6.6.4; all English citations are taken from Buridan, 2001, pp. 490–1; all citations of the Latin text are taken from the critical edition of treatise six, Buridanus 2013, pp. 124–5.
12 Buridan, 2001, 6.1.4, p. 397 – I have slightly modified Klima's translation; Buridanus, 2013, p. 14.
13 Buridan, *Treatise on Consequences*, 1.3, 6 (Buridanus, *Tractatus de Consequentiis*, ed. Hubien, 22). The secondary literature on Buridan's theory of consequence is wide; among the most recent and relevant contributions the following ones are helpful: Joël Biard 1990, pp. 151–68; G. Klima 2004, pp. 95–110; C. D. Novaes, 2005, pp. 277–97; S. Read 2015, pp. 899–912; C. Dutilh Novaes, and B. Bosman 2017, pp. 229–42; M. Crimi 2018 pp. 241–71.
14 'Or, if you want to put it explicitly, a formal consequence is one where every proposition similar in form that might be formed would be a good consequence, e.g. "That which is A is B, so that which is B is A"' (Buridan, *Treatise on Consequences*, 1.4, 68; Buridanus, *Tractatus de Consequentiis*, ed. Hubien, 22–3). An exhaustive list of formal consequences is found in the *Treatise on Consequences*, chapter 3.1.
15 Buridan, *Treatise on Consequences*, 1.4, 68; Buridanus, *Tractatus de Consequentiis*, ed. Hubien, 22–3.
16 Buridan, *Treatise on Consequences*, 1.4, 68, emphasis added (Buridanus, *Tractatus de Consequentiis*, ed. Hubien, 23). Buridan's notion of evidentness is rather sophisticated and a treatment of it goes beyond the scope of this chapter; for an introduction to it see J. Zupko 1993 pp. 191–221; R. Pasnau 2010, pp. 23–41.
17 Buridanus, *Sophismata*, ch. 1, sophism 1; the English translation is taken from Buridan, *Summulae de Dialectica*, p. 952.
18 Buridan, *Treatise on Consequences*, 1.3, p. 67 (Buridanus, *Tractatus de Consequentiis*, ed. Hubien, 22).
19 An absolute generalization is a universally quantified proposition that does not admit exceptions, while a defeasible generalization does for it only holds 'for the most part' (*ut in pluribus*); on defeasible generalization in probable consequences see *infra* §§3–4.
20 Buridan, *Summulae de Dialectica*, 6.2.2, 402; Buridanus, 2003, pp. 20–1.
21 As Buridan says, these generalizations '*more immediately* confirm an argument taken materially than one formed with its terms taken personally, or significatively' (Buridan, *Summulae de Dialectica*, 6.3.5, pp. 418–19), yet due to space constraints, I will take them in personal supposition.
22 Buridan, *Summulae de Dialectica*, 6.5.3, p. 463.

23 Buridan, *Summulae de Dialectica*, 6.2.3, p. 405.
24 Buridan, *Summulae de Dialectica*, 6.5.3, p. 463.
25 Buridan, *Summulae de Dialectica*, 6.6.4, p. 491.
26 Buridan, *Sophismata*, ch. 1, sophism 1 (in: Buridan, *Summulae de Dialectica*, p. 952).
27 Buridan, *Summulae de Dialectica*, 6.2.3, p. 405.
28 Buridan, *Summulae de Dialectica*, 6.3.1, p. 410 (Buridanus, 2003, p. 31); I have slightly modified Klima's translation.
29 'Definitio enthymematis quod enthymema est consequentia ex una propositione ad aliam per medium commune et ab utraque extremitate conclusionis alterum' (Buridanus, *Quaestiones in Analytica Priora*, book 2, q. 22).
30 Buridan, *Treatise on Consequences*, 1.4.
31 Buridan, *Summulae de Dialectica*, 6.2.3, p. 405.
32 Buridan, *Summulae de Dialectica*, 6.5.3, 463.
33 Buridanus, 2003, book 1, q. 3, p. 19; all English translations are mine.
34 Buridan, *Summulae de Dialectica*, 6.1.5, p. 399.
35 The nature and functioning of syllogisms from a hypothesis have puzzled commentators since ancient times; important contributions on this matter are G. Striker 1979, pp. 33–50, and her commentary on the aforementioned chapters in Aristotle 2009; P. Slomkowski 1997; P. Crivelli 2011, pp. 95–184.
36 Buridanus, *Quaestiones in Analytica Priora*, book 2, q. 1.
37 Buridanus, *Quaestiones in Analytica Priora*, book 2, q. 22.
38 'Ponamus ergo quod Socrates, taxillator existens et communiter errabundus de nocte, fuerit in domo Platonis et inspexerit unum fardellum, et iste fardellus per furtum ablatus sequenti die inveniatur in domo Socratis ostio clauso et Socrate habente clavem. Concludetur probabiliter quod Socrates fardellum furatus est. Antecedente enim sic circumstantiato existente vero, consequens ut in pluribus esset verum unde tanta esset probabilitas istius argumenti quod iudex poneret Socratem in tormentis. Possibile est tamen quod Socrates ista nocte cubuit in camera Roberti et de mane in lecto inventus et quod ostium domus erat clausum ut Socrates non posset ipsum aperire; <a> quo detur probare probabiliter quod Socrates fardellum non est furatus', Buridanus, *Quaestiones in Rhetoricam*, book 1, question 8; the English translation is mine; for the Latin text I have used the transcription made by Bernadette Preben-Hansen, accessed April 28, 2016, http://www.preben.nl/BuridanRH.pdf, which I have amended against the manuscript preserved at Leipzig, University Library, ms. 1246, 331v.
39 I take 'weak knowledge' in Goldman's sense of mere true belief as opposed to 'strong knowledge', consisting of 'true belief plus additional elements like justification . . . and the exclusion of alternative possibilities' (A. I. Goldman 1999, pp. 24–5; A. I. Goldman and E. J. Olsson 2009, pp. 19–41, here §1).
40 'Dialectica . . . dividitur ex eo quod propositiones, ex quibus constituitur argumentatio dialectica, possunt respicere intellectum simpliciter vel possunt respicere intellectum in ordine ad appetitum . . . Una ergo et prima pars dialecticae communiter acceptae considerat probabilia secundum quod respiciunt intellectum simpliciter; alia vero secundum quod respiciunt intellectum in ordine ad appetitum. Prima pars traditur in libro Topicorum et Elenchorum Aristotelis, et vocari potest dialectica principalis, quod deservit scientiis primis et principalissimis, scilicet speculativis . . . Secunda pars traditur in libro Rhetoricae, quae vocari potest dialectica moralis, quia deservit per se scientiis moralibus, in quibus appetitus est innatus trahere intellectum. Apparet ergo

in veritate, quod rhetorica est pars dialecticae' (Buridanus, *Quaestiones in Rhetoricam*, book 1, q.2, 325r-v).
41 Buridan, *Summulae de Dialectica*, p. 392 (Buridanus 2013, pp. 8–9); on the notions *argumentum – argumentatio* in Buridan see the subtle analysis made by J. Biard 2009, pp. 359–83.
42 Buridanus, *Quaestiones in Rhetoricam*, book 1, q. 14, 336v.
43 'Non enim exigitur ad dialecticam argumentationem quod ex tali antecedente sequitur tale consequens necessario et inevitabiliter, sed sufficit quod *ut <in> pluribus*' (Buridanus, *Quaestiones in Rhetoricam*, book 1, q.8, 331r).
44 Buridan, *Summulae de Dialectica*, 394 (Buridanus 2013, 11).
45 Buridanus, *Quaestiones Topicorum*, book 1, q. 16, 69.
46 Buridan, *Summulae de Dialectica,* preface, 3. On Buridan's subdivision of science and on view about scientificity see J. Biard 2012.
47 J. Buridanus 1942, pp. 165–6.

Bibliography

Anderson, A. R. and Belnap, N. D. (1961), 'Enthymemes', *Journal of Philosophy* 58, pp. 713–23.
Aristoteles (1962), *Analytica Priora. Translatio Boethii, Recensio Florentina*, L. Minio-Paluello (ed.), Bruges/Paris, Desclée de Brouwer.
Aristotle (2009), *Prior Analytics: Book I*, G. Striker (ed.), Oxford, Oxford University Press.
Biard, J. (1990), 'Matière et forme dans la théorie buridanienne des conséquences', *Archives d'histoire doctrinale et littéraire du Moyen Age* 51, pp. 151–68.
Biard, J. (2009), 'Le lieu de la croyance : le traité sur les Topiques de Jean Buridan', in *Les lieux de l'argumentation. Histoire du syllogisme topique d'Aristote à Leibniz*, J. Biard and F. Mariani Zini (eds), Turnhout, Brepols, pp. 359–83.
Biard, J. (2012), *Science et nature. La théorie buridanienne du savoir*, Paris, Vrin.
Buridan, J. (2001), *Summulae de Dialectica. An Annotated Translation with a Philosophical Introduction*, G. Klima (ed.), New Heaven/London, Yale University Press.
Buridan, J. (1976), *Treatise on Consequences; Buridanus, Tractatus de Consequentiis*, H. Hubien (ed.), Vander-Ouzy, Presses Universitaires de Louvain.
Buridan, J. (2013), *On Topics (De Lociis)*, N. J. Green-Pedersen (ed.). Johannes Buridanus, Summulae de Locis Dialecticis, Turnhout, Brepols.
Buridan, J. (2015), *Treatise on Consequences*, Stephen Read (intro. and trans.), New York, Fordham University Press.
Buridanus, J. (1942), *Quaestiones super libris quattuor de caelo et mundo*, E. A. Moody (ed.), Cambridge, MA, Medieval Academy of America, pp. 165–6.
Buridanus, J. (2003), *Quaestiones Topicorum*, Niels J. Green-Pedersen (ed.), Turnhout, Brepols.
Buridanus, J. (2016), *Quaestiones in Rhetoricam*, transcription made by B. Preben-Hansen, http://www.preben.nl/BuridanRH.pdf, which I have amended against the manuscript preserved at Leipzig, University Library, ms. 1246, 331v (accessed April 28, 2016).
Burnyeat, M. F. (1994), 'Enthymeme: Aristotle on the Logic of Persuasion', in *Aristotle's Rhetoric: Philosophical Essays*, D. J. Furley and A. Nehamas (eds), Princeton, NJ, Princeton University Press, pp. 3–55.

Crimi, M. (2018), 'Formal and Material Consequences in Ockham and Buridan', *Vivarium* 56 (3–4), pp. 241–71.

Crivelli, P. (2011), 'Aristotle on Syllogisms from a "Hypothesis"', in *Argument from Hypothesis in Ancient Philosophy*, A. Longo and D. Del Forno (eds), Napoli, Bibliopolis, pp. 95–184.

Dutilh Novaes, C. (2005), 'Buridan's Consequentia: Consequence and Inference Within a Token-Based Semantics', *History and Philosophy of Logic* 26 (4), pp. 277–97.

Dutilh Novaes, C. and Bosman B. (2017), 'Formal, Material, and Hybrid Grounding for Consequence: Peter Abelard and John Buridan', in *Miroir de l'Amitié: Mélanges offerts à Joël Biard*, Ch. Grellard (ed.), Paris, Vrin, pp. 229–42.

George, R. (1972), 'Enthymematic Consequence', *American Philosophical Quarterly* 9, pp. 113–16.

Goldman, A. I. (1999), *Knowledge in a Social World*, Oxford, Oxford University Press, pp. 24–5.

Goldman, A. I. and E. J. Olsson (2009), 'Reliabilism and the Value of Knowledge', in *Epistemic Value*, A. Haddock, A. Millar and D. Pritchard (eds), Oxford, Oxford University Press, pp. 19–41.

Hitchcock, D. (1985), 'Enthymematic Arguments', *Informal Logic* 7, pp. 83–97.

Hubien, H. http://www.logicmuseum.com/wiki/Authors/Buridan/Quaestiones_in_analytica_priora/Liber_2/Q22.

Klima, G. (2004), 'Consequences of a Closed, Token-Based Semantics: The Case of John. Buridan', *History and Philosophy of Logic* 25, pp. 95–110.

Pasnau, R. (2010), 'Medieval Social Epistemology: Scientia for Mere Mortals', *Episteme* 7, pp. 23–41.

Rapp, Ch. (2002), 'Die Syllogismus-truncatus-Lehre – ein Nachruf', in *Id., Werke in deutscher Übersetzung*, Aristoteles, Rhetorik, C. Rapp (trans. and comm.), Berlin, Akademie Verlag, vol. 2, 187–9.

Read, S. (2015), 'The Medieval Theory of Consequence', *Synthese* 187 (3), pp. 899–912.

Slomkowski, P. (1997), *Aristotle's Topics*, Leiden, Brill.

Sorensen, R. A. (1988), 'Are Enthymemes Arguments?', *Notre Dame Journal of Formal Logic* 29, pp. 155–9.

Striker, G. (1979), 'Aristoteles über Syllogismen "aufgrund einer Hypothese"', *Hermes* 107, pp. 33–50.

Walton, D. and Reed C. A. (2005), 'Argumentation Schemes and Enthymemes', *Synthese* 145, pp. 339–70.

Zupko, J. (1993), 'Buridan and Scepticism', *Journal of the History of Philosophy* 31 (1993), 191–22.

7

The enthymeme from signs and the study of nature in the Renaissance

Marco Sgarbi

7.1 The enthymeme in Aristotle

In the Aristotelian tradition the enthymeme is considered the main argument of rhetorical discourse. In this chapter I want to show (1) how along its history the enthymeme has been employed also in other contexts beyond rhetoric and (2) how it contributed in a major way to epistemological developments in Renaissance philosophy. The specific category of enthymeme for investigation here is that which proceeds by signs. In order to understand in what way this logical argument played a fundamental role in Renaissance epistemology, it is important to reconstruct, albeit briefly, Aristotle's original thinking. My preliminary exposition is intentionally brief and to the point. My aim is to catch the main sense of the Aristotelian doctrine, without diminishing the multiple problems that constellate Aristotle's philosophy and that scholars like Myles Burnyeat and James Allen have drawn our attention to.[1]

The enthymeme is for Aristotle a kind of argument that involves the θυμός (heart/spirit), whose premises are ἔνδοξα (probable opinions) and that concerns a πίστις (belief). In *Rhetoric* 1355a5–8, Aristotle states that this inference is a sort of demonstration (ἀπόδειξίς τις) – a rhetorical demonstration (ἀπόδειξις ῥητορικὴ) – because a belief arises (πίστις) when we consider a thing to have been demonstrated. The enthymeme is therefore a particular kind of demonstration, in the sense that it provides evidence of something. Since for Aristotle demonstration largely takes place through syllogism, then an enthymeme may be considered a rhetorical syllogism.

In *Rhetoric* 1355a10–18, Aristotle explains that rhetorical syllogism has a peculiar affinity with scientific syllogism, which is demonstration properly speaking. While with scientific demonstration the premises are absolutely true and necessary, it is evident for Aristotle that the propositions forming the basic enthymeme, 'though some of them may be necessary, will in the main hold for the most part (ὡς ἐπὶ τὸ πολύ)'.[2] The premises are true opinions 'universally or for the most part (ἢ καθόλου ἢ ὡς ἐπὶ τὸ πολύ)'.[3] Indeed, *Rhetoric* 1395b31–1396a3 establishes that 'we should base our arguments upon what happens for the most part as well as upon what necessarily happens'. Furthermore, Aristotle explains:

> He who is best able to see how and from what elements a deduction is produced will also be best skilled in the enthymeme [...] for the true and the approximately true are apprehended by the same faculty; it may also be noted that men have a sufficient natural instinct for what is true, and usually to arrive at the truth.[4]

Only a person who knows the truth can state that a thing is similar or close to the truth, to the extent that in *Rhetoric* 1396b22–7 Aristotle deals with a peculiar kind of enthymeme called demonstrative or probative, which 'makes an inference from what is accepted (ἐξ ὁμολογουμένων)'.

In the *Prior Analytics* II.27, 70a3–10, it is put rather differently. Aristotle states that the enthymeme is a syllogism based on probable premises, but he adds that these premises can be replaced by signs. I am using the word 'sign' to translate the Greek word τὸ σεμείων. An enthymeme therefore proceeds either from a probable premise or from a sign (ἐξ εἰκότων ἢ σεμείων), although these are not the same thing. Aristotle, indeed, makes clear that the premise that is expressed as a sign has a claim to be demonstrative because

> For anything such that when it is another thing is, or when it has come into being the other has come into being before or after, is a sign of the other's being or having come into being.[5]

Signs can be either necessary or based on opinions that are reputable. Necessary signs cannot be refuted or resolved in any other manner and they are properly called τεκμήρια, while probable signs based on opinions can be refuted. I translate τεκμήρια with 'proofs'. Rhetorical demonstrations through proofs are comparable to statements like 'the fact that he has a fever is a sign that he is ill' or 'the fact that she is producing milk is a sign that she has lately borne a child'.[6] Demonstration by proof as with that by sign assumes thus an epistemic value that exceeds persuasion, extending its scope to topics that concern natural philosophy.[7] In *Physics* II.8 198b35–6, Aristotle is clear in stating that natural events or phenomena take place either always or for the most part. And he further states that it is not only demonstration that deals with things that take place for the most part but also the enthymeme. Therefore, the enthymeme may also be considered a legitimate tool for investigating nature.

In *Rhetoric* II.25 1402b13–1403a15, Aristotle spells out the epistemic value of enthymeme. Enythmemes may be based on probable opinion or verisimile (εἰκος), or on an example (παράδειγμα), or on proof (τεκμήριον), or again on a sign (σημεῖον). In this passage Aristotle introduces a specification that was absent in the *Prior Analytics* II.27, 70a3–10. An enthymeme based on probable opinions concerns what is, or is supposed to be, true for most of the time. Those based on example, however, proceed from a universal generated by induction through the consideration of one or many similar cases and thus proceed by inference to a particular. An enthymeme by means of proof is based on what is necessary and existing (ἀναγκαίον καὶ ἀεὶ ὄντος). Finally, an enthymeme that proceeds by sign deals either with a universal or with a particular, be it true or false. But what is more interesting in relation to Aristotle's explanation is the cognitive import of the enthymeme.

The enthymeme based on the probable – since the probable is what happens most of the time, although it is not necessary – can be refuted. To confute this kind of argument it is not sufficient to state that it is invalid because it is not necessary, by reason of the fact that it is proper to its own nature to be most of the time the case, and not always. Therefore, it needs to be confuted either through facts or over the course of time – that is, by means of experience. Obviously, this confutation is somewhat challenging. To explain this difficulty may take as an example something not immediately related to the enthymeme, yet useful for understanding the value of the enthymeme in Aristotelian epistemology. If we take Karl Popper's famous example of white swans, and we say: 'all swans are white', my statement is epistemologically very strong: indeed, it expresses the idea that every conceivable swan that I might ever set eyes on will be white. However, it is very weak as a logical statement, and its refutation takes no more than the discovery of a single non-white swan. On the other hand, if I say: 'some swans are white', the statement will be weak from an epistemological standpoint but very strong from a logical perspective because in order to demonstrate its falsehood I would need to examine all swans and thus be in a position to state that 'no swan is white'. In the case of the enthymeme, therefore, in order to show that a thing is not probable, one must prove that in no case can a thing happen, not only in relation to the present but at any time. The reason, then, is evident that enthymemes based on examples are easily refutable. Indeed, just one negative instance can invalidate the argument. In contrast, it is impossible to refute enthymemes using proof:

> by showing in any way that they are non-deductive. All we can do is to show that the fact alleged does not exist. If there is no doubt that it does, and that it is a proof, refutation now becomes impossible, for this is equivalent to a demonstration which is clear in every respect.[8]

Enthymemes based on proofs may lead to truth like any other scientific demonstration and can be used to explain natural phenomena that happen in the vast majority of cases. Whether based on signs or proofs, in general terms the enthymeme characterizes a valid inference and shares with the scientific demonstration a capacity to proceed from premises that are always or mostly true. In other words, an enthymeme based on signs represents the perfect candidate for a logical instrument to investigate nature. However, as Donald Morrison remarks, there is a substantial difference between scientific demonstration and enthymeme, in particular regarding proof: the latter leaves the causal explanation totally indeterminate, while for Aristotle all scientific knowledge is knowledge of causes. In instance cited earlier, 'to have fever' is conceived as an effect of the cause of being sick, just as 'to have milk' is conceived as an effect of 'having given birth', but it is not always like this. There may be some cases in which two elements are the effects of the same thing and/or where the causal relation is inverted. In the case of the enthymeme based on proof, what is important to know for Aristotle is not the causal relation so much as the constant conjunction or co-appearance of the two elements. Therefore, at least as far as Aristotle is concerned, the enthymeme (also the enthymeme based on proof) may be of limited value in the study of nature.

Things radically changed with the input of Aristotle's Greek commentators, and in particular with Philoponus and Simplicius. Indeed – according to Morrison – the conception of the enthymeme based on proof comes to be extended more generally to encompass the syllogism from effect to cause – that is, the inference from what is a posteriori to what is a priori. The most important aspect is the introduction of a causal relation that was missing in Aristotle in the inference based on proof. Philoponus explicitly states that 'the syllogism τοῦ διότι infers the effect from the cause, while the syllogism τοῦ ὅτι infers the cause from the effect. The latter are called demonstration by proof'.[9] This idea allows Philoponus to conceive of induction also as a form of reasoning based on proof:

> Demonstration by proof establishes the things that are a priori starting from those that are a posteriori. Of such a kind of proof is induction, which establishes universals from particular – that is, from what is a priori from what is a posteriori.[10]

As we have seen in *Rhetorics*, Aristotle excluded induction from the list of arguments by proof: the two inferences were neatly distinguished.

Furthermore, Philoponus emphasizes how inference based on proof is irrefutable (ἄλυτος).[11] This means that where for Aristotle many demonstrations from effect to cause led to merely probable knowledge, for Philoponus they led to certain knowledge. The certainty for Philoponus did not concern knowledge of the cause as such but was confined to the knowledge that the cause was cause of that particular effect. In order words, it was knowledge of a causal relation between two particular things. To support this, however, cause and effect must needs be 'convertible' – that is, this effect could be generated only by the cause in question, and this cause could generate only the concerned effect. Things are different for Simplicius, as Orna Harari has shown. Indeed, the inference would be based on refutable signs and therefore on an inferential model which would be less scientific and more conjectural in character.[12]

Yet the most striking aspect – as Morrison acutely observes[13] – is that for both Philoponus and Simplicius this kind of argument by proof is the inference that establishes the first principles of science, that foundational inquiry exposed by Aristotle in the proem of *Physics*,[14] although this investigation is carried out in a more deductive manner with Philoponus and more inductively with Simplicius.[15] To sum up, the enthymeme by proof becomes an inference that characterizes the foundations of natural investigation, something that was impossible for Aristotle, lacking the ability to explain the causality of the sign. It is this very idea that Renaissance philosophers will themselves come to exploit in their bid to elaborate the so-called *demonstratio ex signis*, which is in all respects an incorrect interpretation of the Aristotelian enthymeme coming from Greek commentators.

7.2 From the sign to conjecture

Knowledge of Greek commentators of Aristotle during the Middle Ages is fragmentary and thin on the ground. This is all the more true for works of logic, which are well-nigh ignored. Philoponus was known mainly for his thesis on natural philosophy,[16] but his impact on the development of mediaeval logic is virtually negligible. Nonetheless, his theory of demonstration is incorporated into Averroes's works. Even so, it does not receive a proper thematization, limiting itself to distinguishing between demonstration from effect and demonstration *simpliciter* (that of mathematics) and also demonstration *propter quid* (that of natural philosophy).[17]

For a direct knowledge of Philoponus we have to wait until the sixteenth century. His commentary on the *Posterior Analytics* was published in Greek for the first time in 1504 and received its first Latin translation in 1539 by Filippo Teodosio and Andrea Grazioli. The Greek text of the commentary on *Prior Analytics* was published only in 1534 and translated by Guglielmo Doroteo only in 1539. The Greek commentary on *Physics* was published in 1535 and translated in 1539 by Doroteo. This bibliographical information is indicative of the later reception – and therefore development – of the doctrine of demonstration by proof as being a demonstration capable of finding a causal relation. It is even more telling, in fact, the sense that – as Nicholas Jardine has rightly pointed out – the demonstration from effects to cause – that is the syllogism that for Philoponus was based on proof – is called 'coniecturalis syllogismus' in the translation of the commentary to *Posterior Analytics* published by Grazioli and Teodosio,[18] and 'coniecturalis' translates τεκμηριώδης – that is, 'based on proof'. As a further confirmation of this, in the translation of the distinction between demonstrations *propter quid* and *quia* – that is, from cause to effect and from effect to cause – the latter are called 'coniecturales demonstrationes'.[19] And in Simplicius's commentary to *Physics* published for the first time in Greek in 1526 and translated in Latin by Doroteo in 1539 – the argument from what is more known by us is characterized as a conjectural syllogism by proof.[20]

Both translations seem to be influenced by Agostino Nifo's commentary to *Posterior Analytics*, which is based in turn on Philoponus, evidently read and studied directly in the Greek since the Latin version was not yet then available. Indeed, Nifo states that arguments that proceed from what is more known are conjectures or conjectural syllogisms. He points out that, for Philoponus, it is more proper to speak of conjecture than demonstration where the argument can be doubted. Conjectures can be either necessary, and thus they are called demonstrative, or not necessary, and are therefore called rhetorical. The latter are of the kind: 'the woman is pale, so she has given birth' or 'this person wanders at night, so he is a thief'. Nifo thus distinguishes proof from sign according to the Aristotelian dictate, but he calls both conjectures.[21] In another passage he writes that Philoponus characterizes the argument from what is more known as a 'necessary and conjectural syllogism, as in "the woman has milk so she has given birth"'.[22] Nifo adds that 'this syllogism by *signum*, which in Aristotle's *Rhetorics* was the τεκμήριον, Philoponus calls irrefutable'. In Philoponus, according to Nifo, being necessary and being conjectural coexist. This argument is properly called 'demonstrative conjecture'. Nifo then adds that Philoponus identifies four kinds of syllogism: 'demonstrative, dialectic, sophistic, and those by means of sign or necessary conjecture'.[23]

The use of the term 'coniecturalis' is particularly significant because the word was used at the time to translate another Greek adjective, that of στοχαστικός, which characterized properly speaking the argument of medicine from the time of Galen and Celsus onwards.

In his logical works – in the wake of Philoponus and Simplicius – Nifo identifies demonstration by signs with the argument from effect to cause. In speaking of this kind of inference, however, Nifo seems more concerned with signs than proofs, and for this reason he uses the more generic term, sign. Thus, Nifo characterizes demonstration by sign as the logical tool that discovers the cause of an effect within the process of regressus.

> When I consider more diligently the words of Aristotle and the commentaries of Alexander, Themistius, Philoponus and Simplicius, it seems to me that in the *regressus* made in physical demonstrations the first process, by which the discovery of the cause is put into syllogistic form, is a mere conjectural syllogism, since through it the discovery of the cause is syllogized in a merely conjectural fashion.[24]

The conjectural nature of syllogism by sign comes from the eminently provisional character of knowledge provided by experience. It is not mathematical knowledge. For this reason, knowledge of natural phenomena is not *scientia simpliciter* but *propter quid effectus*. Thus Nifo characterizes natural science as the 'science looking for causes that can be inferred by means of conjectural syllogism' – that is, syllogism based on signs. Nifo adds that 'Aristotle in the *Meteorology* says that he did not provide the true causes of natural effects, but those that were possible through conjecture'.[25] In this case Aristotle deals rarely with proofs and more frequently with signs,[26] and for this reason it is possible to say that for Nifo conjectural syllogism was first and foremost a syllogism based on signs, not proofs, and with a lower epistemological, demonstrative value. Thus the use of enthymeme is clearly understood as follows: it allowed for the revision of the concept of science within the Aristotelian tradition – a science, which was no longer considered as being exclusively universal and necessary but could be based on conjectures that needed to be further corroborated and tested. And for this corroboration, the *regressus* theory will become necessary in being the only instrument capable of guaranteeing solid, certain and universal knowledge.

7.3 From conjecture to demonstration from effect

Already before Nifo, however, the philosopher and physician Alessandro Achillini had explored the potentialities of demonstration using signs. Nifo's work is dated 1524, while Achillini died in 1512, and this is the year of his *De physico audito*. Achillini characterizes the 'demonstratio signi' as that demonstration composed of constant propositions – that is, it is necessary – and which proceed from the sign of what is to be demonstrated. By *signum* – Achillini points out – one can signify either the effect itself or the concomitant effect. He states then that all demonstrations from effects are demonstrations *ex signo*, though this does not exclude all demonstrations by proof from being demonstration by effects – indeed, the former could also proceed from a concomitant effect. For instance, consider a woman with yellow skin: the yellow colour of the skin is sign that that woman has cholera. But then we note a whitening of the faeces, which is a sign that has emerged with the yellowing of the skin and this is called a concomitant effect. In future, if the woman observes a whitening of faeces, she may infer that she has cholera.

Achillini adds that if it is true that every demonstration by proof is a demonstration *quia*, the contrary is not true, as is evident in the case of demonstration by remote cause, which is a demonstration *quia*, but cannot be a demonstration by sign because the sign is either immediate and evident or else it is concomitant but never remote.[27]

The physician and natural philosopher Marcoantonio Zimara, in contrast, focuses particularly on the characterization of the demonstration *a signo* in the wake of the Averroistic tradition. In the *Tabula & dilucidationes in dicta Aristotelis & Averrois* (1537), and commenting on the proem of Aristotle's *Physics*, he writes that 'demonstration *ex signo* or of that is (*quia*) occurs when we proceed from the effect more known to us to the existence of the cause'.[28] Zimara evidently shows the influence of Philoponus and Simplicius, but in this case Averroes's filter is even stronger, to the extent that every demonstration that is not *propter quid* is as a matter of fact demonstration by sign. For instance, included among demonstrations by sign are those of an effect generated by a supernatural cause: just as one may infer a lunar eclipse starting from the observation of a lack of shadow from an object on the Earth produced by moonshine. They are demonstrations *a signo* by means of a remote cause and those *ad impossibile* or those that concern efficient cause. These are all kinds of demonstration that Achillini excluded. In Proposition 53 in the *Theoremata seu memorabilium propositionum limitationes* (1539), Zimara writes that there are three modes of demonstration by signs. The first demonstrates the existence of a cause from a known effect: for instance, an eclipse is proof of the interposition of the Earth. The second is where the effect is unknown, but its existence is demonstrated by something other that operates as a sign: as, for example, where an eclipse is shown by a lack of shadows being cast by objects or when milk in the breast shows that a woman has given birth. The third mode of demonstration – *quia* or *a signo* – is by remote cause, a mode that Achillini excluded.

What particularly interested Zimara, however, is the second case, that mentioned by Aristotle in his *Rhetorics*. Zimara emphasizes how this demonstrative argument is that privileged by physicians, whose special concern is experience and sensation, in contrast with natural philosophers, who – he maintains – are more preoccupied with causes. Demonstrations *a signo* as practised by physicians consider things that happen frequently and are based on true experience (*vero experimento*)[29] and which are capable of yielding adequate conclusions by inference for medical purposes – though the true causes may be beyond the immediate concern.

In his commentary on *Physics*, the Aristotelian Ludovico Boccadiferro declares in an Averroistic way that there are three kinds of demonstration: (1) *a signo*, (2) *propter quid* and (3) *simpliciter*. Demonstrations *a signo* are also called improper demonstrations because they infer from the effect to the cause and do not lead to a universal and necessary knowledge. In spite of this, they are most often used in natural investigations, even if they would yield more a precise and exact knowledge if they proceeded from the cause, which is most of the time unknown.[30] Boccadiferro is aware that this demonstration is an enthymeme, but he states that the way in which philosophers use this logical inference differs from how dialecticians and rhetoricians use it in at least three respects: (1) matter, (2) form and (3) end.

In dialectic, matter is seen as contingent and accidental, while that examined by natural philosophers is conceived as being necessary for itself – that is, it shows the essential relation between subject and predicate. This does not mean that knowledge which comes from experience is in itself universal and necessary but only that the proof that such demonstration provides by means of the sign is certain. Regarding form, rhetoricians and dialecticians proceed from a singular to a singular, while natural philosophers proceed from the singular to the universal, finding the necessary connection between subject and predicate with the aim of discovering the first principles of knowledge. The last difference concerns the purpose of demonstration. According to Boccadiferro, dialecticians have intention of demonstrating the unknown, while philosophers pursue what is almost known (*quod quasi notum est*) – that is, the effect by means of the cause.[31]

Girolamo Balduino includes the topic of demonstration *ex signo* within the treatment of the method for discovering the premise of the demonstration *quia*. According to Balduino, Aristotle characterized the sign in a number of ways, but only two of these are epistemologically valid. One concerns a necessary proposition, the other a probable proposition.[32] The value of the signs lay in the fact that they indicated the existence of some or other fact or might provide information on future things that could happen. For instance, sighting many dark clouds in the sky is a sign of impending rain, or seeing milk in the breast of a woman is a sign that she has given birth. The two signs are unequivocally different because one provides information about a future thing which might or might not happen, although there is certainly no necessity about it. The second sign shows something that has already happened or occurred. The ways that these signs are used as premises for the demonstration are therefore very different. It is in the second case that Averroes identified – according to Balduino – the demonstration *quia* with the demonstration *ex signo* because it simply shows the present or past existence of a thing.[33] The other kind of sign, in contrast, has no more than a prognostic function.

Jacopo Zabarella – usually considered the apex of the Paduan logical school – develops his theory of demonstration by sign in his *Tabulae* starting with the enthymeme. The enthymeme – paraphrasing Aristotle – is that imperfect syllogism that proceeds either from verisimile premises or from signs. The difference between the two is while the former are always probable, the latter are always necessary. Enthymeme by sign can therefore be of two kinds: either demonstrative and irrefutable (insolvable in Zabarella's translation) or refutable and probable. Syllogism by means of demonstrative sign – that is, a proof – is imperfect in the case where one states: 'this woman has milk and milk is the sign that the woman has given birth.' This would have been a perfect syllogism if one had added the premise 'every woman, who has milk, has given birth'. A syllogism by means of a refutable sign, or better a solvable sign, would be 'the woman is pale' – where being pale is the sign – and 'therefore she gave birth'. It would be perfect if it had as premise 'every woman who has given birth is pale'.

In his commentary on Aristotle's *Posterior Analytics*, Zabarella points out that Averroes conceived the affections (*affectiones*) of demonstrations as signs, and by signs he meant those accidents which were more known than the causes.[34] Zabarella explains that demonstration by sign is a demonstration that starts from the effect and which does not lead to the knowledge of the reason or cause of the thing. Zabarella points out that demonstration by sign is not exactly the same as syllogism, which infers conclusions from universal and self-evident principles.[35] When Zabarella exemplifies demonstration from the effect, he employs the common example of demonstration *ex signo*: 'there is smoke, therefore there is fire' or 'there is generation, therefore there is prime matter'. The epistemological incompleteness of this demonstration is examined in the book *De regressu*, where Zabarella states,

> From the inspection of smoke, someone argues and shows that there is fire there that he does not see. By this one demonstration, it appears to be demonstrated both that there is fire there and why smoke comes to be. But this is not true. For in knowing these two things, the speed of the understanding deceives him. For the demonstration of fire from smoke, by its very nature, makes clear nothing except that there is fire. And if we appear also to know what that smoke is on account of, it is not by means of the same demonstration but by means of another, one by which we demonstrate smoke from fire and render the reason why there is smoke there.[36]

So even if it seems demonstrative, knowledge produced by inferences through signs does not lead to real scientific knowledge but requires further proof provided by demonstration *propter quid*. Zabarella therefore indicates an epistemic insufficiency in this kind of argument, even if it remains fundamental as the starting point for the epistemological process.

7.4 Conclusion

In conclusion, what for Aristotle should be viewed as a rhetorical inference aimed at persuading and arousing feeling by means of a series of interpretations, misunderstandings and interpolations becomes an instrument for the investigation of nature and the knowledge of particulars coming from experience. The usefulness of this instrument is to characterize the process that proceeds from effects to the cause, either in its entirety or in one of its parts. The discussion about demonstration by signs waned with the rapid decline of the Aristotelian method as a logic of scientific discovery. However, the debate reached the ears of a philosopher, who cannot be listed within the Aristotelian sect – that is, Galileo Galilei. Likely influenced by the reading of these books on logic and by the knowledge of Philoponus's interpretation, Galileo – in his youthful treatise *De demonstratione* – distinguishes demonstration proceeding from effects from demonstration proceeding from the cause. The Pisan philosopher states,

> For, considered from the viewpoint of its middle term, Aristotle calls demonstration *quia demonstratio signi* . . . considered from the viewpoint of its end, he calls it demonstration *quia vel quo*, since it proves the existence of something. Considered

from the viewpoint of its mode of proceeding, Averroes calls it *demonstratio evidentiae*, since it proceeds from what is more known with respect to us; he also refers to it as *demonstratio existentiae*. The Latins call it demonstration *ab effectu vel a posteriori*, the Greeks call it *demonstratio coniecturalis*.[37]

Galileo thus identifies demonstration by sign with the first stage of regressus and provides a functional differentiation that explains the various ways in which this kind of demonstration is conceived. Galileo deals with the various divisions of the demonstration *quia*, and in doing this he characterizes demonstration by sign more specifically.

Demonstration *quia* would proceed either by remote cause or from the effect to the cause. Demonstration by sign is of the latter kind – from effect to cause – and does not involve remote causes. In this, Galileo is perfectly aligned with Zabarella. The example he adduces is that 'if there is smoke, then there is fire'. This kind of demonstration – Galileo warns – proceeds, however, in one of the following ways: from an effect to a cause, from an effect to another effect, from a sign or from any other necessary accident connected to the cause.

In his treatment Galileo establishes the necessary connection and the convertibility between effect and cause, between sign and cause. Thus, in a subsequent division he distinguishes demonstration *quia* according to the convertibility of the middle term. There are demonstrations *quia* which are not by sign and which are not convertible: for instance 'there is heat, then there is fire'. This inference is different from the previous 'there is smoke, then there is fire' on the grounds that, while there cannot be smoke without fire (at least in terms of the Renaissance), heat can be generated by other sources like the sun. In the latter case, there is no direct and necessary correlation. There are then convertible inferences, and among these we find those like 'there is an eclipse, therefore there is an interposition of the Earth'. Of this kind of inference is demonstration by sign.

A third division concerns those that point to the mere existence of something, like the prime mover, or fire, or prime matter, and those that show that certain propositions are true a posteriori. These demonstrations are for Galileo the most important for establishing the first principles of science, and in stating this the Pisan scientist was reiterating a consolidated logical tradition.

The cases that I have investigated in this chapter concern treatises of logic exclusively, but a more thorough investigation would require a deeper inspection of all the rhetorical texts of the period to assess how these topics were considered in parallel. Furthermore, and perhaps most importantly, it would be beneficial to pursue the line of enquiry suggested by Ian Maclean – that is, to check how and when these inferences based on signs came to be applied in practical terms in daily scientific practice. Indeed, all the theoretical reflections that we have examined seem more accurately termed academic debate than an actual instrument for investigating and studying nature.

However, if we consider the case of Giovanni Battista Da Monte – one of the most prominent physicians of the Paduan school who made a fundamental contribution to the development of methodology and epistemology in the Renaissance – the picture changes significantly. Da Monte identifies the demonstration *ex signo* as the main logical instrument of the physician. Demonstration by sign is part of the resolutive method, which proceeds from particulars to universals and leads to knowledge by signs. These signs – which are always particulars – are known through sensation, while their causes, which are always universal, are never known by sensation, but only by means of the intellect, and therefore they remain initially hidden and latent. The sign makes evident and apparent what is not yet perceivable to sensation – that is, the causes themselves. Demonstration by sign would be based on analogism, established between the sign itself and the latent cause. It would constitute a relation that proceeds from the particular (sign) to the universal (cause), but it concludes with a particular – that is, the fact that the cause in question is the specific cause of the sign or that particular effect – in a process that mirrors the Aristotelian *regressus*. The hidden cause is known therefore demonstratively through the sign by means of an external thing, and it is known as the cause of that specific particular. For instance, the intellect knows as a universal that pertains to the nature of fire, the fact that it has as a property the capacity to create smoke. Even if fire were lacking but we see smoke, we would say that there was a fire because smoke is one of its signs.

And so in this way emerges the usefulness and the necessity of signs for Da Monte. The thing that is unknown from the effect would never be known immediately in a universal manner, and therefore its knowledge would never be necessary but always conjectural – that is, based on a supposition. If indeed we were to have knowledge of the nature of all diseases by means of sensation – as happens already with diseases that are manifest and apparent by means of visible and evident signs – there would be no need to look for signs because knowledge of all diseases would be immediate.[38] This kind of procedure requires a proof that traces the particular back to a universal law. Da Monte applies these methods of investigation to the majority of his *consilia medica*, showing how the type of inference embodied in the enthymeme by sign had become an effective and employable instrument for the study of nature.

Notes

1. See M. F. Burnyeat 2001, pp. 3–55; J. Allen 2001.
2. Aristotle, *Rhetoric,* 1357a, pp. 30–1. On the expression ὡς ἐπὶ τὸ πολύ see M. Mignucci 1981.
3. Aristotle, *Rhetoric,* 1356b, pp. 16–18.
4. Aristotle, *Rhetoric,* 1355a, pp. 10–18.
5. Aristotle, *Posterior Analytics,* 70a, pp. 7–9.
6. Aristotle, *Rhetoric,* 1357b, pp. 1–17.
7. See R. Serjeantson 2006, pp. 132–75.
8. Aristotle, *Rhetoric,* 1403a, pp. 13–16.
9. Philoponus 1909, XIII.3, 168, pp. 22–3.
10. Philoponus 1909, 49, pp. 19–21.
11. Philoponus 1909, 31, p. 11.
12. O. Harari 2012, p. 370.
13. D. Morrison 1997, p. 14.
14. Philoponus 1887, XVI-XVII, 9, pp. 15–17; Simplicius 188, IX, 18, pp. 28–9.

15 O. Harari 2012, p. 373.
16 C. B. Schmitt 1989, pp. 210–30.
17 See A. Elamrani-Jamal 2000, pp. 113–31.
18 Philoponus 1542, p. 147.
19 Philoponus 1553, 22v.
20 Simplicius 1539, p. 2.
21 A. Nifo 1526, 15r. Nifo argues differently from the physician Christophorus Vega, calling conjectures only τεκμήρια – that is, irrefutable proofs – and calling signs probable proofs. See C. Vega 1571, p. 1197.
22 A. Nifo 1526, 15r.
23 A. Nifo 1526, 15r.
24 A. Nifo 1549, p. 14.
25 A. Nifo 1549, p. 14.
26 See Aristotle, *Meteorology*, 341a31; 342a30; 346a23; 347a28; 348a34; 350a30; 354a29; 358a5.
27 A. Achillini 1568, 115a.
28 M. Zimara 1565, 39r.
29 M. Zimara 1563, p. 95.
30 L. Boccadiferro 1577, 14r.
31 L. Boccadiferro 1577, 14v.
32 Balduino precedes Capivacci in conceiving the sign as a proposition. See G. Capivacci 1603, p. 282.
33 G. Balduino 1563, p. 295.
34 J. Zabarella 1597, p. 754 e-f.
35 J. Zabarella 1597, p. 751 b-c.
36 J. Zabarella 1597, p. 493 d-e.
37 G. Galilei 1988, p. 107.
38 G. B. Da Monte 1587, p. 50.

Bibliography

Achillini, Alessandro (1568), *Opera*, Venezia, Scotus.
Allen, J. (2001), *Inference from Signs. Ancient Debates about the Nature of Evidence*, Oxford, Clarendon Press.
Aristotle (1970–1993), *Meteorology, Posterior Analytics, Rhetoric*, (trans.) H. P. Cooke (ed.), Cambridge, MA, Harvard University Press, Loeb Classical Library.
Balduino, Girolamo (1563), *Expositio in librum primum Posteriorum Aristotelis*, Venezia, Scotus.
Boccadiferro, Ludovico (1577), *Aristotelis de physico auditu liber primus*, Basel, Perna.
Burnyeat, M. F. (2001), 'Enthymeme: Aristotle on the Logic of Persuasion', in *Aristotle's Rhetoric. Philosophical Essays*, D. J. Furley and A. Nehamas (eds), Princeton, NJ, Princeton University Press, pp. 3–55.
Capivacci, Geronimo (1603), *Opera Omnia*, Frankfurt, Palthen.
Da Monte, Giovanni Battista (1587), *Medicina universa*, Frankfurt, Wechel.
Elamrani-Jamal, A. (2000), 'La démonstration du signe selon Ibn Rushd', *Documenti e studi sulla tradizione filosofica medievale* 11, pp. 113–31.
Galilei, Galileo (1988), *Tractatio de demonstratione*, Padova, Antenore.

Harari, O. (2012), 'Simplicius on Tekmeriodic Proofs', *Studies in History and Philosophy of Science Part A*, p. 43.

Mignucci, M. (1981), Ὡς ἐπὶ τὸ πολύ et nécessaire dans la conception aristotélicienne de la science, in Aristotle on Science. The Posterior Analytics. Proceedings of the Eighth Symposium Aristotelicum held in Padua from 7 to 15, E. Berti (ed.), Padova, Antenore, pp. 173-203.

Morrison, D. (1997), 'Philoponus and Simplicius on Tekmeriodic Proof', in *Method and Order in Renaissance Philosophy of Nature. The Aristotle Commentary Tradition*, D. A. Di Liscia, E. Kessler and C. Methuen (eds), Aldershot, Ashgate, 14, pp. 1–22.

Nifo, Agostino (1526), *Commentaria in Libris Posteriorum Aristotelis*, Venezia, Scotus.

Nifo, Agostino (1549), *Aristotelis Physicarum acroasum hoc est naturalium asuscultationum liber interprete*, Venezia, Scotus.

Philoponus (1909), *Commentaria in Aristotelem Graeca*, Berlin, Reimer.

Philoponus (1542), *Commentaria in libros posteriorum Aristotelis*, Venezia, Scotus.

Philoponus (1553), *Commentaria in libros posteriorum Aristotelis*, Venezia, Scotus.

Schmitt, C. B. (1989), *Reappraisals in Renaissance Thought*, London, Variorum, pp. 210–230.

Serjeantson, R. (2006), 'Proof and Persuasion', in *The Cambridge History of Science. Early Modern Science*, K. Park and L. Daston (eds), Cambridge, Cambridge University Press.

Simplicius (1539), *Commentaria in octo libros Aristotelis Stagiritae De physico*, Venezia, Scotus.

Vega, Cristobal (1571), *Opera*, Lyon, Chard.

Zabarella, Jacopo (1597), *Opera logica*, Köln, Zetzner.

Zimara, Marcoantonio (1563), *Theoremata*, Venezia, Giunta.

Zimara, Marcoantonio (1565), *Tabula & dilucidations in dicta Aristotelis & Averrois*, Venezia, Grifo.

8

The lion's fault

The enthymematic foundation of signatures

Marie-Luce Demonet

The validity of enthymeme is crucial for *semeia eikota* (probable signs): in Montaigne's *Essais* it is the natural mode of discourse for everyone's knowledge, in Renaissance medicine it is the basis of Galenic symptomatology and in the renewal of early modern physiognomony, it justifies 'visual enthymemes', even in Leonardo's sketches and paintings.[1] In the chapter 'La Prose du Monde' of *Les Mots et les Choses* (*The Order of Things*), which develops a bold analysis of Renaissance *epistemè*, Michel Foucault's reasoning from enthymeme appeared as the core of his interpretation of 'signatures'.[2] More recently, Giorgio Agamben expanded the scope of this kind of sign.[3] In what is an important semiotic twist, the forgotten example of the lion's large paws that reveal his fortitude (*Prior Analytics*, II.27/28, 70b) plays a major part within the signature theory, although its value is quite questionable, perhaps no more convincing than Erasmus's adage, 'We know the lion by his fingernails' (Lucian).

8.1 The physiognomic sign in the *Analytica Priora* and the *Physiognomica*

Although it is not unknown during the mediaeval era, pseudo-Aristotle's *Physiognomica* is rediscovered at the end of the fifteenth century, edited and adapted by various authors, together with Adamantius's *Physiognomicon* (fourth century), in Latin translation.[4] They enjoy increasing favour, first among physicians, then among a wider audience at the end of the sixteenth century. But is the physiognomic sign an enthymeme? One of Foucault's weaknesses in his signature theory consists in his reading of two famous treatises published by Giambattista Della Porta, *De humana physiognomonia* (1586) and *Phytognomonica* (1588).[5]

Aristotle devotes a chapter, or the end of a chapter,[6] to the physiognomonic sign in the *Analytica Priora* (70b). It validates syllogisms and enthymemes founded on the observation of the appearance of the body, in order to infer the moral features of an individual, extended by the physiognomers to a social community, and even to a nation. Renaissance editions, translations and commentaries follow the Aldine of 1495, which follows Philoponus's version.[7]

This edition shows the word *atélès* in the definition of the enthymeme as an imperfect syllogism, a word inserted long before in the manuscript tradition. Guillaume Budé, who owned a copy preserved in Leyden University Library, did not amend the text, although Rudolph Agricola had already disputed this definition; afterwards, Julius Pacius underlined the irrelevance of a gloss that contributed to the long-lasting confusion between the logical and the rhetorical definitions of the enthymeme.[8]

The Latin translations offer the same reading. In 1531, Lefèvre d'Étaples modified or copied Boethius's version ('Enthymema ergo est syllogismus imperfectus ex eicotibus et signis'[9]), and later the new translation by Turnèbe retains *atélès* in Casaubon's 1590 bilingual edition: 'Est igitur Enthymema ratiocinatio imperfecta ex verisimilibus vel signis'.[10] For Renaissance authors or rewriters of *Physiognomonica*, the presence of *atélès* did not challenge the status of such learning as *scientia*, for the important issue was the syllogistic/enthymematic nature of the physiognomonic sign. In the *Analytica*, the imperfection could be located in the difference between *eikota* (probable) and *tekmeria* (certain) signs. In contrast, physiognomony claims the certainty or quasi-certainty of the inferences drawn from the senses, in particular from vision. The old art of medical *semeiotike* offers a large register of signs and *indicia*, in order to build reasonings about psychological profiles that seem natural.

The blending of *Physiognomica* and *Analytica Priora* persisted in the medical tradition with the help of Quintilian's *Institutio Oratoria*, and some humanistic dialectics redistributed their definitions in order to stress the certainty of the connection between what is seen and the cause that is inferred. As we know, chapter 27 of *Prior Analytics II* provides the two famous examples of the milk woman and the good Pittacos, respectively, of medical and moral origins. In Aristotle's *Rhetorics* the former is an example of enthymeme, that is, of rhetorical syllogism, because it is technically imperfect, and it builds the oratorical discourse with the *paradeigma*, while Socrates replaces Pittacos; the lion disappears except in the canonical comparison between Achilles and the lion in the case of tropes.

The following chapter (or the end of chapter 27) of *Prior Analytics II* enjoys a special title in sixteenth-century editions, 'De syllogismo physiognomico': it contains the example of the lion's paws that I consider as responsible for the success of signature theory since Foucault. Lefèvre d'Etaples-Boethius's text is:

> Naturas autem cognoscere possibile est, si quis concedat simul transmutare corpus & animam: quaecunque sunt naturales passiones. discens enim aliquis fortasse [musicam], transmutavit secundum quid anima: sed non earum quae natura nobis insunt, haec est passio, sed ut irae & concupiscentiae & naturalium motionum. Si igitur & hoc det & unum unius signum esse, & possumus sumere propriam uniuscujusque generis passionem & signum: poterimus naturas cognoscere. Si enim est proprie alicui generi individuo inexistens passio, ut si leonibus fortitudo: necesse est & signum esse aliquod. compati enim sibi invicem positum est. & sit hoc magnas summitates habere: quod & aliis generibus non totis contingit. nam signum sic proprium est, quoniam totius generis propria passio est & non solius

proprium: sicut solemus dicere. erit ergo & in & alio genere hoc & erit fortis homo, & aliquod aliud animal. habebit ergo signum.[11]

This proemium shows a series of three conditional propositions, here in the Loeb Classical Library translation:

> It is possible to judge men's character from their physical appearance, if one grants that body and soul estimating change together in all natural affections. . . . Supposing, then, this is granted, and also that there is one sign of one affection, and that we can recognize the affection and sign proper to each class of creatures, we shall be able to judge character from physical appearance. For if a peculiar affection applies to any individual class, e.g., courage to lions, there must be some corresponding sign of it; for it has been assumed that body and soul are affected together. Let this be 'having large extremities.' This may apply to other classes, but not as wholes; for a sign is peculiar in the sense that the affection is peculiar to the class as a whole, and not to it alone, as we are accustomed to use the term. Thus the same affection will be found in another class also, and man or some other animal will be brave. Therefore, he will have the sign; for *ex hypothesi* there is one sign of one affection. (Loeb 529)

The hypothetical nature of the reasoning disappears in the physiognomonic *doxa*, as we can see in the French compilation of pseudo-Aristotle, Adamantius and other authors, by Antoine du Moulin, the *Physionomie naturelle* (1550):

> Mais Aristote et Polemon estiment et cuident l'ame par compassion tellement representer & donner à congnoistre le corps, comme l'ame prend et emprunte une espece ou forme de la qualité & disposition du corps.[12]

With the help of assertive modality, the physiognomers since Petrus de Abano (fourteenth century) describe the body as a visible cast of the soul, and they follow the beginning of *Physiognomonica*:

> Quod mores animae corpora ipsa sequantur, quodque a motionibus corporum possint affectionem accipere [. . .] similiter etiam econverso, ipsius animae affectibus, consortii lege compati corpus videtur, ut in amoribus et timoribus, similiter in tristitia et voluptate manifeste videre licet [. . .] tale corpus talis affectio est necessarium.[13]

Della Porta's *De humana physiognomonia* (1586) and *Phytognomonica* (1588) display many engravings that explain the fame of both volumes. Striking as they are with the similarities between men and animals, between human organs and plants, they support a vivid *enargeia* that stands for reality: in Peirce's semiotic vocabulary, they are *icones*. The emergence of illustrated physiognomics precedes the emblematic trend a little[14] and follows the interest painters such as Leonardo and Dürer had shown for this bodily and moral knowledge. It renews the neoplatonic poetics of love as we can see in the emblematic and enigmatic *Delie* by Maurice Scève (Lyon: 1544), to whom Du Moulin dedicated his *Physionomie*. With the emblem books that appeared on the print market from the 1540s and spread the visual (and commonplace) correspondences between animals, objects and plants, in order to signify human qualities or vices, the physiognomonic engravings come under the category of 'visual enthymemes', proposed by Umberto Eco in *La struttura assente*. Nowadays, discussions persist about admitting the compatibility between this kind of enthymeme and Aristotelian definitions.[15]

Giambattista Della Porta is the main agent for the attractiveness of this visual enthymeme. His aim is moral, and his method is both medical and moral: in his preface to the *De humana physiognomonia*, he declares that it is not only a *scientia* but also *diuina*:[16] comparative physiognomony provides proof (*demonstrat*) of what is the deep nature of man and enables one to avoid the dangerous company of impious or mischievous persons by foreseeing their characters, thanks to external signs. Since the soul is the 'cause' of the body, these signs are necessary, even though, in theory, these features reveal only propensities, inclinations; he recalls that Aristotle advised Alexander to choose his ministers from their faces, as physicians diagnose disease or recovery. Della Porta develops these principles in his first chapter with many poetic quotations and medical references, matching the features of men with the characters ascribed to animals: the hunters proceed in just this way when they assess the inner capacities of their hounds, falcons and so on. Moreover, he announces his forthcoming *Phytognomonica*, an encyclopaedia of 'signed' plants, whose form reveals their healing proprieties.[17]

The lion is present in this demonstration, not only for his paws but also for his chest, and Della Porta sets out the following syllogism [*sic*]: 'Omne habens latum pectus, humerosque ac magnas extremitates, forte est, & animosum' (strong and courageous).[18] Why two or three signs for two qualities? He applies the topic of the part to the whole, and before that he enforces another *locus communis*, the similarity between animals and men. He compares the man to the lion on the basis of the corresponding engraving to highlight the difference from the leopard, which is the likeness of a woman. Then, when he has to solve the problem of several signs for the same feature, or whether it is possible to have several *propria* as Aristotle discusses them in the same chapter, he sorts the signs according to their proof value, from the preferable down to the useless. Like Adamantius, he selects three body parts corresponding to decreasing order of certainty: the head, the heart and around, finally the limbs.

In chapter 17 only Della Porta touches on the *ratio* of physiognomics as a method of inferring habits from signs, be they constant or accidental, and the next chapter is entirely devoted to the physiognomic syllogism taken from *Prior Analytics* II. 28. To demonstrate that the conjecture from signs is a *scientia*, he skips the first lines of the Aristotelian chapter (that contain the hypotheses) to quote the lion and his large paws and concludes with a new example applied to an individual, Hector: 'Omne magnas habens extremitates est forte, Hector huiusmodi habet, ergo fortis'. In the Italian translation (1598), Hector gets two companions, Achilles and Hercules, all of them *forti*.[19] Della Porta makes up this last enthymeme in Darii and no more in Barbara and admits our ability to judge a particular creature from its limbs.

8.2 Syllogism or enthymeme?

The academic tradition accepted the physiognomic sign as an enthymeme because the middle term is a sign, at least among the Northern scholars. Gregor Reisch, whose *Margarita philosophica* (1504) was so familiar in colleges and universities, presented the ordinary definition of the enthymeme not only as an imperfect syllogism but also, *aliter*, as a proposition relying on *semeia eikota*, where the conclusion of such a proposition is a necessary conclusion:

> Posset tamen aliter definiri / & taliter: Enthymema syllogismus est ex icotibus et signis. Est autem icos propositio probabilis. Signum autem est propositio necessaria. non quidem in se / sed ratione illationis. Eadem igitur propositio erit icos/ quia probabilis / et signum, quia necessario infert conclusionem. Inveniuntur autem haec signa naturas rerum inquirendo. ut mulier habet lac in mamillis: igitur peperit.[20]

After the predictable milk woman, Reich's second example is physiognomonic, attached to a singular proposition, not for the large paws but for the chest and shoulders (as it is the case in the *Physiognomonica*), not for the lion only but for '*hoc animal*'. Reisch admits that the conclusion here is doubtful, even though the sign is manifest:

> hoc animal habet latum pectus et scapulas: igitur forte, etc. Sunt et aliae quaedam argumentationes imperfectae [...] cum major fuerit manifesta: et minor aeque aut magis dubia conclusione. (ibid.)

Pseudo-Aristotle's *Physiognomonica* begins with the limbs and chest for any animal, without mentioning the lion that appears in a second series, in order to distinguish other clues such as magnanimity one can assume from round nostrils, droopy eyelids and square forehead,[21] a feature Leonardo recalls, in a drawing from 1505 to 1510, as a physiognomic sign of courage.[22] For Adamantius head signs are more probable, and Della Porta provides a twofold portrait where lion and man are paired by their round noses, even though the lion's feature is a *proprium* of his species, whereas the same one is individual and accidental among men.[23] He uses an identical couple: both beings have a pleasant glance, in order to give the meaning of the forehead, the nose, the head size, the place of hair, up to seven features depending on the editions (Figure 8.1).

Did Aristotle open the way to signature theory with such an ending to *Prior Analytics*? It would seem so, since big paws warrant the construction of a valid enthymeme of the first figure: A for courage, B for big limbs, C the lion. But the beginning of the chapter details that the signs are divided into three kinds: demonstrative, necessary (if it is a fact) or probable. The coda does not detail on what kinds the physiognomic sign depends, but the Turnèbe-Casaubon edition uses the term 'coniectura', and the first sentence is a 'if ... then' conditional. As it is a hypothesis, the validity of the conclusion depends (1) on the agreement on the previous hypothesis and (2) on the nature of the sign itself, a condition Della Porta admits with his range of preferable signs. Other

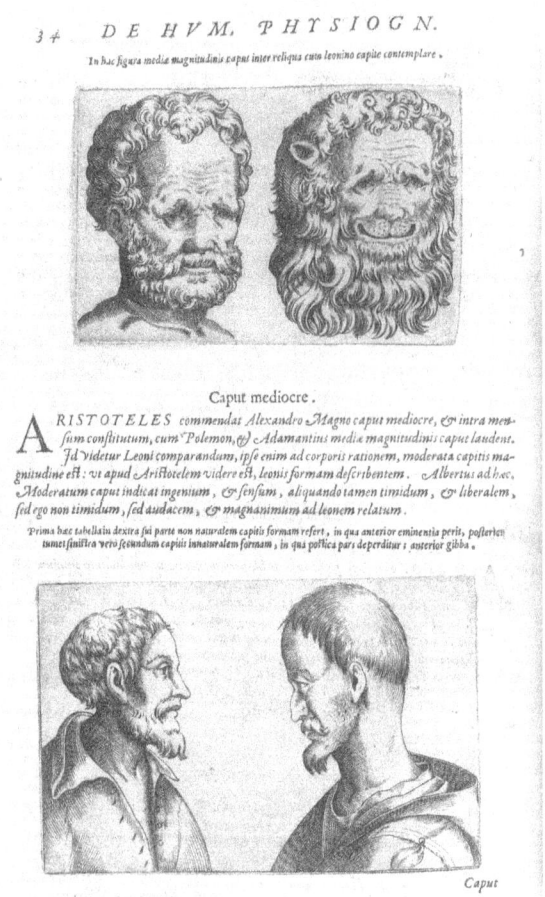

Figure 8.1 Giambattista Della Porta, *De humana physiognomonia*, 1586. Public Domain via Wikimedia Commons. https://commons.wikimedia.org/wiki/File:De_humana_physiognomonia_libri_IIII_-_NLM_NIH_-_page_34.jpg

physiognomers ignore the restriction of the condition, since they admit that body and soul generate the same movements and proprieties.

From a somewhat different corpus, Ian Maclean devoted an entire chapter and an important article to medical physiognomony and the topic. He understood the syllogism of the lion as an enthymeme, valid in Barbara, but the relationship between exterior (body) and interior (soul) is a similitude, whereas physical strength is not a characteristic (*ethos*) of the soul.[24] *Fortis* can be translated either by 'strong' or by 'courageous', an ontological and logical ambivalence, increased by the addition of another feature of the lion, magnanimity, a quality of the soul, not of the body. Moreover, if there is more than one propriety at stake for one *indicium*, the necessity of the connection between body and soul remains questionable: the validity of the enthymeme depends on its uniqueness and on convertibility.

8.3 Foucault's appropriation

Ignoring the initial hypotheses is convenient to move physiognomy from *ars* to *scientia*, and Foucault did not notice the importance of the conditional nature of this kind of enthymeme. Jean-Jacques Courtine took the link between Renaissance physiognomy and the signature theory for granted, as though Foucault had followed Carlo Ginzburg's 'evidential paradigm' ('paradigma indiziario').[25] This is not the case, because according to Foucault the word *is* the thing, and things are attracted or rejected as if they were animate beings. In the evidential paradigm, there is no confusion between the traces of the deer and the animal itself.

Foucault's reading files are now available online: we notice that he used second-hand treatises that blurred the Paracelsian or medical origin of signature: Oswald Croll's *De signatura rerum*, translated in French in 1609, is mistakenly taken by Foucault as a high representative of Renaissance *epistemè*, whereas this book is only a by-product of a follower of Paracelsus.[26] Della Porta adds the visual element, which offers necessary inferences between *signa* and temperament. It is more complex in the *Phytognomonia* since we must go through the influx from the stars of traditional medicine to conclude, from the shape of the plant and of the similar organ, the healing efficacy of the former. Paracelsists add the three principles of sulphur, salt and mercury to plants and to the four elements: their 'signatures' are not visible, but, thanks to the stars and to this debatable notion of 'internal signature', they offer the image of the harmonious body of universe.

As Massimo Luigi Bianchi has shown, authentic signature theory (due to Paracelsus) is widely ignored during most of the sixteenth century, particularly in France.[27] It soon encountered forceful rejection, for example, by the Belgian botanist Rambert Dodoens (1583), for whom these similitudes are fortuitous and dangerous, and the proprieties of the plants can be known only through experience.[28] Foucault was well aware of the syllogism-enthymeme because he assigns a file to Della Porta's development (Figure 8.2), and in *The Order of Things* he hints vaguely at those Greeks who offered the analogy between the strength of the lion's paws and his courage, without acknowledging that such reasoning came from Aristotle's *Prior Analytics*. The title of the file is 'Le syllogisme du signe', and Foucault's paraphrase is: 'De l'argument, ou syllogisme dont se servent les physionomes', taken out of the French translation of Della Porta published in 1655.[29] He copied the text from the second sentence: 'Pour trouver donc ce signe qu'on appelle propre' ('To find the sign one calls proper'). Della Porta had obscured the hypothetical modality, whereas Foucault missed the major source, the *Prior Analytics*.

However, Della Porta often reports diverse interpretations of the same sign, including when the sources contradict themselves, for example, in respect of the round nose, and he expresses the judgements of his authorities with the verbs *tribuire*, *judicare*, *indicare*. Adamantius is the only one to assert that the round nose of the lion reveals

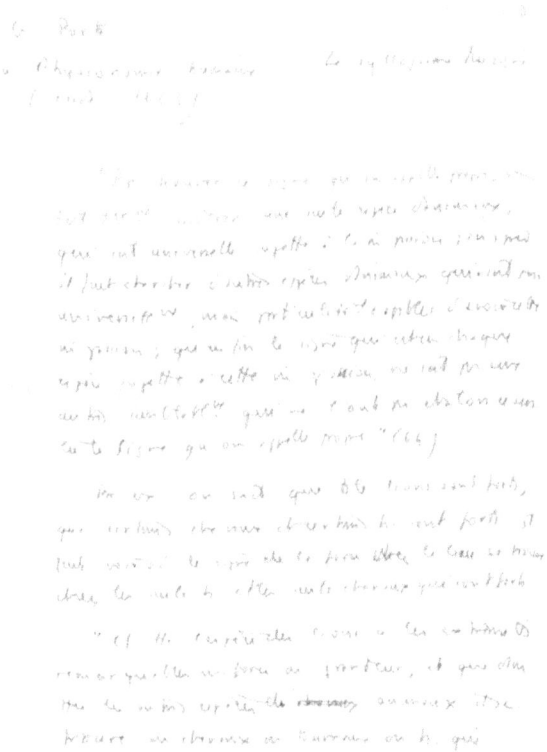

Figure 8.2 Michel Foucault, Bibliothèque Foucaldienne, http://lbf-ehess.ens-lyon.fr/ead.html?c=FRENS_00002_ref6. Reproduced with permission

a boastful character, instead of magnanimity. Martin Porter thinks that the authors did not perceive any discrepancy,[30] but nonetheless the fact that Della Porta devotes a whole chapter to sign rating, according to the level of probability, shows his concern for appropriateness. Eventually, the image plays its part as a visual enthymeme and steers the reader's choice: the accompanying text gives the key term, *relati*,[31] because some men and lions are patently related by their round noses, as *relatio* is a logical category and also a rhetorical topic. This kind of direct *euidentia* achieves a double enthymeme: (1) a sign-enthymeme, <all> the lions are generous/<all> the lions have a round nose/the round nose is the sign of magnanimity; and (2) the topic of similitude: this man displays a round nose, *ergo* this man in generous. Neither magnanimity nor bragging is obvious when we look at the engraving from left to right. Moreover, the head looks like one of the familiar portrayals of Socrates.

The usefulness of such knowledge is advocated by Lefèvre d'Étaples, who asserts that it facilitates the choice of friends, an advantage all the physiognomers are proud of. He sets out at length the way the Arabs, good connoisseurs of physiognomony, select their horses; they are also traders of slaves they know how to value in accordance with their body. Although Lefèvre claims his aversion to the supporters of a science of prediction, he adds he has seen in Aldo Manuzio's workshop how the workforce was chosen, owing to physiognomony. In Greece, pedagogues selected children from their physical abilities, in order to teach them an appropriate occupation, even if the facts could disavow these good or bad natures. Lefèvre ends his commentary with a thorough register of signs taken from Adamantius, and we can find the round nose as a sign of the lion's magnanimity, as well as his large chest as a sign of strength or courage. The big limbs are the legs, that can be *neruosa*, *grossa*, and signify either strength or courage, without any relation to a specific animal, and they are weak signs according to Adamantius's ranking. Renaissance physiognomers were much more interested in the features of the face, as the vogue for portraits increased all over Europe.

Assuming that all these features are signs, they are not *signaturæ*. If Foucault misread and misunderstood Della Porta, some commentators on Foucault's works consider that Agamben misinterpreted *The Order of Things* when he transformed the signature into an universal paradigm, an archetype of all signs, based on singulars.[32] Humanists such as Melanchthon considered that syllogisms built on singulars, '*syllogismi expositorii*', had only a heuristic value,[33] while for Agamben they are promoted, more than ever for enthymemes based on signs, up to an ontological position, a *petitio principii* anchored in a wide use of analogy. Aristotle and his commentators warned about the risk of *fallacia* in the misuse of the topics of equivocation and of similitude, especially in scientific matters, such as the classification of genres and species of animals.[34] Ian Maclean has shown how doctors and physiognomers made a confusion between natural and linguistic signs.[35]

Ultimately, we must concede that the engraving of the man with his fellow lion is rather pleasant: not because of his nose, or forehead, or hair, but because of this thin smile, a lively expression of the face that is not a persistent feature. Less sweet than Mona Lisa's smile, it nevertheless helps us conjecture that this man has a good temper, and that a master could recruit him. To see an actual lion was a rare experience in Western countries during the Renaissance, to see him smiling, all the more so. *Phantasiai* of artists indulge such fictitious visions of philosophers with the unexpected help of Aristotelian enthymeme.

Acknowledgement

I wish to thank John O'Brien, who kindly revised the English version of this text.

Notes

1 See Marie-Luce Demonet, 'Philosopher Naturellement', *Montaigne Studies* XII (2000): 5–24; 'Le signe physionomique chez Montaigne', in *Montaigne. Le signe et le texte*, ed. F. Argod-Dutard (Geneva: Droz, 2003), 153–77.
2 Michel Foucault, *Les Mots et les Choses. Une archéologie des sciences humaines* (Paris: Gallimard, 1966); *The Order of Things. An Archaeology of the Human Sciences* (New York: Pantheon Books, 1970), ch. 2.
3 Giorgio Agamben, *Signatura rerum* (Torino: Bollati Boringhieri, 2008).

4 I prepared an essay on this question: Marie-Luce Demonet, *Les sophismes des signatures, de Foucault à Agamben* (2012, forthcoming).
5 Giambattista Della Porta, *De humana physiognomonia* (Vico Equense: Giuseppe Cacci, 1586); *Phytognomonica* (Napoli: Orazio Salviani, 1588); *La Physionomie humaine* (Rouen: J. and D. Berthelin, 1655).
6 Sixteenth-century editions separate a chapter 28 from the chapter 27 on enthymeme, when the topic moves to physiognomy (Aristotle: Loeb Classical Library, 527–30).
7 See Marco Sgarbi in this volume; Myles Burnyeat, 'Enthymeme: Aristotle on the Logic of Persuasion', in *Aristotle's Rhetoric. Philosophical Essays*, ed. David J. Furley and Alexander Nehamas (Princeton, NJ: Princeton University Press, 1994); 'Enthymeme: Aristotle on the Rationality of Rhetoric', in *Essays on Aristotle's Rhetoric*, ed. Amélie Oksenberg Rorty (Berkeley, CA: University of California Press, 1996), 88–115. About Poliziano's view on enthymeme, see Elisa Saltetto, *Problemi aristotelici nei secondi Miscellanea di Angelo Poliziano: 'universale' ed 'entimema'*, PhD University Ca' Foscari, 2015, 63–244.
8 Aristotle, *Opera graeca* (Venezia: Alde, 1495), I, *Organon*, Guillaume Budé's copy, Leyden University Library, KL 758 A 6. Rudolph Agricola, *De inventione dialectica libri tres*, (Köln: Hero Fuchs, 1527), 253–4; Julius Pacius, *In Porphyrii Isagogen et Aristotelis Organon: commentarius analyticus* (Frankfurt am Main: Claude de Marne and Johann Aubry, 1597), 263–5, relies on four manuscripts, not identified: see Burnyeat 1994, 8; Francesca Piazza, *Il corpo della persuasione. L'entimema nella retorica greca* (Palermo: Novecento, 2000), 90–5.
9 Boethius, 'Latin Translation of *Analytica Priora*', in *Patrologia cursus completus*, vol. LXIV (Paris: Migne, 1847), 711; Aristotle, 'Analytica Priora', in *Logica Aristotelis ex tertia recognitione*, ed. Jacques Lefèvre d'Étaples (Paris: Simon de Colines, 1531), 159r. Since Migne used Lefèvre's revision of Boethius, Lefèvre may have modified the text to confirm an interpolation already admitted; see Minio-Paluello, 'Note sull'Aristotele latino medievale VIII. I Primi Analitici: la redazione carnutense usata da Abelardo e la vulgata con scolii tradotti dal greco', *Rivista di filosofia neo-scolastica* 46 (1954): 211–23, refered to by Saltetto 2015, 124.
10 'De ratione natura coniectanda', in *Analytica Priora*, II, xxviii, *Operum Aristotelis, Graece et Latine*, ed. Isaac Casaubon, trans. Adrien Turnèbe (Lyon: Guillaume Lemarié, 1590), 75.
11 Lefèvre d'Étaples (ed.), *Logica Aristotelis* 1531, 160r.
12 Antoine du Moulin, *Physionomie Naturelle* (Lyon: Jean de Tournes, 1550), 15.
13 *Aristotelis liber de physiognomicis*, ed. Andrés Laguna (Paris: Prigent Calvarin, 1541),
14 They appear in Johannes de Indagine (Jean de Heyn), *Introductiones Apotelesmaticae elegantes in Chyromantiam Physiognomiam, Astrologiam naturalem, Complexiones hominum, Naturas planetarum* (Strasbourg: Johann Schott, 1522), drawings by Hans Baldung Grien.
15 Umberto Eco, *La struttura assente: introduzione alla ricerca semiologica* (Milano: Bompiani, 1968); Georges Roque, 'Comment argumenter à partir d'images?', *Signata*, 'Image et connaissance' (2019): 10, 1–20.
16 Della Porta, *De humana physiognomonia*, 1586, 1.
17 Della Porta, *De humana physiognomonia*, 1586, I, ii, 7.
18 Della Porta, *De humana physiognomonia*, 1586, 9.
19 Giambattista Della Porta, *La Fisonomia dell'huomo*, trans. Giovanni di Rosa (Napoli: Tarquino Longo, 1598), I, xviii, 24.

20 Gregor Reisch, *Margarita philosophica* (Basel: Michael Furter, 1517), II, v, ch. 25, a[8] v.
21 *Aristotelis liber de physiognomicis* 1541, 19.
22 See Domenico Laurenza about the drawing Windsor 12502 in *De figura humana: fisiognomica, anatomia e arte in Leonardo* (Firenze: Olschki, 2001), ch. 2, 'Crani'.
23 Della Porta 1586, 17v-18r.
24 Ian Maclean, *Logic, Signs and Nature in the Renaissance: The Case of learned Medicine* (Cambridge: Cambridge University Press, 2002), iv; id., 'The Logic of Physiognomony in the Late Renaissance', *Early Science and Medicine* 16, no. 4 (2011): 275-95.
25 Jean-Jacques Courtine, *Déchiffrer le corps. Penser avec Foucault* (Grenoble: Jérôme Million), 20.
26 Oswald Croll, *De signaturis internis rerum, die lateinische editio princeps (1609) und die deutsche Erstübersetzung (1623)*, ed. Wilhelm Kühlmann and Joachim Telle (Stuttgart: Steiner, 1996).
27 Massimo Luigi Bianchi, *Signatura rerum: segni, magia e conoscenza da Paracelso a Leibniz* (Roma: Ateneo, 1987).
28 Rambert Dodoens, *Stirpium Historiae Pemptades sex* (Anvers: Christophe Plantin, 1583), ch. xi, 16: « De characterismis sive signaturis ».
29 Della Porta, *La Physionomie humaine*, 1655, I, XVIII, 63 *sqq*. The file shows the wrong year of 1665.
30 William Porter, *Windows of the Soul: The Art of Physiognomy in European Culture 1470-1760* (Oxford: Clarendon Press, 2005), 216.
31 Della Porta 1586: II, 79.
32 Ann Snoek, 'Agamben's Foucault: An Overview', *Foucault Studies*, special issue Foucault-Agamben (November 2010): 44-67.
33 Philip Melanchthon, *Dialecticae præceptiones* (Leipzig: Valentinus Papae, 1545), 102.
34 Aristotle, *Topica* I, 17, 108a; *On Sophistical Refutations*, IV, 165b; *On the Parts of Animals*, IV, 644a; Alessandro Piccolomini, about the enthymeme on signs: *Copiosa Parafrase . . . nel primo libro della Retorica d'Aristotele* (Venezia: Giovanni Varisco 1565), 73 *sqq*.
35 Ian Maclean, *The Logic of Physiognomony*, 2011, 289.

Bibliography

Agamben, G. (2008), *Signatura Rerum*, Torino, Bollati Boringhieri.
Agricola, Rudolph (1527), *De inventione dialectica libri tres*, Köln, Hero Fuchs.
Aristotle (1495), *Opera graeca, Venezia, Aldo Manuzio, I, Organon, Guillaume Budé's Copy*, Leyden, Leyden University Library.
Aristotle (1531), 'Analytica Priora', in *Logica Aristotelis ex tertia recognition*, Jacques Lefèvre d'Étaples (ed.), Paris, Simon de Colines.
Aristotle (1541), *Aristotle's liber de physiognomicis*, Andrés de Laguna (ed.), Paris, Prigent Calvarin.
Aristotle (1590), *Analytica Priora, II, xxviii, Operum Aristotelis, Graece et Latine*, Isaac Casaubon (ed.), Adrien Turnèbe (trans.), Lyon, Guillaume Lemarié.
Bianchi, M. L. (1987), *Signatura rerum: segni, magia e conoscenza da Paracelso a Leibniz*, Roma, Ateneo.

Boethius, Severinus (1847), 'Latin Translation of Analytica *Priora*', in *Patrologia cursus completes*, J.-P. Migne (ed.), vol. LXIV, Paris, Garnier, p. 711.

Burnyeat, M. B. (1994), *Enthymeme: Aristotle on the Logic of Persuasion*, D. J. Furley and A. Nehamas (eds), Princeton, NJ, Princeton University Press.

Courtine, J.-J. (2011), *Déchiffrer le corps. Penser avec Foucault*, Grenoble, Jérôme Million.

Croll, Oswald (1996), *De signaturis internis rerum, die lateinische editio princeps (1609) und die deutsche Erstübersetzung (1623)*, W. Kühlmann and J. Telle (eds), Stuttgart, Steiner.

De Indagine J. (=Jean de Heyn) (1522), *Introductiones Apotelesmaticae elegantes in Chyromantiam Physiognomiam, Astrologiam naturalem, Complexiones hominum, Naturas planetarum*, Strasbourg, Johann Schott.

Della Porta, Giambattista (1586), *De humana physiognomonia*, Vico Equense, Giuseppe Cacci.

Della Porta, Giambattista (1588), *Phytognomonica*, Napoli, Orazio Salviani.

Della Porta, Giambattista (1655), *La Physionomie humaine*, Rouen, J. and D. Berthelin.

Della Porta, Giambattista (1598), *La Fisonomia dell'huomo*, Giovanni di Rosa (trans.), Napoli, Tarquino Longo.

Demonet, M.-L. (2000), 'Philosopher Naturellement', *Montaigne Studies* XII, pp. 5–24.

Demonet, M.-L. (2003), 'Le signe physionomique chez Montaigne', in *Montaigne. Le signe et le texte*, F. Argod-Dutard (ed.), Geneva, Droz, pp. 153–177.

Demonet, M.-L. (forthcoming), *Les sophismes des signatures, de Foucault à Agamben*.

Dodoens, Rambert (1583), *Stirpium Historiae Pemptades sex*, Anvers, Christophe Plantin.

Du Moulin, Antoine (1550), *Physionomie naturelle*, Lyon, Jean de Tournes.

Eco, U. (1968), *La struttura assente: introduzione alla ricerca semiologica*, Milano, Bompiani.

Foucault, M. (1966), *Les Mots et les Choses. Une archéologie des sciences humaines*, Paris, Gallimard; trans. (1970), *The Order of Things. An Archaeology of the Human Sciences*, New York, Pantheon Books.

Laurenza, D. (2001), *De figura humana: fisiognomica, anatomia e arte in Leonardo*, Firenze, Olschki.

Melanchthon, Philipp (1545), *Dialecticae præceptiones*, Leipzig, Valentinus Papae.

MacLean, I. (2002), *Logic, Signs and Nature in the Renaissance: The Case of Learned Medicine*, Cambridge, Cambridge University Press.

MacLean, I. (2011), 'The Logic of Physiognomony in the Late Renaissance', *Early Science and Medicine* 16 (4), pp. 275–295.

Pacius, Iulius (1597), *In Porphyrii Isagogen et Aristotelis Organon: commentarius analyticus*, Claude de Marne and Johann Aubry (eds), Apud heredes Andreae Wecheli, Frankfurt am Main.

Paluello, M. (1954), 'Note sull'Aristotele latino medievale VIII. I Primi Analitici: la redazione carnutense usata da Abelardo e la vulgata con scolii tradotti dal greco', *Rivista di filosofia neo-scolastica* 46, pp. 211–223.

Piazza, F. (2000), *Il corpo della persuasione. L'entimema nella retorica greca*, Palermo, Novecento.

Piccolomini, Alessandro (1565), *Copiosa Parafrase... nel primo libro della Retorica d'Aristotele*, Venezia, Giovanni Varisco.

Porter, W. (2005), *Windows of the Soul: The Art of Physiognomy in European Culture 1470–1760*, Oxford, Clarendon Press.

Reisch, Gregorius (1517), *Margarita Philosophica*, Basel, Michael Furter.

Roque, G. (2019), 'Comment argumenter à partir d'images?', *Signata, 'Image et connaissance'* 10, pp. 1–20.

Saltetto, E. (2015), *Problemi aristotelici nei secondi Miscellanea di Angelo Poliziano: 'universale' ed 'entimema'*, Ph. D. Venice, University Ca' Foscari.

Snoek, A. (2010), 'Agamben's Foucault: An Overview', *Foucault Studies* 10, pp. 44–67.

Index

Abaelard Peter (Peter Abaelard)   8, 12, 58, 75–6, 82–91, 94, 95
abbreviated syllogism   100–1, 108, 111, 136
abduction   7, 15, 120
accident   82, 100, 102, 127, 137, 196
Achillini, Alessandro   16, 192–3, 198
Adam of Bockenfield   112, 137
Adams Mc Cord, M.   157
Adamson, P.   21
added premise   11, 14, 72, 107, 109, 123, 156
adjective   160, 191
affirmation   94
affirmative   56, 61, 65, 81–2, 85, 116–17, 119, 123–4, 150, 155, 158, 160, 162
Agamben, G.   201, 209–11
Agricola, Rudolph   15, 202, 210, 211
al-Ajam, R.   73, 74, 102
'alāma (*signs*)   63
Albert the Great   102–3, 108, 117, 119, 124, 133, 135–6, 138–40
Alcuin of York   27, 43
al-ḍamā'ir/damir (*enthymeme*)   11, 47, 49, 52–3
aletes syllogismus   4
Alexander of Aphrodisias   76, 95, 99, 106, 119, 133, 135, 139, 148, 149, 192, 204, 210
Al-Fārābī (*Alfarabi*)   11, 47–59, 61, 65–8, 71–4, 108–9, 132–6
al-ḥākim (judge)   50
al-iqnā' (persuasion)   48, 58
al-khaṭāba (*Rhetorics*)   11–12, 47–52, 54–69, 71–4
Allen, J.   197, 198
al-mufāwada (debate or discussion)   60
al-taghlīṭ (misleading)   60
ambiguity   23, 25–6, 115, 154
Ammonius   106, 135, 148
ampliative inferences   2, 7–10, 14–16, 179

analogy   7, 11, 47, 197, 207, 209
analysis   10–11, 25, 42, 47, 50, 54, 59, 64, 68, 72, 73, 99, 101, 113, 120, 126–7, 130–1, 133, 138, 149, 158, 185, 201
Anderson, A. R.   17, 43, 182, 185
anima   42, 137, 202–3
animal   3, 31, 40–1, 70–1, 75, 84–7, 89–90, 94, 109–10, 136, 149, 155–60, 162, 171, 173, 175, 177, 203, 205, 207
Anonymus Aurelianensis   139–40
Anselm of Canterbury   34
antecedents   7, 78–80, 82, 86, 93
Aouad, M.   133, 135, 141
apodeixeis   25
apodosis   25, 148
appetite   131, 184
a priori/a posteriori   7, 16, 41, 139, 190
Aquila Romanus   38
Archambault, J.   157
Argod-Dutard, F.   209
argument/*argumentum*   1–4, 6, 8, 10, 12, 14–15, 24–8, 30–1, 33, 35, 37–43, 75–80, 82–5, 87–95, 99–103, 106–11, 115–16, 118–23, 125–7, 130–1, 133, 135, 136, 138, 140, 141, 147–8, 154, 156–7, 161, 169–70, 175–80, 182, 184–7, 190–1, 205
Aristotle   1–6, 11, 16, 18, 30, 34, 39, 47, 49–50, 53, 61, 66–8, 73, 74, 77, 81, 85, 87, 90–5, 100–6, 108–9, 111–12, 119–24, 126–8, 130–1, 147, 149, 154, 180, 184, 185, 187–92, 194–5, 202–4, 209, 210
    Analytics   5, 16, 23, 30, 81, 83, 91, 100–2, 104–6, 108–9, 111–12, 116–17, 119–23, 134–8, 140, 169, 177, 185, 188, 198, 201, 205, 210, 211
    Categoriae   30, 112

De Interpretatione 30
De Sophisticis Elenchis 17, 91, 113, 116
Meteorology 192, 198
Physics 188, 190
Rhetoric 4–5, 36, 50, 59, 61, 64, 66–8, 73, 74, 77, 84, 102, 134, 135, 185, 187–8, 190, 193, 197, 198, 210
Topics 30, 77, 85, 90, 91, 122, 176, 211
Aristoteles latinus 17, 18, 90, 91, 132–6, 138, 141
ars/artes 27–8, 30, 39, 128, 207
assumption 33, 38, 41, 42, 94, 153, 176, 180
Aubry, Johann 210
audience 2, 4–5, 8–9, 11, 48, 50, 53–4, 57–8, 65, 67, 100, 103, 128, 179, 201
Augustine of Hippo 26
Autissiodorensis, Remigius (Remigius of Auxerre) 42
Averroes 74, 112, 132, 136, 137, 194, 196
Avicenna 11–12, 47, 50, 59–74, 132
axioms 91

Bacon, Roger 99, 132
Balduino, Girolamo 16, 194, 198
Barbara 17, 62, 70, 81, 119, 123–4, 204, 206
Barnes, J. 74, 135, 136, 157
Bartocci, B. 14, 132, 169
belief 2, 4–5, 7–11, 14–15, 48, 50–1, 106, 113, 119, 122, 127, 130, 175, 178–9, 182, 184, 185, 187
Bellucci, F. 102, 104, 117, 133, 134, 136, 138, 140, 141
Belnap, N. D. 182
Beltran, E. 141
benefit 60
Bernhard of Clairvaux 43
Bianchi, L. 157
Bianchi, M. L. 17, 18, 207, 211
Biard, J. 157, 160, 183, 185
Bible 11, 35
Bird, O. 18, 133–5, 141
Black, D. 18, 133–5, 141
Bobzien, S. 18, 158
Boccadiferro, Ludovico 193–4, 198

Boethius, Severinus (*Severinus Boethius*) 1, 10, 12–13, 17, 27, 30–2, 34, 40–2, 75–6, 79–85, 87–91, 93, 95–7, 99, 101–3, 105, 109–10, 114–15, 147–8, 157, 210
Boggess, W. F. 132
Borgnet, A. 136
Boskoff, P. S. 92
Bosman, B. 172, 183
brevis conceptio animi or *mentis* 39, 41, 80, 94
brevitas 109, 115
Bronstein, D. 136
Brumberg-Chaumont, J. 12–13, 18, 99, 132, 134–7, 139
Brunschwig, J. 17, 19
Budé, Guillaume 210, 211
Buridan, John (*Iohannes Buridanus*)
Burnyeat, M. F. 18, 36, 75–83, 87, 89–93, 100, 104–7, 122, 133–5, 157, 182, 185, 187, 197, 198, 210
Buttimer, E. 134
Buzzetti, D. 159, 161

Caeneus argument 116, 119–20, 124, 138, 139
Calboli, G. 37, 38
Calboli Montefusco, L. 39
calumny 61–2
Cannone, D. 137, 139
Capivacci, Geronimo 198
Casaubon, Isaac 205, 210, 211
Cassiodorus, Senator 10, 11, 27, 32–3, 35, 42–4, 80, 81, 93
categories 29, 62, 73, 112, 132, 137, 155
Cato Marcius Porcius 30, 40
causes 4, 7, 16, 35, 39, 43, 53, 62, 67, 81, 121–2, 133, 139, 173, 180–1, 189–97, 202, 204
Celsus 192
certainty 11, 14, 52, 58, 101, 113, 117, 131, 178–9, 190, 202, 204
Cesalli, C. 149
Chatti, S. V. 11, 18, 46, 73, 74
Chiaradonna, R. 157
Chrysippus 6
Cicero Marcus Tullius 6–10, 15, 18, 24–7, 31–3, 37–41, 76, 78–80, 82–3,

85, 90–3, 99, 102, 109, 114, 118, 132, 133, 136, 157
circumstantiae 41, 181
Coda, E. 17, 181
commentum/ commentatio 25, 37
common sense 9, 29, 137
completeness/incompleteness 1, 5, 8–13, 15–16, 26, 72, 76, 84–6, 100–1, 148, 169, 195
complete syllogism 1–2, 5–6, 8, 14, 24, 27–8, 32–3, 62–3, 74, 80, 82, 84–6, 111–12, 114, 116, 129, 148, 169–71
complexio 38, 84, 86, 94
conceptio 10, 31, 33, 41–2, 80–1, 94
conclusio/conclusion 25, 28, 33, 37, 40–2, 82, 90, 93–4, 136, 157
conclusive moods 54, 56, 71, 106, 139
conditional argument 5–6, 8–9, 12, 56–7, 81–9, 91, 93, 95, 148, 150, 153, 172, 176–7, 203, 205, 207
conditionalization 12, 86–7
conflict 6, 8, 26, 51–2, 55, 57, 61
conjectures 7, 16, 115, 190–2, 197–8, 204
consequence/consequentia 6–9, 13–15, 26, 35–6, 66, 70–1, 78–86, 93, 105, 122, 147–52, 155–6, 158–65, 170, 174, 178, 182–6
consequents 26, 78–80, 82–3, 93
consilia medica 197
contingent 2–6, 9–10, 14, 108, 178, 194
contradiction 2–3, 6–10, 23, 25, 51, 68
contrary/contrarium 1, 3, 11, 24–6, 31, 33–7, 40, 41, 43, 51, 66, 69, 71–2, 80, 88, 92, 93, 105, 107, 111, 115, 118–19, 121, 125, 127, 134–5, 174, 181, 193
conversion 1, 3–4, 7–10, 12–13, 95, 104, 117–19, 121–2, 124–6, 150, 156, 158, 171–2, 190, 196, 207
Cornificius 26, 36–8, 40, 92
Cosci, M. 21
courage 205, 207, 211
Courtine, J. J. 207, 211
Crimi, M. 157–60, 183, 185
Crivelli, P. 184
Croll, O. 2, 11

Dahan, G. 132, 134
Dal Pra, M. 95
Da Monte, Giovanni Battista 196–8
Danesh Pazuh, M. T. 74
deductio/deduction 1–9, 14, 23, 47, 49, 56, 64, 68–9, 71, 87, 105, 140, 174, 188
Defeasible 7–9, 15, 176–9, 183
defective argument 1, 10, 14, 16, 113, 119, 121, 124, 127–31, 136, 155–6
De Filippis, R. 10–11, 23, 38–41
definition/definitions 5, 7, 12, 23, 31, 33, 40, 52, 76, 80–6, 91, 93, 100, 104–7, 109, 112–13, 120–1, 123, 127, 129, 131, 133–5, 140, 151, 161, 169–71, 175–7, 182, 183, 202, 204–5
De Haas, F. A. J. 157
De Indagine, J. (Jean de Heyn) 210
De Laguna, Andrés 211
Della Porta, Girolamo 17, 201, 204–11
De Marne, Claude 210
Deminitus syllogism 110
Demonet, M. L. 16–18, 201, 209, 210
demonstratio conjecturalis 196
demonstratio evidentiae 196
demonstratio existentiae 196
demonstratio ex signis 16, 190, 192, 195
demonstration 3, 10, 16, 23, 48–9, 53, 61, 72, 77, 81, 100, 103–4, 112, 114, 126–7, 136–8, 174–5, 187–98, 204
demonstratio propter quid 16, 104, 191–3, 195
demonstratio quia 191
deontic logic 2, 8, 10
De Pater, W. A. 18, 19
De Rijk, L. M. 95
descensus/descent 18, 95–6, 185
Desclée, J.-P. 152, 159
dialectic/dialectica 4, 10, 13–15, 18, 32, 36, 41, 49, 53, 57, 59–60, 73, 84–5, 87–90, 94, 95, 100–3, 113–16, 127–8, 130–1, 136, 138, 141, 170, 173, 177–85, 191, 194, 210, 211
dialectical syllogism 3–7, 13–14, 60–1, 76–7, 79, 84, 88, 91, 100–1, 109,

113–16, 118–19, 121–2, 124, 126, 132, 141, 148, 161, 170, 174–6, 178–80, 182
dialectician 32, 57, 60, 77. 81–2, 88, 90, 95, 115, 130
dictum de omni 175–6
difference/differentia 7, 32, 37, 42, 82, 87–8, 91, 95, 133, 136, 148–9, 161
differentia maximae propositionis 148, 161
Diodorus 6
discourse 8, 31–2, 48, 50, 52, 55, 58, 66–9, 71, 103, 114, 122, 149, 187, 201–2
dispositio 40, 114, 135, 139
disputator 114
Dodoens, Rambert 207, 211
Domenicus Gundissalinus 102, 114, 134, 138
D'Onofrio, G. 17, 36, 42
Doroteo, Guglielmo 191
doubt/doubtful 16, 27, 60–3, 71–2, 78, 80, 118, 124, 138, 205
Du Moulin, Antoine 203–4, 210
Dürer, Albrecht 203
Dutilh Novaes, C. 70, 74, 157–8, 162, 172, 183

Ebbesen, S. 17, 90, 91, 141, 161
Eco, U. 204, 210
effects 7, 103, 173, 189, 191–2, 195
eikos, eikota (ikos) 16, 112, 123, 127–9, 201–2, 205
Elamrani-Jamal, A. 198
Elder, E. R. 18, 26, 27
elocutio 27, 38, 114
emblem 17, 203–4
emotions 10, 51
enargeia 203
endoxa 3
entailement warrant 4, 5, 8, 12, 16, 54, 69, 85, 100, 132, 205
enthymema deikticon 28, 39
enthymema elenktikon 28, 39
enthymema gnomikon 28, 39
enthymema paradeigmatikon 28, 39
enthymema pleres 28, 39
enthymema syllogistikon 28, 39

enthymeme 1–2, 4–18, 23–44, 47–9, 52–6, 59, 62–5, 67–71, 75–87, 89–94, 99–112, 115–36, 139–43, 147–50, 152, 154–7, 163–6, 169–75, 177–8, 180–4, 187–90, 192–4, 197, 198, 201–2, 204–11
enthymeme braxy 28, 39
epichirema 26, 28, 37–40, 92
epistemic 2, 6, 8, 10, 12, 14, 170, 172, 178, 180, 182, 188, 195
epistemological/epistemology 2, 9, 14, 17, 182, 187, 189, 192, 195–6
equipollences 172
Eriksson, A. 30
essence 35, 43, 122, 125
Etchmenendy, J. 18, 94
Eunomius 34, 43
Euticius 43
event 27, 50, 67, 79, 92, 173, 188
evidence 11, 16, 23, 50, 67, 78, 84–5, 89, 92, 93, 121, 136, 187, 198
evidentness 172, 175, 183
exegesis 105, 111, 127, 147
exempla/exemplum 30, 38–40, 94, 107, 124
exemplification 51, 173
exergasia 28, 39
expanded syllogism 1, 7, 10, 14, 38, 110, 172, 175, 178–80, 201
experience 16–17, 51, 91, 130, 180, 192–5, 207, 209
exsecutio 27–9, 39

facts 87, 180, 209
faculty 80, 137, 188
faculty of Arts 110–11
fallacia/fallacy 4–5, 13–14, 17, 66–8, 100, 102–3, 106, 115–19, 121, 124, 126, 129, 139, 147, 152, 154–6, 160–5, 172, 209
false/falsity 2–3, 6, 8, 11–12, 14, 43, 48, 51, 54–5, 57, 60, 62, 67–8, 70–2, 77–8, 86–7, 107–8, 115–19, 122, 124, 129–30, 135, 148–50, 153–4, 156, 159, 160, 171–3, 178, 188
felapton 56
fides 7–8, 100, 106, 113, 119, 122, 127, 131, 138

figura/figure 3–4, 12–14, 23–4, 27, 37,
  77, 81, 85–6, 104–9, 111, 113,
  119, 120, 123, 125–6, 128–32,
  134–6, 139, 175–7
finis 32
Flannery, K. L. 157
form 14, 16, 24–5, 29–30, 33, 35, 38, 43,
  54–5, 66, 72, 76, 78–9, 81–6,
  89, 93, 99, 101–3, 107, 113–16,
  119–21, 128–32, 134, 136, 141,
  147–56, 158, 161, 170, 172, 176,
  179, 183, 190, 192, 194, 204
Fortenbaugh, W. 157
for the most part (*ut de pluribus*) 49, 69,
  91, 93, 104, 112, 127, 133, 134,
  178, 183, 187–8
Fortunatianus, Consultus 10, 27–9, 32,
  33, 38, 39
Foster, C. 36
Foucault, M. 202, 207–11
Fredal, J. 157
Frede, D. 157
Freese, J. H. 18
fully-fledged syllogism 121, 176
Furley, D. J. 10, 185, 198, 210

Gabbay, D. M. 74
Galen 6, 18, 49, 148, 192
Galilei, Galileo 195–6, 198
genus 37, 50, 75, 85, 87–8, 94, 110, 133,
  149, 151, 173–5
George, R. 182
Gerard of Cremona 102
Geyer, B. 95
Giles of Rome 13, 99, 101–2, 104, 107,
  126–32, 134, 136, 140, 141
Ginzburg, C. 207
God 35, 153, 160, 180, 181
Goldman, A. I. 184
grammar/grammarians 15, 35, 38, 41,
  93, 111, 113, 132
gratia formae and gratia materiae 43,
  119, 128, 139, 160, 170–1, 174,
  177, 182
Grazioli, Andrea 191
Green, L. D. 17, 157
Green-Pedersen, N. J. 18, 90, 157, 185
Grien, H. B. 210
Grimaldi, W. 90, 91, 157

Guillelmus de Ockham (*Wilhelm of
  Ockham*) 13–14, 74, 147,
  149–67, 185

habitude/habitus 88, 94, 173
Halm, K. 38, 39
Harari, O. 190, 197–9
Hermannus Alemannus 99, 102
hidden premise 11, 17, 51–7, 62, 71–2,
  101, 107–8, 116, 136, 197
Hieronymus Stridonensis 43
Hitchcock, D. 74, 182
Hodges, W. 66, 73, 74
Hubien, H. 70, 182, 183, 185
Hugh of Saint Victor 103, 113–14, 134
hylomorphic 13, 147, 149, 155
hypothesis 32, 42, 67–8, 100, 105, 113,
  134, 176–7, 184, 205
hypothetical syllogism 12, 14, 24–5, 47,
  52–4, 56, 68–9, 81–4, 86, 89, 91,
  155, 170, 176, 203, 207

icons 203
illatio 176, 205
ʿ*ilm* (science) 48, 51
image 17, 207–8, 210
imagination 68
imperfectus syllogismus 3, 9–10, 12–15,
  17, 23, 26, 29, 31–2, 39, 40, 80,
  83–4, 87, 90, 92, 93, 100–1,
  104, 109, 115, 129, 133, 136,
  141, 147–9, 157, 169–70, 172,
  179–80, 182, 194, 202, 205
implications 6, 60, 69, 81, 153
improbabilis 115–16
incomplete syllogism 1–2, 6, 8, 10–14,
  16, 33, 36, 52–3, 71–2, 75–6,
  78–81, 83–9, 92, 93, 99–110,
  116, 129, 131, 135, 139, 141,
  147, 149, 152, 156, 169–72,
  179–80, 194
inconclusive argument 72, 106, 108,
  116–18
indemonstrable 6–8, 11, 78, 83, 92, 93
indicium 17, 118, 202, 208
in dictione and extra dictione 154, 161
induction 4, 12–16, 47, 49, 80, 113,
  120–1, 123, 129, 141, 180, 188,
  190

inference to the best explanation 5
inferential/inference 2, 5–7, 9–10, 12–16, 24, 75, 78–9, 83–90, 113, 141, 147–9, 151, 153–7, 169–70, 172–4, 176–7, 179–82, 187–90, 192–8
in-mood syllogism 106, 123
instinct 188
intellect/intellectum 37, 92, 131, 136, 137, 163, 179, 184, 197
intentiones 33, 173, 181
intrinsic mean and extrinsic mean 13, 147, 149–57, 161
invalid syllogism 12–13, 56, 59, 61–7, 71–2, 91, 100–2, 106–7, 113, 116–20, 123, 125–7, 129–30, 135, 136, 148–9, 169–70, 178, 189
inventio 24, 41, 82, 90–2, 114, 120, 210, 211
Isidorus Ispalensis (Isidor of Seville) 10, 33, 114
Iulius Rufinianus 10, 26–7
Iulius Victor 10, 28–31, 33
Iwakuma, Y. 161

Jacobi, K. 17, 157
John of Jandum 101, 131, 141
John of Salisbury 91, 92
judge 28–9, 32, 35, 50, 67, 115–16, 120, 178–80
judgement 7, 68, 114–16, 120
jurists 63
justification 8, 14, 67, 119, 161, 179–80, 184

Kaufmann, M. 47
Kieffer, J. S. 20
King, P. 157
Klein, J. 18, 38
Kraus, M. 17, 23, 36–8, 43, 157
Kühlmann, W. 211

language 6, 13, 15, 23, 66, 74, 76, 87, 113–14, 147–9
Laurenza, D. 211
law 7, 9, 15, 28, 36, 52, 74, 79, 99, 115, 179–80, 182
lectio cursiva 111, 126
Lefèvre d'Etaples, Jacques 202, 208–11
Leibniz, G. W. 185

Leinkauf, Th. 18, 20
Lennox, J. 136
Leonard of Vinci 203, 205, 211
Leunissen, M. 157
lion 16–17, 201–2, 204–7, 209
listener 29, 48–50, 52–7, 129
locus/loci 5, 9, 12, 24–5, 33, 75–80, 82–3, 85, 87–90, 93–5, 102, 153, 161, 173–4, 176, 180, 204
logic/logica 1, 5–7, 10–13, 15, 17, 30–2, 34, 36, 43, 48, 58–9, 66, 68, 74, 75, 78, 81, 86–7, 94–7, 99–103, 107, 110–11, 113–14, 116, 120, 126, 128, 130–2, 134–6, 138, 147–54, 158–67, 169–71, 175, 178, 181–2, 185, 190–1, 195–6, 198, 210, 211
logicus/logician 15, 24–5, 29, 33, 47, 58, 68, 73, 89, 91, 99–102, 107, 114, 118, 124, 139
Longo, A. 210
Lucilius 38

MacLean, I. 196, 206, 209, 211
Madkour, I. 74
magnanimity 17, 205–7, 209
Magnano, F. 17, 157
Maierù, A. 136
Malink, M. 140
Mandosio, J.-M. 134
Marenbon, J. 17
Mariani Zini, F. 1, 18, 157, 185
Marius Victorinus 32, 42
Marmo, C. 102, 104, 117, 127, 132–4, 136, 138, 140, 141
Martianus Capella 30, 40, 42
Martijn, M. 157
Martin, C. J. 18, 75, 90, 93, 94
Martini Bonadeo, C. 17, 19
material consequence 13–14, 70–8, 81, 147, 148, 150, 153–6, 170–5, 177, 181
material implication 6
material terms 139, 185
matter/materia 32, 35, 42, 43, 54–5, 79, 88, 90, 106–7, 113, 115, 119, 129, 136, 139, 141, 155, 160, 163–6, 170, 177, 179, 181–2, 193–6

maximal proposition 12–13, 75–6, 82–3, 87–8, 119, 122, 148
medium or middle term 2–4, 13, 62–3, 82, 104–5, 112, 117–19, 122–5, 139, 140, 150, 153, 155, 157–61, 163, 170, 175, 178–9, 181, 184, 195–6, 205
Melanchthon, Philipp 209, 211
Middle Age 2, 10–11, 15, 18, 23, 30, 32, 34–5, 76, 80, 99, 105, 107, 110–11, 132, 133, 178, 190
Migne, J.-P. 210
Mignucci, M. 17, 197
mind 5, 8, 26, 31, 33, 35, 48, 51, 53, 55, 61, 65, 78, 80–1, 93, 110, 130, 179
Minio-Paluello, L. 18, 94, 185, 210
minor premise 3, 32, 41, 54, 59, 62–3, 108–10, 117, 135–7, 139, 171, 175, 177, 178, 205
misleading 35, 55, 59–60, 71, 87, 169
missing premise 1, 9, 11–14, 16, 64–5, 68–71, 73, 80, 83, 86, 99–100, 103–13, 115–16, 122, 126–30, 135, 140, 153, 169–75, 190
Modists 111
modus ponens/modus tollens 56, 177
molecular 170–1, 176
Montaigne, Michel 209
moods 3, 11–12, 48, 54, 56, 58, 61, 65, 67–9, 86, 105–6, 111, 119, 129, 131–2, 134, 135, 139
Moody, E. A. 185
Mora Marquez, A. M. 121, 140
Moraux, P. 157
Morison, B. 157
Morrison, D. 189–90, 197
Mulchahey, M. 136
Müller, G. M. 20
Müller, I. 157
Müller, P. 13–14, 18, 147, 158
Murdoch, J. 112, 136

nature 16, 75, 86, 125, 151, 154, 160, 185, 187–9, 192, 195–7, 204, 211
necessarium/necessary 3–5, 7–8, 14, 16, 29, 31, 39, 40, 50–1, 55, 58, 61, 68–9, 77–8, 81, 84, 87–8, 91, 92, 94, 95, 100–1, 103–4, 106, 108–10, 113, 115–16, 121, 123–30, 133, 135, 136, 138–41, 148, 153–7, 159–63, 169–72, 174–7, 179–82, 187–9, 191–4, 196–7, 203–5, 207
negation 2–3, 6, 31–2, 34, 56, 65, 72, 81–3, 100, 127, 131, 150, 155–6, 158, 162, 174, 189
Nifo, Agostino 16, 191–2, 198
Nikitas, D. Z. 90
Nizolio, Mario 15
nomen/nomina 37–41, 163
Normore, C. 161

obliquitas 130
Oksenberg Rorty, A. 210
Olsson, E. J. 184
one-premise syllogism 108, 121, 135, 140, 170–2
opinion/doxa 2, 11, 14, 48–51, 53, 59, 64–5, 71, 100, 110, 113, 127, 134, 179, 188
opponent 3, 32, 50, 88, 115, 174
opposition/opposite 6, 24, 30–1, 55–7, 140, 141
Organon 14, 101–3, 107, 114, 133, 170, 176, 178, 210, 211
ostensio 83, 141
ousia 11, 35

Pacius, Iulius 202, 210
Paduan school 194, 196, 202
Paracelsus 17, 207
paradeigma 202
paradeigmatikon 39
paradoxe 34
paralogism 5, 16, 102, 121, 129
particular 2–4, 6, 10, 16, 27, 31, 49–50, 53, 55–7, 61, 65, 68, 70, 76–7, 79, 81, 84, 88, 93, 110, 113, 116, 150–1, 188, 190, 195, 197, 204
parts and whole 4, 9, 26–9, 33, 66, 69–70, 81–2, 88, 103, 114, 118, 151, 173, 181, 195, 203, 204, 211
Pasnau, R. 18, 183
passions 4, 8, 51, 99, 141
peccantes in forma 155, 163
peccantes in materia 155

perfect syllogism   3, 32, 84, 87, 115, 118, 122, 141, 179–80, 189–90, 194
Perreiah, A. R.   18, 21
persuasion   49–51, 58, 99–100, 103, 107, 109, 114–15, 127–8, 131, 136, 179, 185, 188, 198, 210
Peter Damian   34, 43
Peter of Spain   157
Petrus of Abano   203
phantasiai   209
phantasm   137, 202
philosophy   6–7, 10–11, 15–16, 27, 66, 74, 110–11, 136, 175, 180, 185–8
physiognomy   16, 101, 140, 210, 211
Piazza, F.   17, 36, 157, 210
Piccolomini, Alessandro   211
Pinzani, R.   17, 18, 158
Pittacus/*Pittacos*   106, 108–9, 123, 128, 135, 154, 202
poet   25, 38, 78
poetics   11, 14, 99, 102–3, 132, 134, 178, 203–4
Poliziano, Angelo   15, 210
Porter, W.   208, 211
Preben-Hansen, B.   141, 184, 185
predestination   35
predicable   81
predicate   3–4, 81–3, 114, 120, 123–7, 129, 140, 151, 158, 159, 170–3, 175, 177, 194
premise/premises   1, 3–5, 9–12, 14, 28, 31, 33, 35, 52–7, 62–5, 68–73, 77–8, 80, 82–3, 87–9, 91, 99–101, 103–13, 115–26, 128–30, 135, 137, 140, 141, 148, 153, 155–6, 169–82, 188, 194
principle of bivalence   2
principles   2, 79, 82, 107, 125, 130, 148–9, 154, 161, 174, 176, 179–80, 190, 194–6, 204, 207
probable or plausible (probabilis/probabilitas)   2–5, 8–11, 14, 16, 36, 40, 43, 56–7, 61–2, 64, 68–9, 72, 74, 76–7, 81, 87–8, 91, 95, 100, 103, 112, 116, 138, 141, 154, 170, 175–84, 187–90, 194, 198, 201–2, 205
probationes artificiales   25, 27
pronoun   123, 160
pronuntiatio   114, 154
proof   1, 4–5, 8–11, 15–16, 33, 51, 68, 75, 77–9, 85, 87, 92, 102–4, 112, 123, 127–9, 134, 141–2, 174, 177–80, 188–95, 197, 204
propositio/proposition   2–3, 6, 8, 12, 14, 26–7, 29, 31, 33, 40, 41, 43, 55–6, 63–5, 68, 70–1, 75, 82–3, 85–90, 92–6, 100, 104–5, 108–10, 112, 115–19, 122–4, 137, 148, 150–4, 156–63, 171–6, 179–80, 182, 183, 193–4, 198, 205
proprium   205
Pseudo-Anselmus Cantuariensis   43
Pseudo-Aristoteles   201, 203, 205
Pseudo-Boethius   41

qiyās (syllogisme)   11–12, 47–8, 59, 68–74
quaestio/questiones   7, 27, 41, 42, 114, 138, 183–6
quality   7, 73, 81, 155, 176
Quintilian   8–10, 15, 18, 25–8, 30, 37, 38, 78–9, 81, 92, 93, 133, 138
quod quasi notum est   194

Radulphus Brito   138, 140
Ramus, Petrus   15
Rapp, Ch.   17, 182
ratio   9, 25, 39, 40, 43, 51, 78, 111, 113, 116, 132, 159, 171, 175, 177, 204
ratiocinatio   9, 24, 26–8, 38, 70, 114, 202
Read, S.   18, 70, 74, 158, 183, 185
Reed, Ch. A.   182
refutation   15, 36, 59, 68, 162
regressus   192, 196–7
Reinhardt, T.   74, 79, 92
Reisch, Gregorius   205, 211
Renaissance   2, 10, 15–16, 18, 74, 105, 187, 190, 196, 201–2, 207, 209, 211
rhetores latini minores   10, 27–8, 40, 41
rhetoric/rhetorica   4, 10–15, 18, 23–8, 30–2, 36–7, 39, 41, 47–50, 52–5, 57–61, 64, 66–8, 71–81, 90–2, 99–107, 109, 113–16, 120, 126–36, 138, 140–5, 157, 170, 178, 179, 184, 185, 187–8, 197, 198, 210

rhetorical syllogism 3–4, 6, 12, 16, 23, 25–8, 32, 34, 38, 40, 49–50, 57–8, 60–1, 68–9, 71, 73, 77–81, 90, 91, 99–100, 102–4, 107–9, 111, 113–14, 116–19, 122–4, 126–7, 129–33, 136, 141, 182, 187–8, 191, 195–6, 202, 208
Ricklin, Th. 20
Robert Kilwardby 13, 101, 104, 106–8, 110–26, 128, 130, 133–40
Roest, B. 136
Roque, G. 210
Rose, L. E. 17, 21
Rosier-Catach, I. 132
Russell, D. A. 92

Saltetto, E. 210
Scève, Maurice 198
Schmitt, C. B. 198
Schupp, F. 160
science/scientia 11–12, 35, 48–9, 100, 110–11, 113–16, 120, 125, 132, 140, 178, 185, 190, 192, 196, 208, 211
Scotus Eriugena, John 10–11, 26, 33, 35, 42, 43
sedes argumenti or *argumentorum* 75–6, 90, 92, 173
Sedulius Scottus 43
semantic 13, 71, 113, 135, 147–8, 151–6, 173–4, 177, 182
semeion 91
Seneca the Elder 26
sensation 193, 197
sententia 8, 25, 30, 37, 40, 42, 43, 78–80, 86, 92
Seris, E. 20
Serjeantson, R. 197
Sextus Empiricus 6, 18
Sgarbi, M. 16, 187, 210
signatura/signature 16–17, 201–2, 205, 207, 209, 211
signs 4, 16–17, 30–1, 34, 63, 78, 91, 100–5, 109–10, 112, 116, 118, 123–30, 134–6, 138, 188, 190–8, 201–3, 205, 207–9
Simon of Favesham 110, 136, 138, 210, 211
Simplicius 16, 190, 192–3, 197–9
sintactic/syntax 13, 147, 152, 154, 156

Slomkowski, P. 17, 91, 184, 187
Snoek, A. 211
Socrates 75, 89, 110, 128, 135, 149–53, 155, 174–5, 178, 184, 202, 208
solecism 155
sophism 59, 183, 184
sophistic 55, 57, 60, 73, 102, 113–15, 118–19, 121, 124, 126, 129, 154, 191
Sorabji, R. R. K. 74, 157
Sorensen, Roy A. 17, 169, 182
sorites 34
soul 17, 203–4, 206–7, 211
speaker 9, 14, 24, 36, 49–50, 52–4, 56–9, 65, 71, 100, 122, 179–80
Speca, A. 18, 21
species 36, 50, 75–6, 82–5, 87–90, 94, 110, 114, 149, 151, 173–4, 181, 205, 209
Sprute, J. 157
Spruyt, J. 158, 161
statement 3, 24–5, 34, 54, 131, 151–2, 155, 188
status quaestionis 6–7
Steinkrüger, P. 94
Stoics 5–8, 10, 24–5, 36, 56, 78, 81, 83, 92, 93, 135, 148
Street, Th. 18, 21
Striker, G. 18, 184–6
strong knowledge 6, 14, 178, 180, 184
studia 110, 136
Stump, E. 68, 93, 157
subject 3–4, 6, 14–15, 32, 49, 60–1, 67, 69, 79, 81–2, 84, 89, 93, 114, 118, 120, 124–6, 140, 149, 151, 158, 160, 170–1, 173–5, 177–9, 194
supposition 150–2, 155, 160, 183, 197
suspicion 14, 66–7, 100, 107
syllogism 1–5, 7–17, 23–36, 38–41, 43, 49, 52–7, 59, 62–5, 67, 71, 73–94, 99–100, 102–7, 109–31, 133–9, 141–3, 147–53, 155–7, 159, 161, 169–72, 175–80, 182, 183, 187–8, 190–2, 194–5, 202, 204–7
syllogistics 53
syllogizing 111, 119, 123
syncategoreme 151, 155

Tabarroni, A. 161
Taylor, R. 21
teaching/teacher 25, 38, 48–9, 66–7, 78, 92, 111, 114, 126, 133
Telle, J. 211
Teodosio, Filippo 191
term 2–9, 13, 23, 25–6, 30, 38, 62–3, 67, 70–1, 76, 78–82, 84, 86, 88–9, 92, 104–6, 112–13, 117–19, 121–6, 129, 131–2, 135, 139–42, 147–8, 150–6, 158–60, 170–83, 189, 191–2, 195–6, 203, 205, 208
Theophrastus of Eresus 38, 90
Thiofrid of Echternach 43
Thom, P. 132
Thörnqvist, C. T. 157
Tomitano, Bernardino 16
topica/topics 6–9, 12–13, 17, 24, 30–3, 38, 40, 41, 75–85, 88, 90–3, 95–7, 99–102, 104, 109–11, 113–14, 121–3, 127, 132–3, 136, 138, 141–4, 147, 149, 173–9, 181–2, 185, 188, 196, 209, 211
topical inference/topical syllogism 6, 10–12, 14, 43, 76, 78, 85, 90, 100, 122, 174, 176
topical logic 13, 76, 81, 147–9, 154, 170, 173
topical rules 4, 6–8, 12, 14, 76, 82, 85, 88, 176–8, 180–2
topos/topoi 4
Tredennick, H. 18
trivium 103
truncatus syllogismus 169–70, 182, 183
truth/true 2–6, 8, 11–12, 14, 18, 24, 29–30, 35, 48–51, 53–7, 60–5, 67–73, 76–8, 83–9, 91, 103, 107–8, 110, 113, 116–18, 124–6, 128–9, 136, 148–54, 156, 158–61, 171–3, 175–6, 178, 180, 182, 184, 187–90, 192–3, 195–6
Turnèbe, Adrien 202, 205, 210

universals/universality 2–4, 31, 54–6, 58, 62–3, 108–10, 113, 115–16, 123, 136, 148, 150–3, 159–61, 176, 179–80, 188, 192–5, 197, 209, 210
usus 32
utterances 147, 153, 155–6, 158, 160

Valgius, Rufus 38, 92
validity 1–16, 48, 57, 62–4, 71, 86–8, 111, 148–51, 154–5, 161, 171–5, 201, 205
valid syllogism 1–6, 11, 13–14, 16–17, 48, 53–7, 61–5, 67–73, 77–8, 86–7, 105, 107, 118–19, 126, 130, 147–52, 154–6, 169–75, 180–1, 189, 194, 205–6
Valla, Lorenzo 15, 20
Vega, Cristobal 198
Venantius Fortunatus 43
verisimile 90, 91, 102–6, 112, 123, 127–9, 133, 134, 182, 188, 194, 202
vices 17, 204
virtue 49, 75–86, 100, 128, 135
vis inferentiae 12, 85
visual syllogism 16–17, 201, 204, 207–8
Viti, P. 20

Wallach, L. 43
Wallies, M. 95
Walton, D. 74, 182
Ward, J. O. 92, 132
weak logic 1, 5, 8
William of Moerbeke 99, 126
Woerther, F. 59, 73, 74
Woods, J. 74
Would-be syllogism 99, 104, 107, 111, 116

Zabarella, Jacopo 194–6, 198
Zalta, E. N. 74
Zanatta, M. 157
Zayed, S. 74
Zimara, Marcoantonio 193, 198
ẓunūn (opinion) 51
Zupko, J. 183

www.ingramcontent.com/pod-product-compliance
Lightning Source LLC
Chambersburg PA
CBHW052107300426
44116CB00010B/1562